P9-DIA-535

CULTURALLY RESPONSIVE
COGNITIVE-BEHAVIORAL THERAPY

CULTURALLY RESPONSIVE COGNITIVE-BEHAVIORAL THERAPY

Assessment, Practice, and Supervision

Edited by
Pamela A. Hays and Gayle Y. Iwamasa

American Psychological Association
Washington, DC

Published by
American Psychological Association
750 First Street, NE
Washington, DC 20002
www.apa.org

To order
APA Order Department
P.O. Box 92984
Washington, DC 20090-2984
Tel: (800) 374-2721; Direct: (202) 336-5510
Fax: (202) 336-5502; TDD/TTY: (202) 336-6123
Online: www.apa.org/books/
E-mail: order@apa.org

In the U.K., Europe, Africa, and the Middle East, copies may be ordered from
American Psychological Association
3 Henrietta Street
Covent Garden, London
WC2E 8LU England

Typeset in Goudy by Stephen McDougal, Mechanicsville, MD

Printer: United Book Press, Inc., Baltimore, MD
Cover Designer: Aqueous Studio, Bethesda, MD
Technical/Production Editor: Tiffany L. Klaff

The opinions and statements published are the responsibility of the authors, and such opinions and statements do not necessarily represent the policies of the American Psychological Association.

Library of Congress Cataloging-in-Publication Data

Culturally responsive cognitive-behavioral therapy : assessment, practice, and supervision / edited by Pamela A. Hays and Gayle Y. Iwamasa.
    p. cm.
  Includes bibliographical references and index.
  ISBN 1-59147-360-8
  1. Cognitive therapy. 2. Behavior therapy. I. Hays, Pamela A. II. Iwamasa, Gayle.

  RC489.C63C85   2006
  616.89'142—dc22   2005029626

British Library Cataloguing-in-Publication Data
A CIP record is available from the British Library.

Printed in the United States of America
First Edition

CONTENTS

CONTRIBUTORS

Nuha Abudabbeh, PhD, Court Services and Offender Supervision Agency for the District of Columbia, Washington, DC

Kimberly F. Balsam, PhD, University of Washington, Seattle; private practice

Rebecca P. Cameron, PhD, California State University, Sacramento

Veronica Cardenas, PhD, Sharp Mesa Vista Hospital, San Diego, CA

Daniel Cukor, PhD, State University of New York Downstate Medical Center, Brooklyn

Steven Friedman, PhD, ABPP, State University of New York Downstate Medical Center, Brooklyn

John Gonzalez, PhD, University of Alaska, Fairbanks

Pamela A. Hays, PhD, Central Peninsula Counseling Center, Kenai, AK; Antioch University, Seattle, WA; University of Alaska, Anchorage

Devon Hinton, MD, PhD, Massachusetts General Hospital, Harvard Medical School, Boston

Curtis Hsia, PhD, Azusa Pacific University, Azusa, CA

Gayle Y. Iwamasa, PhD, DePaul University, Chicago, IL

Shalonda Kelly, PhD, Rutgers University, Piscataway, NJ

Lisa M. Kinoshita, PhD, Stanford University School of Medicine, Stanford, CA

Angela W. Lau, PhD, University of California, Neuropsychiatric Institute and Hospital; private practice, Los Angeles

Christopher R. Martell, PhD, ABPP, private practice; University of Washington, Seattle

Justin Douglas McDonald, PhD, University of North Dakota, Grand Forks

Linda R. Mona, PhD, Veterans Affairs, Long Beach Healthcare System, Long Beach, CA

Sumie Okazaki, PhD, University of Illinois at Urbana–Champaign

Kurt C. Organista, PhD, University of California, Berkeley

Shilpa M. Pai, PhD, University of North Carolina at Pembroke

Cheryl M. Paradis, PsyD, State University of New York Downstate Medical Center, Brooklyn; Marymount Manhattan College, New York, NY

Jennifer M. Romesser-Scehnet, PsyD, Rancho Los Amigos National Rehabilitation Center, Downey, CA

Steven A. Safren, PhD, Massachusetts General Hospital, Harvard Medical School, Boston; Fenway Community Health, Boston

Kristen H. Sorocco, PhD, University of Oklahoma Health Science Center, Oklahoma City

Richard M. Suinn, PhD, Emeritus Professor of Psychology, Colorado State University, Fort Collins

Junko Tanaka-Matsumi, PhD, Kwansei Gakuin University, Nishinomiya-City, Japan

FOREWORD

RICHARD M. SUINN

This volume fills a major gap in the clinical literature—a singular focus on adapting cognitive–behavioral therapy (CBT) for people of diverse cultural identities. This goal is important for several significant reasons. First, despite the rapidly increasing numbers of culturally diverse people in the United States, there is a dearth of clinical materials on counseling or psychotherapy using CBT for such populations. The number of African Americans increased from 11.5% of the U.S. population in 1980 to 12.1% in 2000; Latinos/Latinas nearly doubled from 6.4% to 12.6%; Asian Americans rose from 1.5% to 3.6%; and American Indians and Alaska Natives increased from 0.6% to 0.7%. Whereas the number of European Americans increased by only 8% between 1980 and 2000, Asian Americans increased by 190%, Latino/Latinas by 143%, African Americans by 30%, and American Indians and Alaska Natives by 46% (Social Science Data Analysis Network, 2004; U.S. Census Bureau, 1983).

As examples of data on nonethnic culturally diverse persons, it is estimated that about 14% of the New York area population is Jewish (Ukeles & Miller, 2004), individuals with disabilities comprise about 19% of the U.S. population, and about one in eight Americans is 65 years or older (Administration on Aging, 2000; Sotnik & Jezewski, 2005). Despite these significant numbers and despite the efficacy of CBT, very few clinically relevant articles are available regarding CBT applications to such populations. As Hays concludes in the Introduction, "despite its popularity and widespread use, the practice-oriented research on CBT has historically focused almost exclusively on people of European American identities" and "textbooks of CBT now cover a wide range of disorders, but none explicitly integrates cultural considerations throughout the text" (this volume, p. 5).

This book is based on the recognition of the appropriateness of CBT for these particular cultural groups. Such populations often share histories of discrimination or perceptions of being less than adequate; CBT is built on being nonjudgmental, on focusing on strengths, and on empowering clients. Many of these populations have cultural worldviews that are congruent with CBT approaches: a focus on the present, an expectation that healers and help givers will be prescriptive, and an awareness of the importance of the social context. CBT is also relevant for its educational orientation that not only avoids the stigma and shame sometimes associated with seeking help for psychological issues but also provides the client with a more readily understood conceptualization of the issues.

The authors are experienced therapists and scholars as well as being themselves part of the various cultural groups. Using their combined knowledge of CBT and the various cultural norms, they provide concrete and practical advice for the reader. The writings identify important culture-specific variables essential for adapting CBT for each population, such as religion and spirituality concepts, racism and political history, linguistic levels and cognitive style, generation and immigration issues, family structure and gender role assignments, collectivistic orientations, and health belief viewpoints. One of the very special contributions of this volume is the down-to-earth and practical suggestions identified to merge such cultural characteristics with CBT practice, for instance, how to interpret behaviors that seem like denial from an older or Asian American or Orthodox Jewish client, or ways to increase motivation by changing from the individualistic Western-oriented "you need to take care of yourself" to the collectivistic "you can take better care of your family by taking care of yourself." Case histories provide excellent examples of such integration, such as the case of Mr. Lopez, a Latino client experiencing severe back pain (chap. 3). In this one case history, the therapist shows awareness of *respeto* and *personalismo* in the initial encounter, offers a culturally adapted cognitive restructuring assignment, restores motivation through adopting *familismo* values, uses a culturally sensitive approach to set limits, and discusses a culturally appropriate approach to termination.

The writings are not simply uncritical endorsements of CBT. Discussions include consideration of possible deficiencies in CBT's relevance for culturally diverse groups, such as the fact that CBT is not value neutral. For instance, the emphasis on reality testing of beliefs could conflict with the spirituality beliefs of some groups. Also, procedures such as assertiveness training could be at odds with the cultural values of respect for elders and the avoidance of confrontation. However, after identifying such potential deficiencies, the authors then offer advice on overcoming such problems through increasing cultural sensitivity in work with clients.

Although the chapters and case examples may seem somewhat oriented to the cognitive approaches of CBT, careful reading will confirm that the materials cover other behavioral approaches such as parental training, behavioral couple therapy, exposure therapy, response prevention, self-monitoring, and behavioral rehearsal. The book is also unique in being inclusive in its definition of cultural diversity. Hence there are chapters devoted to people with disabilities; lesbian, gay, and bisexual people; older adults; as well as Arab Americans and Orthodox Jews. This decision is a consequence of the recognition that shared cultural experiences are present within such groups, discriminatory experiences based on negative views of others exist, stigmatization is frequently associated with group membership, and despite the increasing numbers, the groups are often viewed as outside the norm. By broadening the target groups considered, this volume offers an enriched approach to enhancing counseling and psychotherapy procedures. Such coverage emphasizes the valid point that the therapeutic encounter demands sensitivity to the core belief system; normative behavioral background; and social, familial, and personal history of the "culture" of any client.

This is a book that informs, conceptualizes, and advises about making CBT culturally responsive with details that make it essential reading for the practitioner.

REFERENCES

Administration on Aging. (2000). *A profile of older Americans*. Washington, DC: Author.

Social Science Data Analysis Network. (2004). *United States population by race*. Retrieved October 2004 from http://www.censusscope.org/us/chart_race.html

Sotnik, P., & Jezewski, M. A. (2005). Disability service providers as culture brokers. In J. H. Stone (Ed.), *Culture and disability: Providing culturally competent services* (pp. 15–36). Thousand Oaks, CA: Sage.

Ukeles, J., & Miller, R. (2004, October). *The Jewish study of New York: 2002, Final report* (Final text, exhibits and an expanded research note on methodology). New York: Ukeles Associates for UJA Federation of New York.

U.S. Census Bureau. (1983). *1980 census of population*. Washington, DC: U.S. Government Printing Office.

ACKNOWLEDGMENTS

We would like to thank our editor Ed Meidenbauer and the excellent staff at the American Psychological Association, and especially Susan Reynolds for her encouragement of this book. Pam would like to thank Marjorie and Hugh Hays and Bob McCard for their support and helpful feedback. Gayle would like to thank Russell, William, and Robert Koch for their patience, understanding, encouragement, and support. We are both grateful to our professional mentors, supervisors, colleagues, clients, and students for all that they have taught and shared with us.

CULTURALLY RESPONSIVE
COGNITIVE-BEHAVIORAL THERAPY

INTRODUCTION: DEVELOPING CULTURALLY RESPONSIVE COGNITIVE–BEHAVIORAL THERAPIES

PAMELA A. HAYS

Julia is a 35-year-old single mother of two teenage boys who came to see a therapist for anxiety related to her new job. She explained to the therapist that she had worked part time and attended school for over 10 years to reach her dream of becoming an occupational therapist (OT). After obtaining her degree, she was hired by a hospital with a large OT staff, and within 3 years she was promoted to department head. But since her promotion, the staff had become increasingly critical of her, and her supervisor had made several pejorative remarks about her qualifications. Julia was feeling a great deal of anxiety about their opinions of her, and although she knew that she was well qualified, she was doubting her ability to do the job. She asked the counselor to help her find a way to decrease her anxiety and "not care so much what other people say or think about me."

If you already use cognitive–behavioral approaches in your work, you probably read this example looking for the cognitive, behavioral, affective, and environmental components of Julia's complaints. In conceptualizing her difficulties, you may have hypothesized that some of Julia's anxiety stems from the newness of her position, the stressors inherent in supervisory work, or the social stressors of parenting two teenagers alone on one income. You may have inferred possible core beliefs and self-talk contributing to her anxiety and doubts. And you may have considered how specific cognitive–

behavioral strategies could help Julia. For example, problem-solving skills training might help her to resolve the conflicts with staff, cognitive restructuring could help to decrease her anxiety and self-doubt, and a coping skills group might provide her with additional social support.

But what if you had been told that Julia is a 35-year-old *Latina* single mother? Would this piece of information have raised some questions and hypotheses that you did not initially consider? For example, what are the ethnic identities of Julia's staff and supervisor, and could this have anything to do with their attitudes toward her? Could Julia's self-doubts emanate from experiences of prejudice and discrimination? Could there be language differences that might account for some communication difficulties? What opportunities, strengths, and supports might be available to Julia and her family, given their cultural heritage, identities, and contexts?

Julia's ethnicity was initially omitted to make the point that when cultural information is not included, the assumption is often made that the client is of European American heritage, and as a result, potentially important questions and hypotheses are often overlooked. Such questions and hypotheses are important to consider with clients of any identity, even European American. Unfortunately, the omission of ethnic and cultural information is the rule rather than the exception in clinical and counseling research, including cognitive–behavioral therapy (CBT).

This neglect is probably due in part to the cultural homogeneity of the field; approximately 85% of psychologists and 94% of American Psychological Association (APA) members are of European American heritage (APA, 2005; Dittman, 2003). In many cases, European American therapists may simply not perceive minority cultural influences because they do not have this experience or close relationships with people from whom they could learn.

However, the dominance of European American perspectives and assumptions in CBT is not due solely to the disproportionate number of European American therapists. It is also related to the reinforcement of dominant cultural values and perspectives by the larger society, of which the field of psychotherapy is a part. Consider, for example, the social and therapeutic emphasis placed on assertiveness in social interactions (i.e., over subtlety), change (over patience and acceptance), personal independence (over interdependence), open self-disclosure (over cautious protection of one's family reputation; Kim, 1985; Pedersen, 1987; Wood & Mallinckrodt, 1990).

CBT is currently the leading theoretical preference among psychologists today. Its effectiveness has been demonstrated in the treatment of anxiety (A. T. Beck, Emery, & Greenberg, 1985), depression (A. T. Beck, Rush, Shaw, & Emery, 1987), obsessive–compulsive disorder (Clark, 2004), chronic pain (Thorn, 2004), eating disorders (Cooper, Fairburn, & Hawker, 2003), marital conflict (Epstein & Baucom, 2002), substance abuse (A. T. Beck, Wright, Newman, & Liese, 2001), personality disorders (A. T. Beck, Freeman, Davis, & Associates, 2003; Linehan, 1993), and many other problems (Barlow, 2001).

However, despite its popularity and widespread use, the practice-oriented research on CBT has historically focused almost exclusively on people of European American identities (Hays, 1995; Iwamasa & Smith, 1996; Suinn, 2003). For example, in 1988, Casas reviewed psychological abstracts of the preceding 20 years, looking for studies of cognitive–behavioral treatment of anxiety in people of racial or ethnic minority groups. He found only three empirically based outcome studies, two of which had samples of only two persons each. Renfrey (1992) conducted a similar search for CBT studies involving Native American participants; his review of 11 major behavioral and cognitive–behavioral journals (from their beginnings to the end of 1990) yielded one case study of one Native American client. In a 1996 survey of the three leading behavioral journals, only 1.31% of the articles were found to focus on ethnic minority groups in the United States (Iwamasa & Smith, 1996). Overview textbooks of CBT now cover a wide range of disorders, but none explicitly integrates cultural considerations throughout the text (e.g., see J. S. Beck, 1995, 2005; Dobson, 2001; Ledley, Marx, & Heimberg, 2005; Greenberger & Padesky, 1995; Salkovskis, 1996).

This neglect of culture in CBT occurs at a time when ethnic minority groups make up approximately 33% of the U.S. population (APA, 2002; U.S. Census Bureau, 2000), and political changes have led to increasing numbers of immigrants and refugees internationally (Marsella, Bornemann, Ekblad, & Orley, 1994). Indigenous groups, people with disabilities, older adults, and gay, lesbian, and bisexual people have become more politically active and visible (Adelson, 2000; Olkin, 1999; Perez, DeBord, & Bieschke, 2000).

With this diversity has come a growing body of research demonstrating how cross-cultural competence facilitates therapy and improves assessment (e.g., see Dana, 2000; Pope-Davis & Coleman, 1997; D. W. Sue, 2001). The APA and the American Counseling Association have published guidelines calling attention to the importance of cross-cultural competence for therapists, educators, and researchers (APA, 2000a, 2000b, 2002, 2004; Roysircar, Arredondo, Fuertes, Ponterotto, & Toporek, 2003). And the Surgeon General's report on mental health in the United States clearly states the need for culturally competent services that address both the uniqueness of the individual and culturally related influences (U.S. Department of Health and Human Services, 1999).

During the past 15 years there has been an enormous increase in the number of books addressing ethnic and cultural minority groups, including those by Aponte, Rivers, and Wohl (1995); Comas-Díaz and Greene (1994); Fong (2004); Hays (2001); Ivey, Ivey, and Simek-Morgan (1997); C. C. Lee (1997); McGoldrick, Giordano, and Pearce (1996); Mio and Iwamasa (2003); Paniagua (1998); Pedersen, Draguns, Lonner, and Trimble (2002); Pipes McAdoo (1999); Robinson and Howard-Hamilton (2000); Smith (2004);

and D. W. Sue and Sue (2002). Texts have also been written on counseling children of color (Johnson-Powell & Yamamoto, 1997); diverse gay, lesbian, and bisexual people (Martell, Safren, & Prince, 2004; Perez et al., 2000); and people of diverse religious and spiritual faiths (Burke & Miranti, 1995; Fukuyama & Sevig, 1999; Miller, 1999; Shafranske, 1996).

In addition, a number of multicultural counseling books have been published regarding specific ethnic groups, including African Americans (Bass, Wyatt, & Powell, 1982; Boyd-Franklin, 2003); Asian Americans (E. Lee, 1997; Uba, 1994); American Indians and Alaska Natives (Droby, 2000; Herring, 1999; Swan Reimer, 1999; Swinomish Tribal Community, 1991); Latinos and Latinas (Falicov, 1998); Arab people (Dwairy, 1998); English-speaking West Indians (Gopaul-McNicol, 1993); and ethnic minority groups in Canada and Australia (Pauwels, 1995; Waxler-Morrison, Anderson, & Richardson, 1990).

The fact that this list is not comprehensive underscores the exceptional growth in this area. However, despite the growth, multicultural researchers have been slow to consider cognitive–behavioral interventions.

The lack of cross-pollination between the fields of CBT and multicultural therapy (MCT) is surprising for several reasons. First, a recent study indicates that CBT and MCT are the top two trends in psychotherapy today (Norcross, Hedges, & Prochaska, 2002). With such a proliferation of research in each area, one would expect to see more overlap between them.

Second, CBT and MCT share a number of basic premises. Both emphasize the need to tailor therapeutic interventions to the unique situation of the individual. Both emphasize the empowerment of clients—MCT through its affirmation of clients' cultural identities, and CBT through recognition of each client's expertise regarding his or her own needs and situation. Both MCT and CBT also emphasize attention to the therapeutic aspects of clients' strengths and supports.

Third, increased interest in evidence-based practices has called attention to the dearth of empirically based studies involving people of minority cultures (Hall, 2001; S. Sue, 2003). The empirical orientation of CBT makes it well suited for such research although, at the same time, it is important to recognize that evidence-based practices also include some broader approaches to research evidence such as clinical expertise and patient values (Levant, 2005).

Fourth, the CBT field has a great deal to gain from cross-cultural research. Culturally sensitive attempts to understand how CBT works and does not work with minority populations offer a multitude of opportunities for CBT researchers to challenge, expand, and refine their theories. Such work could lead to creative approaches that help a much wider range of people.

Recognizing such possibilities also requires a consideration of the potential limitations of CBT with minority cultures. For example, CBT is often assumed to be value-neutral because of its reliance on the scientific method.

However, CBT is as value-laden as any other psychotherapy. Its emphasis on cognition, logic, verbal skills, and rational thinking strongly favors dominant cultural perspectives including definitions of rationality (Kantrowitz & Ballou, 1992). This cognitive emphasis can easily lead to an undervaluing of the importance of spirituality. In addition, CBT's focus on changing oneself can contribute to the neglect of cultural influences that restrict a person's ability to create and implement change. This internal focus, if not balanced by a behavioral perspective that recognizes the power of environmental influences, may contribute to blaming the client for problems that are primarily environmentally based. However, such limitations are not insurmountable, and figuring out ways to address them is part of the process of making CBT more responsive to people of diverse cultural identities.

COGNITIVE–BEHAVIORAL THERAPY: AN OVERVIEW

In the 1950s and early 1960s, the field known as behavior therapy called attention to the ways in which environments could be manipulated to elicit, shape, and reinforce desired behaviors. A number of behavioral researchers subsequently became interested in the influence of cognition on behavior, and it was out of this interest that the field of CBT developed.

CBT involves a consideration of five components to any problem: cognition (thoughts), mood (emotions), physiological reactions (e.g., physical sensations and symptoms), behavior, and the environment (Padesky & Greenberger, 1995). CBT presumes that cognitions (which include perceptions, beliefs, and self-talk) mediate one's mood, behavior, and physiological reactions in response to the environment (Beck, 1995). Dysfunctional cognitions are believed to contribute to maladjustment, whereas functional cognitions contribute to healthy adjustment (Dobson, 2001, p. 27).

It is the role of the cognitive–behavioral therapist to help clients become aware of the relationships between these five areas. Clients learn to recognize how certain negative, unhelpful, or unrealistic thoughts can generate distress in the form of uncomfortable physical sensations, maladaptive behavior, and emotions that feel uncontrollable or out of proportion to the situation. Clients also learn that social and physical aspects of one's environment can contribute to their distress. Once the client understands these connections, the therapist helps the individual to develop more helpful coping strategies, which can be divided into three main categories (Dobson, 2001): (a) problem solving, (b) social skills and support, and (c) cognitive restructuring.

As the three categories suggest, clients may need to take concrete action to solve the problem, learn new social skills to improve their social environments and ability to solve problems, or develop a broader network of support to counteract the negative effects of environmental stressors. In addition, clients learn that there is always the possibility of changing the way they feel by changing the way they think, that is, cognitive restructuring.

The strategy of cognitive restructuring involves more than simply thinking positively (Padesky & Greenberger, 1995). Rather, clients learn to recognize common cognitive errors, automatic dysfunctional thoughts, and cognitive tendencies related to the schema (a sort of cognitive template) by which human beings take in and organize their experience. By considering a broader range of possible interpretations of events and beliefs that one may never before have considered, clients learn to see themselves, the world, and the future more fully and realistically (Beck, 1995; Beck et al., 1987; Padesky & Greenberger, 1995).

Making CBT More Culturally Responsive

A *culturally responsive* approach to CBT begins long before the start of one's therapeutic work with clients. It begins with therapists' attention to those areas in which they may hold biases because of inexperience or knowledge gaps. It may be helpful to think of a lack of knowledge and inexperience (otherwise known as ignorance) as creating a sort of hole or vacuum inside of us. We all know what happens in a vacuum: It sucks in whatever surrounds it to fill itself up. In the case of a lack of experience or knowledge regarding a whole group, the vacuum becomes filled with dominant cultural messages that bombard us every day yet are so subtle and pervasive that we often do not notice them. We then use this information, often without awareness, to make generalizations and draw conclusions about members of particular groups (Hays, in press).

What is important to recognize (and it keeps us humble) is that we *all* have these little vacuum packs of ignorance regarding various groups. The first step is to begin to recognize them. Only then can we actively work to replace our inaccurate beliefs and assumptions with reality-based information. This type of work is personal, and it cannot be accomplished in one course or even in several cross-cultural encounters. Rather, it is an ongoing process that involves exploring the impact of cultural influences on one's own beliefs (i.e., cognitions), behaviors, and identities.

Once a commitment to this personal work is made, it can be facilitated by the following activities: obtaining cultural information from culture-specific sources (e.g., news published by ethnic and other minority communities themselves); attending cultural celebrations and other public events; obtaining supervision from a person who belongs to and is knowledgeable about a minority culture; consulting with a culturally diverse professional group; reading from the wealth of multicultural counseling research now available; and developing relationships with people of diverse cultures. Engagement with these forms of learning facilitates the development of the cognitive schema or template into which client-specific information can be considered and incorporated. The development of this *cultural schema* is the responsibility of the therapist. That is, clients should not be expected to educate the therapist about the broader social and cultural meanings of their identities. However, the therapist *will* need to obtain information from clients regarding each client's unique personal experience of their culture.

Cognitive–Behavioral Assessment

One of the first steps in a cognitive–behavioral assessment involves conceptualization of the problem. CBT divides problems into two general categories. The first category consists of problems in the client's environment (e.g., a difficult task, a conflict, or a stressful situation) that imply an environmental solution (e.g., changing the task, obtaining help, or decreasing stressors in the situation). The second category consists of problems that are more internal, namely, those involving dysfunctional cognitions and undesirable overwhelming emotions. Difficulties in this second category are commonly referred to as cognitive problems. Many problems involve both environmental and cognitive elements, but distinguishing between the two is important in developing the most effective intervention.

Environmental Problems

One would think that cultural influences would be included in the definition of any environment, but this has not been the case with CBT. Cultural aspects of clients' environments have often been overlooked or framed in negative terms.

A culturally responsive assessment takes into account both positive and negative aspects of clients' cultural environments (Hays, 1996a, 1996b). Culturally related *stressors* (i.e., the negative aspects) have been elucidated in Axis IV of the *Diagnostic and Statistical Manual of Mental Disorders* (4th ed., text rev.; American Psychiatric Association, 2000). This list of psychosocial and environmental problems includes difficulties such as acculturation; discrimination; living in an unsafe neighborhood, in inadequate housing, or extreme poverty; receiving insufficient welfare support; inadequate health care or social services; legal problems; and exposure to disasters or war (American Psychiatric Association, 2000).

Positive aspects of a person's cultural environment have received much less attention. These positive aspects can be considered in two categories: *environmental conditions* and *interpersonal supports* (Hays, 2001).

Environmental conditions may be natural or constructed. Examples of natural conditions include rivers, beaches, and land available for subsistence and recreational fishing, hunting, gardening, and farming. Constructed environmental conditions may be an altar in one's home or room to honor deceased family members, a space for prayer and meditation, availability of culturally preferred foods, the presence of culture-specific art and music, a place for animals, and communities that facilitate social interaction (e.g., villages where homes are within walking distance of one another).

Interpersonal supports include extended families (blood related and nonblood related), religious communities, traditional celebrations and rituals, recreational activities, storytelling activities that pass on the history of a group, and involvement in political and social action groups. Having a child who is successful in school can also be an important source of pride and strength for parents and extended family.

The explicit consideration of these positive aspects of cultural environments is important for a number of reasons. For one, helping clients to recognize culturally related supports clearly communicates respect for a client's cultural heritage. Respect is a central concept among many people of minority cultures, and as such it is important for the purposes of establishing a good working relationship (Boyd-Franklin, 2003; El-Islam, 1982; Kim, 1985; Matheson, 1986; Morales, 1992; Swinomish Tribal Community, 1991).

Second, cognitive–behavioral research encourages the incorporation of strengths and supports in the development of effective therapeutic interventions. The use of naturally occurring supports works precisely because the supports *are* naturally occurring and thus easier to implement and maintain. The explicit consideration of culturally related environmental conditions and supports opens up an array of interventions that might otherwise be overlooked from a dominant cultural perspective.

When investigating cultural supports, it is essential to consider the client's personal orientation to his or her culture of origin and to the dominant culture (i.e., competence in each culture). LaFromboise, Coleman, and Gerton (1993) described five models that have been used to explain the psychological processes, social experiences, individual challenges, and obstacles to competence in two cultures: assimilation, acculturation, alternation (i.e., between the two cultures), multicultural, and fusion. In recent years, acculturation has received a great deal of attention, with the concept initially conceptualized as a linear process consisting of two main categories: acculturated and unacculturated/traditional. However, researchers now recognize that acculturation involves a much more complex process that can include a variety of unique adaptations of beliefs, behaviors, and practices (Chun, Balls Organista, & Marín, 2003; Iwamasa & Yamada, 2001; Roysircar, 2003).

Drawing from the alternation model, LaFromboise et al. (1993) proposed a model of *bicultural competence* that emphasizes the reciprocal relationship between the person and the environment, or in this case, *two* environments (the culture of origin and the second culture). They suggested that competence in each of these cultures can be observed in the individual's (a) knowledge of cultural beliefs and values, (b) positive attitudes toward both majority and minority groups, (c) bicultural efficacy, (d) communication ability, (e) role repertoire, and (f) sense of groundedness in a social support system.

This model may be helpful in one's exploration and choice of supports. For example, consider the situation of a middle-aged, urban American Indian woman. If the woman grew up in an American Indian family and cultural context, identifies strongly with her specific Native culture and functions well in the dominant cultural setting in which she works and lives, and currently is well grounded in a social support system that includes Native and non-Native people, the range and types of environmental supports that would be appropriate for her would be quite different from those of another middle-aged, urban American Indian woman who grew up in an adopted European American family with little connection to her cultural heritage. Whereas the first woman might be open to traditional rituals, supports, or healing practices in addition to some dominant cultural approaches, the second woman could interpret the suggestion of traditional rituals, supports, or healing practices as presumptive and thus racist.

Cognitive Problems

This brings us to the second category of problems, namely, those that can be thought of as internal to the client. These include overwhelming emotions, disturbing thoughts, frightening physical sensations, and maladaptive behavior. CBT refers to these problems as cognitive because the disturbance is seen as emanating from dysfunctional cognitions and cognitive processes. As noted earlier, CBT proposes that we can increase our control over disturbing physiological sensations, overwhelming emotions, and self-defeating behaviors if we recognize our unhelpful cognitions and change them to more helpful, realistic, and positive ones.

Attention to cultural influences within this second category of problems is important for several reasons. Culture plays a role in the creation, shaping, and maintenance of cognitions and cognitive processes (Dowd, 2003). Cultural influences can be seen in one's definitions of rationality and in one's view of what constitutes adaptive and maladaptive behavior. Cultural influences are interwoven with beliefs regarding acceptable coping behaviors and forms of emotional expression, and with religious and social values that affect clients' perceived choices.

Because minority cultural influences are often framed as negative by the dominant culture, therapists will want to give deliberate attention to the positive aspects of cultural influences on internal processes. These can be conceptualized as *personal strengths* and include pride in one's culture and identity; a religious faith or spirituality; musical and artistic abilities; bilingual and multilingual skills; a sense of humor; culturally related knowledge and practical living skills regarding fishing, hunting, farming, cooking, and the use of medicinal plants; culture-specific beliefs that help one cope with prejudice and discrimination; and commitment to helping one's group, for example, through social action.

Here again, the client's connection to and competence in his or her culture of origin and the dominant culture are important. For example, consider the situation of a young Vietnamese man in his early 20s who lives in the United States with his parents and younger siblings and who presents with anxiety related to family and work conflicts. From a dominant cultural perspective, the therapist might conceptualize the client's problem as one of individuation and encourage him to question the authority of his parents and find his own place to live. Such an approach could involve challenging culturally based beliefs regarding respect for elders, responsibility to others, and interdependence of family members. If the client and his family are open to alternative cultural perspectives, considering these different views could be helpful. However, if they are not, such an approach would probably diminish the therapist's credibility and lead the young man to terminate therapy. More helpful approaches might involve teaching the client (and possibly the family) skills for problem solving, conflict resolution, and frustration tolerance that do not involve challenging core cultural beliefs.

Addressing the Complexity of Problems

Of course, environmental and cognitive aspects of problems often overlap. An ever-present danger with CBT lies in the inaccurate conceptualization of a client's problem (i.e., distress) as due to dysfunctional cognitions when it is a consequence of unacceptable environmental conditions (e.g., an abusive relationship, a racist workplace, physical obstacles to a person who has a disability). As therapists, we do not want to be in the position of encouraging a client to adapt to an environment that is dangerous or harmful. Attempts to change a client's thinking about such conditions without trying to change the conditions may give the message that the conditions are acceptable and that the client is to blame for them.

Returning to the example of Julia, let's say that her coworkers and supervisor resent her promotion and that their feelings emanate from racial prejudice. In response to this environmentally based problem, the therapist would want to explore with Julia the possibility of taking action aimed at changing her work environment (e.g., talking to someone above her supervisor, filing a complaint, looking for a new job, consulting an attorney). However, if Julia's anxiety is so great that it prevents her from engaging in this type of problem solving, it may be necessary to take a more internal (cognitive) focus to managing the anxiety. This internal focus would involve helping Julia to change her self-defeating thoughts to more helpful ones that decrease her anxiety. Such cognitive restructuring might be conducted first or in combination with the problem solving aimed at changing Julia's environment.

Building on the existing literature in the domains of CBT and multicultural therapy, this book provides clinicians and counselors with practitioner-oriented suggestions, guidelines, and examples illustrating the use of CBT with people of diverse cultural identities. The book is intended for psychologists, counselors, family therapists, social workers, and psychiatrists who are interested in using cognitive–behavioral approaches to assessment, therapy, and supervision with clients and students of diverse identities. It should appeal to those who already hold multicultural expertise and want to learn specific skills and interventions, as well as to cognitive–behavior therapists who wish to expand their approaches to more diverse populations. An underlying premise of the book is that culture influences us all, and the consideration of culture is an essential component of assessment and therapy with everyone. By focusing on the application of CBT with people of minority identities, we hope to call attention to the ways in which cultural considerations can enhance and facilitate CBT with people of minority, dominant, bicultural, and multicultural identities.

OVERVIEW OF THE BOOK

The book begins with chapters 1 through 7 focusing on the use of CBT with specific ethnic cultures, including people of Native, Latino, Asian, and African American heritage, along with chapters on people of Arab and Orthodox Jewish heritage. Chapters 8 through 10 address the use of CBT with people of nonethnic minority groups: older adults, people with disabilities, and sexual minorities. In keeping with the conceptualization of identity as complex and multidimensional, these chapters do not assume a European American norm but rather include people of color who are older, have a disability, or are gay, lesbian, or bisexual.

Whereas nonethnic minority groups are not always conceptualized as minority cultures, we believe that several aspects of these groups justify this conceptualization. All of the groups meet the broader definition of culture used in the multicultural counseling literature (Fukuyama, 1990; Pope, 1995). These groups share some experiences related to their identities and, in the case of sexual minorities and people with disabilities, a history of advocating for equal rights. Sexual minorities and people with disabilities each also have their own within-group terminology. Just as members of ethnic minority cultures are often the targets of prejudice and discrimination, so too are older adults, sexual minorities, and people with disabilities. And, on the positive side, the minority status that goes along with these identities has brought many members of these groups unique forms of knowledge, awareness, emotional and tangible support, and a sense of community (Newman & Newman, 1999).

In chapters 1 through 10, each chapter offers an introductory overview of the respective cultural group, including sociodemographics and information regarding within-group diversity. Chapter authors discuss the advantages of using CBT with each group, potential limitations, and suggested adaptations. Case examples illustrate the practical application of these adaptations. Chapters 11 and 12 address cultural considerations in cognitive–behavioral assessment, supervision, and training.

One final note: Although we have done our best to include a diverse range of cultural influences and minority groups, there is still a long way to go. We recognize the need for more empirically based research involving minority cultures. In the meantime, we hope that the clinically based suggestions and modifications provided in this book will contribute to the search for and consideration of evidence-based practices. We look forward to future research involving an even greater number of cultural groups from a variety of countries.

REFERENCES

Adelson, N. (2000). Re-imagining Aboriginality: An Indigenous peoples' response to social suffering. *Transcultural Psychiatry, 37,* 11–34.

American Psychiatric Association. (2000). *The diagnostic and statistical manual of mental disorders* (4th ed., text rev.). Washington, DC: Author.

American Psychological Association. (2000a). Guidelines for psychotherapy with lesbian, gay, and bisexual clients. *American Psychologist, 55,* 1440–1451.

American Psychological Association. (2000b). *Resolution on poverty and socioeconomic status.* Retrieved November 11, 2001, from http://www.apa.org/pi/urban/povres.html

American Psychological Association. (2002). Guidelines on multicultural education, training, research, practice, and organizational change for psychologists. *American Psychologist, 58,* 377–402.

American Psychological Association. (2004). Guidelines for psychological practice with older adults. *American Psychologist, 59,* 236–260.

American Psychological Association. (2005). APA 2020: A perfect vision for psychology. *American Psychologist, 60,* 512–522.

Aponte, J. F., Rivers, R. Y., & Wohl, J. (Eds.). (1995). *Psychological interventions and cultural diversity.* Needham Heights, MA: Allyn & Bacon.

Barlow, D. H. (2001). *Clinical handbook of psychological disorders.* New York: Guilford Press.

Bass, B. A., Wyatt, G. E., & Powell, G. J. (1982). *The Afro-American family: Assessment, treatment, and research issues.* New York: Grune & Stratton.

Beck, A. T., Emery, G., & Greenberg, R. L. (1985). *Anxiety disorders and phobias: A cognitive perspective.* New York: Basic Books.

Beck, A. T., Freeman, A., Davis, D. D., & Associates. (2003). *Cognitive therapy of personality disorders.* New York: Guilford Press.

Beck, A. T., Rush, A. J., Shaw, B. F., & Emery, G. (1987). *Cognitive therapy of depression*. New York: Guilford Press.

Beck, A. T., Wright, F. D., Newman, C. F., & Liese, B. S. (2001). *Cognitive therapy of substance abuse*. New York: Guilford Press.

Beck, J. S. (1995). *Cognitive therapy: Basics and beyond*. New York: Guilford Press.

Beck, J. S. (2005). *Cognitive therapy for challenging problems*. New York: Guilford Press.

Boyd-Franklin, N. (2003). *Black families in therapy*. New York: Guilford Press.

Burke, M. T., & Miranti, J. G. (Eds.). (1995). *Counseling: The spiritual dimension*. Alexandria, VA: American Counseling Association.

Casas, J. M. (1988). Cognitive–behavioral approaches: A minority perspective. *The Counseling Psychologist, 16,* 106–110.

Chun, K. M., Balls Organista, P., & Marín, G. (Eds.). (2003). *Acculturation: Advances in theory, measurement, and applied research*. Washington, DC: American Psychological Association.

Clark, D. A. (2004). *Cognitive–behavioral therapy for OCD*. New York: Guilford Press.

Comas-Díaz, L., & Greene, B. (Eds.). (1994). *Women of color: Integrating ethnic and gender identities in psychotherapy*. New York: Guilford Press.

Cooper, Z., Fairburn, C. G., & Hawker, D. M. (2003). *Cognitive–behavioral treatment of obesity*. New York: Guilford Press.

Dana, R. H. (Ed.). (2000). *Handbook of cross-cultural and multicultural personality assessment*. Mahwah, NJ: Erlbaum.

Dittman, M. (2003). A changing student body. *Monitor on Psychology, 34,* 42.

Dobson, K. (Ed.). (2001). *Handbook of cognitive–behavioral therapies*. New York: Guilford Press.

Dowd, E. T. (2003). Cultural differences in cognitive therapy. *The Behavior Therapist, 26,* 247–249.

Droby, R. M. (2000). *With the wind and the waves: A guide for non-Native mental health professionals working with Alaska Native Communities*. Nome, AK: Norton Sound Health Corporation, Behavioral Health Services.

Dwairy, M. A. (1998). *Cross-cultural counseling: The Arab-Palestinian case*. Binghamton, NY: Haworth Press.

El-Islam, F. (1982). Arabic cultural psychiatry. *Transcultural Psychiatric Research Review, 19,* 5–24.

Epstein, N. B., & Baucom, D. H. (2002). *Enhanced cognitive–behavioral therapy for couples: A contextual approach*. Washington, DC: American Psychological Association.

Falicov, C. J. (1998). *Latino families in therapy*. New York: Guilford Press.

Fong, R. (2004). *Culturally competent practice with immigrant and refugee children and families*. New York: Guilford Press.

Fukuyama, M. (1990). Taking a universal approach to multicultural counseling. *Counselor Education and Supervision, 30,* 6–17.

Fukuyama, M. A., & Sevig, T. D. (1999). *Integrating spirituality into multicultural counseling*. Thousand Oaks, CA: Sage.

Gopaul-McNicol, S. A. (1993). *Working with West Indian families*. New York: Guilford Press.

Greenberger, D., & Padesky, C. A. (1995). *Mind over mood*. New York: Guilford Press.

Hall, G. C. N. (2001). Psychotherapy research with ethnic minorities: Empirical, ethical, and conceptual issues. *Journal of Consulting and Clinical Psychology, 69*, 502–510.

Hays, P. A. (1995). Multicultural applications of cognitive–behavior therapy. *Professional Psychology: Research and Practice, 26*, 309–315.

Hays, P. A. (1996a). Addressing the complexities of culture and gender in counseling. *Journal of Counseling & Development, 74*, 332–338.

Hays, P. A. (1996b). Culturally responsive assessment with diverse older clients. *Professional Psychology: Research and Practice, 27*, 188–193.

Hays, P. A. (2001). *Addressing cultural complexities in practice: A framework for clinicians and counselors*. Washington, DC: American Psychological Association.

Hays, P. A. (in press). A strengths-based approach to psychotherapy with Middle Eastern people: Commentary regarding Bushra et al. In J. C. Muran (Ed.), *Dialogues on difference: Diversity studies of the therapeutic relationship*. Washington, DC: American Psychological Association.

Herring, R. (1999). *Counseling with Native American Indians and Alaskan Natives*. Thousand Oaks, CA: Sage.

Ivey, A. E., Ivey, M. B., & Simek-Morgan, L. (1997). *Counseling and psychotherapy: A multicultural perspective*. Boston: Allyn & Bacon.

Iwamasa, G., & Smith, S. K. (1996). Ethnic diversity and behavioral psychology: A review of the literature. *Behavior Modification, 20*, 45–59.

Iwamasa, G., & Yamada, A. M. (2001). Special issue: Asian American acculturation and ethnic/racial identity: Research innovations in the new millennium. *Cultural Diversity and Ethnic Minority Psychology, 7*, 203–206.

Johnson-Powell, G., & Yamamoto, J. (Eds.). (1997). *Transcultural child development: Psychological assessment and treatment*. New York: Wiley.

Kantrowitz, R. E., & Ballou, M. (1992). A feminist critique of cognitive–behavioral therapy. In L. S. Brown & M. Ballou (Eds.), *Personality and psychopathology: Feminist appraisals* (pp. 70–87). New York: Guilford Press.

Kim, S. C. (1985). Family therapy for Asian Americans: A strategic structural framework. *Psychotherapy, 22*, 342–348.

LaFromboise, T., Coleman, H. L. K., & Gerton, J. (1993). Psychological impact of biculturalism: Evidence and theory. *Psychological Bulletin, 114*, 395–412.

Ledley, D. R., Marx, B. P., & Heimberg, R. G. (2005). *Making cognitive–behavioral therapy work: Clinical process for new practitioners*. New York: Guilford Press.

Lee, C. C. (Ed.). (1997). *Multicultural issues in counseling: New approaches to diversity* (2nd ed.). Alexandria, VA: American Counseling Association.

Lee, E. (Ed.). (1997). *Working with Asian Americans: A guide for clinicians*. New York: Guilford Press.

Levant, R. (2005). Evidence-based practice in psychology. *Monitor on Psychology, 36*, 5.

Linehan, M. M. (1993). *Cognitive–behavioral treatment of borderline personality disorder*. New York: Guilford Press.

Marsella, A. J., Bornemann, T., Ekblad, S., & Orley, J. (1994). *Amidst peril and pain: The mental health and well-being of the world's refugees*. Washington, DC: American Psychological Association.

Martell, C. R., Safren, S. S., & Prince, S. E. (2004). *Cognitive–behavioral therapies with lesbian, gay, and bisexual clients*. New York: Guilford Press.

Matheson, L. (1986). If you are not an Indian, how do you treat an Indian? In H. P. Lefley & P. Pedersen (Eds.), *Cross-cultural training for mental health professionals* (pp. 115–130). Springfield, IL: Charles C Thomas.

McGoldrick, M., Giordano, J., & Pearce, J. K. (Eds.). (1996). *Ethnicity and family therapy*. New York: Guilford Press.

Miller, W. R. (Ed.). (1999). *Integrating spirituality into treatment: Resources for practitioners*. Washington, DC: American Psychological Association.

Mio, J. S., & Iwamasa, G. Y. (2003). *Culturally diverse mental health*. New York: Bruner-Routledge.

Morales, E. S. (1992). Counseling Latino gays and Latina lesbians. In S. H. Dworkin & F. J. Gutiérrez (Eds.), *Counseling gay men and lesbians: Journey to the end of the rainbow* (pp. 125–140). Alexandria, VA: American Counseling Association.

Newman, B. M., & Newman, P. R. (1999). *Development through life: A psychosocial approach*. Belmont, CA: Wadsworth.

Norcross, J. C., Hedges, M., & Prochaska, J. O. (2002). The face of 2010: A Delphi poll on the future of psychotherapy. *Professional Psychology: Research and Practice, 33*, 316–322.

Olkin, R. (1999). *What psychotherapists should know about disability*. New York: Guilford Press.

Paniagua, F. A. (1998). *Assessing and treating culturally diverse clients*. Thousand Oaks, CA: Sage.

Pauwels, A. (1995). *Cross-cultural communication in the health sciences: Communicating with migrant patients*. Melbourne, Australia: Macmillan Education Australia.

Pedersen, P. (1987). Ten frequent assumptions of cultural bias in counseling. *Journal of Multicultural Counseling & Development, 15*, 16–24.

Pedersen, P. B., Draguns, J. G., Lonner, W. J., & Trimble, J. E. (2002). *Counseling across cultures*. Thousand Oaks, CA: Sage.

Perez, R. M., DeBord, K. A., & Bieschke, K. J. (2000). *Handbook of counseling and psychotherapy with lesbian, gay, and bisexual clients*. Washington, DC: American Psychological Association.

Pipes McAdoo, H. (Ed.). (1999). *Family ethnicity*. Thousand Oaks, CA: Sage.

Pope, M. (1995). The "salad bowl" is big enough for us all: An argument for the inclusion of lesbians and gay men in any definition of multiculturalism. *Journal of Counseling & Development, 73*, 301–304.

Pope-Davis, D. B., & Coleman, H. L. K. (1997). *Multicultural counseling competencies: Assessment, education and training, and supervision.* Thousand Oaks, CA: Sage.

Renfrey, G. S. (1992). Cognitive–behavior therapy and the Native American client. *Behavior Therapy, 23*, 321–340.

Robinson, T. L., & Howard-Hamilton, M. F. (2000). *The convergence of race, ethnicity, and gender: Multiple identities in counseling.* Upper Saddle River, NJ: Merrill.

Roysircar, G. (2003). Understanding immigrants: Acculturation theory and research. In F. D. Harper & J. McFadden (Eds.), *Culture and counseling: New approaches* (pp. 164–185). Boston: Allyn & Bacon.

Roysircar, G., Arredondo, P., Fuertes, J. N., Ponterotto, J. G., & Toporek, R. L. (2003). *Multicultural counseling competencies 2003.* Alexandria, VA: American Counseling Association.

Salkovskis, P. M. (1996). *Frontiers of cognitive therapy.* New York: Guilford Press.

Shafranske, E. P. (Ed.). (1996). *Religion and the clinical practice of psychology.* Washington, DC: American Psychological Association.

Smith, T. (2004). *Practicing multiculturalism: Affirming diversity in counseling and psychology.* Boston: Allyn & Bacon.

Sue, D. W. (2001). Multidimensional facets of cultural competence. *Counseling Psychologist, 29*, 790–821.

Sue, D. W., & Sue, D. (2002). *Counseling the culturally different: Theory and practice.* New York: Wiley.

Sue, S. (2003). In defense of cultural competency in psychotherapy and treatment. *American Psychologist, 58*, 964–970.

Suinn, R. M. (2003). Answering questions regarding the future directions in behavior therapy. *The Behavior Therapist, 26*, 282–284.

Swan Reimer, C. (1999). *Counseling the Inupiat Eskimo.* Westport, CT: Greenwood Press.

Swinomish Tribal Community. (1991). *A gathering of wisdoms, tribal mental health: A cultural perspective.* LaConner, WA: Author.

Thorn, B. E. (2004). *Cognitive therapy for chronic pain.* New York: Guilford Press.

Uba, L. (1994). *Asian Americans: Personality patterns, identity, and mental health.* New York: Guilford Press.

U.S. Census Bureau. (2000). *State and county quick facts.* Retrieved November 24, 2004, from http://quickfacts.census.gov/qfd/states/00000.html

U.S. Department of Health and Human Services. (1999). *Mental health: A report of the Surgeon General—executive summary.* Rockville, MD: U.S. Department of Health and Human Services, National Institute of Mental Health.

Waxler-Morrison, N., Anderson, J., & Richardson, E. (Eds.). (1990). *Cross-cultural caring: A handbook for health professionals*. Vancouver, British Columbia, Canada: University of British Columbia Press.

Wood, P. S., & Mallinckrodt, B. (1990). Culturally sensitive assertiveness training for ethnic minority clients. *Professional Psychology: Research and Practice, 21*, 5–11.

I

COGNITIVE–BEHAVIORAL THERAPY WITH PEOPLE OF ETHNIC MINORITY CULTURES

1

COGNITIVE–BEHAVIORAL THERAPY WITH AMERICAN INDIANS

JUSTIN DOUGLAS MCDONALD AND JOHN GONZALEZ

The degree to which European American and American Indian perspectives differ regarding the topic of mental health could keep an army of cross-cultural psychologists working for decades. Unfortunately, no such army exists, and most of the cross-culturally competent "warriors" have concerned themselves with the larger ethnic minority groups, understandably so. The reasons for this disparity are legion and more fully described elsewhere (see McDonald & Chaney, 2003). The point remains that although much has been anecdotally discussed, very little has been empirically clarified. Nonetheless, as increasing numbers of American Indians receive doctorates in psychology (Benson, 2003), it logically follows that a new generation of culturally competent psychologists will fuel an interest in empirical clarity, and we should build and move in this direction.

In this chapter, we have compiled and synthesized what information is available from the clinical literature with information from traditional American Indian oral history and contemporary practice. We provide the reader with a brief history of American Indian demographic and cultural issues relevant to psychology in general and cognitive–behavioral therapy (CBT) in particular, followed by a case example that integrates consideration of these issues with the clinical application of CBT.

From the beginning we must note that although this chapter is authored by two American Indians representing different tribes, our collective perspectives are inadequate to represent all Native nations on the North American continent. Although many tribes were decimated by military genocide or disease, over 500 Native cultural entities remain (U.S. Department of the Interior, 2002). Current estimates of the numbers of American Indians and Alaska Natives indicate that 2,475,956 citizens identified themselves as such in the 2000 U.S. Census (U.S. Census Bureau, 2001). However, some have questioned the estimates of the data given the procedures used for self-reporting ethnicity and race (see Trimble & Thurman, 2002, for a discussion). Although there are certainly some areas of cultural overlap among all American Indian tribes (i.e., spirituality, collective orientation, reverence of elders and children), some groups are as ethnically diverse as the nations (tribes) of Europe (see Snipp, 1989, 1996). Pan-Indianism, or the notion that all Natives are the same, is the first and perhaps most pervasive stereotype that non-Natives hold.

In the following section, we attempt to establish a historical and cultural context within which our consideration of CBT with American Indians must be placed. We do not present this information to complain or place blame, but rather to help readers unfamiliar with Native American history told from a Native perspective to see the world as we do. We believe that establishment of this context will maximize the potential for readers to both understand and empathize.

HISTORICAL OVERVIEW

Many American Indian cultures have a creation story that indicates their people existed on the North American continent since the beginning of time. Anthropologists and archeologists suggest the earliest inhabitants of North America date back to about 28,000 years ago. Regardless of which timeline is fact, for Indigenous people, history does not begin with European contact (Page, 2003). The oral (and written) histories of American Indians provide accounts of intercultural (tribal) contacts, migrations, and cultural adaptations. For example, the Ojibwe oral history talks of their people originally coming from the west and settling near the gulf of what is now the St. Lawrence River on the east coast. The seven prophecies told the Ojibwe to migrate east and settle in a "place where food grows on the water" (wild rice) and "an island that is shaped like a turtle" (Madeline Island, Wisconsin). There is no doubt that intercultural contact and conflict occurred during this migration. The oral tradition does indicate that conflict occurred with the Iroquois Federation people during the beginning of the migrations and with the Lakota peoples who inhabited the western Great Lakes region prior to the Ojibwe (Benton-Banaii, 1988; Johnson, 1988). The archeological record provides evidence of this migration and the Lakota peoples inhabiting this region prior to the Ojibwe (Morton & Gawboy, 2003). The archeological record also provides evidence of intercultural contact, cultural adaptations, and the rise and fall of complex societies for thousands of years in the Western hemisphere (Page, 2003). The relevancy is that American Indians know their history is one that spans generations and is connected to the land of this continent. At the time of first contact with Europeans, cross-cultural contact was not new to Indigenous cultures. However, the cross-cultural contact with Europeans would prove to be different from anything they experienced in their long histories.

The historical relations between European Americans and American Indians are a mixture of cooperation and conflict (Venables, 2004). More important are the perceptions of these historical relations held by both groups. Until recently, many Americans have held images ranging from those of the "savage Indians" raiding villages of European settlers to Squanto eating turkey with the pilgrims and Sacagawea happily leading Lewis and Clark up and down the Missouri River with a baby on her back (Hanson & Rouse, 1987; Trimble, 1988; Vrasidas, 1997). Perceptions in the Native community are quite different and include recognition of a history of deceit, aggression, betrayal, and broken promises. Whereas most non-Native people have never had any direct experience with American Indian people, every single American Indian person has had experiences with a European American, experiences that shape their perceptions of the dominant culture. Through stories told to them by their elders, nearly all Natives have learned of the history of deceit, betrayal, and mistrust. This is not to say that all Native Americans' experiences with non-Natives are unpleasant; however, it highlights the context in which Native perspectives develop.

For the most part, early relations between Europeans and Natives were collaborative. Within the worldview of many Native tribes, a humanistic ideology existed that is still present today (Gonzalez & Bennett, 2000). This ideology views all people as being similar regardless of race or ethnicity. Therefore, most tribes were initially helpful and welcomed the Europeans with generosity and friendship. However, many Europeans typically had an agenda, whether it was colonization or finding inexistent water passages, cities of gold, or fountains of youth. At the point when tribes began to realize they were being exploited, they would begin to withdraw their support. This resistance was met with swift and sometimes sweeping punishment. Entire bands and tribes were exterminated in the most atrocious, unspeakable manner (for more information, see Faragher, Buhle, Czitrom, & Armitage, 2000).

Manifest destiny provided the holy and legal rationale for the westward expansion. The choices for Eastern tribes were to (a) flee west into unknown and often inhospitable territory, (b) stay and fight, or (c) stay and submit to total domination. In reality, all of these options carried the probability of cultural disintegration and physical annihilation. Those who fled were forced to give up their lands and lifestyles and were often wiped out by unfamiliar climates or disease. Being forced to leave territory that many groups had roamed for centuries was devastating. Those groups who "staked themselves out" ultimately lost either mostly or completely, and if any survived, they were relegated to reservations or chased off and not officially recognized. Treaties were made but were consistently broken by the drafters. By the time of the last major battle between the U.S. Army and a band of starving and freezing Brule Lakota (Sioux) at Wounded Knee, South Dakota in 1891, most tribes had been slaughtered, scattered, or relocated to reservations. The Indian Relocation Act of 1830 marked the beginning of a series of laws and treaties aimed at controlling and quashing Indian resistance and assimilating them as quickly and quietly as possible. This act empowered the federal government to forcibly relocate "friendlies" and punish "hostiles" who resisted relocation.

Soon after forcing Natives on reservations, the federal policy shifted to one of assimilation in an attempt to "civilize" the Native. This assimilation process included teaching and expecting Native Americans to become farmers rather than the hunters and gatherers many of them had been (Collier, 1947; Edwards & Smith, 1979). One of the first policies enacted to force assimilation was the Dawes Act or the Land Allotment Act of 1887, which provided for the allotment of plots of Native American land to "competent" Native Americans. The Dawes Act was disastrous for Native Americans. Because they were unable to properly farm their land and ended up selling it to Whites, the act resulted in the loss of three fifths of all Native American lands (LaDuke, 1999; Meyer, 1994). Life on the reservation became very difficult as tribes were prohibited from using their languages, participating in cultural ceremonies, and fulfilling traditional roles (Collier, 1947). In addition, the transfer of the culture to the next generation was denied when the federal government established the boarding school system. The main objective of the off-reservation boarding school was to assimilate Native American children into "American" culture by teaching them in a closed environment and not allowing them to speak their languages or practice cultural traditions (Choney, Berryhill-Paapke, & Robbins, 1995). The effects of this policy on Native communities have lingered for generations, as one Ojibwe man recalls:

> [W]hen I was sent away to the boarding school in Pipestone [Minnesota], I only spoke Ojibwe and a little French. Now I can only speak a little in my own language and no French. They took that away from me, I was beaten and whipped with a belt if I spoke Ojibwe or French . . . if I did anything in my own [Ojibwe] way. (James Weaver, personal communication, August 17, 2001)

These legislative travesties and personal accounts demonstrate the concept of social dominance theory to the fullest extent (Sidanius, 1993). Suffice it to say, the end result of European contact has been devastating for

American Indians. On the basis of the history of contact alone, these are the perceptions of mainstream society that Indigenous peoples live with. The Native worldview and psyche are further complicated by an environment of continued stereotyping, prejudice, and discrimination by the dominant culture in the United States.

Acculturation and Cultural Identification of American Indians

Throughout the history of postcolonial relations, Natives have struggled to maintain their cultural lifeways and values. However, many of the social policies were created to directly attack and destroy traditional American Indian cultures. In addition, different tribes had varying reactions and responses to Europeans. As a result, significant differences exist between and within tribes regarding the level of acculturation and traditional cultural identification (Trimble, Fleming, Beauvais, & Jumper-Thurman, 1996). For example, the so-called "Five Civilized Tribes" (Cherokee, Chickasaw, Choctaw, Creek, and Seminole) were named as such because they adopted or acculturated into European American lifestyles relatively easily, establishing agricultural systems, constitutions, law codes, judicial systems, churches, and schools primarily on the basis of European ways. However, these tribes learned a bitter lesson that the White man was not necessarily interested in their assimilation but rather their land (Venables, 2004). The boarding school system described earlier has probably had the greatest influence on acculturation and cultural identification of American Indian tribes and members (Choney et al., 1995; Churchill, 2004).

Although few empirical studies exist regarding acculturation and American Indians, some researchers have attempted to delineate a lexicon to describe the possible levels of acculturation of American Indian tribes and individuals. LaFromboise, Trimble, and Mohatt (1990) discussed four possible levels of acculturation or cultural identification: traditional, transitional, bicultural, and assimilated. A *traditional* individual adheres to traditional customs and values and tends to think and speak in his or her Native language. A *transitional* person has maintained some aspects of his or her origin culture and some traits of the dominant culture but does not fully identify with either group. A person who has been accepted into the mainstream or dominant society and still maintains ties to the origin culture in an equal fashion is considered *bicultural*. Finally, an American Indian who is *assimilated* has attempted (or was forced) to adopt the dominant culture and lifestyle, no longer speaking the language or practicing traditional cultural ways.

More recently, Garrett and Pichette (2000) formulated five types or levels of acculturation for American Indians: traditional, marginal, bicultural, assimilated, and pantraditional. Although slightly different in definition, these are similar to those of LaFromboise et al. (1990). The main distinctions are the use of marginal instead of transitional, and the inclusion of the pantraditional category. According to Garrett and Pichette, the *marginal* individual may speak both languages but has lost touch with Native cultural ways and is not fully accepted or comfortable in the mainstream society. The *pantraditional* category of acculturation describes the American Indian who has only been exposed to or adopts some mainstream values but has made a conscious effort to return to the old ways.

Fleming (1992) described the efforts by some Native communities to teach positive Native traditions such as singing, dancing, and Native languages, and at the same time encourage the skills needed to function in the majority culture. Many Native American researchers and practitioners have stressed the importance of forming and strengthening Native cultural identification to ensure positive outcomes in school achievement and coping strategies while protecting against undesirable outcomes such as depression and substance abuse (Dehyle, 1992; LaFromboise & Rowe, 1983; May & Moran, 1995). These efforts and programs would suggest that an acculturation level or cultural identification that is bicultural is desirable for positive mental health in the American Indian community. Later in the chapter we discuss the assessment of acculturation or cultural orientation of Native clients, but for now we turn to the topic of mental health and care.

American Indian Mental Health and Care

Accurate determination of the incidence and prevalence of psychopathology among American Indians is difficult for several reasons. First, the cross-cultural equivalence of many psychological disorders is controversial and poorly understood (Matsumoto, 2000). Differences between Native tribes regarding symptomatology and the diagnostic validity of categories can complicate the most basic assessment efforts. Even for straightforwardly defined problems such as completed suicides, the rates between tribes can be drastically different, making any efforts to generalize misleading. Finally, health care delivery is significantly different for American Indians, particularly those on reservations. The Indian Health Service (IHS), a branch of the U.S. Public Health Service, is responsible for general health care delivery. The IHS is chronically underfunded and understaffed, and the majority of psychologists who work for the IHS are non-Native providers (McDonald, 1996, 1998).

These general issues aside, limited data exists on the prevalence and incidence of mental health problems and substance abuse in Native communities and populations. Only recently have some larger-scale epidemiological reports been published by the National Center for American Indian and Alaska Native Mental Health Research (see Beals, Manson, Mitchell, Spicer, & the AI-SUPERPFP Team, 2003; Beals, Spicer, Mitchell, Novins, Manson, & the AI-SUPERPFP Team, 2003; Mitchell, Beals, Novins, Spicer, & the AI-SUPERPFP Team, 2003 for summaries). This data lends support to what most Native American health providers and leaders would attest to regarding the existence of serious behavioral health problems in their communities. Furthermore, the historical context leading to the current social environment compounds the unique mental health problems in Native communities (Trimble & Thurman, 2002).

Equally lacking is a consistent literature on the appropriate treatment of mental health needs for Native populations. In an article on the difficulties in mental health treatment in Native American communities, Gone (2003) recommended a more comprehensive assessment of therapeutic outcomes—a challenge because the bulk of the literature regarding Native Americans does not subscribe to a cognitive–behavioral approach, making it difficult to establish external validity. Trimble and Thurman (2002) noted a significant increase in the number of published articles related to counseling and psychotherapy with Native populations; however, most of these either educate the reader on Native history and general cultural considerations in treatment (e.g., Anderson & Ellis, 1995; Herring, 1999; Sue & Sue, 1999) or delineate a traditional Native American healing practice (e.g., Colmant & Merta, 1999; Heilbron & Guttman, 2000; Tafoya, 1989). In other words, they do not involve empirically based research.

An online search of the literature revealed only two articles that specifically mention cognitive–behavioral treatment with Native clients. In the first, Renfrey (1992) suggested that CBT is congruent with Native American community mental health needs and made a strong argument for the cognitive–behavioral assessment of the client's cultural identification as a guide to the therapeutic process. Renfrey also called for a bicultural treatment plan that integrates Western practices with a Native worldview. In the second article, Trimble (1992) described a community based, cognitive–behavioral approach to the treatment of substance abuse in adolescents and called for the teaching of bicultural competence in communication skills and coping strategies. Trimble argued that by incorporating the Native American worldview of community and social environments, it is possible to apply cognitive–behavioral concepts from social learning theory to the needs of Native American individuals and communities. A discussion on how this may be possible follows.

COGNITIVE–BEHAVIORAL THEORY AND AMERICAN INDIAN PSYCHOLOGY

Although vastly different in practice, American Indian concepts of healing and the Western model of CBT are compellingly similar in some respects. Many people, including many American Indians, have assumed that the two modalities are entirely orthogonal. In researching the available information, we have concluded that they may instead be thought of as closely related in genotype, yet dissimilar in phenotype. The following sections highlight some issues relevant to understanding wellness and healing from a traditional American Indian perspective.

Worldview

As described by Triandis (1994), most cultural groups can be categorized as either individualistic or collectivistic. Matsumoto (2000) distinguished the two orientations by suggesting that "Members of individualistic cultures see themselves as separate and autonomous individuals, whereas members of collectivistic cultures see themselves as fundamentally connected with others" (p. 41). It is essential for non-Indians to understand that the ontological perspective of traditional American Indians is collectivistic in nature, in that both the well-being and the pathology of the group supersede and sometimes even determine that of the individual. An illustrative example of this point is apparent in the fact that some tribes (i.e., the female Northern Cheyenne dialect) do not have a word in their vocabulary for "I."

Spirituality

In the pursuit of understanding American Indian concepts of wellness and healing, one must acknowledge the significance of spirituality (Swinomish Tribal Community, 1991). Most American Indian belief systems are animistic in that all things are believed to possess a spirit, be it people, animals, trees, wind, or even inanimate, nonliving objects such as rocks. This animistic ontology presumes the existence of a Spirit World, a plane of existence that is both distinct and coexistent with the physical world. People can see, hear, touch, or communicate with other spirits on particular, usually significant occasions (Jackson & Turner, 2004). Whereas many non-Natives find it difficult to appreciate or conceive of two seemingly distinct realities existing in simultaneous harmony, traditional American Indians are quite comfortable with this reality.

The most salient aspect of American Indian spirituality for non-Natives to grasp is that *personhood* is not a unitary construct but a combination of components. Different tribes have subtly different conceptualizations regarding the composition of the person, but most include three facets: the mind, the physical body, and the spirit (Chavez Cameron & Turtle-Song, 2003). Some tribes distinguish the mind from feelings, or the heart from the body, but for the most part the mind, body, and spirit form the three aspects of individual existence.

Harmony and Wellness

Harmony or balance between mind, body, and spirit forms the foundation of the Native conceptualization of wellness (Choney et al., 1995; Cross, 2003; Swinomish Tribal Community, 1991). Conversely, disharmony or imbalance manifests itself in pathology. The challenge in understanding American Indian ideas of pathology lies in conceptually grasping the significance of disharmony. Playing "teeter-totter" is fun and works well if both players are similar in weight. If one is more or less heavy, then some compensation—either moving in or out on the board or one player working harder than the other—must be made. If one player is far too heavy or light, the game goes on but eventually becomes burdensome and frustrating to both for different reasons. Personal disharmony works much the same way in that if, for example, the body is ill, the spirit and mind must compensate in order for life (the game) to go on. The more significant the physical pathology, the more taxing the strain for mind and spirit to keep up, and disharmony and imbalance develop.

Given this scenario, American Indians may perceive such maladies as depression or anxiety as weakness of the mind and body, while the spirit—although intact and fully functional—is seen as being weakened from shouldering the burden of the other two. Eventually, the individual presents as ailing not only physically and mentally but spiritually as well. An individual may also experience spiritual malaise as a result of mentally and physically caused problems. An example is a functional disruption resulting from engaging in behaviors that violate tribally accepted norms, encountering taboo animals or spirits, or having "bad medicine" or witchcraft performed on one (Swinomish Tribal Community, 1991). It is crucial to note that whether a non-Indian practitioner recognizes such possibilities as bad medicine or witchcraft is irrelevant. Working with American Indians, particularly with those who hold traditional beliefs, requires an appreciation of the fact that they believe in the existence of these phenomena and in their power to influence wellness.

It is at this point that we begin to realize the similarity between American Indian psychology and the cognitive–behavioral paradigm. Consider one of the most basic tenets of CBT: Thoughts that occur most frequently are the ones we tend to believe. The rationality, logic, or positive–negative relevance of the thought does not matter; frequency is the key. In this regard, a firm belief that one is "worthless" must be dealt with regardless of its origin. In the same vein, the belief that one is being spiritually punished for a behavioral transgression must also be proactively addressed. The degree to which the first person truly is worthless or the second person is being punished by spirits is inconsequential. The key is that both believe these thoughts are true and real. Thus, the source of people's contributions to their own pathology is the same: their own schema, based on their own worldview.

Oppression, Social Dominance, and Cognition

One of the more damaging aspects of racial and social oppression is the myriad and consistent cognitive assaults on the minority group by the dominant group. Although not dissimilar to the psychological assaults suffered by other minority groups, American Indians have the added sorrow of knowing that they are not only the smallest ethnic minority group in the United States but they were once the dominant group. This distinction provides considerable content for self-deprecation at both the group and individual level. Generations of propaganda waged by the dominant culture often form the basis for negative cognitive, emotional, and behavioral processes. "Indians are _____: lazy, stupid, worthless, drunks, heathens, animals, dirty." Such cognitive assaults have been so consistently reinforced by the dominant culture that Indian people no longer require majority culture members to tell them; they tell themselves. And, as stated previously, the thoughts that occur most frequently are the thoughts we tend to believe and, unfortunately, behave in accordance with. Duran and Duran (1995) conceptualized this belief system, in part, as a result of historical and intergenerational trauma that contributes to suicide, alcoholism, domestic violence, child abuse, and other social problems in Native communities.

Cultural Competence

Much of our research, writing, and teaching is based on the orthogonal cultural identification theory (OCIT) of biculturalism (Oetting & Beauvais, 1990–1991), which suggests that ethnic minority individuals with high levels of cultural competence in both their own traditional culture and the majority culture (i.e., described as bicultural) will demonstrate less psychopathology and higher levels of adaptive functioning in both cultural realms (Oetting & Beauvais, 1990–1991). Conversely, those individuals who have lower levels of cultural competence in traditional and majority cultures (described as marginal) present with more pathology and dysfunction. Those who have low levels of affiliation in their traditional culture but who affiliate highly with the majority culture are described as assimilated and appear more similar to their majority culture peers in terms of diagnosis and treatment preferences.

As an example, consider the scenario described previously in which some traditional Native languages lack the word "I." A mainstream manualized treatment that encourages the use of "I" statements (e.g., assertiveness training) would be inappropriate for a traditional Native client but might be fully appropriate for a more bicultural or assimilated client. Assessment of a Native client's degree of cultural orientation and competence is therefore crucial in developing a valid diagnostic hypothesis and treatment plan. Unfortunately, very few scales exist for assessing cultural orientation with American Indian populations. Most of the research on cultural identification (orientation) with American Indians has been with adolescent populations (Bates, Beauvais, & Trimble, 1997; Moran, Fleming, Somervell, & Manson, 1999; Oetting & Beauvais, 1990–1991).

For American Indian adults, we have used the Northern Plains Bicultural Inventory (NPBI; Allen & French, 1994, 1996) and the American Indian Bicultural Inventory (AIBI; McDonald, 1998). These measures ask the client to indicate how much they engage or participate in American Indian and European American cultural activities, languages, and spiritual events, yielding an American Indian Cultural Identification (AICI) subscale score and a European American Cultural Identification (EACI) subscale score. For example, the client is asked to indicate on a 5-point Likert scale how often they attend Native spiritual events (sweat lodges, sundance, etc.) and a similar question asking how often they attend non-Native religious or spiritual events (church, communion, etc.). A median split procedure is then conducted that attempts to place the individual in one of the four possible cultural orientations defined by OCIT described earlier. For the NPBI, reliability for the AICI subscale was excellent ($r = .82$) and reliability for the EACI subscale was good ($r = .70$).

However, as with any assessment measure there are cautions to consider. The median-split procedure has its limitations in that true differences in cultural orientation may be hard to detect for individuals who score near the median. We have found it useful to supplement the NPBI or AICI data with information gathered from the clinical interview regarding the client's personal and family history, worldview, and current social environment, for example. Therefore, we suggest considerable cross-cultural competence is required for a non-Indian therapist to assess a Native client's biculturalism, particularly if the client is more traditional. Readers are referred to the American Psychological Association's (2002) guidelines for multicultural competence. Simply reading this document will not make a person competent to work with Indian clients. However, the document provides helpful suggestions regarding process and content and a wealth of suggested readings.

As a final note regarding bicultural competence, we suggest that non-Indian therapists be aware that cultural competence should not be judged by skin color. Therapists are advised to avoid jumping to conclusions regarding an Indian client's cultural competence on the basis of how light or dark the client's hair, skin, and eyes are. As a result of Indian removal and the inappropriate placement of Indian children with non-Indians prior to the Indian Child Welfare Act, many with high blood quanta grew up isolated from their Native culture. Conversely, other Native people with lower blood quanta may have grown up on a reservation or in an urban Indian community and be much more traditional than they "look."

Although traditional American Indian and mainstream psychological treatments may differ, they share a primary goal: changing the way the client thinks. If one's negative and dysfunctional thoughts can be changed, so too will one's feelings and behaviors change. In this way, harmony is restored between mind, body, and spirit. The following case highlights the degree to which traditional treatments and CBT may differ but the two approaches can be complementary and their goals the same.

CASE EXAMPLE

Billy was a 45-year-old American Indian from a Northern Plains tribe. He was divorced and unemployed despite being a qualified and bonded electrician. He was a combat veteran who had completed two tours in Vietnam with the second being voluntary. At the time of this assessment, he was receiving veterans' benefits, having been deemed fully service-connected disabled and diagnosed with posttraumatic stress disorder (PTSD). Billy reported graduating from high school on his home reservation. He had been physically and verbally abused by a stepfather in high school and in trouble for truancy, alcohol violations, fighting, and vandalism for which he served a total of 1 year in juvenile detention centers and local jails. He could identify no close relatives with psychiatric disorders and had always been healthy and fit. He had never received psychological or psychiatric services, and none had been offered or court-ordered. A judge (as was not uncommon during this period) had given him the choice of an extended jail sentence or enlistment in the military during the Vietnam War.

Following Marine Corps basic training in San Diego in 1969, Billy was stationed with a unit responsible for providing reconnaissance and fire support for an Army contingent seeking to engage Viet Cong soldiers and identify collaborators. Billy had difficulty speaking about some of the encounters he had survived, and there were others he could not bring himself to articulate. It is unnecessary to graphically describe Billy's accounts. Suffice it to say they were often horrific, and over the course of the 8 weeks of treatment, the depth and scope of what he had endured were astonishing.

Honorably discharged in 1972, Billy spent several years "drifting around" southern California working sporadically as a day laborer for area produce farmers. He reported difficulty sleeping because of intrusive images, racing thoughts, and combat-related nightmares. He began drinking heavily "just to knock myself out; to sleep so I could work more." He found himself becoming increasingly dependent on alcohol and began experiencing flashbacks during the day. The flashbacks involved vivid visual, auditory, tactile, olfactory, and even gustatory sensations connected to his combat experiences. He also began to experience overwhelming feelings of survivor guilt and anger at America's anti-Vietnam War sentiment. Those with long memories can remember how poorly Vietnam veterans were treated on their return home. In Billy's case, he felt ostracized and shunned whenever it became known that he had served in the war.

On his return to the reservation several years after his discharge, Billy fell even deeper into a pattern of alcohol and drug abuse, violence, and general antisocial behavior. He shunned the attention of elders and Native healers who attempted to advise him regarding healing ceremonies and rituals. He spent time solely with other veterans, many of whom were experiencing similar symptoms and thus, were in similar situations. He was admitted to the psychiatric unit of the regional veterans hospital six times for suicidal ideation and two attempts.

Finally, Billy's behavioral tailspin landed him in the state penitentiary for 2 years for aggravated assault. While incarcerated, Billy was befriended by an older veteran who spoke of the "Red Road" approach to healing and living. He learned that walking (i.e., living in accordance with) the Red Road meant embracing his spirituality and traditional values. The Red Road is a "holistic approach to spiritual, mental, physical, and emotional wellness based upon Native American healing concepts and traditions" that uses prayer as the basis of all healing (Gene Thin Elk, 1994, in Arbogast, 1995, p. 319).

On his release from prison, Billy completed an electrician's apprenticeship and worked for 2 years for a mining company in Montana. He reported this as the most productive and positive period of his life, yet he soon began experiencing again the flashbacks, nightmares, and subsequent emotional and social disruptions that had haunted him previously. Ultimately, his employer referred him for therapy through the company's Employee Assistance Program at which point I (McDonald) met him.

Assessment

Following a diagnostic interview, it was determined that Billy was of sufficient bicultural orientation and competence to be administered standardized psychological measures. As suggested previously, it is our contention that determining an American Indian client's degree of cultural orientation and competence is crucial (McDonald, Morton, & Stewart, 1992). If it had been determined that Billy's cultural identity was traditional or marginal, the use of standardized psychological tests may have been deemed inappropriate.

Billy was administered the Beck Depression Inventory—II (BDI–II; Beck, Steer, & Brown, 1996), the State–Trait Anxiety Inventory (STAI; Spielberger, Gorsuch, & Lushene, 1970), and the American Indian Biculturalism Scale (AIBI). The AIBI, which we developed, yields subscale scores for American Indian and European American cultural orientations. A median-split technique allows for placement of the individual into one of the four cultural quadrants defined by the orthogonal theory of biculturalism. As might be expected, Billy's scores on the BDI–II and STAI were clinically elevated, and his AIBI scores suggested he was culturally competent in both his own Native and the majority culture. Some authors suggest utilizing measures of cultural orientation to moderate standardized testing scores (Dana, 2000). This suggestion is intriguing, but there is not currently sufficient research to demonstrate its efficacy. In our view, whether standardized test scores may be moderated by cultural competence or not, their use with traditionally or marginally oriented American Indians is highly questionable.

On the basis of the results of the testing and interview, it was determined that Billy suffered from PTSD. It is at this point that we emphasize the importance of multicultural competence. In working with American Indians, therapists should become fully knowledgeable about the tribes in their area of practice and are encouraged to befriend tribal members in a sincere effort to learn more. This thoughtful and proactive approach to obtaining cross-cultural knowledge and experience for the good of one's practice is strongly encouraged. In this instance, it was known that Billy's worldview contained strong Native values, as evident in his upbringing and his positive response to the Red Road approach. This information was as vital as his psychological testing scores.

Treatment

Billy's high degree of bicultural competence was a key determinant of his treatment plan. With his high degree of orientation toward and affiliation with the majority culture, he appeared to be a good candidate for CBT. However, his traditional competence suggested that therapy would also need to incorporate his Native values. Thus, the *Takes Life* ceremony was considered.

Most American Indian tribes with significant histories of battle and intertribal conflict practice some form of the Takes Life ceremony. (The name of the ceremony has been changed but is generally described later in terms of historical significance and process. This is in accordance with a declaration passed by Lakota spiritual leaders at the Lakota Summit V, aimed at protecting the privacy and preventing the exploitation of American Indian spiritual and ceremonial practices; Mesteth, Standing Elk, & Swift Hawk, 1993.) The intent of these ceremonies is to ease the adjustment of a warrior who has taken the life of an enemy in battle. As discussed previously, Hollywood and other popular media have painted a distorted picture of American Indians in many ways, perhaps most notably in terms of war. By and large, armed and lethal conflict was avoided, and ritualistic and symbolic confrontation was preferred. The practice of "counting coup" was considered more honorable and courageous than actually killing an enemy. When counting coup, a warrior would charge an enemy warrior and touch or strike him with a "coup stick" or their bow and escape unharmed. Only in the most extreme circumstances, such as competition for territory or other resources, were lives taken. The elders knew that although killing enhanced the reputation of the warrior, it also took a heavy psychological toll.

The Takes Life ceremony involves some manner of individual treatment from a spiritual healer, who uses a combination of herbal medicines, songs, prayers, and other sacred procedures. There is a purification process, and in some tribes, prayer for the spirit of the one killed and his family. These ceremonies often end by calling together the warrior's family and friends and having another veteran, such as the one who witnessed the taking of the life, recount the specifics of the fight and the bravery of the warrior. The "narrator" or "testifier" proclaims such points as "I know, I saw, I was there. Here is what I saw my brother do. He is brave—honor him." In the end the crowd accepts this, and often there is an honor song and everyone dances in an ever-closing circle toward the warrior. At the conclusion of the song he is embraced, and there are war cries from other veterans and ululations from the women. The Takes Life ceremony is a perfect example of how a collectivist society helps heal an individual.

On consultation with a spiritual advisor from Billy's tribe, a Takes Life ceremony was arranged during the upcoming Veteran's Day *Wacipi* (powwow). Billy was introduced to the medicine man, who began a series of individual traditional treatments (which were private and therefore unknown to me). Billy also engaged in individual CBT for PTSD and chemical dependency counseling, and he started on an antidepressant medication following a psychiatric consultation.

The CBT consisted of 12 weekly sessions, primarily focused on cognitive restructuring as described by McMullin (1998). This approach is multifaceted and includes education, training, and practice. For the education component, Billy was given extensive reading and video materials describing PTSD and its treatment. The training phase included systematic identification and revision of Billy's typical negative thoughts combined with deep muscle relaxation and guided imagery. The goal of these sessions was to encourage Billy to cognitively experience some of the difficult memories and images he had encountered, while remaining deeply relaxed. As will be seen in the following section, a *countering* cognitive restructuring focus was used. Billy was asked to practice and log all homework exercises, which were gradually increased in frequency over the 12 weeks. He was also administered the BDI and STAI every 2 weeks to monitor symptom remission.

CBT Session 1

The first session is by far the most significant one for the therapist and the Indian client because it is during this session that the client decides whether to trust the therapist and engage in the treatment process or not. The competent therapist, regardless of cultural background, will ask (as the first author did with Billy) many questions about the client's family and family history. The therapist will focus as much on the ground as on the figure, and make it clear he or she understands that this person's social context is key in understanding what the client perceives to be "wrong" (see McDonald et al., 1992). Because I am of the same tribal group as Billy, the therapeutic connection was more easily attained. Also in this initial session, Billy's bicultural competence was clarified, and he was encouraged to reconnect with a traditional healer.

An initial goal of this first session of CBT was to explain the basic principles and process of cognitive restructuring. Kanfer's (1998) description of the components of CBT is helpful in this regard. The first of these is the idea that "the thoughts that occur most frequently are those we tend to believe." A corollary to this is "when a client argues against an irrational thought repeatedly, the irrational thought becomes progressively weaker" (McMullin, 1998, p. 3). The cognitive restructuring process can be drawn as a triangle with thoughts, feelings, and behaviors located at the three points. Examples of the client's negative schema are then elicited and applied to illustrate how the client's negative cognitions fuel his emotional distress and maladaptive behaviors. The process for changing this pattern, along with image-laden metaphors such as "making the engine run smoother," gives the client an idea of what to expect. At this point, Billy was excused with a homework assignment to return the next week with a list of 5 of his most common negative self-statements and 10 sincere, rational positive attributes formed into statements.

Session 2

The first part of this session was used to review Billy's homework. Billy and the therapist then engaged in role-playing, with the therapist reading the negative self-statements to Billy and Billy countering each with the entire list of positive attributes. Billy was asked to practice the list of positive attributes twice daily before the next session.

Billy was also introduced to relaxation therapy with guided imagery. Deep breathing was used for the induction and followed by the strategy of tensing and relaxing each muscle group. Once relaxed, Billy was asked to cognitively visit a calm scene from either his memory or his own creation. An audiotape of the session was made, and Billy was also assigned daily relaxation practice as homework.

At this point, it was also important to monitor the client's efforts toward spiritual healing. Therapists do not need to be fully knowledgeable of the traditional healing rituals and ceremonies being practiced. Instead, their role is to ensure they are occurring, to monitor their impact on the client, and to learn as much as possible in the process. In Billy's case that effort took the following form:

McDonald: So, how's it going with Ralph (the healer, different name)?

Billy: Oh, pretty good.

McDonald: How did you guys hook up?

Billy: I went out to his place the other night. He was working some horses. (pause)

McDonald: What did you do?

> Billy: I offered him some tobacco (a traditional show of respect) and asked if I could talk to him. He asked me some questions first, then said "yes" and took the tobacco.

> McDonald: Great, so what's going to happen from here?

> Billy: He wants to have an *inipi* (sweat-lodge ceremony) tonight and on Tuesdays. He said when he finds out what's wrong he'll know better.

As this brief exchange indicates, cultural knowledge is important in understanding even the smallest amounts of information (e.g., that the offering of tobacco was a demonstration of respect). Cultural knowledge also helps the therapist to know what to ask (e.g., how the connection with the healer was going) and what not to ask (details about the healer's practice).

Sessions 3 Through 8

The focus of these sessions was on practicing and expanding the treatment elements and monitoring the traditional healing efforts and their effects. We began every session by reviewing the homework in terms of content and practice during the week. The role-playing became more intensive, as Billy had memorized the list of positive attributes by Week 3 and could counter negative statements more easily and with greater enthusiasm. His home practice of the list-recall task was increased by one session each week during this phase.

The relaxation sessions also increased in length and time spent in guided imagery. As clients become more skilled at self-induction, more effort can be spent guiding them through specific scenarios related to the traumatic incidents they struggle with. In Billy's case, we revisited some of the scenes he had endured while in combat. As a form of systematic desensitization, Billy was gradually guided to reexperience some of the more distressing encounters he endured while remaining relaxed and retreating to his calm scene when necessary. Each relaxation session was terminated after several minutes in the calm scene.

Billy also participated diligently in the traditional healing regimen. He signed a release allowing for communication between the therapist and the healer that facilitated the flow of communication regarding his case. This practice is strongly suggested both as a show of respect for traditional healers and as a means for less experienced non-Indian therapists to become more competent regarding traditional practices.

Sessions 9 Through 12

Most therapists would agree that the therapy termination process should be considerately and respectfully managed, and this is equally true with Native clients whatever their cultural orientation. Traditional Indian clients may offer a gift to the therapist if the treatment has been beneficial to them. We suggest you accept. To do otherwise is seen as disrespectful in many Native cultures.

By this point Billy was accomplished at self-monitoring his negative thoughts and their subsequent effects on his affect and behavior. His "list of positives" began to occur more frequently in his mind than the negatives, and he expanded them to include positive self-statements aimed at building his confidence in coping with the troubling memories. He was able to relax more readily with each session and home practice, and to induce a relaxation response when negative images or impulses occurred. Eventually the latter decreased in intensity and frequency. These improvements encouraged him to discuss his experiences with others, including other veterans and his family and friends, for which he received a great deal of support.

Billy completed the treatment plan within the 12-week time frame. The Takes Life ceremony took place during Week 10, which allowed several weeks of debriefing and processing prior to termination. Billy's final STAI and BDI–II scores were in the nonclinically elevated range, and although he admitted to "thinking about" his experiences in Vietnam, he described them as "only bad memories now, not nightmares." He continued his sessions with his medicine man and participated in traditional ceremonies on a regular basis for years afterward. On 6-month follow-up, Billy had experienced no recurrences of the flashbacks or nightmares that had plagued him. He was sober, and still employed.

CONCLUSION

We hope this case study illustrates our firm contention that cultural orientation should always be considered when working with American Indian clients and research participants. Billy's successful treatment illustrates several important issues in this regard. First, therapists should become as cross-culturally competent as possible, particularly when they know they will be working with ethnic minorities or those different from themselves. Second, part of that competence should include the ability to measure the level of bicultural competence in a client and incorporate it into all aspects of diagnosis and treatment. Finally, CBT can be a very effective treatment modality for American Indians, particularly if the client displays high degrees of bicultural or assimilated cultural competence. Those Indian clients who are more traditional or marginal may not respond as readily and may prefer more traditional treatments. We admit that case studies of one do not provide much in terms of external validity; however, they can provide guidance and help to clarify ideas for empirically based research.

We began this chapter speaking to differences and misunderstandings. We will close with some straightforward and hopeful suggestions toward reconciliation and clarity. You don't have to "go Native" to help one! And that goes for psychology as a field. There are reasons why so little empirical research exists on the effectiveness of CBT (or anything else) with American Indians. One of the biggest reasons is that training more ethnic minorities and more American Indians in particular has not been a high priority. Doing so would require departments and training programs to shift their academic worldviews. Many have been unwilling to make this shift, whereas some have shifted a little, and very few have shifted significantly. The face of psychology is still White, and so are its values and priorities. As long as this situation remains, empirically based cross-cultural enlightenment will dance away outside our reach, for we know that to dance together we must take each other's hands.

REFERENCES

Allen , J., & French, C. (1994). *Northern Plains Biculturalism Inventory: A preliminary manual*. Unpublished manual, University of South Dakota, Vermillion.

Allen, J., & French, C. (1996). *Northern Plains Bicultural Immersion Scale: Preliminary manual and scoring instructions* (Version 5). Vermillion: University of South Dakota.

American Psychological Association. (2002). Guidelines on multicultural education, training, research, practice, and organizational change for psychologists. *American Psychologist, 58,* 377–402.

Anderson, M., & Ellis, R. (1995). On the reservation. In N. Vacc & S. DeVaney (Eds.), *Experiencing and counseling multicultural and diverse populations* (pp. 179–197). Muncie, IN: Accelerated Development.

Arbogast, D. (1995). *Wounded warriors: A time for healing.* Omaha, NE: Little Turtle Publications.

Bates, S. C., Beauvais, F., & Trimble, J. E. (1997). American Indian adolescent alcohol involvement and ethnic identification. *Substance Use & Misuse, 32,* 2013–2031.

Beals, J., Manson, S. M., Mitchell, C. M., Spicer, P., & the AI-SUPERPFP Team. (2003). Cultural specificity and comparison in psychiatric epidemiology: Walking the tightrope in American Indian research. *Culture, Medicine, and Psychiatry, 27,* 259–289.

Beals, J., Spicer, P., Mitchell, C. M., Novins, D. K., Manson, S. M., & the AI-SUPERPFP Team. (2003). Racial disparities in alcohol use: Comparison of two American Indian reservation populations with national data. *American Journal of Public Health, 93,* 1683–1685.

Beck, A. T., Steer, R. A., & Brown, G. K. (1996). *Manual for the Beck Depression Inventory—II*. San Antonio, TX: Psychological Corporation.

Benson, E. (2003, June). Psychology in Indian country. *Monitor on Psychology, 34,* 56–57.

Benton-Banaii, E. (1988). *The Mishomis book: The voice of the Ojibway*. St. Paul, MN: Indian Country Press.

Chavez Cameron, S., & Turtle-Song, I. (2003). Native American mental health: An examination of resiliency in the face of overwhelming odds. In F. Harper & J. McFadden (Eds.), *Culture and counseling: New approaches* (pp. 66–80). Boston: Allyn & Bacon/Pearson Education.

Choney, S. K., Berryhill-Paapke, E., & Robbins, R. R. (1995). The acculturation of American Indians. In J. G. Ponterotto, J. M. Casas, L. A. Suzuki, & C. M. Alexander (Eds.), *Handbook of multicultural counseling* (pp. 73–92). Thousand Oaks, CA: Sage.

Churchill, W. (2004). *Kill the Indian, save the man: The genocidal impact of American Indian residential schools*. San Francisco: City Lights.

Collier, J. (1947). *The Indians of the Americas*. New York: Norton.

Colmant, S., & Merta, R. (1999). Using the sweat lodge ceremony as group therapy for Navajo youth. *Journal for Specialists in Group Work, 24,* 55–73.

Cross, T. L. (2003). Culture as a resource for mental health. *Cultural Diversity and Ethnic Minority Psychology, 9,* 354–359.

Dana, R. H. (2000). *Handbook of cross-cultural and multicultural personality assessment*. Mahwah, NJ: Erlbaum.

Dehyle, D. (1992). Constructing failure and cultural identity: Navajo and Ute school leavers. *Journal of American Indian Education, 32*(1), 24–27.

Duran, E., & Duran, B. (1995). *Native American postcolonial psychology*. Albany: State University of New York Press.

Edwards, E. D., & Smith, L. L. (1979). A brief history of American Indian social policy. *Journal of Humanics, 7*(2), 52–64.

Faragher, J., Buhle, M., Czitrom, D., & Armitage, S. (2000). *Out of many: A history of the American people*. Englewood Cliffs, NJ: Prentice Hall.

Fleming, C. M. (1992). American Indians and Alaska Natives: Changing societies past and present. In M. A. Orlandi, R. Weston, & L. G. Epstein (Eds.), *Cultural competence for evaluators: A guide for alcohol and other drug abuse prevention practitioners working with ethnic/racial communities* (pp. 147–171). Rockville, MD: Office for Substance Abuse Prevention.

Garrett, M. T., & Pichette, E. F. (2000). Red as an apple: Native American acculturation and counseling with or without reservation. *Journal of Counseling & Development, 78,* 3–13.

Gone, J. (2003). Mental health services for Native Americans in the 21st century United States. *Professional Psychology: Research and Practice, 35,* 10–18.

Gonzalez, J., & Bennett, R. (2000, February). *Self-identity in the indigenous peoples of North America: Factor structure and correlates*. Poster presented at the annual meeting of the Society for Personality and Social Psychology, Nashville, TN.

Hanson, J. R., & Rouse, L. P. (1987). Dimensions of Native American stereotyping. *Native American Culture and Research Journal, 11*, 33–35.

Heilbron, C., & Guttman, M. (2000). Traditional healing methods with First Nations women in group counseling. *Canadian Journal of Counseling, 34*, 3–13.

Herring, R. D. (1999). *Counseling with Native American Indians and Alaska Natives: Strategies for helping professionals.* Thousand Oaks, CA: Sage.

Jackson, A. P., & Turner, S. (2004). Counseling and psychotherapy with Native American clients. In T. Smith (Ed.), *Practicing multiculturalism: Affirming diversity in counseling and psychology* (pp. 215–233). Boston: Allyn & Bacon/Pearson Education.

Johnson, E. (1988). *The prehistoric peoples of Minnesota.* St. Paul: Minnesota Historical Society Press.

Kanfer, G. (1998). *Guiding the process of therapeutic change.* Champaign, IL: Research Press.

LaDuke, W. (1999). *All our relations: Native struggles for land and life.* Cambridge, MA: South End Press.

LaFromboise, T., & Rowe, W. (1983). Skills training for bicultural competence: Rationale and application. *Journal of Counseling Psychology, 30*, 589–595.

LaFromboise, T., Trimble, J. E., & Mohatt, G. (1990). Counseling interventions and American Indian tradition: An integrative approach. *Counseling Psychologist, 18*, 628–654.

Matsumoto, D. (2000). *Culture and psychology: People around the world.* New York: Wadsworth.

May, P., & Moran, J. (1995). Prevention of alcohol misuse: A review of health promotion efforts among American Indians. *American Journal of Health Promotion, 9*, 288–299.

McDonald, J. D. (1996). New frontiers in clinical training: The Indians Into Psychology Doctoral Education (InPsyDE) program. *Journal of American Indian and Alaska Native Mental Health Research, 5*(3), 52–56.

McDonald, J. D. (1998). Completing the circle: Indian health training. *Federal Practitioner, 4*, 22–38.

McDonald, J. D. (1998). *The American Indian Bicultural Inventory (AIBI).* Unpublished instrument, University of North Dakota, Grand Forks.

McDonald, J. D., & Chaney, J. (2003). Resistance to multiculturalism: The "Indian problem." In J. S. Mio & G. Y. Iwamasa (Eds.), *Culturally diverse mental health: The challenges of research and resistance* (pp. 39–54). New York: Brunner-Routledge.

McDonald, J. D., Morton, R., & Stewart, C. (1992). Clinical issues with American Indian patients. *Innovations in Clinical Practice, 12*, 437–454.

McMullin, R. (1998). *Handbook of cognitive therapy techniques.* New York: Norton.

Mesteth, W. S., Standing Elk, D., & Swift Hawk, P. (1993). Declaration of war against exploiters of Lakota spirituality. In W. Churchill (Ed.), *Indians R Us? Culture and genocide in North America* (pp. 273–277). Monroe, ME: Common Courage Press.

Meyer, M. L. (1994). *The White Earth tragedy: Ethnicity and dispossession at a Minnesota Anishinaabe reservation.* Lincoln: University of Nebraska Press.

Mitchell, C. M., Beals, J., Novins, D. K., Spicer, P., & the AI-SUPERPFP Team. (2003). Drug use among two American Indian populations: Prevalence of lifetime use and *DSM–IV* substance use disorders. *Drug and Alcohol Dependence, 69,* 29–41.

Moran, J. R., Fleming, C. M., Somervell, P., & Manson, S. M. (1999). Measuring bicultural ethnic identity among American Indian adolescents: A factor analytic study. *Journal of Adolescent Research, 14,* 405–426.

Morton, R., & Gawboy, C. (2003). *Talking rocks: Geology and 10,000 years of Native American tradition in the Lake Superior region.* Minneapolis: University of Minnesota Press.

Oetting, E. R., & Beauvais, F. (1990–1991). Orthogonal culture identification theory: The cultural identification of minority adolescents. *International Journal of the Addictions, 25,* 655–685.

Page, J. (2003). *In the hands of the Great Spirit: The 20,000-year history of American Indians.* New York: Free Press.

Renfrey, G. S. (1992). Cognitive–behavior therapy and the Native American client. *Behavior Therapy, 23,* 321–340.

Sidanius, J. (1993). The psychology of group conflict and the dynamics of oppression: A social dominance perspective. In S. Iyengar & W. J. McGuire (Eds.), *Explorations in political psychology* (pp. 183–219). Durham, NC: Duke University Press.

Snipp, C. M. (1989). *American Indians: The first of this land.* New York: Russell Sage Foundation.

Snipp, C. M. (1996). The size and distribution of the American Indian population: Fertility, mortality, residence, and migration. In G. Sandefur, R. Rindfuss, & B. Cohen (Eds.), *Changing numbers, changing needs: American Indian demography and public health* (pp. 17–52). Washington, DC: National Academy Press.

Spielberger, C. D., Gorsuch, R. L., & Lushene, R. D. (1970). *Manual for the State–Trait Anxiety Inventory.* Palo Alto, CA: Consulting Psychologists Press.

Sue, D. W., & Sue, D. (1999). *Counseling the culturally different.* New York: Wiley.

Swinomish Tribal Community. (1991). *A gathering of wisdoms; Tribal mental health: A cultural perspective.* LaConner, WA: Author.

Tafoya, T. (1989). Circles and cedar: Native Americans and family therapy. *Journal of Psychotherapy and the Family, 6,* 71–98.

Triandis, H. C. (Series Ed.). (1994). *New directions in social psychology: Individualism and collectivism.* Boulder, CO: Westview Press.

Trimble, J. E. (1988). Stereotypic images, American Indians, and prejudice. In P. Katz & D. Taylor (Eds.), *Toward the elimination of racism: Profiles in controversy* (pp. 181–202). New York: Pergamon.

Trimble, J. E. (1992). A cognitive–behavioral approach to drug abuse prevention and intervention with American Indian youth. In L. A. Vargas & J. D. Koss

(Eds.), *Working with culture: Psychotherapeutic interventions with ethnic minority children and adolescents* (pp. 246–275). San Francisco: Jossey-Bass.

Trimble, J. E., Fleming, C. M., Beauvais, F., & Jumper-Thurman, P. (1996). Essential cultural and social strategies for counseling Native American Indians. In P. B. Pedersen, J. G. Draguns, W. J. Lonner, & J. E. Trimble (Eds.), *Counseling across cultures* (4th ed., pp. 177–209). Thousand Oaks, CA: Sage.

Trimble, J. E., & Thurman, P. (2002). Ethnocultural considerations and strategies for providing counseling services for Native American Indians. In P. B. Pedersen, J. G. Draguns, W. J. Lonner, & J. E. Trimble (Eds.), *Counseling across cultures* (5th ed., pp. 53–91). Thousand Oaks, CA: Sage.

U.S. Census Bureau. (2001). *Census of the population: General population characteristics, American Indians and Alaska Natives areas, 2000.* Washington, DC: Government Printing Office.

U.S. Department of Health and Human Services. (2001). *Mental health: Culture, race, and ethnicity—A supplement to Mental Health: A Report of the Surgeon General.* Rockville, MD: U.S. Department of Health and Human Services, Substance Abuse and Mental Health Services Administration, Center for Mental Health Services.

U.S. Department of the Interior. (2002). Bureau of Indian Affairs. In *Bureau highlights* (pp. 77–85). Washington, DC: Author. Retrieved October 25, 2004, from http://www.doi.gov/budget/2003/03hilites/bh77.pdf

Venables, R. W. (2004). *American Indian history: Vol. I. Five centuries of conflict and coexistence.* Santa Fe, NM: Clear Light.

Vrasidas, C. (1997). The White Man's Indian: Stereotypes in film and beyond. In R. Griffin (Ed.), *VisionQuest: Journeys toward visual literacy* (pp. 63–70). Cheyenne, WY: International Visual Literacy Association. (ERIC Document Reproduction Service No. ED408950)

2

COGNITIVE–BEHAVIORAL THERAPY WITH ALASKA NATIVE PEOPLE

PAMELA A. HAYS

American Indians and Alaska Natives make up approximately 1% of the total U.S. population. However, in Alaska, where the state population is only 626,000, Alaska Natives comprise approximately 19% (119,241) of the state's people (Alaska Division of Planning, Evaluation and Health Statistics, 2002). Thus, therapists living in Alaska are very likely to work with Alaska Native clients. Therapists living Outside (the Alaskan term for places beyond state borders) may also encounter Alaska Native clients, particularly in the area of the Pacific Northwest.

Psychological research regarding the mental health needs and treatment of Alaska Native people is extremely limited. Existing research focuses primarily on American Indians in the Lower 48 (states) and generalizes this information to Alaska Natives. Although there are some similarities, there are also significant geographical, cultural, political, and historical differences between these populations.

A search of the American Psychological Association (APA) journals and books database yielded no empirical studies of counseling or psycho-

I would like to thank Karen Ferguson, Barbara Fleek, Randall Madigan, and Alan Boraas for their feedback regarding this chapter.

therapy with Alaska Native people specifically. To my knowledge, there are only two books that address this topic. In *Counseling the Inupiat Eskimo* (1999), the Inupiaq psychologist Swan Reimer focuses on the importance of the interconnected concepts of personal and community well-being. She offers suggestions for enhancing the effectiveness of counseling that incorporate cognitive–behavioral ideas, although she does not describe them as such. These include an active approach that is focused on the present and aimed at practical problem solving. She also emphasizes the importance of positive thinking as a way to help empower people coping with difficult life events in a harsh environment. The importance of good thoughts in connection with one's actions has also been described in relation to the Alaska Native culture of the Yupiit (Fienup-Riordan, 2000a; Kawagley, 1995).

The second book, *With the Wind and the Waves* (Droby, 2000), emphasizes a strengths-oriented approach and offers information regarding common cultural beliefs and practices among Alaska Native people, along with political and historical information that therapists are advised to know. The appendix consists of numerous handouts organized by topic for use in educational community groups. This and Swan Reimer's book are essential reading for therapists working with Alaska Natives.

Because there is no published research regarding cognitive–behavioral therapy (CBT) with Alaska Natives, I include information drawn from my own experiences working in a community mental health center and in a Native counseling center in rural Alaska, along with the experiences of other Native and non-Native therapists working with Alaska Native clients. I also include references that are not specifically on CBT with Alaska Natives but are relevant to understanding such work. Because Alaska Native communities are so small, I describe only composite case studies that represent real situations but no individual real person.

OVERVIEW OF ALASKA NATIVE CULTURES

This section describes Alaska Native people in the context of their history, religion, political events, cultural identity, and living conditions.

Early History

As noted in the preceding chapter on American Indians, many Alaska Native people have creation stories that place their origins in the land now known as Alaska (e.g., see Kawagley, 1995). According to Langdon (2002), most archeologists believe that sometime between 50,000 and 15,000 years ago, humans began migrating from Siberia to western Alaska across vast Arctic grasslands that existed when sea levels were much lower. These archeologists also believe that the ancestors of Alaska Natives living today migrated to

Alaska more recently, between 10,000 and 5,000 years ago, possibly in an initial wave of Indians and a later wave of Eskaleuts.

These early ancestors followed a traditional way of life that is now called *subsistence*. Although this term is currently used by the dominant culture as a synonym for hunting and fishing rights, Native people commonly define it more broadly to include the traditional worldview and lifestyle. In the Yup'ik language, the word for this worldview and lifestyle is *Yuuyaraq* (Napoleon, 1996), which Kawagley (1995, p. 8) defined as "a complex way of life with specific cultural mandates" that dictate correct behavior between human beings and correct ways of thinking and speaking about all living things. Cooperation and sharing are central, and respectful attitudes, speech, and behavior help to ensure harmony and balance within and between the human, natural, and spiritual realms (Fienup-Riordan, 2000b). The exceptional awareness of one's surroundings that is inherent in this worldview has enabled Native people to survive in and adapt to extremely harsh and continually changing environmental conditions (Fienup-Riordan, 1990, in Kawagley, 1995, p. 9).

Prior to Western contact, the Yupiit believed that following the principles of Yuuyaraq ensured their survival. Yet the arrival of Russian and European explorers turned this belief on end when an influenza epidemic to which the people had no immunity killed an estimated 60% of the Alaska Native population (Napoleon, 1996). Subsequent famine, starvation, and epidemics of measles, chickenpox, polio, and tuberculosis overpowered the efforts of the shamans who had previously been considered the spiritual leaders and healers. In the confusion, shock, and despair that followed, the people abandoned their old beliefs and were more inclined to accept those of the Christian missionaries who promised salvation and deliverance (Napoleon).

Religion

In 1882, the Presbyterian missionary Sheldon Jackson organized a group of Protestant leaders for the purpose of dividing the state into religious territories in which specific denominations would have preeminence without interference from other denominations. Jackson and his colleagues decided on a plan whose legacy continues today. The Presbyterians would take southeast Alaska and the northernmost community of Barrow, the Episcopalians would cover the Yukon River Valley, the Baptists would go to Kodiak Island and Cook Inlet, the Methodists to the Aleutian and Shumagin Islands, the Moravians to the Kuskokwim and Nushagak valleys, and the Congregationalists to the Cape Prince of Wales (Field, n.d., in Tower, 1988, p. 21). The Russian Orthodox Church was already firmly established in several areas (e.g., on the Kenai Peninsula) and was excluded from Jackson's master plan. The Catholics, particularly the Jesuits, made their own inroads.

Despite the colonialist roots of Christianity in Alaska, the current relationship between Alaska Natives and the Church is complex (Fienup-Riordan, 2002b, p. 137). Using the example of the Catholic Church in southwestern Alaska, Fienup-Riordan observed that the incorporation of Yup'ik traditions and concepts into Catholicism benefits both the Church, which becomes more relevant to people's lives, and the Yup'ik people, through support of the revitalization of Yup'ik traditions (e.g., naming ceremonies in baptisms, dancing, drumming, purification rituals). Whatever therapists' personal beliefs, it is important to recognize that Christianity plays a powerful role in the lives of many Alaska Natives today. In rural areas in particular, religion often provides emotional, social, and spiritual support, and at times even financial help. In some small communities, the churches and Alcoholics Anonymous may be the only regular source of nondrinking socialization for people in recovery.

Political Events

In the last century, Alaska Native people have experienced extraordinary sociocultural changes, including a number of political events that continue to affect the lives of Native people today. Boarding schools led to the devaluing of Native languages and traditions, including parenting practices, subsistence knowledge, and survival and coping skills. It was not until 1976 (much later than in the Lower 48) that a lawsuit brought by a Yup'ik student (*Hootch v. Alaska State-Operated School System*, 1975; commonly known as the Molly Hootch decree) forced the state to support the rights of students to be educated in their home villages. The enormous oil revenues in the 1970s subsequently allowed the state to build secondary schools in any village with 15 or more high school age children (Haycox, 2002). (It is important to note that the boarding schools have had some positive aspects, including the opportunity for Alaska Natives to develop relationships and political connections with Alaska Native people from around the state; a few boarding schools continue to operate today [Haycox, 2002].)

Alaska Natives did not become U.S. citizens until 1924, despite the status of Alaska as a U.S. territory since 1867. "White only" signs were present in the state's capital as recently as the 1940s (McClanahan & Bissett, 2002). The development of the Alaska–Canadian highway during the war opened the way for thousands of non-Native people to move to the state and quickly outnumber Native people.

On obtaining statehood in 1958, the state was granted 104 million acres by the federal government and began filing claims to some of Alaska Natives' most important land. The discovery of oil in 1968 led to increased pressure from state legislators and oil developers to resolve the conflicting claims. The Alaska Federation of Natives was formed during this time to fight for Native claims. In 1971, the Alaska Native Claims Settlement Act

(ANCSA) was passed. At the time, the losses from the Act seemed greater than the gains (Native people received only about one tenth of Alaska's 3.75 million acres and a capped sum of $1 billion for all lands given up, with several structural problems embedded in the Act). However, the subsequent financial successes of many of the Native corporations that were formed from this settlement have opened doors for many people (see Haycox, 2002).

Cultural Identity

The term *Alaska Native* refers to a diversity of Native cultures located in Alaska. The organization of these cultures varies depending on whether one considers language, geography, or historical political influences to be primary. At the most general level, Alaska Native cultures can be divided into two language groups, those belonging to (a) the Eska-Aleutian language family, including Eskimo and Aleut; and (b) the Na-Dene languages of the Athabascans, Eyak, and probably Tlingit cultures (Langdon, 2002).

Eska-Aleutian Speakers

Included in the Eska-Aleutian language speakers are the two largest "Eskimo" cultures: the Inupiat, who speak Inupiaq, live in the far north, and are related to the Inuit of Canada and Greenland; and the Yupiit, the majority of whom live in southwestern Alaska (see Figure 2.1). (Note that the "-it" ending in this context signifies nouns referring to the people/culture, whereas "-q" and "-ik" endings refer to adjectives and the languages.) Together, the Inupiat and Yupiit constitute a little over half of the total Alaska Native population (Alaska Conservation Foundation, 2003). It is important to note that although some Native people self-identify as Eskimo, the term is considered pejorative by others; thus, I use the more specific terms.

The Inupiat and the Yupiit are known for their flexibility, knowledge of the environment, and survival skills that enabled them to survive in an extreme climate. The discovery of oil has had an enormous impact on the Inupiat, in both positive ways (e.g., increased resources to fund education, social services, health care, and political activism) and negative ways (easier access to alcohol and drugs, disruption of the subsistence way of life). (See Haycox, 2002, for more on the impact of oil on Alaska Natives.) Hunting, particularly whale hunting, continues to be an important part of community life among the Inupiat (North Slope Borough, n.d., in McClanahan & Bissett, 2002, p. 27).

Owing to a lack of commercially valued resources that drew non-Natives to other areas of Alaska first, Yupiit contact with outsiders occurred later, in the early 1800s (Fienup-Riordan, 2000a). As a result, the Yupiit are among the more traditional cultures and include the largest number of Native speakers (10,000 of the total population of 21,000; The Alaska Native Language Center, n.d., in McClanahan & Bissett, 2002, p. 26). The Yupiit

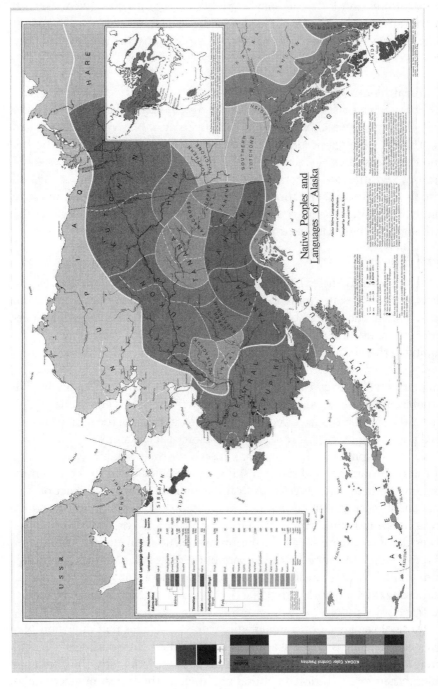

Figure 2.1. Map of Native peoples and languages of Alaska. From *Native Peoples and Languages of Alaska*, by M. E. Krauss, 1982, Fairbanks: University of Alaska Fairbanks, Alaska Native Language Center. Reprinted with permission.

speak three main languages: Central Yup'ik, Siberian Yup'ik, and Alutiiq (Langdon, 2002). The Yupiit hunt marine mammals, including walrus, sea lions, and whales from the Bering Sea; those living more inland also hunt moose and caribou; and the Central Yup'ik fish from the Yukon, Kuskokwim, and Nushagak rivers (Fienup-Riordan, 2000a). The Siberian Yup'ik people, who live on Saint Lawrence Island, are particularly known for their artistic ivory carvings.

The Alutiit or Sugpiat (their original name) of Kodiak Island and Prince William Sound speak Alutiiq and are known for their seafaring skills and traditional reliance on marine mammals, fish, birds, and shellfish (Steffian, n.d., in McClanahan & Bissett, 2002, p. 26). The Alutiit were initially misnamed Aleut by the Russians, but in reality their language is completely unrelated to that of the Aleut (Langdon, 2002).

Also in the Eska-Aleutian language family, the Aleut (Unangan) originated in the Aleutian Islands to the far west of Alaska and were among the first to be invaded. In pursuit of massive numbers of furs during the 1700s, the Russians kidnapped Aleut men for their seafaring and hunting abilities, forcing them to hunt fur seals and sea otters to near extinction while holding the women and children hostage (Alaska Conservation Foundation, 2003). Two centuries later, during World War II, Attu villagers were captured by the Japanese and most of the remaining Aleuts were sent by the U.S. government to internment camps in southeast Alaska, where 1 of every 10 people died. Despite this harsh history, cultural practices including subsistence remain important, the language is spoken by elders and in special church services and schools, Aleut women are known for their weaving of grasses into artistic baskets, and *iqyax*-building (a skin-covered kayaklike vessel) has reemerged (Alaska Geographic Society, 1996).

Na-Dene Speakers

The second broad language grouping of the Na-Dene speakers includes people of Alaska Indian heritage who are genetically more closely related to Indian people in the Lower 48 (i.e., than to the Inupiat or Yupiit; Langdon, 2002). The largest of the Alaska Indian cultures are the Athabascans of the interior and southcentral Alaska. The Athabascans inhabit the largest geographic area with the most diverse environments of any Alaska Native cultures (Alaska Geographic Society, 1996). They hunt caribou and moose and rely heavily on fish from several major rivers. The Athabascans are further divided into a number of cultures whose members speak 11 languages related to those of the Apaches and Navajo (Krauss, 1982).

The remaining Alaska Indian cultures reside in southeast Alaska and are often grouped together: the Tsimshian, Tlingit, Haida, and Eyak. Although the Haida and Tlingit languages were once thought to be related, Haida is now considered unrelated to any Alaska language, and there is evidence that Tlingit diverged from the other Athabascan languages as early as

6,000 years ago (Langdon, 2002). The Tlingit and Haida cultures are known worldwide for their artwork, which includes the carving of totem poles. The Tlingit and Haida are among the more acculturated to European American culture and have the highest number of high school and college graduates of any Alaska Native group (Haycox, 2002).

The Tsimshian came to southeast Alaska from British Columbia in the late 1800s and established a model community on Metlakatla (currently the only reservation in Alaska; McClanahan & Bissett, 2002). This Christian community was known for developing a different approach from other missionary-led groups by emphasizing universal education in the Tsimshian language and collective ownership of transport vessels, a cannery, and a sawmill (Langdon, 2002).

The Tlingit, Haida, and Tsimshian cultures were traditionally matrilineal (as were several other Alaska Native cultures traditionally), with marriage regulated according to social divisions known as *moieties*. Members of the Tlingit and Haida belonged to either the Eagle-Wolf or Raven Moiety, whereas the Tsimshian belonged to one of four: the Wolf, Killer Whale or Bear, Eagle, or Raven moieties. Individuals were allowed to marry only those of the opposite moiety. For example, a Tlingit member of the Eagle-Wolf moiety could only marry someone of the Raven moiety. However, these rules are followed much less today (Ketchikan Museum, n.d., in McClanahan & Bissett, 2002).

Finally, the Eyak people, who were originally from the interior, moved to the coast and, by the time the Russians arrived, were living in the area between Cordova and Yakutat. The Eyaks were a relatively small group, and due in part to similarities in social structure with the Tlingit culture, intermarriages with the Tlingit became common. Presently, there are approximately 120 members who are attempting to revive the Eyak culture and preserve the language (Alaska Geographic Society, 1996).

In addition to the specific cultural identities described earlier, for many Alaska Natives, the geographical location of one's home village may be a primary form of self-identification (e.g., "I'm from Port Graham" rather than "I'm Alutiiq"). For others, self-identification as *Alaska Native* is primary (i.e., over a specific identity). This may reflect a positive connection with people of other Alaska Native cultures. However, in some cases, people do not know their specific cultural origin. High rates of migration and adoption, along with a dominant culture and mass media that lump Native people's cultures together, have contributed to this loss of knowledge and connection.

Many Alaska Native people hold bicultural or multicultural identities. According to the 2000 Census (U.S. Census Bureau, 2000), Alaska has the second-highest proportion (5.4%) of self-identified biracial or bicultural persons in the United States (Hawaii has the first). As Alaska Natives make up the largest ethnic minority group in the state, this statistic suggests that many Alaska Natives are more likely to identify with both (or multiple) aspects of their own cultural heritage. Given the range of possibilities regarding identity, for counseling purposes it is preferable to allow clients to self-identify rather than assuming an identity based on geographical origin, family name, or physical appearance.

It is important to remember that each individual's personal orientation to his or her own culture and to the dominant culture can involve a variety of unique adaptations. For example, the therapist may encounter a client who lives in a rural area and engages in traditional activities such as hunting and fishing but also uses the Internet at home to check e-mail, maintains a responsible position of paid employment in the community, frequently travels Outside, and holds a worldview that includes a combination of traditional Native and mainstream European American beliefs. However, the therapist may also meet individuals who are more traditionally oriented in their behaviors, beliefs, and lifestyles but live in the cities of Anchorage or Fairbanks and have difficulty adjusting to the faster-paced, European American-dominated lifestyles there. These examples do not represent two ends of a continuum but rather examples of the unique and complex ways in which Alaska Native people may interact with their own cultures of origin and the dominant culture.

With some clients, particularly those who are more comfortable with the dominant culture, it may be appropriate and even helpful to ask specific questions about the person's connection to his or her cultural heritage. However, with other individuals, such questions may be perceived as irrelevant or intrusive, particularly coming from a non-Native therapist. In these latter situations, therapists will often be able to obtain information regarding cultural heritage and bicultural competence simply by listening for it, for example, in the clients' use of language, their place of origin and current residence, and in their responses to questions regarding experiences growing up and current activities (Jackson & Turner, 2004). To maximize one's ability to make accurate hypotheses and inferences, therapists will need to do their own work in learning about each client's cultures, and then use this cultural information as background for understanding the client's personal experiences.

Living Conditions

Although approximately 20,000 Alaska Natives reside in Anchorage, the majority live in rural areas, including 225 remote villages accessible only by boat or air (Haycox, 2002). These villages range from communities as small as 50 people to larger hub communities of a few thousand people such as Bethel, Nome, Dillingham, and Barrow. Within most of the villages, a health aide and a safety officer are available, with at least telephonic connection to a doctor and state trooper office in a larger town (Haycox, 2002). Unemployment is high, and limited economic opportunities lead many Native people to migrate to Anchorage, Fairbanks, and other towns, where urban living presents many new challenges (Fienup-Riordan, 2000a). At least 70 villages do not have indoor plumbing (Haycox, 2002). Waste disposal is a major problem owing to the increasing accumulation of nonbiodegradable materials that have accompanied consumer goods, and sewage problems are common, particularly in villages that are barely above sea level (Kawagley, 1995, p. 49).

Alcohol and drug abuse, along with the related problems of suicide, domestic violence, and fetal alcohol syndrome, are chronic problems in many villages (Langdon, 2002). Since the 1980s, a strong sobriety movement has developed, and many villages have asserted their power to take control of alcohol abuse by voting on the legality of alcohol. Villages that have out-lawed the sale and importation of alcohol are referred to as "dry," villages in which alcohol is legally sold are called "wet," and those that allow the impor-tation of alcohol for personal use only are called "damp." Villages that have voted themselves dry (76 as of April 2003) have reported reduced rates of violent behavior including sexual assault (Gay, 2003). However, such votes are often contentious in villages where individualistic community members (often non-Native, although not always) consider alcohol use a personal right and vote for their own personal interest rather than for the good of the com-munity. The bootlegging of alcohol and drugs by individuals also undermines community attempts to reinforce sobriety.

COGNITIVE–BEHAVIORAL ASSESSMENT WITH ALASKA NATIVE PEOPLE

In a workshop I recently conducted, a young African American thera-pist described one of her first clinical experiences with an Alaska Native boy she was attempting to assess. This therapist was compassionate, well inten-tioned, and genuinely wanted to connect with the boy. However, she said that every time she tried to catch his eye, he looked away or moved his body to avoid her gaze. By the end of the session, she made a note that he had low self-esteem and was easily distracted.

Later, with the help of a supervisor who was more experienced with Alaska Native youths, the therapist said that she was able to explore addi-tional hypotheses for the boy's lack of eye contact. She considered the possi-bility that the boy was embarrassed or ashamed to be in the treatment center, that he was fearful (because he had never been away from his village and possibly had never before talked with an African American woman), or that he was trying to be respectful by not looking directly at her.

The therapist recognized that any one of these hypotheses could have been true, including her original one. Yet without the background knowl-edge of and experience with Alaska Native people, she had jumped to a con-clusion that was reinforced by the dominant culture. Not coincidentally, her conclusion reflected negatively on the boy (the negative interpretation of minority cultural influences being common; Stevenson & Renard, 1993). The supervisor's greater number of hypotheses opened up a much broader range of possibilities. With these additional hypotheses in mind, the therapist could return to working with the child and come closer to an understanding of the boy. As this example illustrates, the more knowledge and experience a therapist has about a client's culture, the closer the therapist's hypotheses will be to the client's real situation (Hays, 1996a).

In my attempts to stay mindful of the diversity of cultural influences affecting Alaska Native clients, I use an acronym that spells the word ADDRESSING (Hays, 2001) and stands for the following.

Age and generational influences: These include generational cohort influences (e.g., generations born before and after ANCSA) and generational roles that may be important to a person, such as being a father, an auntie, or an elder.

Developmental and acquired Disabilities: Alaska Native people have disproportionately high rates of disabilities related to accidents (i.e., acquired disabilities). Statistics are unavailable regarding the number of people who have disabilities; however, Alaska in general has the highest injury rates in the United States, and the unintentional injury mortality rate for Alaska Natives is twice as high as the rate for all Alaskans (Alaska Department of Health and Social Services, Division of Public Health, 2001, pp. 22, 35). Regarding developmental disabilities, fetal alcohol spectrum disorders including fetal alcohol syndrome (FAS) are a significant problem. The prevalence rate of FAS for Alaska Natives is 4.8 per 1,000, compared with 1.4 for the entire state (Alaska Department of Health and Social Services, Office of FAS, 2002).

Religion or spiritual orientation: As noted earlier, religious beliefs and affiliations vary widely among Alaska Native people.

Ethnicity: As previously noted, many Alaska Natives hold bicultural or multicultural identities and identify with both or multiple aspects of their cultural heritage.

Socioeconomic status: There are enormous differences among Alaska Natives related to socioeconomic status, particularly between college-educated individuals living in Anchorage and those living in the smaller villages. For examples of these differences, see Velma Wallis's (2002) account of growing up in a Gwich'in village and McClanahan's (2000) stories of the lives of mostly urban business and political leaders.

Sexual orientation: There are Alaska Native people who identify themselves as gay, lesbian, and bisexual. Although American Indians in the lower 48 have described the role of "two-spirit" people (those who self-identify as gay, lesbian, or bisexual) as mediators who moved across genders, I have been unable to find any published information on this identity among Alaska Native people.

Indigenous heritage: As noted earlier, there are many levels to an Alaska Native's Indigenous identity. For example, a particular person may self-identify as Alaska Native *and* Athabascan *and* Dena'ina (one of the Athabascan languages and cultures), *and* Kenaitze (the Dena'ina people living in the Kenai area; although this is a Russian word, it is the identification used by the Kenaitze Tribe). Finally, some Alaska Natives identify with the global movement of Indigenous peoples. (Note that the word *tribe* is generally not used in reference to any of the 11 larger Alaska Native cultures.)

National origin: Most Alaska Natives were born and raised in Alaska and are thus Americans, but there are Alaska Natives who have lived outside the United States or been influenced by a parent who is of another country.

Gender: Traditionally, the roles and activities of Alaska Native cultures (e.g., the Yupiit) were highly gender-specific, although at the same time intricately interdependent. For example, only the men hunted and trapped, and only the women sewed clothes. This meant that whereas women were dependent on men's hunting success for meat, the hunter's success was dependent on the warmth of his clothing that kept him alive (Kawagley, 1995, p. 20). The strictness of these roles has changed significantly during the last few decades.

The influences included in this acronym are not arbitrarily chosen. Rather, they are highlighted in multicultural and related guidelines published by the APA and the American Counseling Association (e.g., see APA, 2000, 2002, 2004; Roysircar, Arredondo, Fuertes, Ponterotto, & Toporek, 2003). Therapists can use the acronym to generate hypotheses about a client's beliefs, values, emotional expression, strengths, and symptom presentation. For example, a therapist working with a client who is responding in a way that a therapist does not understand may ask himself or herself, "Could this client's behavior be explained by age or generational influences, a disability, spiritual orientation, ethnic culture, or other factors that I may be overlooking?" In this way, cultural influences become central to the generation of hypotheses regarding the client.

Advantages and Disadvantages of CBT With Alaska Natives

Several elements of CBT make it especially suited for work with Alaska Native people. The problem-solving focus fits well with the expectations of many clients that the therapist will provide them with some practical solutions to the problems they present. The emphasis on empowerment and attention to clients' strengths can facilitate the clients' sense that they are being respected by the therapist. A careful consideration of the environmental components of the client's situation also fits well, as it can easily include attention to the healing components (or lack of) in the person's environment (e.g., opportunities to spend time outdoors, breathe fresh air, watch wildlife, pick berries, hunt, fish, and observe the sky—all of which are important in Alaska Native cultures). Cognitive restructuring (i.e., the changing of unrealistic, unhelpful, and distressing thoughts to more realistic and helpful ones) has a parallel in the traditional subsistence worldview that one must be "careful in thought and action so as not to injure another's mind or offend the spirits of the animals and the surrounding environment" (Kawagley, 1995, p. 8). Positive, realistic thoughts and correct behavior are also seen as contributing to one's ability to survive in harsh conditions (Kawagley, 1995).

At the same time, several aspects of CBT do not fit well with Alaska Native cultures. The emphasis on logic and rationality, particularly when the rationality of the belief or action is defined by the dominant culture, is clearly problematic. In addition, if specific attention is not given to the role of spirituality in the client's life, the cognitive focus of CBT may seem too narrow or simplistic to the client. Finally, the verbal nature of CBT can be limiting with traditionally oriented clients who speak English less fluently, prefer silence over talking, and are more reserved. The following sections offer suggestions for avoiding or working around these limitations.

Establishing a Relationship

In the introduction to this book, specific suggestions were given for engaging in the personal work that will help therapists to be more open and aware when working cross-culturally. On the basis of the premise that this self-growth process is occurring, one of the first steps in working with Alaska Native clients is the establishment of a respectful and friendly working relationship. The following generalizations regarding relationship-building behaviors are not *the* explanation for Native people's behaviors; many Alaska Native people will fit with these descriptions, but many will not. This information simply opens up a wider range of hypotheses for non-Native therapists to consider in their attempts to understand what facilitates therapeutic relationships with Alaska Native people.

In an initial meeting, introduction of oneself with the first as well as last name is often preferred, keeping in mind that the use of titles and degrees is generally not emphasized, except with some elders. It may be helpful to ask clients how they prefer to be addressed. To show respect for elders, one should generally start with Mr., Mrs., or Ms. and use first names if requested to do so (Hays, 1996c).

Handshake styles may vary significantly from those of European Americans, for whom a handshake is generally intended to communicate information. Specifically, a firm European American handshake is intended to communicate a sense of self-assurance, delight in meeting someone, or social dominance. In contrast, for many Alaska Natives (as for many American Indians) the purpose of a handshake is to *receive* information about the person, and thus a more gentle touch is preferred (Swinomish Tribal Community, 1991).

The role of silence and communication among many Alaska Natives is also important to consider. In the dominant culture, silence is often interpreted as a sign of anger or a signal that the speaker is finished. Among many Alaska Native people, silence is a way to communicate respect for the speaker and what she or he has just said. It may also simply reflect the fact that the listener is thinking, formulating thoughts, or waiting for a sign to speak (Allen, 1998). Aleut instructor Sally Swetzof noted that one of the more offensive responses to silence or a pause occurs when the non-Native speaker "jumps in with another question or, worse yet, asks the question in another way, as if the Native person hadn't understood" (cited in Gerjevic, 2004, p. A-1). She advised simply "waiting a few beats" after asking a question. Recognizing the diversity of communication preferences within Alaska Native cultures, Swan Reimer (1999, p. 91) recommended following the rhythm and tempo of the individual (e.g., regarding eye contact, taking cues from the client about what seems most comfortable for him or her).

Alaska Native psychologist Denise Dillard noted that "some elders have a narrative way of speaking and the intake questions are offensive" (personal communication, September 2003). In such cases, Dillard may not follow the standard intake process but instead allow the elder to provide her with information that the elder deems important. Dillard added that this obviously presents the dilemma that it may not be possible to obtain all of the information desired in an initial session. However, if the client is offended, then the accuracy of the information obtained will be questionable anyway, and it is unlikely the person will return.

Another nonverbal response that can lead to misunderstanding is the raising of one's eyebrows or widening of one's eyes to mean "yes." This is an expression sometimes used by the Yupiit and Inupiat. European American Nick Jans (1993) described a humorous example of such a misunderstanding as he was working in a village store and a 4-year-old Inupiaq girl came in with a handful of change that she silently placed on the counter. He asked if she wanted candy and she looked at him, with widened eyes. She then looked at the candy and he asked "Which one?" More silence. "This one?" Silence. "What about this one?" Exasperated, he picked out some candies and gave them to her, taking the right amount of change. Only later, he said, did he learn that via raised eyebrows and widened eyes she had been nonverbally shouting at him, "Yes, Yes, Yes!" (p. 25).

Clarification of the Problem, Strengths, and Supports

Once a respectful rapport has been established, the next step in a culturally responsive approach to CBT involves clarification of the client's problem, strengths, and supports. Consider the following example:

Mark presented as a friendly, cheerful 25-year-old bicultural young man who came to his college's counseling center requesting career counseling. Specifically, he said that he wanted help in figuring out what jobs to apply for now that he was graduating with his A.A. degree in business. The young European American counselor began the session by asking Mark about his upbringing and background. Mark explained that his mother was Athabascan and father Russian and European American. He lived with both parents in a small town on the road system (i.e., not a village) until they divorced, then he and his brother went back and forth between his father in Anchorage and mother in the rural area. When he was 18, his father died and he decided to stay with his mother for a while before going to college. Two years later, his maternal grandparents died within the same year of one another. Mark became tearful when he talked about their deaths and changed the subject back to his reason for coming in—to obtain help with his career search.

The counselor was familiar with the many losses experienced by Alaska Native people, and he told Mark that he could see that he had experienced many losses in his life and might need an opportunity to grieve more fully. He added that counseling could help with this. At his strong encouragement, Mark made another appointment. Yet the next week at their scheduled time, Mark did not appear and the counselor did not hear from him again.

Although well intentioned, this counselor made a couple of mistakes. At the most basic level, he failed to listen to what the client wanted and instead focused on what *he* thought Mark needed. Although he did hold some knowledge about Alaska Native cultures, his knowledge focused mainly on the negative (i.e., cultural losses) without a recognition of the positive (i.e., culturally related strengths and supports). For example, if he had asked, he would have learned that Mark had good friends and close relationships with his mother, brother, and aunt; and that he was involved in a Native youth dance group that provided him with a positive connection to his Athabascan culture. He was also a positive role model for his brother and several younger cousins. With all of these supports and strengths, he did not need to see a counselor for the grief he experienced at times. All he needed and wanted from counseling was what he requested—help in articulating his work interests and strengths, and then in matching these with potential careers.

Attention to clients' strengths and supports is a core task in any cognitive–behavioral assessment for at least two reasons. One, a problem can often be improved by enhancing, building on, or reinforcing strengths and supports that are already in place and thus easier to maintain. And two, by actively looking for strengths and supports in the client's culture, the therapist communicates a positive regard for the client's culture (Hays, 1996b). As Cross (2003) noted, culture is a resource for healing, self-help, and mental health. (Also see Mohatt et al., in press, for an excellent example of the search for and description of culturally related factors that contribute to a sober and healthy lifestyle among Alaska Natives.)

Another core principle in cognitive–behavioral assessment is the acceptance of the client's presentation of the problem (Hays, 1995). Once a respectful relationship is established, the therapist may offer an alternative perspective, but the therapist's role is generally that of a facilitator and teacher of coping skills. Ultimately, clients decide what is needed and what will work for them in their particular contexts (Wood & Mallinckrodt, 1990). Here again, this empowering stance is especially important with Alaska Native people whose views have often been dismissed, ignored, or demeaned by the dominant culture.

Explaining Cognitive–Behavioral Therapy

As part of my initial assessment, I always explain to clients what I do. I use the term *counseling* more often than *therapy*, because the former seems to be less intimidating and more familiar to people. I rarely use the phrase *cognitive–behavioral therapy*, in part because it emphasizes the cognitive and behavioral aspects of therapy and does not include the words *emotional*, *spiritual*, or *social*. I do not want people to think that these latter areas are not important in counseling. My explanation goes something like this:

> It can be helpful to think of problems in terms of two main categories. The first group includes problems that you can do something about. For example, if your child gets into trouble at school, you could talk with your child, or you could call the teacher, or you could ask your mother for advice, and so on. Counseling can be helpful with these kinds of problems in figuring out what to do and then how to do it.
>
> But there are some problems that we can't do anything about, or we make a decision that we don't want to. This second group of problems includes things like a really stressful job that you have to stay in because you are only 6 months short of retirement, or having to take care of a sick family member. [I try to use an example that the person has already provided.] With these kinds of situations, in which you can't change the problem itself, the one thing people can do is change the way they *feel* about the problem. And one of the ways we can do this is to change how we *think* about the problem. Counseling can be helpful in finding new ways to think about a problem, and this includes new ways of talking to ourselves about problems. [This often leads to the joke that I try to get people to start talking to themselves.]

This general explanation can be adapted to the situation of each individual, couple, or family. For example, oftentimes with single mothers I will add in a piece on self-nurturing activities under the first category of problems. I explain that part of building oneself up and making oneself stronger is good self-care. This includes good nutrition and exercise, but also activities and rewards that help to lift one's mood. If the person looks perplexed, I will say that this is very person-specific but some examples I have heard include taking a hot bath, lighting favorite candles, beading, sewing, going to the women's AA group, going for a walk outside, or taking time to pray or meditate. Most of the people I see do not have much money, so I try to give examples that are free or inexpensive.

To explain the concept of cognitive restructuring further, I often add the following.

> Have you ever had the experience where you start to get down on yourself, and say things to yourself like, "I'm such a loser, that was so stupid of me, I'll never get that job, nobody cares . . . "—that kind of thing—and as you say those things to yourself, you just feel worse and worse? [Pause for a response.] That negative self-talk can really pull you down. But the good news is that we can change that negative self-talk into more positive self-talk, to help us feel better. When we say things to ourselves like "Okay, I can do this, I can get through this, I know that I'll do better next time," and remind ourselves of our past successes and strengths, we build ourselves back up to be stronger.

To illustrate the use of cognitive–behavioral interventions, let's consider a client who is very different from the bicultural young man previously discussed.

CASE EXAMPLE

Clara, a 48-year-old woman of a Yup'ik mother and a Norwegian American father, came to the counselor Beth, a 50-year-old European American woman, with symptoms of crying easily, difficulty sleeping, and worrying "constantly." Clara told Beth that she was worried about her daughter June, who left high school before graduating and was now heavily into alcohol and drugs. In response to Beth's questions, Clara told Beth that she (Clara) was born in a Yup'ik village of about 100 people and lived there until she was 12 years old and her mother died in an accident. Within the year, her father had killed himself and she and her three younger siblings went to live with their paternal grandparents in Bethel (the largest Yup'ik village with a population of about 6,000). Clara described her grandparents as good people who taught her traditional values. They rarely talked about her parents. Clara did well in school, obtained her high school degree, began working as a secretary at the local school, and married at the age of 20. She and her husband wanted children, but she had three miscarriages and then never again became pregnant. However, one of Clara's sisters had chronic problems with alcoholism and was unable to take care of her daughter June. (At this point, Clara explained that June was her biological niece.) June's biological father was physically abusive to both June and her mother and no longer had any contact with either of them. June was initially placed in the custody of child protective services, but when June was 8 years old, Clara and her husband were able to adopt her.

Clara said that "things went good" until June was about 12, and then she began drinking and hanging out with boys. She stopped going to school in her junior year and came and went from the house. At the age of 18, she agreed to go to treatment with the understanding that if she did not, she would not be able to live with Clara and her husband any longer. June completed a 30-day inpatient treatment program and was "clean and sober" for 2 months before she began using again. This had been about 6 months earlier, and now Clara only heard from June when the latter called her needing money or a place to stay. Clara said that after talking with her pastor many times about June, he suggested that she see a counselor. She then went to her doctor, who prescribed medication for her high blood pressure, advised her to lose weight, and also told her to see a counselor. Clara acknowledged her weight problem (about 70 pounds over) but was clearly more concerned about June.

Regarding social supports in her life, Clara described herself as a Christian, said that she attended church regularly, and had two good women friends with whom she talked daily. She described her faith as strong, adding "If I didn't have God in my life, I don't know what I'd do." Her 60-year-old husband Ronald would not go to church with her, but she described their relationship as "we get along good most times." She said he had his own health problems, including emphysema from years of smoking. Clara stated that she had never become "a drinker," and although her husband drank heavily at an earlier point in his life, he had been sober for over 20 years.

One of the most striking aspects of Clara's situation is its complexity. Among Alaska Natives who present to mental health and substance abuse clinics, this complexity intertwined with a history of exceptional loss and trauma is not uncommon (Napoleon, 1996). Therapists need to be especially aware of the possibility of posttraumatic stress disorder (PTSD) in clients who have experienced such an accumulation of loss and trauma. Whether or not PTSD is a primary diagnosis, in such complicated situations the therapist is faced with the question, "In the midst of such an overwhelming number of stressors, both present and past, where does one begin?"

By the end of this assessment session, the therapist Beth had learned enough about Clara to determine that she was not experiencing any immediately debilitating effects of the earlier trauma in her life (i.e., no symptoms of PTSD, and no suicidal or homicidal ideation). Beth summarized the stressors she had heard from Clara, beginning with Clara's childhood difficulties of losing her parents at a very young age, followed by her sister's addiction, June's addiction, Clara's health problems, and her husband's health problems. She suspected that there were other difficulties that Clara had not had time to mention. She expressed amazement at Clara's resilience, making the point that many people would have given up if they had been through what Clara had been through.

Beth then summarized the strengths and supports she saw contributing to Clara's resilience: Clara's relationships with her grandparents (now deceased), her current relationships with women friends and her husband, the Church, and her faith. Beth inquired about fun activities, and Clara said that she enjoyed sewing. When Beth asked about specific culturally related activities by naming them, Clara said yes, she enjoyed berry picking, fishing, and simply being outdoors. She said that she did not use cleansing or purifying rituals, nor did she do drumming, and although she would have liked to dance, she said she did not feel up to it.

Beth asked if there were any personal qualities that Clara liked about herself. With tears in her eyes, Clara modestly shrugged and said nothing. Beth then asked, "What do your best friends like about you?" Clara said "They say I'm a good listener." Beth asked what Clara's husband would say and she said, "He says I take good care of him." This information gave Beth a good list of Clara's strengths and supports to draw from later. The assessment ended with Beth's explanation of how counseling might be helpful to Clara by building on her current strengths and supports, and possibly adding some additional ones. She also stated that she (Beth) could help Clara problem-solve regarding what to do about June. Clara agreed that this would be helpful.

Problem Solving

At the second session, Beth asked for an update on Clara's situation. June had called, and Clara had sent her $50 that June said she needed for food. Clara said that she knew June would probably use it for drugs. Beth asked questions aimed at helping Clara articulate her confused feelings of hurt, anger, fear, and love. She validated these feelings as understandable given her relationship with June and June's behavior. Beth then asked several questions aimed at helping Clara move into the initial stages of problem solving. This included the exploration of Clara's (a) perception of the problem, (b) attributions or beliefs about the causes of the problem, (c) appraisal of the problem (i.e., its level of significance in her life), (d) perception of control regarding the problem (i.e., whether it was solvable, and whether she was capable of solving it), and (e) the amount of time and effort involved in making the situation better and her willingness to put forth this time and effort (D'Zurilla & Nezu, 2001).

Clara perceived the problem to be June's loss of and conflicting feelings toward her mother and father, compounded by the harmful relationships she developed in connection with her alcohol and drug abuse. Clara saw June's alcohol and drug behaviors as symptomatic (i.e., the result rather than the cause) of June's emotional and spiritual pain. When Beth asked, Clara could also see that part of the problem was within Clara, that is, Clara's own pain and emotional difficulties regarding June. Regarding solutions, Clara said that she had hope and faith that things could get better, but she was at a loss as to how to make this happen. She was willing to come to counseling on a weekly basis if it would help, and her history suggested that she was capable of sustaining good effort toward making things better.

Beth initiated a discussion of the parts of the problem that were external to Clara (i.e., June's behavior) and the parts that were internal to Clara (Clara's feelings and thinking about the problem). This led to a discussion of possible solutions for these different parts. Regarding the external part, Clara could not think of any practical actions or changes that she had not already tried, so Beth made a couple of suggestions. One of these concerned June's request for money. Clara was clear that she could not let June starve and was afraid to take the risk of not giving her money when June sounded so desperate. Beth did not pressure her on this point, as she recognized the cultural and personal importance of family to Clara and the need for Clara to keep a connection with June. Instead, Beth suggested finding a way to pay for the food directly, for example, by an arrangement with the grocery store that June frequented. Beth also helped Clara develop a list of social service resources with phone numbers that Clara could periodically give to June when June called. Clara liked these ideas because they allowed her to continue to help June (which was an expression of hope for her) without contributing to June's addiction. (For an excellent book on the importance of hope in physical and psychological healing, see *The Anatomy of Hope* by Grooper, 2003.)

Cognitive Restructuring

As Beth worked with Clara on problem solving the external parts of this situation, she listened for statements that might reflect thoughts that were contributing to or exacerbating Clara's internal conflict and pain. In her explanation of cognitive restructuring (without using the term), she explained that a certain amount of frustration, fear, and pain were understandable when someone you love is on such a destructive path. This validation of Clara's negative feelings was important to avoid the self-blame that is so often reinforced by the dominant culture. At the same time, Beth explained how changing some of Clara's negative thoughts could help her feel better and stronger.

Remembering that Clara had said her grandparents taught her traditional values, Beth asked if they had talked about the relationship between one's thoughts, attitudes, and behaviors. Clara said yes, she knew about the importance of holding "right attitudes" particularly when hunting and fishing. She knew that if one behaves respectfully toward animals and the environment, "things will work better." For example, she said, "If you act respectfully toward the fish, it will give itself to you." As they talked more about this idea, Beth made the connection between the Yup'ik beliefs and the cognitive–behavioral idea that "what you think affects how you feel, and how you think and feel affect your behavior." Building on Clara's example, Beth said,

> If you think to yourself, "I'll never catch this stupid fish," you will prob-
> ably feel discouraged and a little angry and this will lead you to be sloppy
> in how you fish, whether you're setting a net or using a dipnet or a line.
> This sloppy, disrespectful behavior will decrease the chances that you
> will catch the fish. On the other hand, if you respect the fish and the
> river and yourself, you will be careful and thoughtful in what you do, and
> your chances of catching a fish will be greater.

Clara added that it is possible that the fish knows that you are being respectful and is thus more willing to give itself.

Beth and Clara then talked about how one's attitude and thoughts could
help or hinder a person's well-being. Regarding Clara's thoughts about June,
Beth gave an example of one thought that she had heard Clara state, which
Beth thought might be hurtful to Clara:

> If I don't give June money, she won't be able to eat, and she could get
> into even worse trouble. She could have to stay with bad men, she could
> kill herself because she gives up, or one of those bad people could kill
> her.

This statement illustrates the problem with using the cognitive–behavioral
concept of rationality as a way to categorize the helpfulness or unhelpfulness
of a thought. Namely, definitions of what is rational and irrational are culture specific and situational. Whereas a middle-class European American
might judge Clara's statement to be an irrational "jumping to conclusions,"
it is just as likely that Clara's assessment of what might happen is quite rational. It is clear that the more therapists know about a client's cultural context,
the more able they will be to figure out how rational the feared thought is.
However, there is still the problem of judgmentalism that can creep into
one's beliefs about what is rational, particularly when the therapist is of the
dominant culture and the client is not. To avoid this problem, the therapist
can use the concept of helpfulness rather than that of rationality (i.e., asking
the client, "Is it helpful to think this?"). From a theoretical perspective, this
approach can be conceptualized as challenging the utility of the thought
rather than its validity (Beck, 1995).

Beth began directing Clara toward the process of cognitive restructuring by asking her how she felt when she thought about this statement. Clara
acknowledged, with tears in her eyes, that she felt "very bad and very sad."
There was a long silence as they both experienced the sadness of her thought.
Beth asked Clara, "Is there anything that you tell yourself, that helps you to
feel better about the situation with June?" Clara said yes, that when she feels
very low, she tells herself, "God doesn't give you more than you can handle."
Beth allowed for another silence to indicate her appreciation of this statement and then said, "Well, God sure must think you're strong!" which made
both of them laugh. Beth then asked questions aimed at helping Clara to
elaborate on this helpful thought (i.e., adding information regarding the evi-

dence for it and other helpful thoughts). This led Clara to articulate the following beliefs:

> I'm a strong person. I've been through a lot, and with God's help, I've survived and helped other people and even had good times along the way. I can't control June's behavior but I will still love her and help her when I can. I'm doing my best.

Subsequent sessions focused on this cognitive restructuring process, reinforcing Clara's helpful thoughts about herself and June. Beth pointed out how counseling served as a reminder for Clara throughout the week to pay attention to her own thoughts, because she knew that Beth would be asking her about them. Beth also frequently called attention to Clara's personal strengths, to reinforce Clara's awareness of her positive qualities and the supports around her.

A person's problems are never easily compartmentalized, and the internal and external aspects of Clara's pain overlapped throughout therapy sessions. At times, there was more focus on cognitive restructuring, at times on problem solving regarding the latest encounters with June, and at times on strengthening and adding to the self-nurturing activities in Clara's life. The external aspects of Clara's problem changed very little during the course of therapy (i.e., June continued to drink, use drugs, and call and ask her for money). However, Clara began to feel stronger, and although each call from June brought her some sadness, Clara reported feeling less distressed on an ongoing daily basis and more able to enjoy the pleasurable activities and relationships in her life.

CONCLUSION

With its emphasis on client empowerment, practical problem solving, the development of positive coping skills, and the reinforcement of strengths and supports, CBT offers therapists tools for working more effectively with Alaska Native people in treatment. However, for CBT to be truly helpful with Native people, it must be combined with culture-specific knowledge, flexibility, and creativity. This chapter discusses only a few of the many possibilities in the development of culturally responsive CBT with Alaska Native people.

REFERENCES

Alaska Conservation Foundation. (2003). *Guide to Alaska's cultures.* Anchorage, AK: Author.

Alaska Department of Health and Social Services, Division of Public Health. (2001). *Healthy Alaskans 2010: Vol. 1. Targets and strategies for improved health.* Juneau, AK: Author.

Alaska Department of Health and Social Services, Office of Fetal Alcohol Syndrome. (2002, July 3). *Alaska's comprehensive FAS project, prevalence of FASD in Alaska.* Retrieved May 16, 2004, from http://www.hss.state.ak.us.fas/AKfiveyrgoal/default.htm

Alaska Division of Planning, Evaluation and Health Statistics, Indian Health Service, U.S. Department of Health and Human Services. (2002, December 19). *Special report: Key facts—Alaska Natives.* Retrieved May 22, 2004, from http://www.ihs.gov/facilitiesservices/areaoffices/alaska/dpehs/ak-dpehs-sp-ak-natives.asp

Alaska Geographic Society. (1996). *Native cultures in Alaska.* Anchorage, AK: Alaska Geographic.

Allen, J. (1998). Personality assessment with American Indians and Alaskan Natives: Instrument considerations and service delivery style. *Journal of Personality Assessment, 70,* 17–42.

American Psychological Association. (2000). Guidelines for psychotherapy with lesbian, gay, and bisexual clients. *American Psychologist, 55,* 1440–1451.

American Psychological Association. (2002). Guidelines on multicultural education, training, research, practice, and organizational change for psychologists. *American Psychologist, 58,* 377–402.

American Psychological Association. (2004). Guidelines for psychological practice with older adults. *American Psychologist, 59,* 236–260.

Beck, J. S. (1995). *Cognitive therapy: Basics and beyond.* New York: Guilford Press.

Cross, T. L. (2003). Culture as a resource for mental health. *Cultural Diversity and Ethnic Minority Psychology, 9,* 354–359.

Droby, R. M. (2000). *With the wind and the waves: A guide for non-Native mental health professionals working with Alaska Native communities.* Nome, AK: Norton Sound Health Corporation, Behavioral Health Services.

D'Zurilla, T. J., & Nezu, A. M. (2001). Problem-solving therapies. In K. S. Dobson (Ed.), *Handbook of cognitive–behavioral therapies* (pp. 211–245). New York: Guilford Press.

Fienup-Riordan, A. (2000a). Continuity and change in southwestern Alaska. In A. Fienup-Riordan, W. Tyson, P. John, M. Meade, & J. Active (Eds.), *Hunting tradition in a changing world: Yup'ik lives in Alaska today* (pp. 3–28). New Brunswick, NJ: Rutgers University Press.

Fienup-Riordan, A. (2000b). Mixed metaphors in the new Catholic Church. In A. Fienup-Riordan, W. Tyson, P. John, M. Meade, & J. Active (Eds.), *Hunting tradition in a changing world: Yup'ik lives in Alaska today* (pp. 109–141). New Brunswick, NJ: Rutgers University Press.

Gay, J. (2003, April 18). Villages back off booze experiment. *Anchorage Daily News,* p. A-1.

Gerjevic, S. (2004, April. 3). Native language classes teach manners in addition to words. *Canku Ota* [Many Paths]: *An Online Newsletter Celebrating Native America.* Retrieved November 21, 2005, from http://www.turtletrack.org/Issues04/Co04032004/CO_04032004_Manners_Words.htm

Grooper, J. (2003). *The anatomy of hope*. New York: Random House.

Haycox, S. (2002). *Alaska: An American colony*. Seattle: University of Washington Press.

Hays, P. A. (1995). Multicultural applications of cognitive–behavior therapy. *Professional Psychology: Research and Practice, 26*, 309–315.

Hays, P. A. (1996a). Addressing the complexities of culture and gender in counseling. *Journal of Counseling & Development, 74*, 332–338.

Hays, P. A. (1996b). Cultural considerations in couples therapy. *Women and Therapy, 19*, 13–23.

Hays, P. A. (1996c). Culturally responsive assessment with diverse older clients. *Professional Psychology: Research and Practice, 27*, 188–193.

Hays, P. A. (2001). *Addressing cultural complexities in practice: A framework for clinicians and counselors*. Washington, DC: American Psychological Association.

Hootch v. Alaska State-Operated School System, 536 P.2d 793 (Alaska 1975).

Jackson, A. P., & Turner, S. (2004). Counseling and psychotherapy with Native American clients. In T. B. Smith (Ed.), *Practicing multiculturalism: Affirming diversity in counseling and psychology* (pp. 215–233). New York: Pearson Education.

Jans, N. (1993). *The last light breaking: Living among Alaska's Inupiat Eskimos*. Anchorage: Alaska Northwest Books.

Kawagley, O. A. (1995). *A Yupiaq worldview: A pathway to ecology and spirit*. Prospect Heights, IL: Waveland Press.

Krauss, M. E. (1982). *Native peoples and languages of Alaska* [Map]. Fairbanks: University of Alaska Fairbanks, Alaska Native Language Center.

Langdon, S. J. (2002). *The Native people of Alaska*. Anchorage, AK: Great Land Graphics.

McClanahan, A. J. (2000). *Growing up Native in Alaska*. Anchorage, AK: The CIRI Foundation.

McClanahan, A. J., & Bissett, H. L. (2002). *Na'eda: Our friends*. Anchorage, AK: The Cook Inlet Regional Foundation.

Mohatt, G. V., Rasmus, S. M., Thomas, L., Hazel, K., Allen, J., & Hensel, C. (in press). *Tied together like a woven hat: Protective pathways to sobriety for Alaska Natives*. Fairbanks: University of Alaska, The People Awakening Project.

Napoleon, H. (1996). *Yuuyaraq: The way of the human being*. Fairbanks: University of Alaska, Alaska Native Knowledge Network.

Roysircar, G., Arredondo, P., Fuertes, J. N., Ponterotto, J. G., & Toporek, R. L. (2003). *Multicultural counseling competencies 2003*. Alexandria, VA: American Counseling Association.

Stevenson, H. C., & Renard, G. (1993). Trusting ole' wise owls: Therapeutic use of cultural strengths in African American families. *Professional Psychology: Research and Practice, 24*, 433–442.

Swan Reimer, C. (1999). *Counseling the Inupiat Eskimo*. Westport, CT: Greenwood Press.

Swinomish Tribal Community. (1991). *A gathering of wisdoms, Tribal mental health: A cultural perspective*. LaConnor, WA: Author.

Tower, E. (1988). *Reading, religion, reindeer: Sheldon Jackson's legacy to Alaska*. Anchorage, AK: Author.

U.S. Census Bureau. (2000). *Alaska quick facts*. Retrieved May 16, 2004, from http://quickfacts.census.gov/qfd/states/02000.html

Wallis, V. (2002). *Raising ourselves: A Gwich'in coming-of-age story from the Yukon River*. Kenmore, WA: Epicenter Press.

Wood, P. S., & Mallinckrodt, B. (1990). Culturally sensitive assertiveness training for ethnic minority clients. *Professional Psychology: Research and Practice, 21*, 5–11.

3

COGNITIVE–BEHAVIORAL THERAPY WITH LATINOS AND LATINAS

KURT C. ORGANISTA

In her writings on the Latino family, Falicov (1998) used the term *culture* to refer to a community of people that partially share the same meaning systems used to describe and ascribe meaning to the world (e.g., values, norms, role prescriptions). She noted that the ecological niche or unique combination of multiple contexts and partial perspectives define each individual's and each family's variation on major cultural themes. The ecological niche guides the evolution of values and behaviors (for better or worse) given its link to the social and physical environment (e.g., social class), as well as access to power and the resources necessary for healthy development. The beauty of this definition is that it recognizes within-group similarities that constitute culture and variations from central cultural tendencies and pays proper attention to the social environment. With this in mind, Organista and Muñoz (1996) described Latinos as follows:

> We fully recognize that each Latino is in some ways like no other Latino, and that there are subgroups of Latinos that are quite different from one another. Nevertheless, there are elements of shared history, of language, customs, religion and moral values, and of self-identity and identity attributed by others, which define, however imperfectly, a recognizable

subgroup in society which must be properly served. The more clinicians know about a particular subgroup of Latinos (e.g., Mexican Americans, Puerto Ricans, etc.), the more they can conceptualize and treat the mental health problems of that group in a culturally sensitive manner. (p. 255)

The knowledge referred to earlier should include a basic socioeconomic status (SES) profile, as described subsequently, and awareness of the historical and social experience of the Latino group(s) with whom one practices. Organista and Muñoz (1996) further noted that

> Latinos are individuals with personal and family roots in Latin American countries. Many Latinos speak Spanish and most partake of the blended cultural traditions of the Spanish colonists and the indigenous peoples of the Americas. Latinos may belong to any racial group including those with roots in Europe, Africa, Asia, and the Middle East. (p. 256)

The term *Latino* is now commonly used by Latinos and non-Latinos to refer to both immigrant and U.S.-born Americans of Latino ancestry.

SOCIOECONOMIC PROFILE

Intimations of mental health needs, as well as more general psychosocial and health problems, can be gleaned by reviewing the sociodemographic and acculturation profiles of different U.S. Latino groups. For example, the well-documented inverse relation between psychopathology and SES (e.g., Bruce, Takeuchi, & Leaf, 1991; Kessler et al., 1994) should alert us to the mental health needs of Latinos who are disproportionately affected by poverty and the challenges in adjusting to life in the United States.

With the 2000 Census report fresh in our minds (U.S. Census Bureau, 2000), we know that Latinos now comprise 13% of the U.S. population, a dramatic population growth rate of almost 60% between 1990 and 2000 (Marotta & Garcia, 2004; Therrien & Ramirez, 2000). Mexican Americans comprise almost two thirds of Latinos (58%), followed by Puerto Ricans (10%), Cubans (4%), and several other smaller groups such as Central and South Americans and Dominicans (28%). Table 3.1 provides socioeconomic profiles for Latinos and non-Hispanic Whites, with attention to within-Latino variance in income and education levels, as well as rates of poverty. As can be seen, poverty levels are considerably higher for Latinos as compared with non-Hispanic Whites, and this is especially true for Puerto Ricans, followed by Mexicans, with Cubans closer to non-Hispanic Whites in SES. We should presume different levels of SES-related mental health needs in these major Latino groups, partly rooted in their very different acculturation histories in the United States.

TABLE 3.1
Socioeconomic Profile of Latinos and Non-Hispanic Whites

Group	Median income	% in poverty	High school completion	College graduation
Latinos	$26,179	29.4	57.0	10.6
Mexican	25,347	31.0	51.0	6.9
Puerto Rican	23,646	35.7	64.3	8.0
Cuban	35,616	17.3	73.0	23.0
Central and South American	29,960	20.8	64.3	15.1
Other Hispanic	26,171	29.9	71.6	15.1
Non-Latino Whites	49,636	8.6	88.4	28.1

Note. From Marger (2000); Therrien and Ramirez (2000).

ACCULTURATION AND MENTAL HEALTH

In their review of the literature on acculturation and mental health among major American minority groups, Balls Organista, Organista, and Kurasaki (2003) found two major patterns in the available epidemiological data for Latinos. The first pattern showed between-group differences in mental health that ran parallel to the different levels of SES reviewed earlier. That is, mental health problems such as major depression and alcohol abuse were consistently higher in Puerto Ricans and Mexican Americans as compared with Cuban Americans. Although more comparative mental health research is needed, this pattern of mental health differences between Latino groups reflects their acculturation histories, which vary considerably in terms of degree of acculturative stress and challenges to adaptation. For example, whereas Puerto Ricans have experienced over a century of colonization by the United States, including industrial exploitation of the island and segregation of Puerto Ricans alongside African Americans on the mainland, Cuban American history reveals high investment on the part of the United States in facilitating the adjustment of a predominantly professional and upperclass group of legal refugees who fled the Castro regime beginning in 1959.

The second pattern found by Balls Organista et al. (2003) was that within Mexican Americans, acculturation to the United States is consistently related to higher levels of a broad array of diagnosable mental health problems. This pattern was attributed to a process of Mexican American acculturation often characterized by labor force participation in the service sector of the working poor, consequent segregation and poverty, and the breakdown of traditional cultural supports such as the extended family and community. Thus, whereas the mental health needs of Latinos vary between and within major Latino groups, they are considerable and increasing, warranting concerted efforts on the part of mental health professionals to conduct the necessary outreach, development, and evaluation of Latino-focused services.

ADVANTAGES OF COGNITIVE–BEHAVIORAL THERAPY

Although there is no empirical evidence to suggest that some forms of psychotherapy are superior to others when working with Latinos, various dimensions of cognitive–behavioral therapy (CBT) appear to be consistent with many of the traditional cultural characteristics and social experiences of Latino clients. The didactic emphasis in CBT is helpful in orienting Latino clients to therapy by educating them about how mental disorders are conceptualized (e.g., from the perspective of the American Psychiatric Association's [2000] *Diagnostic and Statistical Manual of Mental Disorders* [4th ed., text rev.; DSM–IV–TR]) and treated with CBT. Not only is an educational approach helpful in demystifying psychotherapy, it is also consistent with what Orlinsky and Howard (1986) call *role preparation*, in which clients unfamiliar with therapy learn what they can expect and what will be expected of them, as a way of enhancing treatment compliance and preventing premature termination. Consider the example of a traditionally oriented Latino client who meets criteria for depression yet defines her symptoms as *nervios* (nerves). Nervios is a culture-bound idiom of distress in response to overwhelming stressful experiences, particularly grief, threat, or familial conflict, characterized by dysphoria and multiple somatic symptoms (Guarnaccia, Good, & Kleinman, 1990). CBT can offer such a client an acceptable conceptualization of her problem and treatment that do not necessarily negate her experience and perception of the problem and potential solutions (e.g., increasing meaningful activities, changing thoughts that make one feel bad, and improving relationships). CBT also seems to be less abstract than some other forms of therapies (e.g., psychodynamic) and thus easier for clients to understand.

The typical use of therapy manuals, homework assignments, and in-session chalkboard work helps Latino clients to think of therapy as more of a classroom experience, thus decreasing the stigma so often attached to therapy. For example, the Latino clients with whom I have worked generally referred to their CBT depression group as *la clase de depresión* (the depression class). These predominantly Mexican immigrant and Central American refugee clients frequently communicated that mental health services in their countries of origin were scarce and reserved mostly for *personas locas* (crazy people) in mental institutions.

Traditionally oriented Latinos often expect their doctors and other health professionals to prescribe medications or to recommend a course of action to improve their health and well-being. Professionals are viewed as authority figures who are sanctioned to be active and directive in delivering services. Such expectations are more readily met in CBT as opposed to non-directive forms of therapy.

Given that CBT is short term, oriented toward problem solving, and focused on the present, it seems to fit better with the lives of low-income people who are overly affected by poverty-related problems, frequent crises, and limited resources. CBT can be flexibly applied to such multiple problems even when they are not the immediate focus of treatment. For example, therapy may center on helping a client cope with panic disorder while simultaneously helping the client to improve related problems in domains such as family, work, and school. Such flexible applications of CBT to clients' pressing concerns help them to feel that therapy is worthwhile and responsive to their immediate lives.

LIMITATIONS OF COGNITIVE–BEHAVIORAL THERAPY

Cultural competence includes being able to size up or consider how well an intervention may or may not fit with a client's or a family's social and cultural reality. In the case of Latinos, a few possible disadvantages of CBT are considered subsequently as a first step in generating dialogue on this topic and thinking of ways to minimize potential obstacles.

Limited Outcome Evaluation Research on Latinos

Although the efficacy of CBT for a variety of mental disorders is impressive (e.g., refer to *A Guide to Treatments That Work*, by Nathan & Gorman, 2002), there continues to be very little CBT outcome research that includes Latino participants. The handful of studies that do exist suggests that CBT is a promising approach for Latinos, but much more research is needed. For example, Miranda, Azocar, Organista, Valdes Dwyer, and Areán (2003) published the results of a randomized clinical trial comparing group CBT for depression, with and without case management, in a sample of 199 low-income medical outpatients, about 40% of whom were Latinos. Results showed that participants in the CBT plus case management condition had lower dropout rates than those receiving only group CBT. Comprehensive case management services were provided by social workers who addressed general client needs and also participated as CBT group cofacilitators (Organista & Valdes Dwyer, 1997). Group CBT plus case management was also associated with greater improvements in depression and general client functioning than CBT alone, but only for the 77 Spanish-speaking Latino patients.

These findings are consistent with the landmark study by Sue, Fujino, Hu, Takeuchi, and Zane (1991), who assessed the effects of linguistic and ethnic matching of therapists and clients by reviewing the mental health charts of 12,000 Los Angeles County mental health patients (3,000 charts per race or ethnic group of Latino, Anglo American, African American, and Asian American). Results revealed that linguistic or ethnic matching improved treatment outcome, decreased dropout from therapy, and increased the total number of therapy sessions attended by clients, but only for Latinos and Asians who were low in acculturation (i.e., recent immigrants who were less likely to speak English, less familiar with the mental health system, etc.). Thus, the presence of bilingual or bicultural mental health professionals appears imperative for the significant numbers of Latinos low in acculturation who have special language and adaptation-related needs.

Prior to the study by Miranda et al. (2003), but at the same site, Organista, Muñoz, and González (1994) conducted a preliminary outcome study of CBT with 175 low-income medical outpatients, nearly half of whom were Spanish-speaking Latinos. Results revealed pre- to posttreatment reductions in major depression but to a lesser extent than results reported in the outcome literature on non-Hispanic White and typically middle-class samples. That is, study participants went from severe to moderate symptoms. Organista (1995) also described a detailed case study in which CBT was moderately successful in treating a severe case of major depression and panic disorder (with subthreshold agoraphobia) in a Central American woman overwhelmed by divorce, single parenthood, and her recent arrival in the United States. Given the naturalistic setting of the research, reductions in depression from severe to moderate were clinically significant changes.

Comas-Díaz (1981) compared cognitive therapy with behavior therapy in a small sample of depressed, Spanish-speaking, single Puerto Rican mothers from low-SES backgrounds ($N = 26$). Results showed significant and comparable reductions in depression for both cognitive and behavioral treatments compared with a waiting list (WL) control group.

A few studies have also begun to demonstrate promising results with CBT applied to Latino youths experiencing various mental health problems. Kataoka et al. (2003) developed a school-based CBT group for recent Latino immigrant children exposed to community violence and found a modest decrease in symptoms of depression and posttraumatic stress disorder (PTSD). This intervention program was implemented in nine public schools with third-through eighth-grade students. The 152 students in the group CBT condition showed significantly greater improvement than the 47 students assigned to a WL control condition. Piña, Sliverman, Fuentes, Kurtines, and Weems (2003) used exposure-based CBT to treat phobic and anxiety disorders in 52 Latino and 79 non-Latino White youths between 6 and 16 years of age. Results showed excellent treatment effects (more than 80% recovery) and maintenance gains at 3- and 6-month follow-up for both Latino and non-Latino White youths who did not differ from each other in outcome.

In a randomized controlled trial to compare individual CBT and interpersonal psychotherapy (IPT) in the treatment of 71 clinically depressed Island Puerto Rican adolescents, Rossello and Bernal (1999) found that both therapies reduced symptoms, as compared with a WL control condition, and that IPT was also superior to WL in increasing self-esteem and social adaptation. The authors concluded that although both culturally adapted treatments were efficacious for Puerto Rican youths, IPT might be especially congruent with Latino cultural values (see Table 3.2 for a listing of such values,

TABLE 3.2
Sampling of Mainstream American Values Inherent in Cognitive–Behavioral Therapy and Traditional Latino Values

Mainstream American values	Traditional Latino values
Task orientation, especially to business and professional relations (e.g., "Never mix business with pleasure")	Personalismo, or a personal orientation that emphasizes the personal dimension to all human relations, including business and professional
Individualistic orientation	Collective or familial orientation
Verbal expressiveness; expression of feelings	Stoicism; resignation; control of emotions; nonverbal communication
Assertiveness	Traditional communication protocol based on deference to those higher in status; cultural script of *simpatía* (sympathy) or goal of smooth versus confrontational relations
Egalitarian, democratic relationships	Nonegalitarian gender and age group roles based on traditional hierarchy
Scientific, intellectual reasoning	Religious faith, importance of emotions

which are discussed later in the chapter). That is, although treatment manuals for both therapies included salient traditional Latino values such as respect (*respeto*) and emphasis on the centrality of family (*familismo*), IPT may have more directly emphasized such values given its main objective of reducing symptoms within interpersonal relations and contexts. However, these researchers recently conducted a second trial of CBT and IPT, this time comparing individual and group formats of each therapy, with 112 Puerto Rican adolescents. This time Rossello and Bernal found that while individual and group formats were both effective in decreasing depression symptoms, CBT produced greater improvement in depression than IPT (unpublished study cited by Miranda et al., 2005). In summary, although the limited literature on CBT is promising, much more outcome research is needed to substantiate its effectiveness relative to other forms of therapy.

Individual Versus Social Change

Another potential limitation of CBT is that it emerges from the behavioral science tradition of focusing on individual-level variables (i.e., cognitions, skills, behaviors, etc.) to effect therapeutic change. Although clients can be empowered with new knowledge, deeper understanding, and self-efficacy enhancing skills, their behavior may still be considerably influenced by structural–environmental, social, and cultural contexts that shape problems and behaviors in ways that may at times be outside of an individual's volitional control. Macrosocial changes (e.g., laws, policies, institutional arrangements, national norms, and societywide values) are needed to improve Latino mental health in addition to microlevel therapeutic interventions.

For example, in a policy analysis of Latino mental health in the state of California, Organista and Snowden (2003) noted that only 29 Latino clinicians are currently available for every 100,000 Latinos in the state as compared with 173 per 100,000 for their non-Latino counterparts in the state. These authors made several recommendations, including the need to advocate for policies designed to increase the number of bilingual therapists. For example, they recommended loan forgiveness programs whereby the state pays a portion of loans incurred by bilingual graduate students in exchange for 2 years of postgraduate services in public or nonprofit agencies serving low-income clients in languages other than English (a policy already in place in the field of education that has resulted in thousands of bilingual teachers working in language minority schools).

Thus, although not usually an explicit part of training or supervision, therapists and agencies working with Latino populations may want to think about ways they can promote Latino mental health at mesocommunity and macrosocietal levels (e.g., increasing Latino political participation and public policy benefit). Through such advocacy work, clinicians working with Latino clients will be more likely to empathize with the social context of Latino mental health problems, and less likely to attribute such problems solely to individual, psychological mechanisms.

Mainstream American Versus Traditional Latino Values

Table 3.2 lists a number of modern American and traditional Latino cultural values that, if not considered and creatively negotiated, could undermine the flow and effectiveness of CBT with Latino clients. Obviously such values and role prescriptions are cultural norms and not people, thus considerable variation exists across Latino clients as well as therapists. However, because they do arise, advanced preparation and vigilance are important, as discussed later in the chapter.

PRACTICAL SUGGESTIONS FOR ADAPTING CBT

Suggestions for adapting CBT to Latino clients are listed briefly here, followed by a case study.

Use a Traditional Latino Relationship Protocol to Engage Clients

Successful engagement in therapy is a fundamental first step that can be enhanced with Latino clients by incorporating the salient Latino value of *personalismo* into a culturally sensitive relationship protocol. Personalismo refers to a valuing of and responsiveness to the personal dimension of relationships, including task-oriented professional relationships such as psychotherapy. As such, the mainstream practice of immediately focusing on the presenting problem in therapy can be perceived as impersonal by Latino patients especially if it is at the expense of the social lubrication needed to build *confianza*, or trust (Roll, Millen, & Martinez, 1980).

Because personalism is not informality, it would be a mistake to come across too casually or overly friendly. As described by Roll et al. (1980), the task of the culturally sensitive psychotherapist is to find the balance between task-oriented formality and warm personalized attention to the client. To achieve such a balance, it is frequently necessary for therapists working with Latino clients to engage in sufficient small talk, or *plática*, that includes judicious self-disclosure.

Pretherapy Orientation

Taking the time to orient clients to therapy can also enhance engagement. At the hospital-based depression clinic where I work, therapy preparation videos were developed in both Spanish and English by Gayle Iwamasa (this book's coeditor). These films depict the process of therapy, beginning with the referral made by medical staff that have been trained by the clinic director to screen for symptoms of depression. In addition, a mock group therapy session is shown, described by the film's narrator and later discussed by actual clients. Client discussions include how they felt before and after their experience, the types of problems addressed, and how helpful they found therapy. The films have been shown in the waiting room of the general medical clinics and to patients who were recommended therapy following psychological evaluation.

Recognize and Address Values Underlying CBT and Traditional Latino Culture

As noted in Table 3.2, being conscious about the many implicit values underlying *both* CBT and Latino culture can facilitate their integration into therapy, open discussions of these issues as they arise, and result in finding the "bicultural middle ground" for intervention modifications:

- Advocate activity schedules for the client with and without other family members, rather than solely for the client, to respond to the collectivist value of familismo or familism with its strong emphasis on family centrality and loyalty. Rationales such as "You need to take care of yourself first" are not as culturally compatible as those that link self-care to family care: "You can take better care of your family by taking care of yourself." Also, make sure to generate a list of enjoyable things to do that do not require much money for low-income clients (e.g., free admission to museums first Wednesday of the month, walk in the park, visiting friends, etc.).

- Streamline cognitive restructuring by using the "Yes, but" technique in which unhelpful thoughts and beliefs are considered half-truths that need to be made into whole truths, rather than labeling patients' thinking as irrational or distorted (see Organista, 1995).

- Conduct culturally sensitive assertive training in ways that are mindful of the culture-based protocols for communication between people at different levels of traditional social status (e.g., older vs. younger; bosses and professionals vs. workers; men vs. women). For example, Comas-Díaz and Duncan (1985) described how to preface assertive communication in ways that convey traditional forms of deference and respeto while still being assertive: "With all due respect" and "Would you permit me to express how I feel about that?" Such entrées into assertiveness also increase the chances of integrating the Latino value of *simpatía*, or smooth, less confrontational communication.

CASE STUDY

The client was a middle-aged, first-generation, married Mexican American man who spoke mainly Spanish and a little English (i.e., he was born in Mexico and immigrated to the United States as a young man). I refer to my client as Mr. Lopez. He was referred to the depression clinic at San Francisco General Hospital by the pain clinic for suspected depression and because he was not following through with physical therapy, which he believed was too painful and physically harmful to perform. The client's referral to the pain clinic was part of his medical treatment plan, which had included back surgery to alleviate back pain following a work-related injury the year before when he had fallen and damaged two spinal discs. The lack of bilingual Latino staff in the pain clinic only added to the problem of noncompliance. The depression clinic is located within the division of psychosocial medicine and is staffed by bilingual and bicultural clinicians and staff members who called the client by phone to set up the appointment.

The client and his wife had emigrated from a small rural city in Mexico and adhered strongly to traditional Mexican culture. The client's wife had mainly been a homemaker but began working full time at a local restaurant shortly after the client's disability. Although the client did not like his wife working, he recognized the financial necessity now that his only source of income was disability insurance.

Client Factors

Several client factors need to be considered before CBT, including the client's strengths and challenges, social support, and risk and protective factors.

Client Strengths and Challenges

With regard to strengths, Mr. Lopez was fairly intelligent and communicative despite having little formal education (8 years). He was also likable and responsive to being treated with respect and kindness. He stated that he was committed to "finishing what I begin," including the new experience of therapy.

With regard to challenges, the client felt extremely angry about his physical disability, related chronic pain, and inability to continue working as an auto mechanic. His anger and depression would often result in withdrawal from family activities and angry outbursts in which he would yell at his wife and adult son and strike or break objects in the home. On one occasion he punched his son in the shoulder for not doing an automotive task to his satisfaction. Recently he had even fractured the small finger on his right hand as a result of punching a wall when angry. The client also appeared to be overly controlling in family activities (e.g., he would insist that the family return home from outings if his pain became intense).

Client Social Support

The client had an extended family in the Latino Mission District of San Francisco consisting of two adult married daughters with young children in addition to the single adult son living at home. With regard to friends, the client socialized with coworkers while healthy and working but had little contact with these friends during the past year following his injury.

There were many Latino-oriented centers and activities in the client's community, but the client claimed to be physically unable to avail himself of these activities. Although the community was rich in Latino cultural resources, it was also a typical low-SES environment with high crime statistics, rendering the client especially vulnerable and needing to take extra precautions (e.g., staying in more at night, doing more activities in the company of others).

Client Risk Versus Protective Factors

With regard to risk factors, the client's limited work skills, education, and English greatly diminished the possibility of nonlabor intensive work. He said that he was open to speaking English and to computer classes but that his pain did not allow him to sit for very long. With regard to protective factors, the client's extended family offered many forms of social support but were growing weary of his negativism and disruption of family activities.

Engaging the Client

Especially with less acculturated and presumably more traditional Latino clients, emphasis should be placed on enacting a traditional Latino relationship protocol based on the values of respeto and personalismo. Although clients higher in acculturation may need less of such traditional engagement, it seems best to err in this direction.

For example, I went out to meet Mr. Lopez in the waiting room by formally addressing him by his last name and shaking his hand in a manner that acknowledged the respect that his older age accorded. I also asked if he had any trouble finding the clinic and if he would like a glass of water or coffee. He agreed to a cup of coffee, and we began talking about the pleasure of *un cafesito* (a small coffee), a Spanish term of endearment for coffee, as I joined him in a cup.

I asked Mr. Lopez where he was from and when he answered Jalisco, Mexico, I smiled and told him that my family came from the same state and that I still visited cousins there. We spent the next few minutes talking about the capital city of Guadalajara and some of our favorite places to visit such as Lake Chapala and the arts and crafts town of Tlaquepaque (just being able to pronounce the latter confers a degree of ethnic authenticity!).

Eventually I mentioned the concerns of his doctor at the pain clinic regarding his adjustment to the severe back injury and chronic pain and his decision to discontinue physical therapy. I also assured the patient that I had read his medical chart and empathized with his predicament (i.e., ruptured spinal discs, loss of work, chronic pain) by noting that it was quite serious, or *muy grave*. The patient felt reassured that I did not think the pain was "in his head," although he still questioned the need for psychotherapy for a physical problem. I asked Mr. Lopez how he normally coped with his chronic pain, and he stoically replied that all he could do was "resign himself" to it. Although such an answer might be viewed as maladaptive, it is worth noting that Latino values such as resigning oneself to pain beyond one's control and controlling consequent negative emotions are viewed as strengths (see Table 3.2). The trick is to redirect such values toward the more verbal and action-oriented values inherent in CBT.

Thus, I explained that the therapy we practice could be helpful in teaching him how to better cope with or control his chronic pain as well as decrease his *coraje* (which roughly translates to angst). The patient replied that if he didn't have the pain and injury, then he wouldn't be upset, and to illustrate the pain he held out a tightly clenched, slightly tremulous fist. Such if-then thinking is common under stress and a prime target for cognitive restructuring. The nonverbal image of the fist was also worth noting for future use.

Before he left our first meeting, I told Mr. Lopez that I had worked with many patients with similar medical conditions who had very different levels of adjustment, ranging from anger, depression, and self-neglect to living as good a life as possible under the circumstances. I asked him to think about why some people have better and worse adjustment to similar medical conditions.

Therapist–Client Differences in Acculturation and Values

Although both the client and I are of Mexican ancestry, our acculturation differences were evident in our language use, which for my part involved speaking Spanish like an English-dominant Chicano or Mexican American (i.e., occasional literal translations of thoughts from English into Spanish, mixing English and Spanish as in terms such as *chequiar*, a corruption of the English verb "to check"). I dealt with the language differences by letting Mr. Lopez know up front that I spoke Spanish like a *pocho*, or a poached (i.e., half-baked) Mexican. Like the majority of my patients, Mr. Lopez laughed and was quick to compliment my Spanish in a sincere appreciation of having a member of the staff with whom he could communicate.

Mr. Lopez was as respectful of my professional status as I was of his higher age status, yet there were other acculturation-related differences of which to remain mindful. For example, although I could understand the client's traditional orientation to family life, my own orientation as a third-generation American of Mexican descent has become quite egalitarian (e.g., with regard to sharing household chores, child care, and decision making). Thus, our considerable mutual respect was later tested by angry outbursts on his part and limit setting on mine.

Central Role of Empathy

Research on CBT has documented the considerable therapeutic effect of empathy, an element traditionally lacking in the CBT literature that implicitly conveys that if you apply the right techniques to the problem, a positive outcome follows. For example, Burns and Nolen-Hoeksema (1992) found that clients with depression who rated their cognitive–behavioral therapists the warmest and most empathic improved significantly more than the clients of therapists rated as less empathic, even when controlling for factors such as initial depression severity and homework compliance.

With chronic pain, generous amounts of empathy need to be communicated for clients to feel that they are being understood. It was not difficult to empathize with the client's anger and depression in response to his pain and disability in view of the high value he placed on working. He was, in a sense, culturally as well as physically dislocated.

Streamlining Cognitive Restructuring

In the experience of the author, cognitive restructuring can be streamlined—without sacrificing its effectiveness—when working with low SES and ethnic minority clients. Methods of cognitive restructuring such as Albert

Ellis' well-known A-B-C-D method can sometimes overwhelm patients by requiring them to think about multiple relations between Activating events (e.g., stressors) and emotional Consequences (e.g., negative mood) that are mediated by irrational Beliefs about the activating events, and are thus in need of being Disputed. This method of cognitive restructuring often requires much effort to master and is frequently discarded by clients in the process. Following are examples of more client-friendly, streamlined approaches.

Small Steps Toward Pain Tolerance

Enacting the aforementioned culture-based relationship protocol helped the client to feel comfortable and respected, thereby enhancing engagement. The client also became more open to the idea of using therapy to better manage his chronic pain and depression. Although he initially insisted that his severe pain was constant and intolerable (i.e., "¡No puedo soportarlo!" [I can't stand it!]), self-monitoring revealed that it was more severe when attempting physical tasks and that he paid less attention to the pain when absorbed in interesting activities such as watching a movie or reading. I spent time in the first couple of sessions teaching the client some relaxation techniques (e.g., deep breathing) with the rationale that if his body was less tight, his pain would be less bothersome. We used his own nonverbal symbol of his back pain to promote relaxation by having him tightly clench his fist and then slowly relax it along with deep breathing and verbal cues such as "calm" or *tranquilo* (tranquil; a popular Mexican Spanish term of choice for describing the state of being relaxed).

Finally, we discussed how automatic it is for us to think, "I can't stand this!" when experiencing intense pain but how such thoughts can actually exacerbate pain. We discussed countering such automatic thoughts with those that help us cope, such as "It feels like I can't stand it but I can" and "This pain is very uncomfortable but not intolerable." After the first week of therapy, the patient reported "a little" improvement in his back pain consistent with his daily self-monitoring scores, which were beginning to drop a couple of points from the maximum pain rating.

Addressing Anger-Related Pain

Addressing the client's anger was very touchy, but I began by empathizing with the seriousness of his physical problems and noting how understandable it was that he felt frustrated and angry about his predicament. Next, I asked him to describe how getting angry affected his body, and he was able to describe muscle tightness that made his back pain worse. I also added that if he expressed his anger by striking objects, he also ran the continued risk of increasing his physical injuries, such as his fractured finger. Here the empathic logic was, "Look, you already have enough pain and physical problems. You don't have to add to them by hurting yourself when angry."

Thus, we agreed that less anger would be beneficial to his health, although he could not see how to escape the vicious cycle of pain causing anger and vice versa. I empathized that reaching this goal would not be easy but that it was possible. I asked him to continue with the relaxation training but also to monitor situations and thoughts related to his anger. In addition to "I can't stand it!" another troublesome automatic thought identified was "I can't do anything!" Cognitive structuring with this thought proceeded by using what I call the "Yes, but" technique in which unhelpful thoughts are described to the patient as "half-truths" that are partly but not completely true.

The "Yes, But" Technique

To teach the patient how to change such unhelpful thoughts, I asked him to complete the following thought: "Yes, my pain does make it very difficult to do many things, but . . . ," to which the patient eventually responded ". . . but I guess I can do some things." He was instructed to use the new restructured thought to counter the negative automatic thought whenever the latter emerged and to convey how changing his thinking made him feel. Here it is important to explain that although restructuring thinking may not provide immediate relief, consistent practice can provide relief by the end of the day or over the course of a few days (i.e., the positive effects tend to be cumulative).

Restructuring the previous two thoughts was also helpful in increasing the client's daily activities to further reduce symptoms of depression. He agreed to experiment with trying to do more daily activities on his own, such as walking two blocks to a café near his home to have coffee in the morning. He reported that this was very difficult, that he had to stop many times along the way, but that he did enjoy his cafesito. We discussed this as a very important lesson to take many breaks when trying to do ordinary things that are no longer easy to perform (e.g., washing dishes).

Less Bothersome Pain Versus Less Pain

By about midway through our 16 weeks of therapy, the client began to accept how his pain, anger, and depression were affected by his activities, thinking, and interactions with family members. Yet on days when his pain was particularly severe or when a lack of activities led to ruminating about his limitations, Mr. Lopez seriously questioned the extent to which therapy would help him adjust to his pain and disability. We discussed adjustment to disability as a lifelong process requiring not perfect but consistent practice of new skills to manage his very difficult situation. He accepted the idea that the goal of his therapy was to try to live as good a life as possible under the circumstances.

Mr. Lopez's depression had dropped from severe to moderate as indicated by weekly Beck Depression Inventory scores, but his pain ratings remained high. Because he seemed averse to ever admitting to less pain, we discussed how it would be better for him to do daily ratings of how much his pain bothered him. That is, without challenging the patient's claim of constant pain, we could assess his coping in terms of being less bothered by the pain as a result of activities (i.e., distractions) and thinking patterns.

Addressing the Client's Sense of Uselessness

Whereas the previously discussed thoughts were relatively easy to identify, core beliefs are by definition more central and less consciously available to patients. Often they are activated only during stressful events, can elicit catharsis when identified, and require considerable assistance identifying them and their role in causing and maintaining psychological distress. To begin identifying such core beliefs, I asked Mr. Lopez perhaps the most probing question in therapy: Could he help me understand what was the hardest part of living with his pain and disability? He quickly answered, "¡Porque ya no sirvo para nada!" (Because I am no longer good for nothing!) and "¡No valgo!" (I don't have any worth or value). On exploring the roots of such a belief, it emerged that Mr. Lopez's father had frequently made similar statements when talking about manhood and its relation to hard work and providing for one's family. We discussed how common this belief was in Mexican culture and among those who perform physical labor. We also sketched out on paper the relation between such a belief and depression in the event of injury and disability.

I asked the client what we should do with men in our families who can no longer work in a manner that made him laugh: "¿Debemos echarlos pa' fuera?" ("Should we throw 'em out?"). However, when the laughter subsided, Mr. Lopez became teary eyed and asked, "What good is such a man?" I answered that everybody becomes unable to work eventually yet can remain valuable to others. I then asked him to consider the value of retired elderly family members, and he was able to name some of their important functions, such as giving advice to younger family members and being good *compañeros* (companions) to spouses and friends. I strategically amplified his answer by adding that they also serve as examples of how to cope with problems such as chronic illnesses to which younger family members eventually succumb. I then asked him to think about what he wanted to teach his son at home about coping with chronic pain and disability.

Giving the central value of familismo in Mexican–Latino culture and the respect accorded elders in the family, the previously discussed reasoning made cultural sense to the client. We eventually constructed a counter to his core beliefs "I'm not good for anything" and "I don't have any value" with the following: "Yes, it's true that I can no longer work and earn money like before my injury, but . . ." (How would the reader complete this adaptive counter-belief?)

To give the restructuring of his problematic core beliefs a "testing ground," we wrote up a behavioral contract in which the client was assigned to stop by the auto shop where he used to work to visit some of his old friends. I told him that he could expect his negative core belief to interfere with attempting this assignment but that he was now prepared, given the positive counter belief that we had written on an index card for him to carry in his shirt pocket and practice during the week. In addition, we did some role-playing in which he practiced responses to questions that his friends were likely to ask, such as what was wrong with him, whether he is going to recover, and what he is doing now.

Culturally Sensitive Assertiveness Training

Although it would seem that something as modern and American as assertiveness training would be contraindicated for people from traditionally oriented cultural backgrounds, more clients were inclined to respectfully defer to those higher in authority—not engage in confrontational discussions or arguments and so forth. Yet as illustrated in the next section, there are ways of teaching assertiveness that are sensitive to the client while at the same time push the boundaries of traditional cultural norms in the best interest of the client.

Limit Setting With the Client

At first, the client was happy to see me and on two occasions brought small 4-ounce cans of Folgers coffee for me to try at home because it was his favorite. I graciously accepted these gifts in a manner consistent with Latino culture. However, as therapy became more difficult in challenging the client to do more activities to lift his mood and to help out at home, he often became angry.

At one point in therapy Mr. Lopez again balled his fist but this time struck my desk when he felt that I was suggesting something unreasonable (i.e., we were discussing his need for more physical therapy). I recall having to monitor and control my impulse to admonish him so that I could seize the moment to illustrate the role his thoughts played in driving his anger and hostility, which could result in physical harm to himself as well as others. I was also aware that assertively setting limits with Mr. Lopez might deviate from the value of simpatía, or the Latino cultural preference for smooth, pleasant, and nonconfrontational communication that we had enjoyed thus far (see Table 3.2). I said, "With all due respect, I see that you're very angry, but instead of hitting my desk, can you help me understand what I said that made you so angry?" When the client answered that I did not understand how painful physical therapy was for him, I sketched out on paper how such a belief would make anybody in his position angry but that there might be other ways to interpret my comment (e.g., concern).

The incident also made me consider the possibility that Mr. Lopez was expressing anger at me in a manner similar to the way he behaved toward his adult son at home. As such, I had to think about how to assertively set limits with him as a prelude to addressing such family issues.

Family-Focused Interventions

The client described how he would get angry at his adult son, whom he would ask to do things but who was either too busy to do them immediately or could not do them to his satisfaction (e.g., car and home repairs). There appeared to be few challenges to the client from wife, son, and other family members. Midway through treatment, I asked the client to invite his wife and son to therapy so that I could better assess and address family dynamics.

In response to my suggestion, the client brought his wife and adult son to two sessions of therapy. To accommodate their work schedules, I arranged two evening sessions in which I was able to gain more information regarding my hypothesis about the patient's possible secondary gain (i.e., attention) for complaining about his pain. Although our clinic is not set up for family therapy per se, it is important in working with Latino clients to be open to inviting key family members to therapy sessions.

Mrs. Lopez and her son Héctor expressed considerable concern for Mr. Lopez but also expressed some exasperation about how to help. With regard to Mrs. Lopez, her biggest frustration was dealing with her husband breaking things in anger when she asked him to help with household chores such as washing the dishes. The son similarly expressed frustration with his father's anger when he could not do tasks to Mr. Lopez's satisfaction or as quickly as his father desired. In both cases, I saw the need for assertive limit setting with Mr. Lopez's anger but realized that the wife and son ran the risk of being perceived as rude and disrespectful. As indicated in Table 3.2, the potential culture clash here is that American assertiveness training is based on egalitarian democratic principles and a person's (equal) "right" to express one's thoughts and feelings that can run counter to the nondemocratic, traditional hierarchy of many Latino families. In such families, a wife's deference to her husband, as well as a son's deference to his father, can minimize modern assertive communications that are critical of a husband's or father's behavior. Hence, I needed to teach assertiveness in a culturally sensitive manner and relied on the informative work of Comas-Díaz and Duncan (1985) to pursue this strategy.

I began by informing Mrs. Lopez and Héctor that anger made Mr. Lopez's pain worse and that although his frustration and irritability were understandable, he could use their help in managing his anger. I then asked Mr. Lopez if he would "permit" his wife and son to help him by occasionally giving their opinions on family matters and by expressing their feelings to him about how he was handling difficult situations. Phrased this way, he could hardly say no because the term *permit* within Latino culture acknowledges the respect he deserves as head of the family (i.e., permitted vs. unsolicited criticism).

Next, I attempted to model culturally sensitive assertiveness by reminding Mr. Lopez of the time he struck my desk with his fist, asking him to role-play this event. With an embarrassed smile, he pretended to strike the desk and I said to him, "Con todo respeto, papá, por favor no pegue mi escritorio. No es bueno para tu salud y también me hace sentirme mal cuando prefería sentirme bien contigo" [With all due respect, dad, please don't hit my desk. It's not good for your health and also it makes me feel upset when I would prefer to feel good with you]. Note how this communication begins with an acknowledgment of respect before making a request and expressing one's reactions to the father's hostile behavior.

When I asked Mr. Lopez how he felt about such a communication, he said that it was okay. After helping the son to practice such communication, we also did a little added problem solving, such as suggesting to the son that he give his father an alternate time when he could do a chore if he was too busy to do it when requested. I also told Mr. Lopez that nobody was going to do things for him to his satisfaction until he became less frustrated with his own diminished ability to do things (i.e., that perhaps he was taking his frustration out on his wife and son).

With regard to secondary gain for disrupting family outings with his pain, I addressed this topic with Mrs. Lopez and Héctor, and they noted that if Mr. Lopez experienced great pain during a drive or while at a family gathering he insisted that they all return home. This demand was typically met by unsuccessful attempts to console Mr. Lopez. I asked the family if they could think of a way to achieve balance between taking care of Mr. Lopez and taking care of the family's need to relax and spend time together. The son offered the idea of taking two cars to such activities in the event that Mr. Lopez absolutely felt the need to leave (he still drove, albeit with pain and effort). I asked everybody if this was acceptable, and they agreed to try it.

I also emphasized that Mrs. Lopez and Héctor should continue encouraging Mr. Lopez's involvement with family activities but should resist being overly attentive to his bouts of pain and discomfort because sometimes too much attention can increase irritability (i.e., sometimes paying less attention to a chronic problem is better). I added that they should not wait until a severe bout of pain to check in with Mr. Lopez to see how he is doing. Again I checked this out with everybody, and all agreed to implement this new strategy. I warned them that this would take practice because it was not the natural way that they had dealt with things.

In the ensuing weeks, Mr. Lopez reported less complaining at family gatherings and on one occasion leaving a gathering early by himself in his car. Although he continued to report continued irritability, he had stopped breaking things and was permitting his wife and son to express their opinions on his behavior. We discussed how important it was for him to promote more open communication in view of his family's need to be more bicultural in the United States (with assertiveness being an important skill for his son and wife to have in their places of work, etc.). Here the emphasis was not on replacing Latino communication styles with American styles but on enhancing bicultural skills for maximum flexibility.

Activity Interventions

Mr. Lopez came to his session smiling about completing his behavioral contract assigned the week before, and he shared how enjoyable it was to talk with his old friends at work again. He even recalled giving some input into an automotive problem that a friend of his was trying to solve. I asked Mr. Lopez how "bothersome" his pain was on this day, and he had rated it a 6 on the 10-point scale ranging from *pain not bothersome* (1) to *pain very bothersome* (10), his lowest rating yet.

Toward the latter part of therapy, I opened up the topic of resuming physical therapy by trying to use an analogy that my client as a mechanic might appreciate. I told him that I realized that there were problems with his physical therapy but that, just as it is important to regularly maintain and drive a car, it would be in the best interest of his health to resume physical therapy. The client immediately became red faced, raised his voice, and said that they requested too much of him in the pain clinic. I asked Mr. Lopez to forget the pain clinic for a moment and to consider what happens to a car when one goes on vacation and stops using it for weeks. He noted how the battery might go dead, and we continued to discuss engine problems that would occur over the course of months of inactivity. Next, I conveyed his physical therapists' concern that without such therapy he could wind up with more pain and disability. Thus, the argument for physical therapy was pitched more in terms of "cutting losses" rather than improvement per se. With respect to Mr. Lopez's concern about the painfulness of exercising, we discussed the analogy of dental visits, which can be painful at the moment but which prevent more pain and problems in the long run.

I offered to meet with the client and his physical therapist "just to discuss areas of disagreement." I told him that before he makes the decision whether or not to return, it would be important to make sure that all parties involved understand each other (especially given the language differences). In preparation for the meeting, I pressed Mr. Lopez to consider other ways of looking at his physical therapists' insistence that he do some very difficult exercises. Although he insisted that they could not feel and understand his pain, he was able to acknowledge the possibility that they were concerned about his health and wanted to prevent him from becoming inactive and worse.

I reminded Mr. Lopez that the pain clinic was providing a service to him and that, as a consumer, he could express his thoughts and desires to them. We again did some role-playing in which we practiced communications that he could use with his physical therapists. Such communications included the request for an explanation of the day's exercises as well as responses to requests that he perceived as too demanding. Role-playing was expedited by replaying his last encounter at the pain clinic in which he claimed that certain exercises landed him in bed for a couple of days. I asked him to role-play the therapist's requests and modeled sample assertive responses (in broken English) such as the following: "Can we slow down please?" "What is this exercise for?" and "Can we try it another way?"

The actual meeting with pain clinic staff went fairly well, with the staff eventually being able to convey their sincere concerns about Mr. Lopez's health and the client asserting his worry about hurting himself. In the beginning, however, things almost went awry when a frustrated pain clinic staff member unintentionally challenged Mr. Lopez's machismo by saying, "If you don't do your physical therapy, your back is going to get worse!" to which Mr. Lopez argued that it was his business. When I asked the staff person the motivation behind his statement, he said that he wanted Mr. Lopez to get better and that he knew he could be helpful to him.

All eventually agreed to a "trial" return to the clinic in which exercises would be thoroughly explained and Mr. Lopez could elect not to attempt certain exercises (i.e., have some control over the situation). This particular intervention is an example of the flexibility required of therapists working with clients with multiple problems that need support and "culture brokering" from therapists who are overly accustomed to providing only an hour of weekly, in-session assistance.

Culturally Appropriate Termination

During our last month of treatment, I began to prepare Mr. Lopez for termination by reviewing our problem list and therapeutic strategies. The client was generally positive about the CBT treatment plan as applied to his pain, depression, and anger. He had no trouble "buying" the important role of behaviors and activities in the management of his situation and of the lifelong need to continue these techniques after terminating therapy. The posttreatment evaluation revealed mild to moderate depression, a clinically significant gain for our low-income, frequently overwhelmed, and severely depressed patient population.

With regard to termination, we routinely tell our clients that they are free to drop by and say hello, and in the case of Mr. Lopez, treat me to a cafesito. This flexible approach to termination is based on our hospital-based location where we frequently see our many patients coming in for various medical appointments. Yet it is also based on Latino relationship protocol in which it would seem abnormal to completely terminate a positive and personalized relationship.

Whereas most clients do not come by, Mr. Lopez did eventually return and offer to buy me a cup of coffee downstairs in the cafeteria. Although busy at the moment, I graciously accepted the offer and asked if we could meet at a nearby cafe that brewed extra-good coffee. He responded that the cafe was a bit out of his way but that if the coffee was really that good, it would be worth the trip.

CONCLUSION

In their authoritative review of the literature on psychosocial interventions for ethnic minorities, Miranda et al. (2005) concluded that, with respect to outcomes for minority adults, "Both naturalistic and large randomized trials with Latinos and African American participants have found that well-established psychotherapies, such as CBT and IPT, are effective for those populations" (p. 132). With regard to modifying mainstream treatment approaches, as advocated and illustrated in this chapter, Miranda et al. (2005) also concluded that "Adapted interventions have been shown to be effective; however, tests of adapted versus standard interventions aren't yet available to guide care" (p. 134). Thus, we should feel both encouraged and challenged to continue testing standard and culturally responsive applications of CBT, as well as other treatment approaches, with different Latino groups and their varied mental health needs.

And while waiting for outcome research to better inform our clinical directions, we should continue to be encouraged by the apparent advantages that CBT appears to possess with respect to Latino clients (i.e., orienting Latinos to therapy with a didactic approach that appears to decrease the stigma commonly associated with mental health services). CBT also appears responsive to expectations on the part of traditionally oriented Latino clients such as immediate symptom relief, an active and directive therapist, and a problem-solving approach to current concerns. Although disadvantages of CBT include too little attention to the social and political context of Latino mental health in the United States, as well as implicitly communicating modern mainstream American values to traditionally oriented client populations, such potential problems are not insurmountable, as illustrated in this chapter.

Culturally competent CBT with Latinos requires that we learn more about the historically rooted living legacies of Latino discrimination and exclusion in the United States, and even becoming involved in advocacy work on behalf of Latino clients and communities. Such actions help develop sensitivity to and empathy with Latinos in therapy, while addressing issues of social injustice that can increase a population's risk for various psychosocial and health problems.

REFERENCES

American Psychiatric Association. (2000). *Diagnostic and statistical manual of mental disorders* (4th ed., text rev.). Washington, DC: Author.

Balls Organista, P., Organista, K. C., & Kurasaki, K. (2003). The relationship between acculturation and ethnic minority health. In K. M. Chun, P. Balls Organista, & G. Marín (Eds.), *Acculturation: Advances in theory, measurement, and applied research* (pp. 139–161). Washington, DC: American Psychological Association.

Bruce, M. L., Takeuchi, D. T., & Leaf, P. J. (1991). Poverty and psychiatric status: Longitudinal evidence from the New Haven Epidemiologic Catchment Area Study. *Archives of General Psychiatry, 48*, 470–474.

Burns, D. D., & Nolen-Hoeksema, S. (1992). Therapeutic empathy and recovery from depression in cognitive–behavioral therapy: A structural equation model. *Journal of Consulting and Clinical Psychology, 60*, 441–449.

Comas-Díaz, L. (1981). Effects of cognitive and behavioral group treatment on the depressive symptomatology of Puerto Rican women. *Journal of Consulting and Clinical Psychology, 49*, 627–632.

Comas-Díaz, L., & Duncan, J. W. (1985). The cultural context: A factor in assertiveness training with mainland Puerto Rican women. *Psychology of Women Quarterly, 9*, 463–476.

Falicov, C. J. (1998). *Latino families in therapy: A guide to multicultural practice*. New York: Guilford Press.

Guarnaccia, P. J., Good, B. J., & Kleinman, A. (1990). A critical review of epidemiological studies of Puerto Rican mental health. *American Journal of Psychiatry, 147*, 1449–1456.

Kataoka, S. H., Stein, B. D., Jaycox, L. H., Wong, M., Escudero, P., Tu, W., et al. (2003). A school-based mental health program for traumatized immigrant children. *Journal of the American Academy of Child and Adolescent Psychiatry, 42*, 311–318.

Kessler, R. C., McGonagle, K. A., Zhao, S., Nelson, C. B., Hughes, M., Eshleman, S., et al. (1994). Lifetime and 12-month prevalence of *DSM–III–R* psychiatric disorders in the United States. *Archives of General Psychiatry, 51*, 8–19.

Marger, N. N. (2000). Hispanic Americans. In N. N. Marger (Ed.), Race and ethnic relations: American and global perspectives (5th ed., pp. 282–321). Belmont, CA: Wadsworth.

Marotta, S. A., & Garcia, J. G. (2004). Latinos in the United Sates in 2000. *Hispanic Journal of Behavioral Sciences, 25*, 13–34.

Miranda, J., Azocar, F., Organista, K. C., Valdes Dwyer, E., & Areán, P. (2003). Treatment of depression in disadvantaged medical patients. *Psychiatric Services, 54*, 219–225.

Miranda, J., Bernal, G., Lau, A., Kohn, L., Hwang, W., & LaFromboise, T. (2005). State of the science on psychosocial interventions for ethnic minorities. *Annual Review of Clinical Psychology, 1*, 113–142.

Nathan, P. E., & Gorman, J. M. (2002). A *guide to treatments that work* (2nd ed.). New York: Oxford University Press.

Organista, K. C. (1995). Cognitive–behavioral treatment of depression and panic disorder in a Latina patient: Culturally sensitive case formulation. *In Session: Psychotherapy in Practice, 1*, 53–64.

Organista, K. C., & Muñoz, R. F. (1996). Cognitive behavioral therapy with Latinos. *Cognitive and Behavioral Practice, 3*, 255–270.

Organista, K. C., Muñoz, R. F., & González, G. (1994). Cognitive behavioral therapy for depression in low-income and minority medical outpatients: Description of a program and exploratory analyses. *Cognitive Therapy and Research, 18*, 241–259.

Organista, K. C., & Snowden, L. (2003). Latino mental health in California: Policy recommendations. In D. Lopez & A. Jimenez (Eds.), *Latinos and public policy in California: An agenda for opportunity* (pp. 217–239). Berkeley: University of California, Institute for Governmental Studies.

Organista, K. C., & Valdes Dwyer, E. (1997). Clinical case management and cognitive–behavioral therapy: Integrated psychosocial services for depressed Latino primary care patients. In P. G. Manoleas (Ed.), *The cross-cultural practice of clinical case management in mental health* (pp. 119–143). New York: Haworth Press.

Orlinsky, D. E., & Howard, K. I. (1986). Process and outcome in psychotherapy. In S. L. Garfield & A. E. Bergin (Eds.), *Handbook of psychotherapy and behavior change* (3rd ed., pp. 311–381). New York: Wiley.

Piña, A. A., Sliverman, W. K., Fuentes, R. M., Kurtines, W. M., & Weems, C. F. (2003). Exposure-based cognitive–behavioral treatment for phobic and anxiety disorders: Treatment effects and maintenance for Hispanic–Latino relative to European-American youth. *Journal of the American Academy of Child and Adolescent Psychiatry, 42*, 1179–1187.

Roll, S., Millen, L., & Martinez, R. (1980). Common errors in psychotherapy with Chicanos: Extrapolations from research and clinical experience. *Psychotherapy: Theory, Research and Practice, 17*, 158–168.

Rossello, J., & Bernal, G. (1999). The efficacy of cognitive–behavioral and interpersonal treatment for depression in Puerto Rican adolescents. *Journal of Consulting and Clinical Psychology, 67*, 734–745.

Sue, S., Fujino, D. C., Hu, L., Takeuchi, D. T., & Zane, N. W. S. (1991). Community mental health services for ethnic minority groups: A test of the cultural responsiveness hypothesis. *Journal of Consulting and Clinical Psychology, 59*, 533–540.

Therrien, M., & Ramirez, R. R. (2000). *The Hispanic population in the United States: March 2000* (Current Population Reports, P20-535). Washington, DC: U.S. Census Bureau.

4

COGNITIVE–BEHAVIORAL THERAPY WITH AFRICAN AMERICANS

SHALONDA KELLY

The common historical threads shared by African Americans present them with challenges not typically experienced by other groups. First, their unique history of slavery has left an ongoing legacy of racism and oppression (see Hollar, 2001, for a thorough historical review). Slavers actively attempted to eradicate African culture and break up family units for profit and convenience (Black, 1996). Since the end of slavery in 1870, racially hostile laws and practices have continued in such forms as the dehumanizing Jim Crow laws of the late 1800s, lynchings into the 1930s, and school segregation that did not become illegal until the *Brown v. Board of Education* Supreme Court decision in 1954 (Hollar, 2001). Moreover, from the early to mid-1900s, many African Americans migrated from the rural south to the urban north to escape this brutality and segregation and to find employment, which resulted in wide-scale disruption of their families and communities (Young, 2003). African Americans continue to experience discrimination in employment and housing (Coleman, 2003; Ross & Turner, 2005), exclusion and negative stereotyping by the media (e.g., Coltraine & Messineo, 2000), inferior health services (Hollar, 2001), and higher morbidity rates (Hines & Boyd-Franklin, 1996). Such assaults and challenges contribute to a poverty rate

97

that is higher than that of all other ethnic groups except Latinos (Dalaker, 2001) and mental health disparities between African Americans and other groups (e.g., U.S. Department of Health and Human Services, 2001).

COMMONALITIES RELEVANT TO TREATMENT

African Americans are very aware of racism and report significantly more chronic stress related to discrimination than do Whites (Schulz et al., 2002; Troxel, Matthews, Bromberger, & Sutton-Tyrrell, 2003). In one study, African American women reported experiencing racism an average of 75 times per year (Clark, 2000). Such experiences are also pervasive in mental health research and treatment, and many African Americans know that the field historically has held a pathological and deficit view of them (R. T. Jones, Brown, Davis, Jeffries, & Shenoy, 1998).

Across the life span, African Americans' reports of racism and discrimination are negatively associated with psychological and physical health and positively associated with substance use (Bowen-Reid & Harrell, 2002; Krieger & Sidney, 1996; Kwate, Valdimarsdottir, Guevarra, & Bovbjerg, 2003). In one study, racist events accounted for 15% of the total variance in psychological symptoms expressed by 520 African Americans (Klonoff, Landrine, & Ullman, 1999). The associations between perceived racism and psychological functioning are partially mediated through the effects of perceived racism on stress and self-esteem (DuBois, Burk-Braxton, Swenson, Tevendale, & Hardesty, 2002; Guthrie, Young, Williams, Boyd, & Kintner, 2002). In addition, the relationship between perceived racism and psychological functioning tends to remain even when demographics and stressors are controlled (Klonoff et al., 1999; Schulz et al., 2002). Although these associations are derived from correlations, such factors are relevant to treatment because anger at perceived racism and discrimination is one of the primary reasons that many African Americans seek therapy (Clark, 2000).

African Americans' experiences of inequity and stress adversely affect their psychological adjustment and can lead to particular symptom presentations. For example, many African Americans experience rage that may be expressed toward White therapists or therapists of color who are seen as representatives of the dominant culture. Anger may also be directed toward family members because they are safer targets, or because family members fail to support one another, for example, arguing over who experiences the worst racism or how racist incidents should be handled (e.g., Boyd-Franklin & Franklin, 1998; Kelly, 2003). Many African Americans feel a deep distrust of Whites rooted in generations of negative experiences. Often referred to as a "healthy cultural paranoia," this distrust is associated with an unwillingness to seek mental health services, negative attitudes toward White therapists, and premature termination rates (Whaley, 2001).

African Americans also may present with worldviews related to the pain of oppression. For example, some may exhibit internalized racism as manifested in negative in-group statements and a preference for White therapists whom some may perceive as more competent than African American therapists (Boyd-Franklin, 2003; Hardy, 2004; Kelly, 2003, 2004). Some African Americans become demoralized by racism, leading to feelings of nihilism, an external locus of control, or a fatalistic perspective (e.g., Hines, 1998). It is easy for therapists to misinterpret these worldviews and related coping responses as blaming others, self-pitying, or lacking motivation. Laszloffy and Hardy (2000) described such an example in the following summary.

> In the first session between a therapist and an 11-year-old African American boy diagnosed with conduct disorder, the child described his misbehavior as related to his dislike of his teacher, who he felt was racist. After hearing his examples, the therapist, who was White, told him that he may have misunderstood the teacher's intentions and actions and that his anger was no excuse to break the rules. Moreover, the predominantly White supervisory team behind the two-way mirror agreed with the therapist; they all viewed the boy's behavior through the lens of his disorder, and none considered race or racism in their discussion. Not surprisingly, the child and his family discontinued treatment.

Several common cultural tendencies among African Americans may present challenges to traditional psychotherapy. A focus on the present can result in a lack of planning for a future that seems uncertain owing to racism (Hardy, 2004). Beliefs that "the future will wait" and experiences with social services that require people to wait for hours may foster excessive lateness and missed appointments (Hardy, 2004). In valuing direct experience in deciding whom to trust, African Americans may ignore a therapist's academic degrees and suggestions until they are sure of the feeling or "vibes" they get from the therapist (Boyd-Franklin, 1998). Despite therapists' training against corporal punishment, data from large samples show that it is not associated with negative outcomes in African American communities in which it is prevalent (Simons et al., 2002) and in which the children do not view it as a sign of caregiver rejection (Rohner, Bourque, & Elordi, 1996). Finally, therapists may misinterpret emotional expressiveness, nonverbal communication, and nonstandard language as an inability to regulate emotions and communicate effectively (e.g., Boyd-Franklin, 2003; Kelly & Boyd-Franklin, 2004).

Cultural Strengths

Cultural strengths and supports among African Americans can help to offset the adverse effects of racism and discrimination. The extended family is an important source of strength and support originating in African cultures that can include blood kin such as cousins and "fictive kin" who are unrelated by blood (e.g., members of a "church family" or a "play mama";

Boyd-Franklin, 2003). The extended family may engage in reciprocal assistance with money, goods, and services that increase the economic viability of African American families (Taylor, Chatters, & Jackson, 1997). Extended family members may share their homes with each other for short-term stays during times of financial hardship or longer periods, as in the case of informal adoption (e.g., Boyd-Franklin, 2003). Extended family members may also serve as mediators, judges, or networkers, flexibly adopting these roles as needed. African American parents also prepare their children for the race-related struggles they will encounter (Fischer & Shaw, 1999). Overall, surveys show that proximity, subjective closeness, and frequency of kinship interaction contribute to the physical and emotional well-being of African Americans (Taylor et al., 1997).

Religious institutions and spiritual beliefs are additional sources of strength for African Americans, and data have consistently demonstrated greater levels of religiosity and spirituality within African Americans as compared with other ethnic groups (e.g., Taylor, Mattis, & Chatters, 1999). African American churches provide formal and informal supports such as childcare and educational programs that help to improve the welfare of African Americans (Ellison, 1997). Churches enable African Americans to achieve status in their communities, for example, through leadership roles that compensate for the lack of occupational and educational opportunities and status in the dominant culture (Boyd-Franklin, 2003). Churches also encourage and support the development of organizational skills and social activism (Taylor et al., 1999). For many African Americans, religion and meaning-enhancing attributions regarding God are significantly associated with individual and family well-being (Blaine & Crocker, 1995; Ellison, 1997).

A positive racial or ethnic identity is another source of strength for African Americans. Multicultural research shows that a positive ethnic identity is associated with increases in self-esteem, coping, mastery, and optimism, and with lower levels of loneliness, anxiety, and depression (Carter, Sbrocco, Lewis, & Friedman, 2001; Phinney, Cantu, & Kurtz, 1997; Roberts et al., 1999). In addition, for African Americans, a positive ethnic identity acts as a buffer against perceived discrimination and racism (Wong, Eccles, & Sameroff, 2003).

Individual Differences

Many demographic factors including but not limited to skin color, gender, and socioeconomic status profoundly affect the experiences of African Americans (Celious & Oyserman, 2001). Data show that socioeconomic gaps between light and dark African Americans are of the same magnitude as the gap between Whites and Blacks in the United States. Those who are light may be considered prettier, are more affluent, and receive better treatment in society. Still, both very light and very dark African Americans can experience bias. For example, those who are dark are sometimes prized within the community because they are considered to be racially pure (Celious & Oyserman, 2001). Societal stereotypes of African American men elicit fear and hostility (e.g., violent criminals), whereas those of African American women elicit derision and sexual intrigue (e.g., welfare queens and "Jezebels"). Such treatment results in differing experiences for each gender (Celious & Oyserman, 2001). African Americans' socioeconomic status is positively associated with their perceptions of discrimination, perhaps because the economically privileged have greater contact with the larger society that discriminates against them (Cutrona et al., 2003). Conversely, poorer African Americans are less likely to benefit from government programs that tend to go to their brethren of higher socioeconomic status, perhaps because many in the larger society assume that all African Americans are poor (Celious & Oyserman, 2001). Given these and other differences, it is important to note that there is no single "African American experience" (Black, 1996).

Although the primary focus of this chapter is on African Americans, differences between African Americans and immigrants from the African diaspora deserve mention (for further reviews, see McGoldrick, Giordano, & Pearce, 1996; Stephenson, 2004). Unlike African Americans, many Black immigrants have not experienced American slavery and racism or the loss of many cultural connections. Many Black immigrants (e.g., West Indians and Africans) are the majority group in their country, so they may define race more broadly than African Americans, and they often do not experience it as an indicator of success or social mobility. Often, these groups immigrate voluntarily to partake in the American dream, and many have the option of maintaining ties with home or of returning home (Stephenson, 2004). Finally, whereas all Blacks share an African cultural legacy, Black immigrants also have unique cultures related to their country and its history of colonization. For example, many Caribbean Blacks are influenced by British culture, and South American Blacks are influenced by Spanish culture (Black, 1996).

Initially, these differences often result in less awareness of racism, a greater belief in meritocracy, more positive feelings about White Americans, and more varied notions of identity as compared with African Americans (Phinney & Onwughalu, 1996; Stephenson, 2004). Thus, when confronted with racism, some Black immigrants may experience shock, may distance themselves from African Americans because of their differing national identities, or may circumvent the adoption of what they view as a restrictive, inferior status (Stephenson, 2004). Still, data show that American-born children of Black immigrants, and the immigrants who stay in the United States for long periods, often develop racial identities and stances that are more similar to those of African Americans (Phinney & Onwughalu, 1996; Stephenson, 2004).

Often, African Americans with the same backgrounds may behave in radically different ways owing to their different levels of acculturation and different racial identities. Acculturation refers to the extent of adoption of the dominant culture versus one's indigenous culture (Klonoff & Landrine, 2000). Studies show that African Americans' level of acculturation is associated with how they cope with stress, their level of social support, psychological symptoms, and health-related behaviors (Klonoff & Landrine, 2000). Acculturation also can produce stress that affects psychological functioning beyond the effects of general life stress (Joiner & Walker, 2002). In treatment, knowledge of acculturation can indicate the likelihood that a given African American client might present in ways more common to African Americans or ways more common to White clients. Overall, acculturation levels often account for much more variance in African Americans' behavior than do education and income combined (Klonoff & Landrine, 2000).

> Jim, a White male, had his first session with Larry, an African American male in his early 20s, who was born and raised in Los Angeles, California. In his attempt to develop rapport with Larry, Jim mentioned how the West Coast was really cool because West Coast rappers made the best hip-hop music. To Jim's surprise, Larry said, "I have no idea what you are talking about. I play the cello and study classical music." Jim told his supervisor, who gave him readings on acculturation theory and other aspects of diversity among African Americans, which they then discussed. Thereafter, Jim learned to ask questions aimed at obtaining a better understanding of his clients' levels of acculturation.

Similar to acculturation, consideration of racial identity is important in treatment, as it also involves one's orientation toward one's own group and toward the dominant group (for a review, see Vandiver, Cross, Worrell, & Fhagen-Smith, 2002). Clinical observations indicate that therapists of color who see African American clients may receive questions as to their competence, responses conveying distance and dissimilarity, or responses conveying feelings of similarity and connection (Boyd-Franklin, 2003). White therapists commonly encounter reluctance to receive treatment, anger related to oppression, or an ingratiating, deferential style (Boyd-Franklin, 2003). Racial identity can explain these observations; data show that racial identity predicts the degree of preference for African American versus other therapists (e.g., Goodstein & Ponterotto, 1997).

ADVANTAGES OF COGNITIVE–BEHAVIORAL THERAPY

With its emphasis on tailoring therapy to the particular individual, CBT has the potential to positively address African Americans' treatment needs. Assessment data are gathered from multiple sources, such as interviews and questionnaires, and are used in a functional-analytic approach that recognizes the diversity of environmental influences and paths to symptom reduction (Jacobson & Christensen, 1996). A CBT approach can help therapists to avoid a judgmental stance toward differences and help clients to do the same (Jacobson & Christensen, 1996). For example, as radical Black behaviorism states, observable behavior should never be explained by unobservable mentalistic events such as motivation or intelligence but rather understood in light of its environmental consequences (Fudge, 1996).

A second advantage of CBT with African Americans is the collaborative nature of the treatment; the therapist is the expert on the treatment, but clients are the experts on themselves and their problems (e.g., Briesmeister & Schaefer, 1998). For example, in cognitive–behavioral parent training, therapists provide parents with the skills to become effective cotherapists in facilitating change with their children. The therapist and parents share their expertise to benefit the child and family. Parent training is problem focused, with everyone working together on problems defined by the parents. Parents also have control over the duration of treatment, as it ends when the parents report that their child's symptoms are no longer a problem. Similarly, therapists conducting behavioral couple therapy seek to establish a collaborative set using data to develop shared conceptualizations, rationales by which behavioral principles can help, and encouragement of mutuality in goal setting and choice of intervention. Therapists assist partners in taking a hypothesis-testing stance toward resolving their issues (Sayers & Heyman, 2003). This emphasis on a collaborative set was speculated to be the reason that observers in one study rated CBT significantly higher on the therapeutic alliance than psychodynamic treatments (Raue, Goldfried, & Barkham, 1997).

A third potentially beneficial characteristic of CBT with African Americans is its emphasis on empowerment. CBT empowers African American clients by helping them to build strengths, supports, and skills to meet their goals more effectively (Sayers & Heyman, 2003). Therapists actively help clients look for ways to build on and expand social support, and to recognize coping skills that have worked for them in the past and may work again (Epstein & Baucom, 2002). Clients are also taught to look for and expect evidence of ongoing improvement and to use behavioral experiments that provide evidence to replace their cognitive distortions with realistic, noncatastrophic appraisals (e.g., Briesmeister & Schaefer, 1998).

In summary, the advantages of CBT with African Americans include an emphasis on nonjudgmental, collaborative problem solving and empowerment of the client through skill building and strengthening of natural support systems. These key components are illustrated in this example:

> Peter was an African American first-generation college freshman who sought treatment at the university clinic for depression and difficulties completing schoolwork. His therapist was John, a White, third-generation Italian American. As Peter was attending college locally, part of his problem involved the racial differences between his college peers and him,

and the pressure he felt from his high school friends who had not "made it" to college. His friends gave him messages to "keep it real and stop acting like those preppy White boys." John avoided the assumption that Peter's friends were bad. Nor did he try to break Peter's friendships by encouraging him to behave more like his White peers in college. Instead, John encouraged Peter to talk about his friendships and normalized his experiences by suggesting that it is not an uncommon coping mechanism for friends to denigrate experiences that they have not had together, as a way of preventing the loss of the friendship. Following John's normalizing, psychoeducational reframe, Peter described several times when his high school peers had applauded his academic efforts. They then began to problem-solve how to maintain his old friendships as a means of improving his depression and academic performance.

LIMITATIONS OF COGNITIVE–BEHAVIORAL THERAPY

A major criticism of CBT addresses the claim by many cognitive–behavioral therapists and researchers that the approach is neutral and universally applicable owing to its scientific orientation. Sue (1999) challenged this myth by noting researchers' and therapists' selective enforcement of the scientific principles of skepticism and convincingness, for example, the lack of skepticism regarding the generalizability of findings for White Americans to ethnic minority groups. Conversely, some claim that findings obtained from ethnic minorities are not generalizable if they lack a White control group. Another bias is the assumption that one must take a "colorblind" approach to ensure the fair treatment of ethnic minorities, an assumption that works against the consideration of cultural influences on human behavior (Iwamasa, 1997).

Fudge (1996) noted that science continues to sanction the use of many nonscientific concepts to explain African Americans' behavior. For example, subjective assertions of negative innate or genetic tendencies have long been made regarding African Americans, and even today deficit models regarding African Americans' differences from Whites are readily believed and investigated. For example,

> Sheila, an African American student, began treatment at a local counseling center because of the stress of her first year of graduate school in biology. In an early session describing her feelings of alienation on campus, she complained to her therapist that one of her professors described research investigating genetic causes of Black violence, as if African Americans were inferior and genetically prone to violence. Although her White female therapist empathized with her, being a cognitive–behavioral scientist-practitioner, the therapist tried to explain the teacher's perspective by saying, "It may help you to know that in the pursuit of knowledge, scientists should be able to study any topic." The

student was offended and angrily quipped, "Well, I never heard about studies of a gene for violence in Whites back when they were lynching and conquering everybody."

Beyond the therapist's discounting of her client's experience of oppression, this vignette highlights the Eurocentrism embedded in CBT and in the research base on which it is founded. African Americans are underrepresented as research participants and as researchers (Baucom, Shoham, Mueser, Daiuto, & Stickle, 1998), and as such exert little influence on the topics, direction, and value placed on areas of psychotherapy research. The psychotherapy research that does exist regarding African Americans is still at the descriptive and understanding phases, far behind the prediction and control phases of research regarding White Americans. This lag perpetuates the circular reasoning that cultural adaptations of CBT are not needed because no evidence exists regarding its cross-cultural effectiveness.

Eurocentrism is also a problem in some applications of cognitive–behavioral theory. For example, the emphasis on rational thinking can be interpreted in ways that devalue African Americans' spirituality and tendencies toward emotional expressiveness. One African American client reported that her depression would increase if she could not cry and let out her emotions periodically. This sounded illogical and too much like catharsis for her therapist, who challenged her belief and tried to help the client to see the value in regulating her emotions. The client then felt chastised and began to try to hold in her tears, even though they functioned as a stress reliever in her life.

Similarly, mainstream values regarding the importance of personal independence and autonomy tend to be reinforced by cognitive–behavioral orientations. Cognitive–behavioral therapists who fail to recognize the importance of family and community for their African American clients may be seen as reinforcing dominant cultural values. At the same time, they may overlook important sources of familial and community support that could be incorporated into cognitive–behavioral interventions. This individualistic focus also may inhibit therapists from addressing factors in the larger African American community that are relevant to African American clients.

African American therapists have noted additional reasons why attention to the larger African American community is important in the treatment of African American clients, beyond its usefulness as a source of strength and support (e.g., Fudge, 1996; McNair, 1996). First, the ability of African Americans to effect positive change in their communities can be empowering. Second, the notion of working for or healing the community is consistent with an African-centered perspective that encourages responsibility and self-determination. Third, the promotion of positive external change can help to heal painful feelings and perceptions related to a negative ethnic identity. Fourth, from a behavioral perspective, involvement in the community can help African Americans to actively change the contingencies in their environment that maintain their current symptoms of distress (Fudge, 1996; McNair, 1996). Finally, at times, larger social issues are directly relevant to African Americans' presenting problems. For example, African American men often hold anxiety related to their abilities as providers that negatively affects both their couple and family functioning (Kelly, 2003; Kiecolt & Fossett, 1995).

In summary, it is only fair to note that many of the preceding criticisms pertain less to the theory of CBT than to those who practice it without cross-cultural knowledge and awareness. Moreover, being a therapist of color is no guarantee against cultural biases, as therapists of color receive the same training as White American therapists, and treatments in the United States are often exported internationally (Iwamasa, 1996). Although there is no substantial literature on culturally adapted CBT with African Americans, the results of a recent nonrandomized study are promising. Kohn, Oden, Munoz, Robinson, and Leavitt (2002) found that the Beck Depression Inventory scores of depressed, low-income African American women who received culturally adapted group CBT decreased twice as much as those of their counterparts who received traditional CBT.

MODIFYING COGNITIVE–BEHAVIORAL THERAPY FOR AFRICAN AMERICANS

Given the Eurocentric biases embedded in cognitive–behavioral research and theory, along with therapists' documented diagnostic and treatment biases regarding African Americans (e.g., Atkinson et al., 1996), the first essential modification of CBT involves therapists' self-exploration and education. This includes exploration of one's own racial and cultural identity, as well as education regarding institutional and structural aspects of racism including the concepts of White privilege and power (McIntosh, 1998). Therapists should gain knowledge of and exposure to African Americans and immigrants of African descent in real-world settings in which the therapist is not in a dominant role, such as that of a teacher or therapist. Supervision and case consultation are also important, particularly when therapists lack knowledge of culturally acceptable and normative behaviors and beliefs (e.g., Kelly, 2003).

Regarding modifications of CBT, it is useful to return to the preceding cases wherein therapists, in their attempts to be helpful, gave their clients benign interpretations of the clients' reported racist experiences. When therapists dismiss clients' beliefs about the presence of racism, they prevent themselves from conducting a complete functional analysis of the client's behavior. Furthermore, they decrease clients' willingness to further disclose how racism is related to their problems. Even in optimal conditions, African American clients may be reluctant to consider how racism may be related to their symptoms. Thus, one of the most important actions a therapist can take is to begin with the supposition that the racist incident occurred and assess how it is relevant to the problem.

The next key action is to validate the client's experience of racism and discrimination (Laszloffy & Hardy, 2000; McNair, 1996). An example is provided by Fink, Turner, and Beidel (1996), which I summarize here:

> A 39-year-old African American female physician was diagnosed with social phobia based on her description of her fear of speaking in front of her colleagues, and the belief that they would view her as stupid and not cut out to be a physician. In an intervention using imaginal exposure, early exposure sessions did not produce the expected arousal levels, indicating that the presented cues were not salient in invoking her symptoms. However, further exploration revealed that she was the only African American resident at her job, and that her symptoms were elicited in situations primarily involving middle-aged White male colleagues. In particular, she reported believing that these colleagues viewed her as incompetent and undeserving of being a physician largely because of her race, and that they thought she was admitted to medical school only because she was African American. Fink et al. (1996) noted that "racially relevant cues enhanced the social-evaluative, fear-producing quality of the scene as reflected by the patient's verbal report, behavior, and an index of arousal" (p. 208). Subsequently, racial cues were used systematically in her in vivo homework exercises, resulting in the extinction of her core fear, which was racially based.

Once a therapist recognizes the reality of racism in African Americans' lives, he or she will be better prepared to join with African American clients to form a collaborative therapeutic alliance. This joining must occur early in treatment if it is to prevent dropout, which is significantly higher among African Americans than among Whites (Fudge, 1996). Therapists are encouraged to give every indication of respect to African Americans via supportive and noncritical statements, a lack of jargon, and asking clients whether they prefer to be addressed by first or last name (Wright, 2001). Nonthreatening psychoeducation regarding the purposes, course, and process of therapy, along with clear expectations regarding therapist and client roles, can help to increase the therapeutic alliance. Also important is the avoidance of affiliation with agencies that have a negative reputation in the community.

Therapists must gain the courage to raise the topic of race and ethnicity in a way that is comfortable for them and communicates to the client that anything can be discussed (Hines & Boyd-Franklin, 1996). In some cases, the therapist may choose to identify his or her own racial, ethnic, and cultural background, and then ask the client to do the same. In other situations, open-ended questions may be more appropriate, for example, "Are there aspects of your race or culture that you think are important for me to know about in working with you?" Questions regarding specific cultural influences may also be helpful, for example, "Do you have any spiritual or religious beliefs that are important to tell me about?" Questionnaires aimed at assessing racial identity, level of acculturation, or Afrocentricity can provide information regarding individual differences and the extent to which the client participates in his or her own ethnic traditions and in those of the larger American culture (e.g., Vandiver et al., 2002). When working with couples and families, the therapist should make such assessments for each individual, noting similarities and differences between family members.

In reference to the lack of empirical clarity regarding how race and culture affect treatment, Sue and Zane (1987) hypothesized two essential conditions for effective cross-cultural counseling. The first of these is therapist *credibility*, which refers to the client's beliefs that the therapist is capable of helping. The second condition involves *giving* and refers to the client's sense that the therapist has offered something valuable, such as a shift in perspective or a new solution to the problem. On one hand, therapists who do not acknowledge these factors will be at a disadvantage in understanding the function of their behavior for the client. They may also miss opportunities to allay fears related to cultural distrust and to address negative or irrational beliefs that the client may hold regarding the therapist. On the other hand, attention to the importance of credibility and giving for African American clients can significantly facilitate the therapeutic process.

> A good friend recommended that Judy, an African American, seek treatment from Carol, a White therapist. In the first session, Judy was initially nervous but admitted to Carol that much of her problem stemmed from the racism and disrespect that she experienced at her job. She stated that she had begun to doubt her abilities. Carol told Judy how sorry she was that Judy was victimized by racism and made genuine statements affirming Judy's worth. During treatment, Carol conducted self-management and self-advocacy training with Judy to enhance her effectiveness in managing and connecting with her coworkers. Notably, Carol did not imply deficiencies in Judy, nor did she ignore or excuse any racism. Carol also helped Judy to challenge her self-doubts via positive statements about her race and culture. In hearing that Judy coped with the situation by working long hours and praying, Carol's interventions included asking Judy to put the work that she could not get done in the "something for God to do" box and pray on it. By the end of treatment, Judy reported a decrease in her feelings of stress and depression and stated that her relationships with the people that she managed were "much better."

COGNITIVE–BEHAVIORAL THERAPY WITH AFRICAN AMERICAN FAMILIES

Jacobson and Christensen (1996) noted that couples composed of partners of different racial or cultural backgrounds may not recognize when their conflicts stem from differing cultural norms, and that these conflicts can be exacerbated during times of stress. They asserted that CBT can be helpful with couples through attention to the environmental (i.e., cultural) influences on the couple. Conflicts can be reframed as at least partially related to larger social stressors affecting the couple, and to the ways in which each partner's views have been shaped by their own cultural heritage (Jacobson & Christensen, 1996). This attention to larger, external influences can help to decrease defensiveness and increase understanding, thus facilitating collaborative problem solving.

Even when family members are both African American, such conflicts can easily arise as a result of individual differences in how each perceives and copes with racism and other social stressors (e.g., Kelly, 2003; Kelly & Boyd-Franklin, 2004). Boyd-Franklin and Franklin (1998) suggested use of the reframe that clients are "letting racism win" instead of uniting together to fight against it.

> Kim and Terrance were an African American couple who sought therapy because of their frequent fights involving finances. Kim reported that Terrance did not bring her flowers, as some of her White coworkers' partners did at their workplace. Terrance angrily replied that Kim was "always wanting something and testing my manhood." The therapist, Sheila, tried a communication intervention that met with limited success in reducing the couple's blaming of one another. Although she commonly used reframing to normalize stress for couples who were new parents, Sheila did not normalize the socioeconomic stressors of this couple. Neither did the couple think about their periodic unemployment as a chronic socioeconomic stressor.

In this case, the therapist might have been more effective if she had reframed the problem as described earlier. She could have observed that Kim and Terrance were letting racism win by turning their frustration regarding limited economic opportunities on each other. Furthermore, she could have encouraged them to work together and support each other toward coping and thriving in the face of discrimination and unfair treatment.

The idea of working together and supporting one another fits well with CBT's emphasis on building strengths and supports. Toward this end, therapists may respectfully ask African Americans to share aspects of their heritage and background of which they are proud, and then acknowledge and validate those strengths (McGoldrick et al., 1996; Wright, 2001). It is also important to elicit information regarding strengths and supports that may have been disrupted over time but can be reinstated or rebuilt, for example, reconnecting with a "church family" or relatives.

Even when both partners are African American, therapists should assume that cultural similarities and differences may exist and thus encourage

> (a) a conscious awareness by both partners of the role that culture plays in relationships; (b) the ability of both partners to experience ethnic and

cultural energies as an expansion rather than a threat to the self; and (c) the paradoxical ability of both partners to develop their own uniqueness because of the other partner's different cultural background. (A. C. Jones & Chao, 1997, pp. 169–170)

As part of these tasks, therapists should help clients to develop shared meanings, rituals, and spiritual understandings that transcend their cultural differences (A. C. Jones & Chao, 1997).

Incorporating clients' natural support systems may involve the inclusion of elders or other respected family members and clergy to collaborate in treatment (Boyd-Franklin, 1998). For some clients, forming an alliance with the person's pastor or religious leader can enhance treatment outcomes and provide additional therapeutic leverage. Therapists need to be aware of the supports offered by local African American churches and mosques, including couple and family ministries. Home visits, outreach to community organizations, and the identification of community role models can be helpful in developing realistic goals and supporting positive change. For African Americans who are not involved in organized religion, therapists should ask about the role of spirituality in their lives, and if this is significant, build on these beliefs as part of the therapy (Boyd-Franklin, 1998).

Research indicates that a negative racial identity is strongly associated with greater personal distress (e.g., Kelly, 2004). Given the chronic influences of racism and socioeconomic stressors in many African Americans' lives, therapists need to assess the degree to which their African American clients internalize racist and self-blaming societal messages. At times, clients may spontaneously express negative internalized stereotypes, as in the aforementioned case in which Terrance stated that Kim was testing his manhood. Unfortunately, the therapist did not recognize this statement as a common negative stereotype that depicts African American women as psychologically castrating of African American men.

In the case example of an African American man being treated for substance abuse, Fudge (1996) identified several key themes that revealed the client's negative racial identity. These included "Being Black means I'll never be good enough" and "Being Black means acting in a particular [negative] way" (p. 328). To counter such myths, the therapist used standard rational emotive therapy (RET) to help the client develop more realistic and positive self-statements. In addition, the therapist provided the client with culturally relevant readings, including *The Autobiography of Malcolm X* (1966) and Gordon Parks's autobiography, *A Choice of Weapons* (1965/1986), that were integrated into RET as bibliotherapy. These materials provided examples to which the client could relate, demonstrated African American men's transition from a negative to a positive racial identity, and helped the client to shift his own racial identity to a more positive direction. The therapist also empowered the client by encouraging him to take action on larger social factors that he felt were related to his problem. This work involved problem solving, coaching, and role-playing, and eventually resulted in the client talking with the teens who drank and disturbed the residents in his building to decrease their noise level (Fudge, 1996).

CONCLUSION

CBT's theory, philosophy, and use of idiographic data make it supportive of and suitable for use with African Americans. However, CBT is often conducted within mainstream America, which endorses a Eurocentric framework that is oppressive and damaging to African Americans. As a result, CBT has been tainted by myths of neutrality and universality that promote White privilege and justify the failure to include African Americans in clinical research. A burgeoning literature has begun to demonstrate the need for therapists to gain knowledge about and experience with African Americans. By calling attention to the unique experiences and strengths of African Americans, this training can help to counter therapists' personal biases and the systemic biases within the field of CBT. Additional clinical research is needed to understand the ways in which racial and ethnic constructs are influential in the treatment of African Americans and how such factors are associated with outcomes.

REFERENCES

Atkinson, D. R., Brown, M. T., Parham, T. A., Matthews, L. G., Landrum-Brown, J., & Kim, A. U. (1996). African American client skin tone and clinical judgments of African American and European American psychologists. *Professional Psychology: Research and Practice, 27,* 500–505.

Baucom, D. H., Shoham, V., Mueser, K. T., Daiuto, A. D., & Stickle, T. R. (1998). Empirical supported couple and family interventions for marital distress and adult mental health problems. *Journal of Consulting and Clinical Psychology, 66,* 53–88.

Black, L. (1996). Families of African origin: An overview. In M. McGoldrick, J. Giordano, & J. Pearce (Eds.), *Ethnicity and family therapy* (2nd ed., pp. 57–65). New York: Guilford Press.

Blaine, B., & Crocker, J. (1995). Religiousness, race, and psychological well-being: Exploring social psychological mediators. *Personality and Social Psychology Bulletin, 21,* 1031–1041.

Bowen-Reid, T. L., & Harrell, J. P. (2002). Racist experiences and health outcomes: An examination of spirituality as a buffer. *Journal of Black Psychology, 28,* 18–36.

Boyd-Franklin, N. (1998). Application of a multisystems model to home and community based treatment of African American families. In R. L. Jones (Ed.), *African American mental health* (pp. 268–281). Hampton, VA: Cobb & Henry.

Boyd-Franklin, N. (2003). *Black families in therapy: Understanding the African American experience* (2nd ed.). New York: Guilford Press.

Boyd-Franklin, N., & Franklin, A. J. (1998). African American couples in therapy. In M. McGoldrick (Ed.), *Re-visioning family therapy: Race, culture, and gender in clinical practice* (pp. 268–281). New York: Guilford Press.

Briesmeister, J. M., & Schaefer, C. E. (Eds.). (1998). *Handbook of parent training: Parents as co-therapists for children's behavior problems* (2nd ed.). New York: Wiley.

Brown v. Board of Education, 347 U.S. 483 (1954).

Carter, M. M., Sbrocco, T., Lewis, E. L., & Friedman, E. K. (2001). Parental bonding and anxiety: Differences between African American and European American college students. *Anxiety Disorders, 15,* 555–569.

Celious, A., & Oyserman, D. (2001). Race from the inside: An emerging heterogeneous race model. *Journal of Social Issues, 57,* 149–165.

Clark, R. (2000). Perceptions of interethnic group racism predict increased vascular reactivity to a laboratory challenge in college women. *Annals of Behavioral Medicine, 22,* 214–222.

Coleman, M. G. (2003). Job skill and Black male wage discrimination. *Social Science Quarterly, 84,* 892–905.

Coltraine, S., & Messineo, M. (2000). The perpetuation of subtle prejudice: Race and gender imagery in 1990s television advertising. *Sex Roles, 42,* 363–389.

Cutrona, C. E., Russell, D. W., Abraham, W. T., Gardner, K. A., Melby, J. N., Bryant, C., et al. (2003). Neighborhood context and financial strain as predictors of marital interaction and marital quality in African American couples. *Personal Relationships, 10,* 389–409.

Dalaker, J. (2001). *Poverty in the United States: 2000.* Washington, DC: U.S. Census Bureau.

DuBois, D. L., Burk-Braxton, C., Swenson, L. P., Tevendale, H. D., & Hardesty, J. L. (2002). Race and gender influences on adjustment in early adolescence: Investigation of an integrative model. *Child Development, 73,* 1573–1592.

Ellison, C. G. (1997). Religious involvement and the subjective quality of family life among African Americans. In R. J. Taylor, J. S. Jackson, & L. M. Chatters (Eds.), *Family life in Black America* (pp. 117–131). Thousand Oaks, CA: Sage.

Epstein, N. B., & Baucom, D. H. (2002). *Enhanced cognitive–behavioral therapy for couples: A contextual approach.* Washington, DC: American Psychological Association.

Fink, C. M., Turner, S. M., & Beidel, D. C. (1996). Culturally relevant factors in the behavioral treatment of social phobia: A case study. *Journal of Anxiety Disorders, 10,* 201–209.

Fischer, A. R., & Shaw, C. M. (1999). African Americans' mental health and perceptions of racist discrimination: The moderating effects of racial socialization experiences and self-esteem. *Journal of Counseling Psychology, 46,* 395–407.

Fudge, R. C. (1996). The use of behavior therapy in the development of ethnic consciousness: A treatment model. *Cognitive and Behavioral Practice, 3*, 317–335.

Goodstein, R., & Ponterotto, J. G. (1997). Racial and ethnic identity: Their relationship and their contribution to self-esteem. *Journal of Black Psychology, 23*, 275–292.

Guthrie, B. J., Young, A. M., Williams, D. R., Boyd, C. J., & Kintner, E. K. (2002). African American girls' smoking habits and day-to-day experiences with racial discrimination. *Nursing Research, 51*, 183–190.

Hardy, K. V. (2004, June). *Worlds apart: Family therapy with low-income and minority families.* Paper presented at the American Family Therapy Academy, San Francisco, CA.

Hines, P. M. (1998). Climbing up the rough side of the mountain: Hope, culture, and therapy. In M. McGoldrick (Ed.), *Re-visioning family therapy* (pp. 78–89). New York: Guilford Press.

Hines, P. M., & Boyd-Franklin, N. (1996). African American families. In M. McGoldrick, J. Giordano, & J. Pearce (Eds.), *Ethnicity and family therapy* (2nd ed., pp. 66–84). New York: Guilford Press.

Hollar, M. C. (2001). The impact of racism on the delivery of health care and mental health services. *Psychiatric Quarterly, 72*, 337–345.

Iwamasa, G. Y. (1996). On being an ethnic minority cognitive behavioral therapist. *Cognitive and Behavioral Practice, 3*, 235–254.

Iwamasa, G. Y. (1997). Behavior therapy and a culturally diverse society: Forging an alliance. *Behavior Therapy, 28*, 347–358.

Jacobson, N. S., & Christensen, A. (1996). *Integrative couple therapy: Promoting acceptance and change.* New York: Norton.

Joiner, T. E., Jr., & Walker, R. L. (2002). Construct validity of a measure of acculturative stress in African Americans. *Psychological Assessment, 14*, 462–466.

Jones, A. C., & Chao, C. M. (1997). Racial, ethnic, and cultural issues in couples therapy. In W. K. Halford & H. J. Markman (Eds.), *Clinical handbook of marriage and couples interventions* (pp. 157–176). New York: Wiley.

Jones, R. T., Brown, R., Davis, M., Jeffries, R., & Shenoy, U. (1998). African Americans in behavioral therapy and research. In R. L. Jones (Ed.), *African American mental health* (pp. 413–450). Hampton, VA: Cobb & Henry.

Kelly, S. (2003). African American couples: Their importance to the stability of African American families, and their mental health issues. In J. S. Mio & G. Y. Iwamasa (Eds.), *Culturally diverse mental health: The challenge of research and resistance* (pp. 141–157). New York: Taylor & Francis.

Kelly, S. (2004). Underlying components of scores assessing African Americans' racial perspectives. *Measurement and Evaluation in Counseling and Development, 37*, 28–40.

Kelly, S., & Boyd-Franklin, N. (2004). African American women in client, therapist, and supervisory relationships: The parallel processes of race, culture, and family. In M. Rastogi & E. Wieling (Eds.), *The voices of color: First person accounts of ethnic minority therapists* (pp. 67–89). Thousand Oaks, CA: Sage.

Kiecolt, K. J., & Fossett, M. A. (1995). Mate availability and marriage among African Americans: Aggregate- and individual-level analysis. In M. B. Tucker & C. Mitchell-Kernan (Eds.), *The decline in marriage among African Americans* (pp. 121–135). New York: Sage.

Klonoff, E. A., & Landrine, H. (2000). Revising and improving the African American acculturation scale. *Journal of Black Psychology, 26,* 235–261.

Klonoff, E. A., Landrine, H., & Ullman, J. B. (1999). Racial discrimination and psychiatric symptoms among Blacks. *Cultural Diversity and Ethnic Minority Psychology, 5,* 329–339.

Kohn, L. P., Oden, T., Munoz, R. F., Robinson, A., & Leavitt, D. (2002). Adapted cognitive behavioral group therapy for depressed low-income African American women. *Community Mental Health Journal, 38,* 497–504.

Krieger, N., & Sidney, S. (1996). Racial discrimination and blood pressure: The CARDIA study of young Black and White adults. *American Journal of Public Health, 86,* 1370–1378.

Kwate, N. O., Valdimarsdottir, H. B., Guevarra, J. S., & Bovbjerg, D. H. (2003). Experiences of racist events are associated with negative health consequences for African American women. *Journal of the National Medical Association, 95,* 450–460.

Laszloffy, T. A., & Hardy, K. V. (2000). Uncommon strategies for a common problem: Addressing racism in family therapy. *Family Process, 39,* 35–50.

McGoldrick, M., Giordano, J., & Pearce, J. K. (Eds.). (1996). *Ethnicity and family therapy* (2nd ed.). New York: Guilford Press.

McIntosh, P. (1998). White privilege: Unpacking the invisible knapsack. In M. McGoldrick (Ed.), *Re-visioning family therapy: Race, culture, and gender in clinical practice* (pp. 147–152). New York: Guilford Press.

McNair, L. D. (1996). African American women and behavior therapy: Integrating theory, culture, and clinical practice. *Cognitive and Behavioral Practice, 3,* 337–349.

Parks, G. (1986). *A choice of weapons.* Minneapolis: Minnesota Historical Society Press. (Original work published 1965)

Phinney, J. S., Cantu, C. L., & Kurtz, D. A. (1997). Ethnic and American identity as predictors of self-esteem among African American, Latino, and White adolescents. *Journal of Youth and Adolescence, 26,* 165–185.

Phinney, J. S., & Onwughalu, M. (1996). Racial identity and perception of American ideals among African American and African students in the United States. *International Journal of Intercultural Relations, 20,* 127–140.

Raue, P. J., Goldfried, M. R., & Barkham, M. (1997). The therapeutic alliance in psychodynamic–interpersonal and cognitive–behavioral therapy. *Journal of Consulting and Clinical Psychology, 65,* 582–587.

Roberts, R. E., Phinney, J. S., Masse, L. C., Chen, Y. R., Roberts, C. R., & Romero, A. (1999). The structure and ethnic identity of young adolescents from diverse ethnocultural groups. *Journal of Early Adolescence, 19,* 301–322.

Rohner, R. P., Bourque, S. L., & Elordi, C. A. (1996). Children's perceptions of corporal punishment, caretaker acceptance, and psychological adjustment in a poor, biracial southern community. *Journal of Marriage and the Family, 57,* 842–852.

Ross, S. L., & Turner, M. A. (2005). Housing discrimination in metropolitan America: Explaining changes between 1989 and 2000. *Social Problems, 52,* 152–180.

Sayers, S. L., & Heyman, R. E. (2003). Behavioral couples therapy. In G. P. Sholevar (Ed.), *Textbook of family and couples therapy: Clinical applications* (pp. 462–500). Washington, DC: American Psychiatric Association.

Schulz, A., Williams, D., Israel, B., Becker, A., Parker, E., James, S., et al. (2002). Unfair treatment, neighborhood effects, and mental health in the Detroit metropolitan area. *Journal of Health and Social Behavior, 41,* 314–332.

Simons, R. L., Lin, K.-H., Gordon, L. C., Brody, G. H., Murry, V., & Conger, R. D. (2002). Community differences in the association between parenting practices and child conduct problems. *Journal of Marriage and the Family, 62,* 331–345.

Stephenson, E. (2004). The African diaspora and culture-based coping strategies. In J. L. Chin (Ed.), *The psychology of prejudice and discrimination: Racism in America* (Vol. 1, pp. 95–118). Westport, CT: Praeger.

Sue, S. (1999). Science, ethnicity, and bias. *American Psychologist, 54,* 1070–1077.

Sue, S., & Zane, N. (1987). The role of culture and cultural techniques in psychotherapy. *American Psychologist, 42,* 37–45.

Taylor, R. J., Chatters, L. M., & Jackson, J. S. (1997). Changes over time in support network involvement among Black Americans. In R. J. Taylor, J. S. Jackson, & L. M. Chatters (Eds.), *Family life in Black America* (pp. 293–316). Thousand Oaks, CA: Sage.

Taylor, R. J., Mattis, J., & Chatters, L. M. (1999). Subjective religiosity among African Americans: A synthesis of findings from five national samples. *Journal of Black Psychology, 25,* 524–543.

Troxel, W. M., Matthews, K. A., Bromberger, J. T., & Sutton-Tyrrell, K. (2003). Chronic stress burden, discrimination, and subclinical carotid artery disease in African American and Caucasian women. *Health Psychology, 22,* 300–309.

U.S. Department of Health and Human Services. (2001). *Mental health: Culture, race, and ethnicity—A supplement to mental health: A report of the Surgeon General.* Rockville, MD: Substance Abuse and Mental Health Services Administration, Center for Mental Health Services.

Vandiver, B. J., Cross, W. E., Jr., Worrell, F. C., & Fhagen-Smith, P. E. (2002). Validating the Cross Racial Identity Scale. *Journal of Counseling Psychology, 49,* 71–85.

Whaley, A. L. (2001). Cultural mistrust: An important psychological construct for diagnosis and treatment of African Americans. *Professional Psychology: Research and Practice, 32,* 555–562.

Wong, C. A., Eccles, J. S., & Sameroff, A. J. (2003). The influence of ethnic discrimination and ethnic identification on African American adolescents' school and socioemotional adjustment. *Journal of Personality, 71*, 1197–1232.

Wright, E. M. (2001). Substance abuse in African American communities. In S. L. A. Straussner (Ed.), *Ethnocultural factors in substance abuse treatment* (pp. 31–51). New York: Guilford Press.

X, Malcolm. (1966). *The autobiography of Malcolm X.* With the assistance of Alex Haley. New York: Grove Press.

Young, C. (2003). Assimilation and social change dynamics in African and African American communities. *Western Journal of Black Studies, 27*, 164–175.

5

COGNITIVE–BEHAVIORAL THERAPY WITH ASIAN AMERICANS

GAYLE Y. IWAMASA, CURTIS HSIA, AND DEVON HINTON

Asian Americans are one of the most diverse and fastest growing ethnic groups in the United States, having grown 204% between 1980 and 2000 (U.S. Census Bureau, 2002). Asian Americans consist of over 30 different ethnic groups, comprise approximately 4.4% of the U.S. population, and are expected to continue growing (U.S. Census Bureau, 2003). Although the number of groups that collectively make up Asian Americans is large, unfortunately, the amount of treatment research focused on them is quite limited (Iwamasa, 1996, 1999, 2003). An additional complication is that because of the diversity within the Asian American population, existing research has limitations.

Although people of diverse Asian ethnicities are often grouped together because of a lack of available participants, studies often do not address ethnic or generational differences, and many of the studies are conducted on English-speaking students attending U.S. universities. Thus, any information gleaned from these studies has limited generalizability. Acknowledging these limitations, researchers have identified some similarities across Asian ethnic groups that can be useful to clinicians. In addition, awareness of the marked cultural, political, and environmental differences among and within groups may assist therapists in providing culturally competent treatment. However, it must be stressed that each culture as well as each individual has unique characteristics that need to be fully explored and understood; this chapter merely serves as a guide.

This chapter briefly reviews basic history and culturally based information on Asian American groups, including immigration experiences and generational differences. Cognitive–behavioral therapy (CBT) is then discussed in the context of working with Asian Americans, using a case example of how CBT was adapted to be effective with one Southeast Asian client.

HISTORICAL AND CULTURAL BACKGROUND

The histories of many Asian countries significantly overlap because of their close proximity and mutual conquests that have occurred. For example, part of the Japanese language is based on the Chinese language, and many still use the Asian lunar calendar. Negative sentiment sometimes still remains between different Asian countries because of past political conflicts (e.g., Japan and China) and current ones (e.g., Taiwan and China). It is not atypical for Asian American parents to forbid their children to marry into specific ethnic groups because of personal or social beliefs and previous interactions with members of that ethnic group. Competent clinicians are aware of the potential for historical issues to influence the Asian American client's perceptions, beliefs, and behaviors. A comprehensive review of the histories of specific Asian American cultures is beyond the scope of this chapter, and readers are encouraged to consult Uba (1994) and Lee (1997) for concise reviews of many Asian American groups.

Immigration

Some Asian Americans, such as Japanese Americans, have been established in the United States for many generations, whereas others, such as the Hmong Lao, are relatively new (Chan, 1991). Among first-generation Asian Americans, clinicians must be cognizant of the individual's immigration or refugee status and consider how the client's pre-, during, and postmigration experiences may be related to the current level of distress.

Asian American immigration to the United States has occurred in large waves, mainly in response to economic and political issues. The first Asian immigrants were the Chinese, who were recruited to build railroads and work in agriculture in the mid-1800s. The 1882 Chinese Exclusion Act barring further Chinese immigration was enacted when the Chinese began to settle in the United States and prosper by owning businesses and land. Subsequently, Caucasian businesses and landowners, who demanded cheap labor, began recruiting workers from other Asian countries. This continued until the 1924 Asian Exclusion Act, which barred all Asian immigration, again because some of the workers of Asian descent began settling in the United States and acquiring property. Following these two anti-Asian immigration acts, immigration to the United States from other countries increased.

The 1965 Immigration Act was specifically designed to increase European immigration, but it also allowed for an increase in immigration from Asian countries. The mid-1970s saw the beginning of Southeast Asian immigration, mainly Vietnamese refugees, followed by voluntary immigration of Koreans and Asian Indians in the 1980s. The 1980 Refugee Act provided states with funding for refugee assistance programs, and in 1987 the Amerasian Homecoming Act was established. This Act allowed those Asian children born to U.S. military personnel between 1962 and 1976 (and some family members) to apply for U.S. visas prior to 1990.

It is essential that clinicians be aware of the differences between *immigrants* and *refugees* (Lee, 1997; Uba, 1994). Immigrants typically desire and plan to move to the United States. They often have family members who already live in the United States, higher levels of education, and greater financial resources. Many of these individuals have familiarity with the United States, including the English language. They are more likely to immigrate with their entire family and have support for employment and housing when they arrive. They often settle in areas near family, sometimes in or near an already established ethnic community in which others speak their native language and where culturally familiar foods, activities, and events are readily available.

Refugees, however, typically have no previous interest or experience with the United States and leave their homes without planning, mainly because of political and social violence and upheaval. Many of these individuals are less educated and poor, and they often leave with only the clothing they are wearing. They are often separated from loved ones and come to the United States with no resources. They often speak little or no English, and this, in combination with their lack of formal education and skills, results in an inability to obtain employment or adequate housing. Many refugees find themselves living with other refugees from their same village, and in places unfamiliar with Asian culture (e.g., the Hmong Lao in Minnesota). Economic opportunities for them are limited, and because of this, they also tend to live in communities where poor U.S. ethnic minority groups live. In addition to experiencing racism and discrimination from the dominant U.S. society, many Asian refugees experience racism and discrimination from other ethnic minorities, many of whom are ignorant of their traumatic experiences and erroneously believe that the refugees are being unfairly supported and subsidized by the U.S. government.

Culture-Specific Issues

It is important for clinicians to understand the various culture-specific issues in the lives of Asian American clients. These include religion, family structure and roles, gender roles, acculturation, ethnic and racial identity, values, language and cognitive styles, health beliefs, and social behaviors. We discuss each in the following sections.

Religion

There are many religious belief systems in Asia that are not specific to any geographical area. Much like Europe, many ideas and ideologies spread across Asia, resulting in myriad belief systems. Additionally, there is a range of depth of faith, and some do not believe in any religion at all (e.g., in China, where the official state religion is atheism). Thus, religious and spiritual affiliation among Asian Americans is likely to be quite diverse.

However, one of the major spiritual themes in Asian religions is balance. Most widely known in the West are the concepts of yin and yang and the need to balance them (Tseng, 2003). Whereas yin represents passivity, yang represents activity (Kazarian & Evans, 2001). This concept permeates all domains of traditional Chinese, Japanese, and Vietnamese society, from the conception of the body (as noted by the need to balance the intake of food with yin and yang qualities), to emotions, society, and the environment (Atkinson, 2004; Spector, 2004). To achieve balance, an individual is expected to have moderation in all things, similar to Buddhism, and not to engage in any one area to excess (e.g., not exercise to exhaustion; Spector, 2004).

Many Asian Americans are open about their spiritual life and have a worldview that includes the belief that the spiritual realm has a direct effect on their lives. Also, many Asian Americans are active in their local church or temple, considering religion to be an important part of their lives.

Family Structure and Roles

Historically and currently, most traditional Asian cultures are best represented by a patriarchal authoritarian system. The father (and to a lesser extent the mother) make decisions for the family often without the input of the children, as it is assumed that parents have greater wisdom and will be able to make better decisions, even after the children reach adulthood (Tien, 2003; Uba, 1994; Wu, 2001). Additionally, each person in the family has a specific role that he or she is expected to fulfill (Chao, 2002; Yeh, 2003). For example, the typical role of the father is to provide financially and make decisions for the family but not be involved in the day-to-day operations of the household as this is the domain of the mother. The mother's role can include preparing the food, cleaning and caring for the house, managing finances, and rearing the children (Uba, 1994). Children are expected to help with daily chores, especially the daughters, who are taught how to manage their own home for the future.

In general, traditional Asian American parents do not display their emotions or affection to their children as openly as do Western parents. For example, it is common for Asian American children never to hear their parents say "I love you." It is expected that children understand that their parents love them by the parents providing for them and not through overt expression of affection. As an example of the patriarchal nature of Chinese families, it is not atypical for a Chinese American father to choose the college that his child will attend, and that the child will not see this as an imposition but rather as a judicious choice based on an understanding of what is best for the adult child and the family (M. Liao, personal communication, October 11, 2003). Parents may also play a large role in choosing a spouse for their children (either directly or indirectly influencing the decision) and make other important decisions throughout a son's or daughter's life. Of course, all Asian American families differ in terms of their adherence to these more traditional practices.

Current research suggests five types of Asian American families: traditional, cultural conflict, bicultural, American, and interracial (Lee, 1996). *Traditional* families follow the traditional patriarchal structure described earlier. *Cultural conflict* families are those in which parents and children are of different generational status, and thus, may have differing opinions and expectations of family roles (Chao, 2002; Yu, 1999). *Bicultural* families are those who engage in both traditional Asian and "American" activities and combine the value systems in family life. *American* families are those that do not integrate traditional Asian practices and roles into everyday family life. Finally, *interracial* families are those in which one parent is of Asian heritage and the other parent is not. An additional family type is the *parachute child* family in which the parents send their child to the United States to live with a relative, or buy a house for the child and let him or her live alone during the teenage years without direct supervision. This is done with the belief that the child will have a better education, opportunities, and lifestyle in the United States than he or she would in the home country.

Intergenerational differences can cause conflicts based on values and a sense of responsibilities (Wu, 2001). This may be illustrated by the differing levels of commitment to the family. Often the older generation, being more collectivistic, expect that the younger generation will take care of the elders (e.g., go to college near home, move back home after college, and stay near home after marrying). The younger generation, being more individualistic, may feel unfairly imposed on by the older generation, believing that certain responsibilities to their parents have ended. For example, these adult children may refuse to assist with household chores when no longer living with their parents. Sometimes these conflicts directly or indirectly influence the presenting problems of Asian American clients.

A leading theory for the underutilization of mental health services is that for most Asian Americans, having a mental illness brings shame not only on oneself but also on the family. Not uncommonly, Asian Americans may present to medical doctors with somatic complaints that may be psychological in origin. Because of the stigma associated with seeking help for a "mental" problem, some Asian Americans may be more likely to seek help from a medical doctor of the same culture (T. Luu, personal communication, June 12, 2003). Getting to know physicians within Asian American communities can be quite helpful. Additionally, working within the Asian American community itself can be a way to limit the stigma associated with psychology. This can be done by interacting with the community nonprofessionally (e.g., spending time at the community center or ethnic churches) and by gaining the trust of those within the community.

Being part of a collectivistic society, the Asian American client may experience one of two extremes: (a) not wanting anyone to know he or she is in therapy or (b) being from a family that wants to be very active and involved in the therapy. In the former case, it is important to reassure the client of confidentiality, often across several sessions. Also, if the therapist can reframe the problem as a physiological disorder with a behavioral solution (e.g., depression is a chemical imbalance in the brain, which can be treated with behavioral activation and challenging irrational thoughts), both the client and the family may conceptualize the problem in a context that is more culturally acceptable.

However, it is not surprising to see an Asian American client present with the entire family, including aunts, uncles, and grandparents. When this occurs, it is important to remember that deference and respect should be shown to the elders. Family members may have questions, and the therapist might have to budget extra time to spend with the entire family. If an interpreter is used, the client should be addressed directly rather than the interpreter. The effectiveness and ethics of using interpreters for non-English speakers in therapy are beyond the scope of this chapter, and readers who encounter such situations should be familiar with the research and issues in these situations. For a summary of issues, see Angelelli and Geist-Martin (2005), Bradford and Muñoz (1993), and Goh (2004).

Gender Roles

As might be expected, individuals from more traditional Asian families are more likely to adhere to traditional gender roles. A review of the published literature reveals that only recently have psychologists begun to address gender issues among Asian Americans. As discussed by Chin (2000), many myths continue to exist regarding the "mystique about Asian American women, and stereotypes that objectify and disempower them remain" (p. 6). Indeed, until recently, discussions about gender roles and the experiences of Asian American women were largely absent from many of the primary sources in Asian American psychology. However, therapists must be aware of how media portrayals affect societal perceptions and stereotypes of Asian American women, how immigration and refugee experiences affect Asian American women and their children, how relationships between Asian

American mothers and daughters change over time, and how ethnic identity and the acculturation process influence dating and marriage practices.

Acculturation and Ethnic and Racial Identity

In the Asian American psychology literature, major advances in examining the concepts of acculturation, ethnic identity, and racial identity among Asian Americans are being made (Chun & Akutsu, 2003; Iwamasa & Yamada, 2001; Marín & Gamba, 2003). For the purpose of this chapter, these concepts are briefly reviewed so that clinicians can be aware of how such processes and personal identity issues may affect the client and, hence, the therapy process. Of particular importance is the erroneous assumption that these concepts are similar and can be used interchangeably.

Acculturation is often defined as the process of change over time when individuals encounter a different culture (Moyerman & Forman, 1992). Of importance is that it is not just the individual who undergoes acculturation; individuals in the dominant culture also undergo change as a result of interacting with someone of a different cultural background.

Ethnic identity is often defined as a sense of belonging based on beliefs, communication styles, values, attitudes, and behavioral norms shared by a group (Chun & Akutsu, 2003; Phinney, 2003; Uba, 1994). It is both self- and other-defined. The development of ethnic identity is influenced by factors such as cognitive development, age, and experiences with one's own ethnic group, exposure to other ethnic groups, and experiences of racism and discrimination. Ethnic identity is believed to develop over time and tends to remain strong throughout the acculturation process (Phinney, 2003).

Racial identity has been defined by Helms and colleagues (Helms & Cook, 1999; Helms & Talleyrand, 1997) as one's identification with one's racial group and includes how individuals recognize and overcome the psychological effects of racial oppression as a result of being identified racially by others. The concept of racial identity incorporates the experience of the negative societal messages about one's race into the identity formation process, whereas ethnic identity tends to be viewed as an internal and individualistic process. Although clinicians may not personally value such concepts themselves, the culturally competent clinician understands that these concepts may be important to the client and thus considers them accordingly (Helms, 1992).

Collectivistic Values

Many traditional Asian societies are collectivistic by nature, meaning that the emphasis of life is placed on the good of the collective. The size of the collective may range from the nuclear family to the extended family, village, city, and even country. In contrast to most Western societies, the focus is not on the rights of the individual but rather the good of the group (Kim, Atkinson, & Yang, 1999; Marin & Gamba, 2003). For example, a popular American phrase is "The squeaky wheel gets the grease," whereas a well-known Japanese proverb is "The protruding nail will be pounded down." *Individual-level collectivism* is when an individual makes a personal sacrifice for the good of the group, such as attending a nearby college to be able to continue helping out at home (e.g., with younger siblings or the family store) when he or she would prefer to go away to college. On a larger scale, the idea of human rights in the sense of the individual is relatively new to some Asian countries such as China, and a new word had to be developed to represent the concept (Y. Hsia, personal communication, November 5, 2003).

The idea of the in-group extends beyond the nuclear family, often encompassing the extended family and close family friends who have been "adopted" into the family and given titles such as "aunt" or "uncle" (D. Sue, 2005). It is not uncommon to have three generations living in one house, with many relatives living within walking distance (Uba, 1994). This pattern may originate from Asian countries, where in some areas whole villages could consist of one family group. Therapists should be aware of how collectivistic values influence their clients' everyday lives and be cognizant that stressing independence and individual problem solving may not be culturally appropriate. For instance, in the example indicated earlier, it may not be in the best interest of the individual to disregard the family's wishes and go away to college. Therapists should be able to assist clients with being able to evaluate the consequences of the decisions that they make, keeping in mind familial and cultural values and ethnic and gender roles, so that clients will be comfortable with and aware of the results of their choices.

Language Issues and Cognitive Styles

Language plays a significant role in how an individual views the world. How concepts are expressed varies from one language to the next, and some languages do not contain concepts present in other cultures. In translating from one language to another, often words or concepts that do not exist in one language need to be constructed or further explained to make sense in another language. A well-known example exists in the contrast between the three Greek words for love (*eros* for sexual love, *phileo* for brotherly love, and *agape* for unconditional love) and the sole word in English (*love*). There are many words and ideas not easily expressed in English that exist in Asian languages and vice versa (Hannas, 1997; Huang, 1996). For example, a common linguistic mistake made by Mandarin speakers occurs in the use of *he* and *she*. In spoken Mandarin, there is no differentiation between *he*, *she*, or *it*, and therefore, when Mandarin speakers use English, there may be confusion regarding the gender of the pronoun. Clinicians should be aware that clients may engage in a process of translating what has been said into their first language, thinking about it, then translating it back into English, with the possibility that some concepts will need to be clarified or explained.

Additionally, Asian Americans may not think in a cause-and-effect manner as do Westerners. As part of the yin/yang concept, one's well-being involves harmony with the world. If one is not in balance with others (i.e., family, friends, or nature), the result can be an imbalance in health. Western thought is often mechanistic and reductionistic (e.g., looking for a direct cause by observing a system and reducing it to its smallest parts), whereas many traditional Asian cultures view systems holistically, often focusing on indirect causes for a result (Shiraev & Levy, 2004). Thus, although a therapist may see a direct causal link between a thought and an action, an Asian American client may take into consideration additional causes that may not have occurred to the therapist but that are valid and make sense to the client.

A related issue is locus of control. In the dominant individualistic U.S. society, people are often assumed to have an internal locus of control, and this focus is believed to be the healthiest. However, in Asian American cultures, the opposite may be true. For example, it is more common for Chinese people to have an external locus of control, and when certain events occur, to believe that the source was an outside factor and that their own actions had a minimal effect. Therapists must be aware of this when using cognitive approaches that stress cause and effect (Park & Kim, 2003). What the therapist may see as a logical outcome may not be as clear to an Asian American client, and vice versa. For instance, even though an illogical thought pattern may seem obvious to the therapist, the client may be taking into account how his or her own thoughts and behaviors also affect his or her family.

Health Beliefs

In contrast to Western culture, traditional Asian cultures have a different understanding of medicine and health. Similar to the collectivist emphasis on relationships with others, individuals with traditional Asian beliefs and values also believe that they are interconnected with the universe. One's own health is related not only to direct causes as seen by Western medicine (e.g., influenza caused by a virus) but also to disharmony within the world (Spector, 2004). This includes relationships with other people, the earth, and the environment. It may also include how one thinks about the world and the forces beyond one's control (e.g., luck). On the basis of a presenting problem, many different traditional treatments may be suggested, ranging from dietary changes, acupuncture, coining, cupping, and medicinal herbs. An example of coining is provided in the case example that follows. *Cupping* is the placing of a cup (sometimes heated) on the body and suctioning of air so that the skin is drawn in the cup. The practice is believed to stimulate blood flow and relieve pain and is often used in acupuncture. Many traditional Asian Americans do not view their physiological well-being separately from other parts of their life (Spector, 2004). It is interesting to note that this is similar to the biopsychosocial model of health. With this in mind, understanding traditional Asian medical approaches and incorporating them into the therapy may be useful for some Asian American clients. For example, progressive muscle relaxation, often used to treat generalized anxiety disorder, may be paired with or replaced by meditation, tai chi, or yoga.

Some clinicians may be aware that the *Diagnostic and Statistical Manual of Mental Disorders* (4th ed., text rev.; *DSM–IV–TR*) contains an appendix of "culture-bound syndromes" (American Psychiatric Association, 2000). The inclusion of such syndromes was probably an attempt to facilitate clinicians' consideration of clients' cultural contexts in assessing symptoms. However, reliance on this section of the *DSM–IV–TR* may reinforce stereotypes about Asian Americans, for example, the idea that culture contributes to the development of particular symptoms in ethnic minority cultures but not in the dominant culture (Hays, 2001).

Social Behaviors

For a number of reasons, Asian Americans may be perceived as less active and verbal than their Western counterparts in various settings, including meetings, class, work, and therapy. For clients who speak English as a second language, it is important to assess the individual's language ability, as the client may not understand the therapist's vocabulary, especially psychological terminology. Asian American clients may also ask fewer questions and interact less with the therapist because of cultural norms. For example, in many Asian cultures, it is considered inappropriate to question elders or authorities, as it may be perceived as doubting their abilities (Atkinson, 2004). Furthermore, it is possible that a client may verbally or nonverbally agree (e.g., nod) to what is being said while actually being in disagreement. This may be done to avoid confrontation and to maintain a harmonious relationship with the therapist. For example, after being assigned homework, the client may agree to do the task yet not have any intention of completing it. Querying the client about the feasibility of the homework is useful in assessing the likelihood of it being completed. It is also helpful for the client to understand clearly why the assignment is important to complete and how it is directly connected to the therapy goals.

COGNITIVE–BEHAVIORAL THERAPY AND ASIAN AMERICANS

We hope clinicians will combine knowledge of the heterogeneity of Asian Americans with clinical skills to understand how each individual is unique and that these individual differences take precedence over generalized assumptions about a client's particular ethnic group. As always, at the outset of treatment, conducting a thorough initial assessment will allow the clinician to better understand the individual and the problems he or she is experiencing. In addition to understanding the presenting problem, the therapist should understand the client's existing cultural and belief systems and how these are expressed behaviorally.

Advantages and Disadvantages of CBT

CBT is advantageous in the treatment of Asian Americans for several reasons. Its short-term, problem-focused orientation is appealing, as many Asian Americans will seek treatment for a specific acute problem that is currently interfering with their ability to function. CBT's focus on addressing specific symptoms with specific interventions and breaking down goals into small doable steps is also helpful. In contrast to other cultural groups, most Asian Americans would not be comfortable with long-term or open-ended therapy and would likely see such therapy as a failure. They may wonder, if it takes so long for improvement to occur, why continue? CBT's emphasis on contextual factors also makes it a culturally consistent treatment approach.

However, CBT's solution-focused treatment may result in clinicians initially attending more to the problem behaviors rather than ensuring the establishment of a strong therapeutic alliance. As indicated previously, for many Asian American clients, such an alliance is crucial to establishing the therapist's credibility (S. Sue & Zane, 1987). Also mentioned previously, CBT's reductionistic approach to solving problems may result in miscommunication and misunderstanding if the therapist seeks to solve problems in what he or she believes to be the most efficient and linear way. An additional limitation of CBT is its emphasis on individualism and an internal locus of control in contrast to the Asian American emphasis on the family unit, collectivism, and spirituality. A final limitation is CBT's reliance on written assignments such as daily activity scheduling and thought records, as well as on reading and reviewing handouts and self-help books. Reliance on interventions such as these, particularly for those Asian Americans for whom English is a second language or who have had little or no formal education in the United States, may be inappropriate.

Therapist Issues

Of importance in working with individuals from a different culture is not only how the client interprets symptoms and their effects but also how the therapist interprets the situation. These differences may be significant, and what the therapist may view as abnormal and needing change may be part of the client's culture. S. Sue and Consolacion (2003) noted the importance of the therapist's awareness of the role that minority status may play in the development of psychological distress for Asian Americans. In particular, the effects of stereotypes, racism, anti-Asian violence, immigration experiences, and language issues may contribute to or exacerbate distress (Austria, 2003).

Each person sees the world through a set of filters, and the therapist conducting therapy is no different. The therapist must be able to understand his or her own worldview (e.g., collectivistic vs. individualistic perspective, communication style, beliefs about parenting, family obligations, gender roles) to be able to recognize biases. To impose one's values and beliefs (e.g., "liberating" the wife from a patriarchal system or decreasing "enmeshment" in a family) may be seen as imperialistic. It is also unethical and likely to fail.

Counselors of Caucasian descent should become aware of what is known as "White privilege," or the concept of having unique privileges within the American culture because of being part of the dominant culture (Ancis & Szymanski, 2001; McIntosh, 1998). Becoming self-aware of everyday privileges not afforded to minorities (e.g., seeing people of your ethnicity represented positively in the media, being able to rent or buy a home in any neighborhood, never being asked to speak for one's ethnic group) will also help the therapist better relate to the day-to-day realities of an Asian American client.

For Asian Americans, a potential therapy issue is that of being a visible minority, termed *visible racial ethnic group* by Helms (1994). Because of this, most Asian Americans have experienced racism sometime during their lives. This may vary from overt racism (e.g., verbal abuse and physical beatings) to more subtle forms of racism (e.g., glass ceilings in the workplace). The general message communicated by many non-Asians is that Asian Americans are inferior, they are perpetual foreigners, and they will always be different in a negative way when compared with the dominant culture. Consequently, non-Asian therapists (especially older White men) need to be aware that they may be seen as an unfriendly figure, or at least viewed as an outsider unable to understand the client's situation (Kiselica, 1998).

Probably the most important aspect of working with Asian Americans is to have cultural sensitivity. Although research has shown that Asian Americans perceive other Asian Americans as more culturally sensitive (Gim, Atkinson, & Kim, 1991), having an Asian American counselor is not always feasible, thus it behooves all therapists to become more aware of their own cultural beliefs and the cultural norms of the clients with whom they are working. Indeed, this responsibility of the therapist is so important that the American Psychological Association (2002) adopted the *Guidelines on Multicultural Education, Training, Research, Practice, and Organizational Change for Psychologists* as organizational policy. Of the six guidelines, the following three pertain most to our point:

> Guideline 1: Psychologists are encouraged to recognize that, as cultural beings, they may hold attitudes and beliefs that can detrimentally influence their perceptions of and interactions with individuals who are ethnically and racially different from themselves.
>
> Guideline 2: Psychologists are encouraged to recognize the importance of multicultural sensitivity and responsiveness, knowledge, and understanding about ethnically and racially different individuals.
>
> Guideline 5: Psychologists strive to apply culturally-appropriate skills in clinical and other applied psychological practices. (See http://www.apa.org/pi/multiculturalguidelines.pdf)

Treatment Plan

Although the following information is tailored for Asian American clients, therapists familiar with CBT approaches will recognize much of the material as being similar to their own approach. It is hoped that the information contained in this chapter will provide therapists with some suggestions to help the therapeutic process without introducing a completely new methodology.

Initial Sessions

Initial therapy sessions should focus on assessment, development of rapport, goal-setting, psychoeducation, and achieving success with short-term goals. A thorough assessment is critical to understanding the presenting complaint and the cultural context in which the client (and therefore the therapist) will have to work. See Okazaki and Tanaka-Matsumi in chapter 11, this volume, for specific issues and suggestions related to assessment.

In the first session it is important to communicate to the client that you understand the presenting issue. Essence reflection may be a useful tool to reassure both yourself and the client that the problem is understood and that you are able to treat it. Therapists should discuss the treatment plan and schedule in an interactive manner, asking the client, "At the end of treatment, what would you have liked to have accomplished?" In this way, unrealistic goals may be discussed and more reasonable goals determined. This also helps to set longer term goals for therapy that are clearly understood by both therapist and client.

With Asian American clients, one should inquire about the presence of any problems in addition to the initially presented problem, as the client may be reticent about other areas of dysfunction. Additionally, contextual information may not be as forthcoming, especially if it may cause embarrassment to the family. In making judgments about how the client is functioning, it is important to keep in mind that what may seem maladaptive in one culture may be adaptive and useful in another. Therefore, it is important to examine the functionality of any behavior in context. This means that the therapist may need to ask questions about whether or not a behavior is specific to the person and his or her culture. Asking questions about the client's cultural values and practices demonstrates an interest and willingness to learn on the part of the therapist, which is preferable to the therapist assuming that such personal characteristics of the client are unimportant.

Once long-term goals have been agreed on, it is important to discuss the short-term goals so that the client understands the therapy process and the idea that long-term goals are achieved through the short-term goals. If the treatment plan is clearly laid out for the client, he or she will likely feel more comfortable, which will enhance therapy attendance.

During the first few sessions, success is imperative to reassure the client that therapy is beneficial. An Asian American client unaccustomed to counseling may expect something akin to herbal or Western medicine in which the problem is quickly assessed and addressed. Setting achievable short-term goals will increase the likelihood that the client will return. Engaging in behaviors that are successful and useful to the client will build trust and rapport. Examples include behavioral activation for clients with depression, interoceptive conditioning for panic disorder, and systematic desensitization for phobias. Each can be done in the first few therapy sessions, in or out of the therapy session.

If language is an issue, it may be prudent to rely more on behavioral interventions. For example, the second author (Curtis Hsia) has limited skills with Cantonese and worked successfully with a Cantonese-speaking client who had limited English skills and was diagnosed with obsessive–compulsive disorder (contamination issues) by focusing on systematic desensitization. Even with a language barrier, the client saw success by decreasing his anxiety in handling "contaminated" items and, thus, he regularly attended therapy.

Psychoeducation is also important in initial sessions. Many clients do not have an understanding of their disorder and experience relief when they understand the etiology of their disorder and that their problem is not unique. Sharing what you have learned from the empirical literature about the efficacy and effectiveness of therapy techniques can make clients feel more at ease as they learn that their disorder is well known, is researched, and that a viable solution exists. Teaching clients the CBT model and how it will address their problems increases comfort with therapy and will enable Asian American clients to be able to anticipate what therapy will be like. It is useful to ask clients about their own beliefs about the problem, as this will help the therapist better understand how the client perceives the problem and the underlying issues that support behaviors. This may also help when engaging in cognitive countering, by providing the therapist with a solid starting point.

Middle Sessions

The focus of middle sessions should be on continued behavioral interventions, cognitive challenging, preparation for in vivo exposure if necessary, and preparation for termination. If good rapport has been established, it is not uncommon during the middle sessions for other issues to arise. Once the client has observed the effectiveness of therapy and experienced a decrease in symptoms along with an increase in quality of life, the Asian American client may become more open about other issues. For example, after a few successful sessions, a Chinese client divulged to the therapist that she was in the United States illegally, currently living with her mother, and needed help finding alternative housing. In such a situation, it is necessary to make some decisions: Does the new problem interfere to such an extent that treatment for the initial problem should be put on hold? Can someone else (family, friends) help with the new problem? Should treatment continue?

This decision-making process should be nonconfrontational and collaborative, with the therapist and client together reviewing the original treatment plan and deciding if it needs to be altered to address more immediate problems. It can be helpful to remind the client that as one problem becomes resolved, typically other problems also resolve without a direct focus of therapy. The therapist can emphasize how such a process indicates the client's increased ability to generalize and apply skills learned in treatment.

The hallmark of the middle sessions, once behavioral interventions have been successful, is a focus on learning cognitive skills. Both in terms of ease of use and language issues, cognitive challenging can be simplified, and thus more easily remembered and used. One approach is to focus on three areas:

- Core cognitions: "What is your underlying concern?"
- Probability overestimation: "What's the likelihood of your underlying concern occurring?"
- Catastrophizing: "If your underlying concern does occur, will it really be that horrible?"

The therapist can have the client practice these statements so that it becomes second nature to ask himself or herself such questions. Ideally, these cognitive tools will become ingrained to such an extent that in any situation, the client can critically assess the problem and select the necessary action, thus increasing the client's ability to cope on his or her own after therapy ends.

In cognitive challenging with Asian Americans, if the client speaks English as a second language, he or she may approach situations differently than clients for whom English is their first language. Whereas American English makes significant use of slang, many Asian languages (e.g., Chinese) express thoughts through the use of idioms. Thus, it may be useful to learn some idioms or proverbs from the client's background to use as examples in therapy. Additionally, Asian Americans may not always approach situations on the basis of whether it is a logical choice. They may take into consideration how decisions will affect their family and others around them. Even if an action seems logical to the therapist, an Asian American may perceive it as potentially embarrassing or as bringing shame to the family and may refuse the suggestion. If this occurs, or if the client objects to the intervention, a different approach should be taken.

Clinicians need to assess how the client has dealt with the problem behavior and discuss why such approaches may not have been successful. The therapist can then suggest a new approach to the problem by critically assessing the problem and breaking it down into more manageable steps that can be addressed individually. Once this is done, the relational aspects of changing one's behavior and how this might affect others may be discussed.

A helpful cognitive reframe is that, without change, the whole family will experience some level of dishonor because the client's difficulties are not being addressed, but by addressing the problem, harmony and honor for the family can be achieved. Some compromises may need to be made, especially in implementing in vivo practices, because of possible concerns about looking foolish in public. If the client and therapist can discuss what is helpful and what is not working well in therapy, it is likely that acceptable alternative approaches can be found.

During the middle sessions it is also important to begin laying the groundwork for the client's final sessions and beyond. Therapy should focus on the cognitive skills learned while training the client to become his or her own therapist.

End Sessions

The last few sessions should focus on the practice of behavioral and cognitive skills, continued preparation for termination, and assisting the client to increase his or her social support. In particularly challenging situations, practicing "dry runs" or role-plays will increase the likelihood of success in the real situation. For in vivo practice, one may have to begin with imaginary exposures and build toward in vivo exposures. The therapist may need to be inventive in finding sites for in vivo practice away from locations where the client may be seen by other community members.

If the client is still reluctant to engage in behaviors seen as potentially embarrassing, another approach is to address the consequences if no change occurs. Using the "What if . . . " approach and asking the client to brainstorm the positives and negatives about changing the behavior can be useful. Although the client may want to avoid short-term shame, long-term consequences may become more problematic. Discussing what aspects of the intervention make it embarrassing and examining its pros and cons will provide the therapist with more information about how to revise the intervention to make it more comfortable for the client.

Therapists should discuss termination and what to expect after treatment ends. Although the client may indicate that he or she does not want any further interaction, the therapist should still stress future availability regardless of circumstances. An Asian American client may feel that if gains are not maintained, he or she has failed and may experience shame in admitting problems after therapy has ended. Emphasizing realistic cognitions will help the client understand that life will continue to be stressful and that experiencing future difficulties is normal.

In ending therapy with Asian American clients, three steps are suggested. The first is to increase the time between final sessions. The second is, after termination, to maintain contact with the client through several monthly follow-up phone calls. During these calls, remind the client that life will continue to have its ups and downs and that difficulties are common and should be expected. This way, when the client encounters problems, he or she may be more willing to contact the therapist if a problem moves beyond his or her ability to cope. Finally, if the client agrees, use his or her support system. Ideally, the client can explain to a trusted friend or family member what has been accomplished in therapy and how to maintain gains, which reinforces the learning for the client and provides him or her with social support.

CASE EXAMPLE

To provide culturally sensitive treatment, the therapist must understand the sociopolitical history of the client's ethnic group and how it may influence the experience and expression of psychological distress. For example, for Cambodian and Vietnamese refugees, unique forms of panic attacks may occur (e.g., *orthostatic panic*, i.e., dizziness on standing that causes a panic attack, and *neck-focused panic*, i.e., neck sensations that cause a panic attack; Hinton, Chau, et al., 2001; Hinton, Um, & Ba, 2001). Research has shown that for these individuals, panic attacks combine posttraumatic stress disorder (PTSD) characteristics (e.g., flashbacks) and those of panic disorder (e.g., fear of death from physiological dysfunction; Hinton, Ba, Peou, & Um, 2000; Hinton et al., 2004).

The *multiplex model of panic generation* (see Figure 5.1) can be used to explain how panic attacks are generated among Southeast Asian refugees (Hinton, Chau, et al., 2001; Hinton et al., 2004, in press). The model is based on the psychological conceptualization of panic attack generation (Barlow, 1988; Clark, 1986) and fear network theory (e.g., Foa & Kozak, 1986). According to the model, a panic attack may begin after the induction of an arousal-reactive symptom, that is, a symptom made worse by arousal (e.g., dizziness; Taylor, Koch, & McNally, 1992). The symptom may be induced by various causes, such as a worry episode, hyperventilation, exertion, anger, overeating, head rotation, or thinking about a traumatic event.

The arousal-reactive sensation may activate one or more fear networks: (a) trauma associations, (b) catastrophic cognitions, (c) metaphoric associations, and (d) interoceptive conditioning directly to somatic and psychological fear. Anxiety generated by the activation of one or more of these four types of fear networks aggravates the arousal-reactive symptom, which leads to further activation of the fear networks. Through this positive feedback loop, an escalating spiral of arousal may ensue, leading to a panic attack. When all four types of fear networks are simultaneously activated and create an escalating spiral of panic, it may be called a *TCMIE panic attack* ("T" for trauma associations; "C" for catastrophic cognitions; "M" for metaphoric associations; "I" for interoceptive conditioning of an arousal-reactive sensation to psychological and somatic fear; and "E" for escalating arousal). The

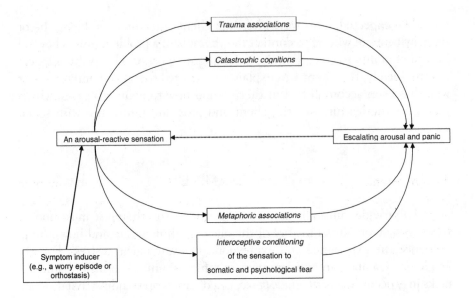

Figure 5.1. The generation of the TCMIE (multiplex) panic attack. T = trauma associations; C = catastrophic cognitions; M = metaphoric associations; I = interoceptive conditioning of an arousal-reactive sensation to somatic and psychological fear; and E = escalating arousal and panic.

following is a case description of a Cambodian refugee with orthostatically induced panic, with the formulation and treatment on the basis of the TCMIE model.

On initial presentation to a psychiatric clinic, 59-year-old Chan was experiencing hour-long orthostatic panic attacks three times a week. During the attacks, on standing, he experienced severe dizziness, along with cold hands, palpitations, and neck soreness. He would immediately sit down, fearing "wind overload" (Cambodians consider "wind" to be an airlike substance that runs in the body alongside blood, which may surge upward in the body, with disastrous results; Hinton et al., 2004). Chan also worried about cardiac arrest, neck vessel rupture, and stroke. During a third of these panic attacks, Chan had flashbacks of either his brother's execution or stacks of body parts.

To relieve the symptoms, Chan would "coin" himself to remove excessive inner wind. Chan considered cold extremities, dizziness, and other symptoms to result from the blockage of vessels in the limbs and an inner accumulation of wind. Coining is thought to remove wind and restore proper blood and wind flow in the vessels. One takes a coin, dips the edge in wind oil, and drags the coin's edge in a proximal to distal direction, either along the ribs of the front or the back of the body, along the limbs, or both, resulting in streaks. The color of the streaks reveals how much wind accumulated in the body.

In the Khmer Rouge period, Chan worked 12 hours a day under hot sun. Twice a day he was fed a watery rice broth. The work was mainly of two types: digging and carrying dirt in a bucket, and rice transplantation. Chan often felt dizzy, especially after bending over, and he saw many people collapse while doing the work. In the Pol Pot period, Chan, like most Cambodians, suffered severe malaria. Malaria may predispose individuals to panic disorder by forming a trauma association to symptoms of autonomic arousal such as dizziness, and by causing interoceptive conditioning of fear to sensations of autonomic arousal such as chills, dizziness, and palpitations (Hinton, Pham, Chau, Tran, & Hinton, 2003). Chan had malaria attacks every day for 6 months. These episodes essentially formed a "cold" panic attack lasting 45 minutes and were marked by rigors and palpitations, followed by 30-minute "hot" panic attacks marked by palpitations, headache, extreme dysphoria, and severe dizziness. As were most Khmer, Chan was frequently accused of feigning illness. Consequently, even after a malarial attack commenced, he was forced to work. Chan would struggle to work and, suddenly dizzy, would often collapse.

Just before the Vietnamese invasion of his village, Chan and his two brothers were farming rice about an hour's walk from their village. Six Khmer Rouge suddenly arrived and arrested them. The soldiers knew Chan's brothers had served as soldiers prior to the Khmer Rouge invasion. Chan was charged with the crimes of being related to a soldier and not revealing his brothers' identities to the authorities. Three soldiers escorted Chan's brothers a distance away while the other three guarded Chan. One of the guards lit a cigarette and, while exhaling smoke into Chan's face, told him they would kill and eviscerate his two brothers and consume their livers. Chan was forced to watch his brothers' hands being bound, his being shot in the chest, and then his being eviscerated. Chan was overcome with panic, nausea, dizziness, and leg weakness. The soldiers released him, saying that this would be his fate if he committed any errors. On arriving at his village, Chan found the Khmer Rouge assembling the villagers to view the corpses of two people who tried to escape. A pile of limbs, severed at the knee and elbow, was next to the two heads. When the Vietnamese invaded his village a few hours later, he escaped and managed to reach the Thai border.

Once the therapist understood the etiology of Chan's panic attacks, the treatment plan could be established. Seven core elements were stressed during Chan's treatment:

1. Provision of information about PTSD and panic disorder, such as how trauma reminders and catastrophic cognitions generate panic attacks.
2. Training in muscle relaxation and diaphragmatic breathing procedures, including relaxation techniques.
3. Framing relaxation techniques as a form of mindfulness, while attending to specific sensory modalities (i.e., muscular tension and the kinesthetics of breathing).

4. Cognitive restructuring of fear networks, especially trauma memories and catastrophic misinterpretations of somatic sensations (including culture-related fears).
5. Interoceptive exposure (including reassociation) to anxiety-related sensations to treat panic attacks generated by catastrophic cognitions, interoceptive conditioning, and trauma associations to such sensations.
6. Provision of an emotional processing protocol to use during times of trauma recall (e.g., flashbacks), bringing about a shift from an attitude of pained acceptance to one of mindfulness.
7. Specifically exploring orthostatic panic, both the investigation of initiation sequences and the determination of catastrophic cognitions and trauma associations.

Chan was educated about the autonomic nervous system and how fright could generate symptoms such as cold extremities or dizziness. He also was educated about trauma-related disorders, including a discussion of TCMIE panic attacks. His catastrophic cognitions about somatic symptoms were addressed, and the trauma associations to dizziness and other symptoms elicited by standing were explored. As adjuncts to CBT, a selective serotonin reuptake inhibitor (paroxetine) and a benzodiazapine were provided as treatment adjuncts. After this treatment, Chan experienced complete resolution of his panic attacks and a substantial decrease in his PTSD severity, such that his symptoms no longer met diagnostic criteria for either disorder.

CONCLUSION

This chapter summarized issues related to conducting CBT with Asian Americans. The heterogeneity among Asian Americans, including their historical context and immigration history, was briefly presented. In addition, we provided clinicians with information on culture-specific issues such as religion, family structure and roles, gender roles, acculturation, ethnic and racial identity, values, language and cognitive styles, health beliefs, and social behaviors, and how these cultural factors may influence clients' behaviors and perceptions of therapy and the therapist. We also discussed the advantages and disadvantages of CBT with Asian American clients, along with therapist issues. Finally, a case example of successful CBT with an Asian American client was presented.

REFERENCES

American Psychiatric Association. (2000). *Diagnostic and statistical manual of mental disorders* (4th ed., text rev.). Washington, DC: Author.

American Psychological Association. (2002, August). *Guidelines on multicultural education, training, research, practice, and organizational change for psychologists*. Retrieved December 20, 2005, from http://www.apa.org/pi/multiculturalguidelines.pdf

Ancis, J. R., & Szymanski, D. M. (2001). Awareness of White privilege among White counseling trainees. *The Counseling Psychologist, 29*, 548–569.

Angelelli, C., & Geist-Martin, P. (2005). Enhancing culturally competent health communication: Constructing understanding between providers and culturally diverse patients. In E. Ray (Ed.), *Health communication in practice: A case study approach* (pp. 271–283). Mahwah, NJ: Erlbaum.

Atkinson, D. (2004). *Counseling American minorities* (6th ed.). New York: McGraw Hill.

Austria, A. (2003). People of Asian descent: Beyond myths and stereotypes. In J. Robinson & L. James (Eds.), *Diversity in human interactions: The tapestry of America* (pp. 63–75). London: Oxford University Press.

Barlow, D. H. (1988). *Anxiety and its disorders: The nature and treatment of anxiety and panic*. New York: Guilford Press.

Bradford, D. T., & Muñoz, A. (1993). Translation in bilingual psychotherapy. *Professional Psychology: Research and Practice, 24*, 52–61.

Chan, S. (1991). *Asian Americans: An interpretive history*. Boston: Twayne.

Chao, R. (2002). Parenting of Asians. In M. Bornstein (Ed.), *Handbook of parenting: Vol. 4. Social conditions and applied parenting* (pp. 59–93). Mahwah, NJ: Erlbaum.

Chin, J. L. (2000). *Relationships among Asian American women*. Washington, DC: American Psychological Association.

Chun, K., & Akutsu, P. (2003). Acculturation among ethnic minority families. In K. M. Chun, P. B. Balls-Organista, & G. Marin (Eds.), *Acculturation: Advances in theory, measurement, and applied research* (pp. 95–119). Washington, DC: American Psychological Association.

Clark, D. M. (1986). A cognitive approach to panic. *Behaviour Research and Therapy, 24*, 461–470.

Foa, E., & Kozak, M. J. (1986). Emotional processing of fear: Exposure to corrective information. *Psychological Bulletin, 99*, 20–35.

Gim, R. H., Atkinson, D. R., & Kim, S. J. (1991). Asian American acculturation, counselor ethnicity and cultural sensitivity, and ratings of counselors. *Journal of Counseling Psychology, 38*, 57–62.

Goh, M. (2004). Bias in counseling Hmong clients with limited English proficiency. In J. Chin (Ed.), *Psychology of prejudice and discrimination: Vol. 2. Ethnicity and multiracial identity* (pp. 109–136). Westport, CT: Greenwood.

Hannas, W. (1997). *Asia's orthographic dilemma*. Honolulu: University of Hawaii Press.

Hays, P. A. (2001). *Addressing cultural complexities in practice: A framework for clinicians and counselors*. Washington, DC: American Psychological Association.

Helms, J. E. (1992). *A race is a nice thing to have: A guide to being a White person or understanding the White persons in your life*. Topeka, KS: Content Communications.

Helms, J. E. (1994). The conceptualization of racial identity and other "racial" constructs. In E. J. Trickett, R. J. Watts, & D. Birman (Eds.), *Human diversity: Perspectives on people in context. The Jossey-Bass social and behavioral science series* (pp. 285–311). San Francisco: Jossey-Bass.

Helms, J. E., & Cook, D. A. (1999). *Using race and culture in counseling and psychotherapy: Theory and process.* Needham Heights, MA: Allyn & Bacon.

Helms, J. E., & Talleyrand, R. (1997). Race is not ethnicity. *American Psychologist, 52*, 1246–1247.

Hinton, D., Ba, P., Peou, S., & Um, K. (2000). Panic disorder among Cambodian refugees attending a psychiatric clinic: Prevalence and subtypes. *General Hospital Psychiatry, 22*, 437–444.

Hinton, D., Chau, H., Nguyen, L., Nguyen, M., Pham, T., Quinn, S., & Tran, M. (2001). Panic disorder among Vietnamese refugees attending a psychiatric clinic: Prevalence and subtypes. *General Hospital Psychiatry, 23*, 337–344.

Hinton, D. E., Chean, D., Pich, V., Safren, S. A., Hofmann, S. G., & Pollack, M. H. (in press). A randomized controlled trial of CBT for Cambodian refugees with treatment-resistant PTSD and panic attacks: A cross-over design. *Journal of Traumatic Stress.*

Hinton, D., Pham, T., Chau, H., Tran, M., & Hinton, S. (2003). "Hit by the wind" and temperature-shift panic among Vietnamese refugees. *Transcultural Psychiatry, 40*, 342–376.

Hinton, D., Pich, V., So, V., Pollack, M., Pitman, R., & Orr, S. (2004). The psychophysiology of orthostatic panic in Cambodian refugees attending a psychiatric clinic. *Journal of Psychopathology and Behavioral Assessment, 26*, 1–13.

Hinton, D., Um, K., & Ba, P. (2001). *Kyol goeu* ("wind overload"): Part I. A cultural syndrome of orthostatic panic among Khmer refugees. *Transcultural Psychiatry, 38*, 403–432.

Huang, J. (1996). Visual perception in Chinese people. In M. Bond (Ed.), *Handbook of Chinese psychology* (pp. 15–29). London: Oxford University Press.

Iwamasa, G. Y. (1996). Asian American issues in behavioral therapy: Current status, future directions and resources. *The Behavior Therapist, 19*, 136.

Iwamasa, G. Y. (1999). Behavior therapy and Asian Americans: Is there a commitment? *The Behavior Therapist, 22*, 196–206.

Iwamasa, G. Y. (2003). Recommendations for the treatment of Asian American/Pacific Islanders. In Council of National Psychological Associations for the Advancement of Ethnic Minority Issues (Eds.), *Psychological treatment of ethnic minority populations* (pp. 9–13). Washington, DC: Association of Black Psychologists.

Iwamasa, G. Y., & Yamada, A. M. (2001). Asian American acculturation and ethnic/racial identity: Research innovations in the new millennium—Introduction to the special issue. *Cultural Diversity and Ethnic Minority Psychology, 7*, 203–206.

Kazarian, S., & Evans, D. (2001). *Handbook of cultural health psychology.* San Diego, CA: Academic Press.

Kim, B. S. K., Atkinson, D. R., & Yang, P. H. (1999). The Asian values scale: Development, factor analysis, validation, and reliability. *Journal of Counseling Psychology, 46*, 342–352.

Kiselica, M. S. (1998). Preparing Anglos for the challenges and joys of multiculturalism. *The Counseling Psychologist, 26*, 5–21.

Lee, E. (1996). Asian American families: An overview. In M. McGoldrick, J. Giordano, & J. Pearce (Eds.), *Ethnicity and family therapy* (pp. 227–248). New York: Guilford Press.

Lee, E. (1997). *Working with Asian Americans: A guide for clinicians.* New York: Guilford Press.

Marín, G., & Gamba, R. (2003). Acculturation and changes in cultural values. In K. M. Chun, P. B. Balls-Organista, & G. Marin (Eds.). *Acculturation: Advances in theory, measurements, and applied research* (pp. 83–93). Washington, DC: American Psychological Association.

McIntosh, P. (1998). White privilege: Unpacking the invisible knapsack. In M. McGoldrick (Ed.), *Re-visioning family therapy: Race, culture, and gender in clinical practice* (pp. 147–152). New York: Guilford Press.

Moyerman, D. R., & Forman, B. D. (1992). Acculturation and adjustment: A meta-analytic study. *Hispanic Journal of Behavioral Sciences, 14*, 163–200.

Park, Y., & Kim, U. (2003). Locus of control, attributional style, and academic achievement: Comparative analysis of Korean Chinese and Chinese students. *Asian Journal of Social Psychology, 1*, 191–208.

Phinney, J. S. (2003). Ethnic identity and acculturation. In K. M. Chun, P. B. Organista, & G. Marin (Eds.), *Acculturation: Advances in theory, measurement, and applied research* (pp. 63–82). Washington, DC: American Psychological Association.

Shiraev, E., & Levy, D. (2004). *Cross-cultural psychology.* Boston: Allyn & Bacon.

Spector, R. (2004). *Cultural diversity in health and illness.* Upper Saddle River, NJ: Prentice Hall.

Sue, D. (2005). Asian American/Pacific Islander families in conflict. In W. George (Ed.), *Race, culture, psychology, and law* (pp. 257–268). Thousand Oaks, CA: Sage.

Sue, S., & Consolacion, T. (2003). Clinical psychology issues among Asian/Pacific Islander Americans. In J. S. Mio & G. Y. Iwamasa (Eds.), *Culturally diverse mental health: The challenges of research and resistance* (pp. 173–190). New York: Brunner-Routledge.

Sue, S., & Zane, N. (1987). The role of culture and cultural techniques in psychotherapy: A critique and reformulation. *American Psychologist, 42*, 37–45.

Taylor, S., Koch, W. J., & McNally, R. J. (1992). How does anxiety sensitivity vary across the anxiety disorders? *Journal of Anxiety Disorders, 6*, 249–259.

Tien, L. (2003). Confucian past, conflicted present: Working with Asian American families. In L. Silverstein & T. Goodrich (Eds.), *Feminist family therapy: Empowerment in social context* (pp. 135–145). Washington, DC: American Psychological Association.

Tseng, W. S. (2003). *Clinician's guide to cultural psychiatry*. San Diego, CA: Academic Press.

Uba, L. (1994). *Asian Americans*. New York: Guilford Press.

Uba, L. (2002). *A postmodern psychology of Asian Americans: Creating knowledge of a racial minority*. Albany: State University of New York Press.

U.S. Census Bureau. (2002, November). *Demographic trends in the 20th century: Census 2000 special reports*. Retrieved August 20, 2004, from http://www.census.gov/prod/2002pubs/censr-4.pdf

U.S. Census Bureau. (2003, May). *The Asian and Pacific Islander population in the United States: March 2001: Population characteristics*. Retrieved June 27, 2005, from http://www.census.gov/prod/2002pubs/censr-4.pdf

Wu, S. (2001). Parenting in Chinese-American families. In N. Webb (Ed.), *Culturally diverse parent–child and family relationship: A guide for social workers and other practitioners* (pp. 235–260). New York: Columbia University Press.

Yeh, K. (2003). The beneficial and harmful effects of filial piety: An integrative analysis. In K. S. Yang, K. K. Hwang, P. B. Pederson, & I. Daibo (Eds.), *Progress in Asian social psychology: Conceptual and empirical contributions* (pp. 67–82). Westport, CT: Praeger.

Yu, M. (1999). Multimodal assessment of Asian families. In K. Ng (Ed.), *Counseling Asian families from a systems perspective* (pp. 15–26). Alexandria, VA: American Counseling Association.

6

COGNITIVE–BEHAVIORAL THERAPY WITH PEOPLE OF ARAB HERITAGE

NUHA ABUDABBEH AND PAMELA A. HAYS

People of Arab heritage are among the most neglected in the psychological literature regarding assessment and psychotherapy. To date, there are no empirical studies of psychotherapy including cognitive–behavioral therapy (CBT) with Arab people. However, there is at least one book (Dwairy, 1998, on Palestinians) and a growing number of articles and chapters that offer suggestions for increasing the effectiveness of therapeutic practice based on their authors' clinical experiences (Abudabbeh, 1996, 2005a, 2005b, 2005c; Abudabbeh & Aseel, 1999; Abudabbeh & Nydell, 1993; Bushra, Khadivi, & Frewat-Nikowitz, in press; Dwairy & Van Sickle, 1996; El-Islam, 1982; Erickson & Al-Timimi, 2001; Hays, 1996, 2001, in press; Nassar-McMillan & Hakim-Larson, 2003; Sayed, 2003a, 2003b; Simon, 1996). This chapter draws from these sources as well as our own experiences working with people of Arab heritage, with a focus on Arab Americans. Although not all Arabs are Muslim, more attention will be given to Islam owing to many therapists' lesser familiarity with Muslim people and beliefs.

Pamela A. Hays would like to thank Jawed Zouari, Habib Hachem, Mohamed Sayed, and Fatima Al-Darmaki for their helpful feedback regarding this chapter.

UNDERSTANDING ARAB CULTURES

In beginning a discussion of Arab cultures, one must first define what is meant by the term *Arab*. Arab cultures are often described synonymously with Islam; however, these terms are not identical in meaning. For example, although most of the Arab League countries are predominantly Muslim, approximately one third of the population of Lebanon is Christian, nearly 6 million Egyptians belong to the Christian Coptic Orthodox Church, and large Christian populations can be found in Syria, Jordan, and Palestine (Abudabbeh & Aseel, 1999; The World Almanac, 2005). In addition, the majority of Arab Americans are Christian (Zogby, 1990). (Note that the term *Islam* refers to the religion, whereas *Muslim* refers to a member of the religion. The term *Mohammedan* is inaccurate and offensive, as it implies that one is a follower of the Prophet Mohammed rather than a follower of God.)

The most commonly used definition of Arab people includes those who can trace their origins to the nomadic tribes of Arabia and who speak Arabic as their native language. According to the Arab American Institute (n.d.), approximately 300 million Arabs live in 22 countries in the Middle East (Palestine, Jordan, Syria, Lebanon, and Iraq), the Gulf region (Saudi Arabia, Kuwait, Oman, Qatar, Bahrain, Yemen, and the United Arab Emirates), and Africa (Morocco, Algeria, Tunisia, Libya, Egypt, Sudan, Somalia, Djibouti, Comoros, and Mauritania). Arabic is the primary language of all of these countries, although each has its own dialect. The Arabic language is a source of pride for speakers who point to its beauty, subtlety, and poetry and who consider it one of Arab cultures' greatest achievements (Nydell, 1987).

Several historical events are important in an understanding of Arab cultures. The most significant of these is the life of the Prophet Mohammed (570–632 AD), the revelations he received that ultimately comprised the book of the Qu'ran, and the emergence of the religion of Islam. The Prophet Mohammed called on the people of the Arabian Peninsula to submit to the will of God and united the tribes of Arabia in the name of Islam (the term *Islam* means *surrender* in Arabic, as in surrendering to the will of God). At the time, people were worshiping pagan gods, women were considered property, and only male descendants were recognized for inheritance purposes. The social reforms introduced by Islam were thus considered extraordinary and included the obligation of husbands to provide for their wives and children, inheritance rights for women as well as men, financial independence for wives, and rights for women after divorce or the death of their husband (Lamchichi, 2003).

From the 7th through the 10th centuries, Islam and the Arabic language spread as far as China in the East and Spain in the West (Abudabbeh, 1996). This period was known as the Golden Era of Islam owing to the extraordinary cultural advances that occurred, including the development of

Arabic literature, poetry, philosophy, architecture, mathematics, science, hospitals, and medical practices (Ashrif, 1987; Hourani, 1970). This flourishing of Arab Muslim culture occurred at the same time that the period known as the Dark Ages was occurring in Europe. Later, during the European renaissance, many of the scientific and literary developments of the Arabs and Muslims were claimed as European, a practice that persists to the present day in academia and public education (Ashrif, 1987).

The last Muslim empire was that of the Ottomans, with its capital in Istanbul, which reached its zenith during the 16th century and thereafter began to decline. During the late 1800s and early 1900s, the decline accelerated as European powers began colonizing the Middle East and North Africa (e.g., Algeria, Tunisia, and Morocco by France, Egypt by England, and Libya by Italy). In 1916, the British and French divided the remaining area into zones of permanent influence via the Sykes–Picot Agreement, and the British took control of Palestine and pledged in the Balfour Declaration of 1917 to support a Jewish national home in Palestine "provided this did not prejudice the civil and religious rights of the other inhabitants of the country" (Hourani, 1970, p. 318). During and after World War II, Jewish immigration to Palestine increased dramatically, as Jewish refugees fled Nazi persecution. In 1947, the United Nations General Assembly voted to partition Palestine into an Arab and a Jewish state. Britain ended its protectorate status over Palestine and withdrew. The Jewish population declared the existence of the independent state of Israel in 1948. The Arab population rejected the partition, and war ensued. During this period, over 70% of Palestinians were expelled from their homeland and became refugees to the Israeli military-occupied territories of the West Bank and Gaza, the surrounding Arab countries of Jordan, Syria, Lebanon, and Egypt, and other countries around the world (Dwairy, 1998).

Since 1991, sociopolitical events profoundly affecting Arab people have included the Gulf War, involving a U.S.-led coalition against the Iraqi invasion of Kuwait; the attacks on the World Trade Towers and the Pentagon on September 11, 2001 (henceforth 9/11); the U.S. invasion of Iraq in 2003; and more recently the abuse of prisoners by U.S. soldiers at Abu Ghraib. Unilateral actions by the United States (i.e., the invasion of Iraq without seeking United Nations support) have been perceived by many in the Arab world as an attack on Arabs and Muslims and symbolic of the arrogance of a world power that acts with only its own interests in mind (i.e., hegemony in an oil-rich region).

Obviously, such events place Arab Americans in an exceedingly difficult position. Even before 9/11, negative stereotypes and prejudice against Arabs were commonplace (Mansfield, 1990; Suleiman, 1999). Since then, people of Arab heritage have been further marginalized. After 9/11, the FBI reported that hate crimes against Muslims increased 1,600% and against people of Arab heritage by 500% (Zogby, 2003). Dominant cultural biases in the media are commonplace (Hays, in press). Since passage of the Patriot Act in 2001, Arab Americans also face the fear of possible questioning, arrest, and deportation.

Arab Americans

Arab Americans are estimated to comprise approximately 3.5 million people in the United States today (Arab American Institute, n.d.). The largest concentration of Arab Americans can be found in Detroit, Los Angeles, New York/New Jersey, Chicago, and the Washington, DC area. The majority of Arab Americans are Christian (Catholic 42%, Protestant 12%, Orthodox 23%), and 23% are Muslim (Arab American Institute, n.d.).

The first wave of Arab immigration to the United States occurred between 1890 and 1940 and consisted mainly of merchants and farmers who emigrated primarily from Lebanon and Syria for economic reasons. They were mostly Christian, poor, uneducated, and did not identify themselves as Arabs (Abudabbeh, 1996, 2005b). These individuals assimilated into U.S. culture with less difficulty than did subsequent immigrants (Suleiman, 1999).

The second wave of Arab immigrants began after World War II and consisted of many university students and professionals seeking refuge in the United States after the creation of the state of Israel or for other political reasons. This group included a larger percentage of Palestinians and Muslims who also had a stronger Arab identity (Abudabbeh, 1996, 2005b).

A third wave began after the 1967 Arab–Israeli war. These individuals came from a variety of Arab countries primarily to escape political conflict in their countries of origin. They included more Lebanese (as a result of the civil war that lasted 17 years) and Iraqis following the Gulf War. They too have tended to hold a strong Arab identity that, along with the multicultural movement in the United States, the Arab–Israeli conflict, and U.S.-led war on Iraq, contributed to the increasing cultural separateness of Arab Americans (Abudabbeh, 2005b).

Approximately 85% of Arab Americans hold a high school diploma, and more than 40% hold a bachelor's degree or higher (compared with 24% of the U.S. population). Approximately 17% hold a postgraduate degree (twice the U.S. average). About 73% of working Arab Americans maintain jobs in managerial, professional, technical, sales, or administrative fields. In sum, Arab Americans are a highly educated, economically successful population in relation to the American norm (Arab American Institute, n.d.).

Cultural Values and Beliefs

One of the core values shared by people of diverse Arab cultures concerns the centrality of family. The Arab family is typically patriarchal, organized hierarchically by age and gender (Barakat, 1993; Sharabi, 1988). Final authority rests with the father, whose power and responsibilities place him at the top of the pyramid. Both men and women are expected to contribute to the support and maintenance of the family unit. Fathers are expected to provide for the family, mothers to care for their husbands and children, and children to honor their parents. In Arab countries, the extended family often provides a great deal of emotional, social, and financial support. The actions of one family member reflect on the entire family. Members are expected to place the family's welfare above their own, and family values often include self-sacrifice and the pursuit of satisfaction through the happiness of others (Abudabbeh, 1996).

Although family cohesion has been challenged by rapid social change, it continues to be the primary socioeconomic unit in Arab cultures, including among Arab Americans (Barakat, 1993). Outside the United States, arranged marriage is still the norm, with parents choosing their child's future spouse. Ideally, this process involves input from both the young woman and man and is intended to ensure that the two families are as well matched as the individuals. A dowry is paid by the man to his future wife, which is interpreted by some to be a form of financial insurance for her in the case of divorce. However, in practice, the dowry is frequently given to the wife's family and thus provides her with little security. Moreover, in most Arab countries it is relatively easy for a man to divorce his wife but nearly impossible for a woman to divorce her husband without his consent (Barakat, 1993).

Within Islam, marriage is considered a sacred ceremony, central to the growth and stability of Arab culture. A Muslim man is allowed to marry a non-Muslim woman as long as she belongs to the "people of the Book" (i.e., is Jewish or Christian). Traditionally, women join the family of their husband, and it is assumed that the woman will become Muslim. A Muslim woman is not allowed to marry a non-Muslim man (Esposito, 1982), although a non-Muslim man can convert to marry a Muslim woman. The Qu'ran gives a man the option to have more than one wife as long as he can treat all of them equally; however, it also states that a man can never maintain fairness and equality between women no matter how hard he tries. Thus, polygyny is controversial, with some arguing that the Qu'ran supports it while others counter that the Qu'ran discourages it. (*Polygyny* refers to the right of a man to have more than one wife; *polygamy* refers to either spouse's right.) Although polygyny is legal in most Arab countries (with the exception of Tunisia), in practice it is now relatively rare (Barakat, 1993, p. 112).

Within the marriage, the husband holds the ultimate authority and connection to the outside world; however, the wife can wield a great deal of power within the family. This is particularly true when polygyny is not an option and divorce is considered shameful for both parties. For example, in Tunisia, divorce may be seen as a sign that a man is unable to "satisfy" his wife. A woman may express disagreement with her husband's behavior by going to her parents' house for a day (or several days, depending on the severity of his transgression) without first fixing dinner for him and, if she is especially angry, without taking the children with her (Hays & Zouari, 1995). In tightly knit rural communities where few behaviors are private, the wife's brief departure serves as an embarrassment (or source of public amusement) that pressures the husband to make amends. Erickson and Al-Timimi (2001) cited a similar example in which an Arab American homemaker briefly left home at mealtime without fixing the family's dinner in response to their complaints about the meal being overdone the night before. The family recognized this as a nonverbal communication that they needed to be more respectful of her contributions. The point here is that therapists need to be cautious about assuming powerlessness on the part of Arab women (Friedman & Pines, 1992; Hays, in press).

Children are considered an essential part of marriage and one of the primary joys of family life. Child rearing is relatively lax compared with European American norms, with young children frequently indulged, and boys often favored. Common forms of discipline include shaming, instilling fear that something bad will happen if the child misbehaves, and physical punishment. Children are expected to obey their parents, and it is not uncommon to observe parents lecturing children rather than inviting them to discuss a problem. Rote learning is valued over innovative forms of self-expression. Children are encouraged to maintain close ties with their families through adulthood and are not encouraged to be individualistic or separate from their parents. (An exception to this pattern can be found in rural Bedouin families in which children are encouraged to be more individualistic [Barakat, 1993].) Younger children spend more time with their mother than with their father and are likely to be more open with her, at times using her as the messenger or go-between with their father (Abudabbeh, 1996).

Identity and Acculturation

Although the values described earlier are common among Arab people, therapists need to be aware of within-group differences related to national identity and social status. Each Arab country (i.e., those in which a majority of the inhabitants are of Arab heritage) has its own unique constellation of values, beliefs, and traditions. These differences have emerged in the context of particular geographical locations, natural resources, and political histories. For example, the French colonization of Morocco, Algeria, and Tunisia contributed to the strong French influence in these countries and the greater tendency for individuals to immigrate to France or French-speaking Québec than to the United States. In contrast, the British colonization of Iraq, Jordan, Egypt, and the Arabian Peninsula has resulted in closer economic ties and greater immigration to the United Kingdom and United States.

Social status in Arab societies is linked to social class; however, social class involves a more complex and dynamic set of variables that include but extend beyond income, occupation, and education (Barakat, 1993). Land ownership and occupational autonomy (i.e., working for oneself, for example, as a business owner) have traditionally conferred a higher status, and currently, particular professions often hold an especially high status (e.g., engineer, physician, attorney). Religious piety and a familial connection to the Prophet Mohammed have also historically contributed to the status of a family. Greater respect is typically given to and expected by individuals who are older, well educated, wealthier, and religious, as well as to those who belong to a family that has "a good name" (i.e., a reputation for integrity based on benevolent works or religiousness). The practice of arranged marriages tends to reinforce class differences.

In recent decades, oil revenues have also contributed to the socioeconomic differentiation of Arab cultures. For example, the relatively rapid growth of the economies of Qatar, the United Arab Emirates, Kuwait, and Saudi Arabia has led to increased urbanization, opportunities for international travel, and greater exposure to Western ideas, goods, and media for middle- and upper-middle-class citizens of these countries. The disparity in wealth has resulted in the loss via emigration of many well-educated and skilled laborers from the poorer countries (e.g., Morocco, Algeria, Tunisia, Egypt, Jordan, and Palestine) to the United States, Canada, Europe, and the wealthier Arab nations (Barakat, 1993).

One other social division requires mention, and that is the distinction between the settled rural populations and the culturally nomadic Bedouins. The Bedouins originated in the Arabian Peninsula and migrated to other parts of the Arab world with the spread of Islam. During the last few decades, Bedouins in most Arab nations have been pressured by their national governments to settle into permanent dwellings and communities. Bedouins are seen by some Arab people as a threat to "civilized" lifestyles because of the lesser importance they place on class differences and their lack of religious establishment. However, others consider them to be the embodiment of the core Arab values of tribal solidarity, chivalry, hospitality, and simplicity (Barakat, 1993). In contrast to these shared Arab values, Bedouin society is also known for its emphasis on individual independence, autonomy, and freedom (Barakat, 1993).

Within the United States, an individual's national and ethnic identity will often be related to their generational status (i.e., how far back their roots in the United States extend) and degree of connection to their country of origin. It is not uncommon to find Arab Americans whose family members immigrated several generations ago (during the first wave from Syria or Lebanon) and who are assimilated into European American culture; these individuals tend to be Republican and conservative in their political affiliation (Erickson & Al-Timimi, 2001). In contrast, more recently immigrated individuals often identify strongly with their national origins. Therapists may also encounter individuals who are bilingual and identify with both cultures. Therapists should not be surprised if Arab clients from these latter two groups appear distrustful. Autocratic leadership and the abuse of civil rights in clients' countries of origin, as well as governmental actions within the United States (e.g., the Patriot Act), may contribute to distrust that can extend to the therapist who is seen as an authority figure (Bushra et al., in press). Furthermore, when a client's refugee status is a result of direct U.S. intervention or the use of U.S. resources to facilitate the collapse of their country, as in the case of Iraq, it should not be surprising that clients feel angry toward the United States and toward the American therapist (Nassar-McMillan & Hakim-Larson, 2003).

Because political histories and current events can strongly affect clients' attitudes toward therapy, it is essential that therapists consider the interaction of their own identities with those of their clients. For example, the initial feelings and beliefs held by a recently immigrated Christian Palestinian client toward a European American Christian therapist will be different from those of a fourth-generation Syrian Muslim client toward a European American Jewish therapist. In some cases, a similar identity (e.g., when both therapist and client are Arab or Muslim or Christian) can create a sense of connection; however, therapists must also be aware of the possibility of over-emphasizing similarities and missing important differences (Chin, 1994). In sum, the more the therapist knows about the political history of and current events in a client's specific Arab culture, the more able he or she will be to understand and address the client's concerns and reservations regarding the therapist and therapy.

COGNITIVE–BEHAVIORAL THERAPY WITH ARAB CLIENTS

Therapists need to be aware of specific issues when counseling Arab clients. A few of these include pretherapy considerations of their own attitudes and knowledge of people of Arab heritage, commonly presented problems, establishing a respectful and caring relationship, and the advantages and disadvantages of CBT with Arab clients. We address each in the following sections.

Pretherapy Work

The need for therapists to examine their own attitudes is as important with Arab people as with any other group. However, given the pervasiveness of anti-Arab sentiment in the United States today, along with the lack of clinical information regarding Arab populations, U.S. therapists will have to work extra hard to obtain information that is accurate and helpful. Toward this goal, several suggestions are offered. First, therapists are advised to engage in an ongoing process of individually oriented work that includes introspection, self-questioning, research, and reading across disciplines. Erickson and Al-Timimi (2001) provided a list of informational resources regarding Arab people. This individually oriented work is necessary but not sufficient for uncovering one's own biases and knowledge gaps.

A second suggestion involves the use of critical thinking about one's sources of information. The following questions can help to facilitate this process. Who wrote (or directed or funded) this article or movie or program? What is its purpose or goal? Who is represented in this report, and who is not represented? What voices are heard or not heard? An additional source of information that can facilitate critical thinking is supervision by or consultation with an Arab or Arab American therapist.

A third suggestion is to seek out experiences and relationships with people of Arab heritage, if this is a possibility in the therapist's social environment. It is often only through close relationships with people that one learns the subtleties of individual and family variations within a culture. At the same time, it is important to remember that power differentials can affect what and how much a person will share. In relationships with people who are in a less powerful position than oneself (e.g., clients, students, support staff), the person in the less powerful position may feel less able to speak openly. Some of the best learning comes from intimate relationships in which both parties hold enough power to honestly and safely share their feelings and thoughts (Hays, 2001).

Commonly Presented Problems

As is true in many other groups, mental illness carries a heavy stigma in Arab cultures. In more traditional households, attempts to hide psychological problems may be related to a desire to protect the family's reputation or concern about a young person's marriage opportunities if the problem becomes known by others (Al-Darmaki & Sayed, 2004). Individuals may also be unaware of mental health treatment options, particularly those who have emigrated from countries where psychological services were unavailable.

When Arab people do come to counseling, it is often with the expectation that the therapist will be in an authoritative position, offering specific suggestions and providing help with problem solving. In Arab countries where few psychological services exist, people will often present with somatic complaints to their physician (El-Islam, 1982; Racy, 1970). A similar tendency exists among Arab Americans. Among the latter, typical problems presented include the following (Abudabbeh, 1996):

- generational conflict between parents who expect their children to follow traditional norms of behavior and children who feel pulled between these expectations and the norms of their U.S. peers;

- gender-related conflicts between spouses as women become exposed to a wider range of lifestyles, behaviors, and opportunities;
- struggles between parents and adult children over the choice of a spouse, with parents insisting on their right to choose for their child, and the dilemma when a child is in love with someone the parents do not choose;
- cross-cultural marriages that often involve conflicts over child-rearing practices, spousal responsibilities, and behavioral expectations; and
- legal entanglements related to diverse problems, such as asylum seeking, competency to stand trial, or sexual abuse.

Nassar-McMillan and Hakim-Larson (2003) noted the increasing number of Arab Americans diagnosed with posttraumatic stress disorder. In a survey of therapists working at a community services agency serving a large Arab American population, many individuals were reported to be exhibiting severe postwar trauma. These individuals were primarily Iraqi refugees and immigrants from the Lebanese civil war. Similarly, Dwairy (1998) described high rates of trauma among Palestinian children, noting that 40% of the Palestinians killed during the Intifada have been children. Since 1987, childhood problems of depression, fear, sleep disturbances, and fighting with others have increased by 15% to 26% over the pre-Intifada occupation levels, which were already high (Dwairy, 1998, p. 98).

Establishing a Respectful and Caring Relationship

As noted earlier, Arab people pride themselves on their generosity and hospitality. These values often enter the therapy relationship in the form of clients giving the therapist small gifts or inviting the therapist to the client's home for a meal. Within-gender physical touch and kissing on both cheeks as a form of greeting are common (i.e., with women touching only women, men touching only men, the exception being within the family wherein men and women may also use this form of greeting). Questions about one's marital status, children, country of origin, or family name (if the latter two appear Arab) are to be expected. Turning down a gift, shrugging off a hug, or refusing to answer such questions will often be perceived as rejection or arrogance (Bushra et al., in press). Therapists are advised to be responsive to these preferences and flexible in their adaptation of mainstream procedures. For example, Abudabbeh and Aseel (1999) suggested that therapists be willing to go to clients' homes, and in cases of family therapy in which one family member does not want to attend, to call and attempt to persuade that family member to join the family session.

Advantages and Disadvantages of CBT With Arab Clients

Several authors have articulated the characteristics of CBT that make it well suited for work with Arab people. These include CBT's structured educational approach, its emphasis on problem solving, and its focus on the here-and-now (Abudabbeh, 1996; Abudabbeh & Aseel, 1999; Erickson & Al-Timimi, 2001; Nassar-McMillan & Hakim-Larson, 2003). In addition, CBT is adaptable to work with couples, families, as well as individuals. This is especially important given the tendency of Arab Americans to present with family and marital problems. Finally, CBT's emphasis on the enhancement and reinforcement of strengths and social supports fits well with Arab values regarding family involvement. The latter also communicates an appreciation of Arab culture, which is especially important in the United States during this time when Arab people face negative portrayals of their culture in the media on a daily basis.

Therapists also need to be aware of the potential limitations of CBT with Arab people. The term itself, cognitive–behavioral therapy, emphasizes the cognitive and behavioral aspects of the situation, and thus may be interpreted by Arab clients as overlooking areas of life that they consider central, namely family and religion. In addition, CBT is permeated with European American cultural norms, including the high value placed on personal independence and autonomy, behavioral change, and rationality (Hays, 1995). In contrast, many Arab clients place a higher priority on family interdependence and harmony, patience, acceptance, and faith. Finally, cognitive restructuring may be seen as offensive and disrespectful if it is conducted in a confrontational manner, or if it is aimed at challenging core cultural beliefs. The following case example provides suggestions for avoiding or minimizing these problems.

CASE EXAMPLE

Fatima was a 35-year-old married Arab American woman who presented with symptoms of depression (poor sleep, decreased appetite, irritability, and a sense of foreboding regarding the future). At the time of the assessment, she was 5 months pregnant with her first child. Her husband, Ahmed, accompanied her to the appointment. The Arab American therapist noted that Ahmed was dressed in Western clothes, and Fatima was wearing a long-sleeved shirt, long skirt, and headscarf.

Fatima told the therapist that she was the youngest daughter in a family of six children, all of whom were married with children. Her Palestinian parents had emigrated to the United States before she was born, and she grew up in a large midwestern city, attended public schools, was an honor student, and completed a bachelor's degree in science education. She worked as a teacher for several years before marrying her Palestinian husband. He had come to the United States as a college student on scholarships and obtained permanent residency after they married. Both she and her husband defined themselves as devout Muslims, and before moving had maintained an active connection to a local mosque. Fatima said that her family was "not very religious," but she considered them close and missed seeing them on a daily basis. Her husband's family was living in Jordan, and they spoke occasionally by phone.

Fatima and Ahmed had been married approximately 6 months when she became pregnant. Fatima had just ended her teaching year, and they agreed that she would not renew her contract. During the summer, they moved out of her parents' home into their own house in a city approximately 2 hours away. The commute for Ahmed took the same amount of time that it had before the move. Ahmed worked long hours in a biotech company and enjoyed his work, but this meant that Fatima was alone much of the time. They both acknowledged missing her family, neither had friends in the new place, and since the move they had begun having arguments. Fatima was not looking forward to the baby's birth, although Ahmed said that he thought things would improve because she would be busier with the baby. Still, he was concerned that she was not happy and had difficulty carrying out her normal activities of housecleaning, cooking, and grocery shopping.

At the end of the assessment, the therapist summarized her perspective beginning with the stressors she had heard from Fatima and Ahmed, along with those that she inferred on the basis of her knowledge of Arab Muslim culture. These included the stress of a new marriage with all of the interpersonal adaptations required, the pregnancy (a physical and possibly psychological stressor), the move to a new city, and the losses of Fatima's family's daily support, their involvement with the mosque of their former town, and Fatima's work and collegial friendships. The three of them talked about the stressful nature of these changes. Fatima and Ahmed had not previously recognized the degree of stress involved because, as they noted, many of the changes involved good things.

Next, the therapist described the strengths and supports she saw in their lives, namely, their concern for one another, their caring families, their financial stability which she attributed to a sense of family responsibility, their faith, and their strong identities as Muslims, including their connection to the Muslim community. With regard to the last, she did not say "former connection" because although they were no longer involved in the mosque of their prior home, they still had a strong sense of connection to the *umma*, or worldwide community of Muslims. Fatima and Ahmed seemed to appreciate the therapist's recognition of these positive aspects of their lives, particularly those related to their faith.

The therapist then described her approach as one that involved "problem-solving regarding those things that a person can change, and learning to cope better with those things that you can't or choose not to." Regarding the former, she said "practical problem solving often involves figuring out a way to change something in your environment to make the problem less stressful." She used the example of their current lack of social support and emphasized how important interactions with family and friends are for people to be happy and healthy. She said that counseling could be useful in helping them figure out ways to increase their support.

Regarding problems that cannot be solved by changing something in one's environment, she explained how cognitive restructuring works without using the term itself. She said: "One thing we know in psychology is that what we think affects the way we feel. Oftentimes, people are unaware of what they're thinking and how their thoughts are affecting their stress level." She gave an example in which a wife calls her husband when he is at work, and the husband is short with her, saying that he has to get back to work.

> If the wife thinks to herself, "He'd rather be at work than with me, I know he doesn't really love me," she will probably feel pretty low, and the more she tells herself this, the worse she will feel to the point that she may be all upset and crying by the time he gets home. On the other hand, if she tells herself, "He must be feeling really pressured at work. I must have caught him at a bad time," she may feel some concern for him but will not work herself into such an emotional state that she starts questioning her marriage and his love for her.

The therapist asked Fatima and Ahmed if this made sense to them. They both said yes and Fatima added "I know I do that." The therapist continued:

> Well, we all have tendencies to say these kinds of things to ourselves sometimes, especially when we're under a lot of stress or experiencing some big transitions in our lives. Counseling can be helpful because it gets people to start to recognize the negative and hurtful things that may be pulling them down or increasing their anxiety. It can also help in figuring out more positive and helpful things to say to yourself. Now this may sound pretty easy, and in my experience most people are able to do this part, but the hard part comes in keeping it up. And that's another place that counseling can be helpful. You know that you're coming back in a week so you're more apt to practice it during the week, because you know that I'm going to ask you whether it helped or not.

The therapist explained to Fatima and Ahmed that she could work together with them as a couple or individually with Fatima, and that her recommendation was to try two to three couple sessions first, then if it felt appropriate, she would meet alone with Fatima for three to four sessions. She said that she did not recommend an evaluation for medication at this point given Fatima's pregnancy and the possibility that counseling might help without it. However, she said, after the pregnancy, medication could be an option if the depression persisted. Fatima and Ahmed agreed to follow her suggestions and returned together the next week.

Environmental and Behavioral Interventions

In the first counseling session, the therapist helped Fatima and Ahmed to generate a broad range of possible solutions to their need for more support. It was explained that this increased support could help to improve their relationship and Fatima's mood. Their ideas included moving back to live with Fatima's parents, Ahmed looking for a different job that would require fewer hours, or Ahmed decreasing his hours at the current job. The therapist asked questions aimed at helping them to look at the advantages and disadvantages of each possible change. Ahmed insisted that decreasing his hours was not possible given the type of job he had, and he did not want to look for another job. Fatima was accepting of his decision on this. Through the questioning process, they remembered the reasons they had decided to move out of her parents' home (not enough physical space for them and a baby, along with some times of irritation because of the lack of privacy). They did not rule out moving back to the area in which her parents lived but decided that for the time being this would not be a sound financial decision given the purchase of their new house. (Another financial responsibility they had both committed to was sending money on a monthly basis to Ahmed's family in Jordan.)

Through the course of this brainstorming process, Fatima and Ahmed recognized their need to find a new mosque, a task that they were able to accomplish within a couple of weeks. However, it was clear that although making friends would be helpful, Fatima still missed her family. Attention was given to ways that she might increase her family connections without moving. They came up with a plan whereby Fatima would visit her family overnight once during the week when Ahmed was working long hours anyway. Ahmed was quite self-sufficient when it came to preparing his own meals because he had lived in the United States as a single young man for several years before marrying, and cooking had been one of the most enjoyable ways he stayed connected to his culture. In addition, Fatima's mother came to stay with them every other week on a weeknight so that Fatima and Ahmed still had some time alone together on weekends. Fatima and Ahmed continued to visit her family for celebrations and family dinners at least once a month.

It is important to note that the therapist did not push Fatima and Ahmed to decrease their connections with her family. Whereas a mainstream European American perspective might have emphasized the need for this young couple to "individuate," this therapist recognized that they needed more support and that enlisting her family's support was the most culturally congruent strategy, particularly in that the family was able and willing to be involved. Obviously, the couple's plan was possible because the physical distance was not too great. Yet even if the family had been much farther away, the point would still be the same. That is, the therapist would have helped the couple to enlist greater family support rather than discourage it.

Similarly, the therapist raised questions for Ahmed and Fatima to think about regarding his commitment to his job, but once they made their preferences clear, she did not push either of them on this point. Although the therapist preferred the economic independence she had in her own marriage, she did not want to impose her value priorities on Ahmed and Fatima. Rather, she accepted their more traditional relationship. She was aware that in such relationships, couples often have more realistic expectations regarding what needs their spouses can and cannot meet. Such realism is rooted in traditional Arab marriages in which each spouse's social needs are met primarily within the family, by other same-gender family members. Although immigration and the exportation of Western values into Arab countries are changing this pattern, it was still a preferred mode for Fatima and Ahmed and it was possible given the proximity of her family.

Cognitive Restructuring

Regarding the second part of the therapist's approach (i.e., learning to cope better with those things that do not have an environmental solution), the therapist met individually with Fatima to find out more about her feelings and thoughts regarding marriage, her role as wife and mother, and the loss of her work outside the home. Fatima shared that she had always expected to stay home with her children as her mother had done. She added that for many years, she had felt strong pressure to marry and have children, and now at the age of 35, she was long past the "ideal" age. However, her mother had never been to college or worked outside the home, and Fatima found that she enjoyed her studies and work. At the same time, she said that her mother strongly encouraged her career, and Fatima had the feeling that her mother experienced a great deal of vicarious satisfaction through Fatima's professional accomplishments.

As the therapist asked questions aimed at helping her to articulate these expectations, Fatima was able to recognize the strongly conflicting messages she had received from her family and culture. These included "As a wife and mother, I should be devoted to my husband's and children's well-being" and "As an Arab American woman, I have to take advantage of all the opportunities that were never available to my mother, and I should achieve as much as possible to make my parents proud."

The therapist did not challenge the idea that these were good or acceptable things to want (i.e., the validity of the beliefs) but rather asked questions that raised Fatima's awareness of the subtle imperative in these statements (i.e., the "shoulds" and "have to's"). In addition, she questioned the helpfulness of such absolute expectations. They talked about the variety of adaptations Fatima saw other women making, including women doing career-oriented work outside the home and inside the home, single mothers, and women focused on homemaking. The therapist asked if Fatima could think of any women she knew who were completely devoted to their families but not particularly happy. Fatima could think of one such woman and was able to make a link to the idea that one needs to take care of oneself to be a better mother and wife. She eventually reworded her earlier statement to say "I want to be a loving wife and mother who cares for her husband and children, and I need to take care of my spiritual, physical, and social needs in order to be a good wife and mother."

The therapist encouraged Fatima to think about the ways in which she might take better care of herself in each of the domains she mentioned. Regarding her spirituality, Fatima said now that she was going to the new mosque, she was praying more regularly again and felt that this was good spiritual self-care. Regarding her physical self, she said that she ate healthy food according to Muslim dietary rules, but she acknowledged her need for more exercise. However, she did not want to make a change in this area at the time, and the therapist did not push her to do so.

Regarding her social needs, Fatima expressed a desire to talk about the loss of her work and friends. She had not thought about the possibility that she would miss her work and coworkers until after she was gone. However, now she could see that she missed the social activity as well as the sense of accomplishment. Regarding the latter, it was apparent to her and the therapist that she had a strong achievement orientation, as do many Arab Americans, particularly first- and second-generation immigrants.

As Fatima explored her beliefs about what exactly would be involved in being a good mother and wife, she recognized that she could probably be both, and work outside the home, at least part time. As this idea became more real to her and as she talked more about it, her mood began to improve. She knew it would be several months until she could seriously explore part-time work possibilities (because of the upcoming birth), but having the goal in mind gave her something to look forward to. She talked with Ahmed, and he agreed on the condition that she wait until the baby was a year old. She preferred 6 months but agreed to wait with the intention that she would begin exploring possibilities before then. In the final session held with Ahmed and Fatima about 2 months before the baby's birth, they were regularly attending services at the new mosque, Fatima had met a new friend at the mosque who was also pregnant, the visitation plan with her family was working well, and Fatima was looking forward to returning to part-time work in a year. Ahmed continued to work long hours but felt more satisfied with Fatima and the marriage.

CONCLUSION

This case illustrates some of the key components of culturally responsive CBT with people of Arab heritage. These include the following:

- a focus on the present and on the problems as presented by the clients;
- an educational approach (e.g., the therapist's explanation of the relationship between stressors, social support, and mental health);
- respect for the clients' assessment of their own situation and needs;
- flexibility (in this case, a willingness to see the clients both individually and as a couple depending on their needs);
- behavioral interventions used to solve environmentally based problems; and
- cognitive restructuring that challenged the helpfulness (i.e., utility) of beliefs rather than their validity.

It is clear that this is a new area that requires a great deal of clinical research to clarify what works and what does not with the diversity of people who define themselves as Arab and Arab American. This chapter has attempted to provide some beginning suggestions for this work.

REFERENCES

Abudabbeh, N. (1996). Overview on Arab families. In M. McGoldrick, J. Giordano, & J. K. Pearce (Eds.), *Ethnicity and family therapy* (pp. 333–346). New York: Guilford Press.

Abudabbeh, N. (2005a). Arab families. In E. Congress & M. Gonzalez (Eds.), *Multicultural perspectives in working with families* (pp. 228–241). New York: Springer Publishing Company.

Abudabbeh, N. (2005b). Arab families: An overview. In M. McGoldrick, J. Giordano, & N. G. Preto (Eds.), *Ethnicity and family therapy* (pp. 423–436). New York: Guilford Press.

Abudabbeh, N. (2005c). Palestinian families. In M. McGoldrick, J. Giordano, & N. G. Preto (Eds.), *Ethnicity and family therapy* (pp. 487–498). New York: Guilford Press.

Abudabbeh, N., & Aseel, H. A. (1999). Transcultural counseling and Arab Americans. In J. McFadden (Ed.), *Transcultural counseling: Bilateral and international perspectives* (pp. 283–296). Alexandria, VA: American Counseling Association.

Abudabbeh, N., & Nydell, M. (1993). Transcultural counseling and Arab Americans. In J. McFadden (Ed.), *Transcultural counseling: Bilateral and international perspectives* (pp. 261–284). Alexandria, VA: American Counseling Association.

Al-Darmaki, F., & Sayed, M. A. (2004, July). *Practicing polymorphism in traditional gender-role Emirates: Conflicts and challenges*. Paper presented at the 112th Annual Convention of the American Psychological Association, Honolulu, HI.

Arab American Institute. (n.d.). *Arab American demographics*. Retrieved November 14, 2005, from http://www.aaiusa.org/demographics.htm

Ashrif, S. (1987). Eurocentrism and myopia in science teaching. *Multicultural Teaching, 5,* 28–30.

Barakat, H. (1993). *The Arab world: Society, culture, and state.* Berkeley: University of California Press.

Bushra, A., Khadivi, A., & Frewat-Nikowitz, S. (in press). Multiple perspectives on the Middle Eastern identity in psychotherapy. In J. C. Muran (Ed.), *Dialogues on difference: Diversity studies of the therapeutic relationship.* Washington, DC: American Psychological Association.

Chin, J. L. (1994). Psychodynamic approaches. In L. Comas-Díaz & B. Greene (Eds.), *Women of color: Integrating ethnic and gender identities in psychotherapy* (pp. 194–222). New York: Guilford Press.

Dwairy, M. A. (1998). *Cross-cultural counseling: The Arab-Palestinian case.* Binghamton, NY: Haworth Press.

Dwairy, M. A., & Van Sickle, T. (1996). Western psychotherapy and traditional Arabic societies. *Clinical Psychology Review, 16,* 231–249.

El-Islam, F. (1982). Arabic cultural psychiatry. *Transcultural Psychiatric Research Review, 9,* 5–24.

Erickson, C. D., & Al-Timimi, N. R. (2001). Providing mental health services to Arab Americans: Recommendations and considerations. *Cultural Diversity and Ethnic Minority Psychology, 7,* 308–327.

Esposito, J. L. (1982). *Women in Muslim family law.* Syracuse, NY: Syracuse University Press.

Friedman, A., & Pines, A. (1992). Increase in Arab women's perceived power in the second half of life. *Sex Roles, 26*(1/2), 1–9.

Hays, P. A. (1995). Multicultural applications of cognitive behavior therapy. *Professional Psychology: Research and Practice, 26,* 309–315.

Hays, P. A. (1996). Addressing the complexities of culture and gender in counseling. *Journal of Counseling & Development, 74,* 332–338.

Hays, P. A. (2001). *Addressing cultural complexities in practice: A framework for clinicians and counselors.* Washington, DC: American Psychological Association.

Hays, P. A. (in press). A strengths-based approach to psychotherapy with Middle Eastern people: Commentary regarding Bushra et al. In J. C. Muran (Ed.), *Dialogues on difference: Diversity studies of the therapeutic relationship.* Washington, DC: American Psychological Association.

Hays, P. A., & Zouari, J. (1995). Stress, coping, and mental health among rural, village, and urban women in Tunisia. *International Journal of Psychology, 30,* 69–90.

Hedayat-Diba, Z. (2000). Psychotherapy with Muslims. In P. S. Richards & A. E. Bergin (Eds.), *Handbook of psychotherapy and religious diversity* (pp. 289–314). Washington, DC: American Psychological Association.

Hourani, A. (1970). *Arabic thought in the liberal age: 1798–1939.* London: Oxford University Press.

Lamchichi, A. (2003, July). Claiming independence, asserting personal choice: Islam's rebel women. *Le Monde Diplomatique* (English version). Retrieved December 20, 2005, from http://mondediplo.com/2003/07/16lamchichi?var_recherche=lamchichi

Mansfield, P. (1990). *The Arabs*. New York: Penguin.

Nassar-McMillan, S. C., & Hakim-Larson, J. (2003). Counseling considerations among Arab Americans. *Journal of Counseling and Development, 81*, 150–159.

Nydell, M. K. (1987). *Understanding Arabs: A guide for Westerners*. Yarmouth, ME: Intercultural Press.

Racy, J. (1970). Psychiatry in the Arab East. *Acta Psychiatrica Scandinavica, 221*(Suppl.), 1–171.

Sayed, M. A. (2003a). Conceptualization of mental illness within Arab cultures: Meeting challenges in cross-cultural settings. *Social Behavior and Personality, 31*, 333–342.

Sayed, M. A. (2003b). Psychotherapy of Arab patients in the West: Uniqueness, empathy, and "otherness." *American Journal of Psychotherapy, 57*, 445–459.

Sharabi, H. (1988). *Neopatriarchy*. New York: Oxford University Press.

Simon, J. (1996). Lebanese families. In M. McGoldrick, J. Giordano, & J. K. Pearce (Eds.), *Ethnicity and family therapy* (pp. 364–375). New York: Guilford Press.

Suleiman, M. W. (1999). *Arabs in America: Building a new future*. Philadelphia: Temple University Press.

The World Almanac. (2005). New York: World Almanac Books.

Zogby, J. (1990). *Arab Americans today: A demographic profile of Arab Americans*. Washington, DC: Arab American Institute.

Zogby, J. (2003). *Hearing on America after 9/11: Freedom preserved or freedom lost?* (The statement before the United States Senate Committee on the Judiciary, November 18). Retrieved August 12, 2004, from http://www.aaiusa.org/PDF/JZtestimony111803.pdf

7

COGNITIVE–BEHAVIORAL THERAPY WITH ORTHODOX JEWS

CHERYL M. PARADIS, DANIEL CUKOR, AND STEVEN FRIEDMAN

Little has been published concerning the cognitive–behavioral therapy (CBT) of Orthodox Jews, a group of individuals who define themselves in terms of their religious lives. It is estimated that there are approximately 650,000 Orthodox Jews worldwide and 250,000 in North America (Gall, 1998). As of 2002, approximately 14% of the New York region's population was Jewish, and 19% identified themselves as Orthodox (Ukeles & Miller, 2004). In our experience, Orthodox clients often consider CBT, with its emphasis on symptom reduction, as their first choice of treatment modalities. Clients are usually less interested in long-term, insight-oriented treatment.

This chapter provides an overview of the Orthodox Jewish community and reviews the many cultural issues that affect treatment, including views of mental illness, confidentiality, family relationships, collaboration with religious leaders, therapeutic alliance, and observance of the Sabbath and holidays. Many of these issues are relevant for the treatment of individuals of other faiths; thus, much of this chapter may have utility for people from other religious groups. Clinicians have emphasized the importance of understanding, respecting, and integrating religious and cultural beliefs in treat-

TABLE 7.1
Glossary of Terms

Chumrah	An acceptable, stringent religiosity.
Frum	Orthodox, religious.
Halacha	Religious movement founded in the first half of the 18th century in Eastern Europe.
Holocaust	The organized mass persecution and annihilation of European Jewry by the Nazis (1933–1945).
Kosher	Ritually permitted food, for example, meat and dairy are never mixed, no pork or shellfish.
Mitzvah	Refers to a commandment to perform certain deeds. Also used to refer to good or charitable deeds.
Nidah	A woman during the period of menstruation and 7 days after cessation when no physical contact between husband and wife is permitted.
Reb, rebbe	Yiddish form for rabbi, applied generally to a teacher or a Hassidic rabbi.
Shanda	Shame, disgrace, "marked" by a secret.
Synagogue	Place of worship, the center of religious and social life for Orthodox Jews.
Talmud	"Teaching," the authoritative body of Jewish law and tradition codified in the third to fifth century comprising both Halacha and Aggadah ("folklore").
Torah	Scroll containing the first five books of the Bible for reading in the synagogue; can also refer to the entire body of traditional Jewish teaching.
Yeshiva	An academy devoted to the study of religious and rabbinic literature. In the Orthodox tradition, sexes are educated separately. Currently, in these schools, children receive both religious and secular education.

ment (Heilman & Witztum, 2000; Shafranske, 1996; Witztum & Buchbinder, 2001). A glossary of terms is included (Table 7.1). Given that our clinic focuses on the treatment of anxiety disorders, the case examples used in this chapter primarily involve the treatment of anxiety disorders. Although to the best of our knowledge there are no epidemiological studies looking at the incidence of psychiatric disorders in the Orthodox Jewish population, it is our clinical experience that the prevalence of Axis I psychiatric disorders is similar to the distribution in the general U.S. population. However, our chapter focuses on the provision of CBT for people diagnosed with "neurotic" disorders in outpatient settings.

OVERVIEW OF THE ORTHODOX JEWISH COMMUNITY

There are two main divisions within Jewish Americans: Ashkenazi Jews who emigrated from Europe and Sephardic Jews who emigrated from North Africa and the Middle East (Rosen & Weltman, 1996). Sephardic Jewish immigration to the United States began in the mid-17th century. Their descendants are a small proportion of the current Jewish population in the United States of approximately 5.5 million. The earliest Ashkenazi Jewish immigrants came to the United States in the mid-1800s and were primarily from Germany. The majority of American Jews are descendants of Eastern European Jews who immigrated to the United States during the late 1800s and early 1900s. In addition, a recent wave of approximately 300,000 Jewish immigrants have come from the former Soviet Union (Rosen & Weltman, 1996).

There are several different subgroups of Jews, including Orthodox, Conservative, Reconstructionist, Reform, and those not affiliated with any specific denomination. Individuals within both the Ashkenazi and Sephardic lineage may define themselves as Orthodox. This chapter focuses on the CBT of Orthodox Jews (Paradis, Friedman, Hatch, & Ackerman, 1996).

Shared Beliefs of Orthodox Jews

Within the Orthodox Jewish community, there are subgroups that vary in their cultural and familial traditions; however, all hold a core set of beliefs stemming from the conviction that the Torah and the laws of God are unchangeable and nonnegotiable (Hirsch, 1967). The Torah consists of the five books of the Bible believed to be given by God directly to Moses. The Torah and its laws are interpreted in the Talmud and other written commentaries in the rabbinical literature. These laws dictate Orthodox Jews' relationships with others and with God and include precise prescriptions for family relationships, marriage, sexual behavior, observance of the Sabbath and holidays, dietary laws, financial and business relationships, and all aspects of life.

Orthodox Jews value the religious way of life and recognize no differences between civil and religious obligations. They view their laws and requirements not as a burden but rather as a source of strength.

Orthodox Jews share important cultural and religious values that differ from those of the modern secular community. For example, Orthodox Jews are generally less focused on individual happiness, self-actualization, and autonomy. Their goals and decisions are often viewed from the position of what is good for the family and community. They also strive to lead a life, acting in the service of God, that focuses on community and group solidarity.

Orthodox Jews define themselves primarily as members of a community, often striving to isolate themselves from mainstream American society. This separation serves to maintain their adherence to their cultural and religious beliefs and traditional way of life. The separation is achieved through choices regarding where they live and school their children and whom they marry. For example, because Jewish law forbids traveling in cars on the Sabbath and many of the holidays, individuals need to live within walking distance of their synagogue. This need fosters a close-knit community and favors locating the community in urban settings. Recently, there has been an expansion of Jewish Orthodox communities to the suburbs.

Orthodox Jews almost always send their children to private schools called *yeshivas*, which are segregated by gender. The children are educated in both Jewish studies and the usual American school curriculum. After high school graduation some may continue to attend religious schools, whereas others pursue more mainstream college and graduate school education. Marriage to non-Orthodox Jews is not acceptable, and marriage within the community fosters separation from the secular world. Separation is also fostered by dietary restrictions. Orthodox Jews follow the laws of *kashrut*, which include dietary laws both inside and outside of the home.

Although Orthodox Jews share much in common, the term *Orthodox* does not describe a monolithic group. There are many subgroups that differ in the degree to which they assimilate into American society (Margolese, 1998). Individuals may vary in the strictness of their interpretation of Jewish law or belong to sects that also range in strictness. At one end of the continuum are the Hasidic Jews, which includes the Lubavitch and Satmar communities. Members of this community often speak Yiddish and continue the traditions of 18th and 19th century in their dress. There is a large ultra-Orthodox community in Israel (Witztum & Buchbinder, 2001). There are a variety of differences in the social mores and beliefs between Hasidic sects. For example, most Lubavitch do outreach to nonaffiliated Jews, whereas other Hasidic groups rarely interact with others outside their community. Many Lubavitch Hasidic Jews believe that their rabbi was the Messiah as prophesied in the Torah, whereas other Lubavitch Hasidic Jews do not have this belief. An extensive description of the Israeli ultra-Orthodox communities is provided by Heilman (2000).

At the other end of the spectrum are the Yeshivesh and Modern Orthodox groups. The Modern Orthodox believe in the assimilation of secular culture into their religious framework. It is important to recognize that religious identification can be very personal and complex. A therapist should never make assumptions about an Orthodox Jew's religious life based on his or her appearance. This overview is provided to help the therapist place in context the client's description of his or her religious world and to provide a point of reference for normative Orthodox beliefs and behaviors.

Family Relationships

Orthodox Jews place a very high value on community, family, and traditions. This is similar to other family-oriented ethnic and religious groups. Therefore, to be effective, the therapist must frame the CBT within the family values of the Orthodox community. In many Orthodox Jewish families, men and women have different roles and requirements as prescribed by the Torah and tradition. Women are primarily responsible for running the household and caring for children, whereas men are primarily responsible for financial support and religious obligations including the study of Torah and certain prayers. Men are encouraged to continue a lifelong study of religious learning. Often a young married couple is financially supported by relatives and the wife, allowing the husband to continue his pursuit of Torah study.

Orthodox Jews follow rules of segregation of the sexes, and no physical contact is allowed between men and women outside the immediate family. A married couple follows the laws of *Taharat Hamishpocho*, or family purity. This includes the laws of *nidah*, which proscribes physical intimacy for the couple from the start of the wife's menstruation until 7 days after cessation of menstruation. Sexual activity is resumed after the *mikvah*, or ritual bath.

Children are educated separately by gender, and men and women do not sit together at synagogue. For Hasidic Jews, segregation by gender may be more encompassing (Silverstein, 1995). For example, Hasidic Jews may avoid the use of public transportation because of the mingling of sexes, and many Hasidic women do not drive because it is considered immodest.

Recent changes in American society have led to an increase in the percentage of women entering the workforce. In contrast to mainstream American women, Hasidic women are less likely to work outside the home. Women in the modern Orthodox sects may pursue careers or employment, but their primary responsibility remains their family. Achievement for women is also more likely to be gained through defined roles within the community, including volunteer work such as *bikor cholim* (visiting the sick) or teaching in the yeshivas (Loewenthal et al., 1995). Therapists need to be aware of this value and not routinely encourage Orthodox women to find self-esteem and fulfillment that work against their values (Heilman & Witztum, 1997). This point is illustrated in the following example.

A 30-year-old Orthodox mother of six entered CBT for panic disorder. She presented with depression, low self-esteem, and a perception that she "did nothing important" in her life. In addition to CBT for panic symptoms, the therapist naively encouraged her to seek career opportunities. The client experienced these suggestions as insensitive and further confirmation of her inadequate achievements. Her husband expressed the belief that the therapist did not appreciate or value the importance of his wife's role within the family. Both became resistant to behavioral homework assignments. Prior to these suggestions, the woman's anxiety symptoms and the frequency of the panic attacks had lessened with a combination of relaxation training and exposure. Supervision with an Orthodox therapist helped the therapist become more knowledgeable about the values of Orthodox Jews and also to examine her own beliefs about women's roles. The treatment got back on track when the primary therapist helped the client choose her own culturally acceptable work opportunities. The client began volunteer work and found it enabled her to develop leadership skills and improved her interpersonal effectiveness. Her self-esteem improved and her depressive symptoms lessened.

The Orthodox Jewish community places great importance on the respect of elders and parents, and individuals are often reluctant, and in fact forbidden, to express criticism of parents. Concomitantly, the law against *loshon hora* (translated literally as "evil speech" and figuratively meaning gossip) can complicate the taking of a complete history during psychotherapy. An inexperienced therapist might mistake a client's desire to avoid criticism of parents as denial, avoidance, or uncooperativeness. For example, a 24-year-old Orthodox man reported that he lived at home with his parents but would not comment on their mental health, stating "It's not for me to judge." On consultation with the family, the therapist learned that the father was in treatment for major depression. His depression affected the entire family, particularly the client, as many of the interactions within the home were marked with criticism and hostility stemming from the father's low mood. The therapist viewed the client's reluctance to discuss his father's mental illness as a culturally appropriate attempt to pay honor to his father by not speaking poorly of him. The therapist also showed the client's values sufficient sensitivity by not forcing him to say something he was not prepared to say, which would have disrupted the therapeutic rapport. As a strong working alliance developed, the client became increasingly able to discuss his father's depression and how it affected him. He realized that he was not merely speaking ill of his father but relaying vital information about the family dynamic that was a contributing factor to his own depression.

Generally, before marrying, Orthodox couples date for a short period of time, typically not for romantic love but for the purpose of selecting an appropriate marriage partner. A "date" may in reality be a brief meeting in the home of the young woman, chaperoned by both sets of parents. However, within the different subgroups there are considerable differences in courtship and marriage practices. In Hasidic communities, the couple may only meet one to three times and marriages are essentially arranged. In Modern Orthodox communities, the couple may date for a longer period of time but usually not more than a year.

When a young man or woman reaches a certain age, he or she begins the courtship process, and parents are actively involved in finding a suitable partner. Young men may begin dating about the age of 20 or 21, and young women between the ages of 18 and 20. Premarital sex or any physical contact is forbidden. Marriage is considered a lifelong commitment, and divorce is proscribed except in cases of severe abuse or continuous irreconcilable strife.

Following the Torah's commandment "Be fruitful and multiply," the Orthodox community places great value on having many children. The practice of having large families is supported by religious beliefs and the motivation to psychologically replace relatives murdered during the Holocaust (Heilman, 2000). Different subgroups of Orthodox Jews have different numbers of children according to the strictness with which this commandment is interpreted.

A large number of children may place great stress on both parents and exacerbate a variety of anxiety disorders. Contraception is permitted, with rabbinical consultation, for situations in which having more children would be a threat to health.

Individuals with anxiety disorders are usually reticent about discussing the exact nature of their disorder with their rabbi because of their feelings of shame and embarrassment. In treatment, we encourage our clients to honestly discuss their feelings and symptoms with their rabbi. We have found that when the rabbi fully understands how the client's anxiety symptoms would be adversely affected by more children, he often encourages the client to use contraception.

TREATMENT ISSUES

There are a number of treatment issues that occur when working with the Orthodox community. These include the importance of building trust in the therapist, the need for confidentiality, and the importance of understanding cultural mores which are similar to issues with non-Orthodox clients but should receive greater emphasis. Issues specific to working with Orthodox clients include consulting with the client's rabbi and focusing on dating and marriage issues (which are central to Orthodox communal values) and issues surrounding holiday observances. We discuss these issues in detail in this section, as well as the advantages and limitations of CBT with this population.

Relationship With the Therapist

Orthodox clients may find it difficult to trust a therapist from outside the community and usually wonder whether even a *Jewish*, non-Orthodox therapist understands and respects their values and way of life (Cinnirella & Loewenthal, 1999; Wikler, 1986). They may ask whether the therapist is Jewish or understands Jewish law. Therapists need to be prepared for these questions and consider the impact of open disclosure. In our experience we have found it helpful to answer these questions honestly, providing information about our own religious backgrounds. Answering such questions is an important means of establishing rapport.

It is important for the therapist to be aware of social and political events that may affect the Jewish and particularly the Orthodox Jewish community. The readily identifiable dress and traditional clothes may make Orthodox Jews, especially Hasidic Jews, vulnerable to anti-Semitism. It is also important for therapists to examine whether they hold any anti-Semitic or antireligious biases or beliefs.

Regarding attire, therapists need to be aware of their own way of dressing. We do not recommend that therapists try to "pass" as Orthodox. Instead, we have found that dressing modestly is perceived by our clients as a sign of respect. Therapists also need to be aware of appropriate behaviors related to touching. For example, therapists should refrain from touching a client of the opposite sex, including even shaking hands. Laws of modesty also require the therapist to leave the office door closed but unlocked if one is treating a client of the opposite sex.

Views of Mental Illness and Confidentiality

Although confidentiality is an important aspect of treatment of all individuals, it is especially important for the Orthodox Jewish client. There is a widespread prejudice within this community against those with mental illness (Wikler, 1986). *Shanda* is a term that means shame or disgrace and is used to describe being "marked" by a secret such as mental retardation or mental illness in the family. It is essential that therapists not underestimate the widespread prejudice against those with mental illness in this community. The stigma against mental illness makes it especially important to maintain confidentiality. Open disclosure of psychological symptoms can affect the reputation of the family and marriage prospects of the client, their children, and immediate relatives.

The importance of confidentiality affects CBT in a variety of ways. Clients may refuse to do in vivo work in their neighborhood because they may be observed by neighbors. In addition, Orthodox Jewish therapists are often known within the community. A client doing in vivo work with a recognized mental health professional will be noticed and their reputation may be adversely affected. If the therapist is not an Orthodox Jew, neighbors will speculate about the person's relationship with an individual who is clearly not from the community. Therapists are also advised to avoid scheduling consecutive office visits for clients within the same Orthodox community, as a chance meeting could cause unnecessary embarrassment.

The stigma against mental illness also affects the help-seeking behaviors of Orthodox individuals who have anxiety disorders. Individuals are unlikely to discuss their anxiety symptoms or treatment with individuals outside their immediate family. Individuals usually attempt to conceal symptoms and postpone seeking treatment. Treatment is sought only when symptoms grossly interfere with functioning in the family, at work, or at school. Initially, individuals often seek help from family or rabbinical leaders. Rabbinical leaders may be concerned that a mental health professional, ignorant of Orthodox Jewish values and religious obligations, would recommend that the client break with the religion or community. Rabbinical leaders may recommend an Orthodox therapist or a non-Jewish therapist rather than a nonreligious assimilated Jewish therapist who is perceived as having negative attitudes or unresolved conflicts about Judaism.

Rabbinical Consultation

It is often helpful to include rabbinical consultation or collaboration in the cognitive–behavioral treatment of Orthodox clients with anxiety disorders. Collaboration can enhance treatment by educating the non-Orthodox therapist about Jewish law and clarifying misunderstandings. Collaboration with a rabbi also demonstrates to the client that the therapist is willing to work within the Orthodox system of values. It will certainly lessen or alleviate the anxiety associated with some homework assignments if the client is aware that his or her rabbi has consented to the exercise.

Consultation with a rabbi can be ineffective or counterproductive if the rabbi is not accepting of mental health intervention. This can occur if he senses that the therapist does not respect religious priorities or might encourage Orthodox clients to defer from religious requirements or question their faith. One way to avoid such pitfalls is to discuss the treatment with the rabbi prior to meeting together with the client. During this meeting the therapist needs to begin with psychoeducation about the CBT process. The therapist needs to emphasize the severity of the client's anxiety symptoms, explain how it interferes with religious and community obligations, and focus specifically on what the rabbi can say to the clients to assist treatment. If the rabbi understands that the consultation is being done out of respect for religious values, he may be more open to establishing a collaborative relationship.

Collaboration is especially critical for clients with obsessive–compulsive disorder (OCD) who have difficulty differentiating between *chumrah* (a culturally acceptable, extrastringent religiosity) and a form of OCD termed *scrupulosity*. Scrupulosity is an overly strict interpretation of what is religiously moral or proper. Research has found that Orthodox Jewish clients with OCD experienced a greater number of religious symptoms than nonreligious symptoms (Greenberg & Shefler, 2002). Clients with OCD may consult with a series of rabbis, doubting their advice. Before the consultation, it is important for the therapist to encourage the client with OCD to agree to follow the advice of their chosen rabbi and avoid "rabbi shopping" (Greenberg & Witztum, 2001).

Because of their anxiety or OCD, some Orthodox clients may misinterpret Halachic rules, leading to increased anxiety symptoms. For example, a 40-year-old Orthodox man had had a history of OCD since the age of 13. During adolescence he was "plagued by doubts whether I had properly recited my prayers." For hours he recited prayers that should have taken only a few minutes. His rabbi referred him for CBT because "his many concerns regarding preparation for Passover are unrealistic and symptoms of a disorder." Throughout the year the client had obsessive thoughts that the crumbs of *chometz* (unleavened bread) would be dropped in his house and make it impossible to clean correctly for Passover. (Orthodox Jews remove all leaven products from their homes prior to Passover.) He completed numerous compulsions that involved checking for bread crumbs that might be left on furniture and engaged in hand-washing rituals to prevent the spread of crumbs. CBT included conjoint sessions with his wife and a consultation with his rabbi. Exposure and ritual prevention exercises were very effective, and his compulsive rituals decreased dramatically.

The importance of rabbinical consultation is also illustrated in the case of an 18-year-old man who had experienced a recent onset of OCD involving obsessions about his rabbi. He visualized his rabbi as an "evil person." He continually used mental compulsions to reduce anxiety and avoided prayer and study because he was convinced that it was a sin to study Torah or pray while experiencing these abhorrent obsessions. The client was resistant to treatment with exposure and ritual prevention until a rabbinical consultation was arranged. The rabbi explained that his OCD and obsessive thoughts were not a sin and did not prevent prayer and study. The rabbi instructed him to continue normal daily prayer and engage in the exposure and ritual prevention components of treatment. After the rabbinical consultation, treatment was effective in eliminating compulsions and lessening the frequency and severity of his obsessive thoughts.

Dating and Marriage

An Orthodox Jewish individual with a severe anxiety disorder will often be deemed not ready to marry and the dating process postponed until the condition improves. In our experience, many individuals with mild to moderate anxiety disorders can fulfill their marital responsibilities. Their symptoms may only interfere with travel or participation in large religious or social gatherings. It is important to address these issues directly in treatment as illustrated in the following case.

A 23-year-old Orthodox man who was being seen for a mild case of trichotillomania (repetitive hair-pulling) reported that despite a strong urge to marry, he was not going to date because of his mental illness. With some cognitive restructuring and a rabbinic consultation, the man was able to begin dating within a few weeks. However, when the therapist suggested a pharmacological consultation to augment treatment, the young man was told by his rabbi to either not take the medicine or postpone his dating until he was off the medication. The rabbi explained that although the diagnosis had not changed, potential partners would be more put off by the use of medication than by short-term psychotherapy. This caused great conflict within the client, but he decided not to pursue pharmacotherapy as he felt ready to date and marry.

If a client is dating, the timing of disclosure to a possible marriage partner is an important issue in treatment. Premature disclosure of the existence of an anxiety disorder, or of current or past psychological treatment, is not usually recommended until the couple is seriously considering marriage. This protects the client's reputation and future marriage prospects in the community. Again, this is an issue in which rabbinical guidance can be helpful to the client and therapist.

For example, a 20-year-old man began CBT because of his avoidance of dating. His panic disorder with agoraphobia, which began at age 18, caused difficulty in synagogue attendance. He had fled on numerous occasions during panic attacks. During treatment he had begun to date a young woman and contemplated marriage; however, he was concerned about whether and how to discuss his anxiety disorder with her. After receiving a written release from the client, the therapist scheduled a consultation with both the client and prospective spouse. The focus of the consultation session was to educate both about the course and treatment of anxiety disorders. They both reported that this session was helpful. They felt reassured with the information that panic disorder did not indicate a severe character disorder that would cause him to be unable to be a good husband and father. Eventually, they became engaged and married.

Marriage is considered a bond for life, and divorce is rarely an option. Making radical changes in family dynamics is usually not a preferred focus of treatment. Because clients with anxiety disorders and marital problems are often referred to marital therapy, a more helpful focus is on improving the marital relationship. It can be especially helpful to promote intimacy through verbal communication during times of physical separation (Ostrov, 1978).

The cultural value of having many children can lead to increased stress and anxiety. Therapists should not routinely encourage Orthodox women with anxiety disorders to use birth control. Therapists need to encourage the client to consult with his or her rabbi, who may or may not counsel the use of contraception. As noted earlier, a threat to health often relieves the couple of the obligation of having more children.

A client's embarrassment about an anxiety disorder may be so intense that the client may avoid discussing the anxiety disorder within his or her family. For this reason, we have found it necessary to include the spouse to some extent in the treatment. The importance of timing in the inclusion of family members is illustrated in the case of a 28-year-old Orthodox man who had been experiencing undiagnosed OCD his entire life but had hidden the disorder from his wife and children. When he was 14 he had discussed his problems with a trusted adult who counseled him to "keep the bizarre thoughts and actions as hidden as possible from everyone." The client believed that he had successfully hidden his problem despite such obvious rituals as checking the alarm clock before bed nearly 100 times or putting on and removing his shoes five times whenever he dressed. The client was terrified by the therapist's suggestion to include his spouse in treatment. After cognitive restructuring regarding beliefs about his wife's possible reaction, the patient agreed and found inclusion of his wife liberating. He was finally able to speak openly about his OCD with her. She was also relieved to be included in the treatment process and to receive information regarding OCD, as she had worried that her husband had a psychotic disorder.

Holidays and Sabbath

Therapists working with Orthodox clients need to be knowledgeable about the Jewish calendar and the rules and rituals associated with daily events, Sabbath, and holidays. These rituals are time consuming and may cause additional stress for clients with anxiety disorders. However, it is essential that therapists appreciate the sense of continuity and source of joy associated with these religious observances, and the embarrassment and pain suffered if the person cannot perform what he or she believes to be a "simple" thing.

The Sabbath or day of rest begins at sundown on Friday and ends one hour after sundown on Saturday. This day of rest is dedicated to studying religious texts, praying in synagogue, and spending time with the family. Worldly activities including working, driving, turning on lights, and using the telephone are proscribed. Individuals are forbidden to carry any object in public unless medically required or unless the community has created an *eruv* (a ritual fence around the neighborhood that creates one private domain). These restrictions often lead to increased anxiety because clients are usually proscribed from carrying water, nonvital medications, or any security object. A security object is something an individual with phobias carries to lessen anxiety and may include a bottle of water, sucking candies, a cell phone, and so on. Individuals are also to refrain from calling their therapist for reassurance, except in life-threatening situations.

Visiting family for lengthy and elaborate meals can also be difficult for individuals who experience the urge to flee when anxious. Avoiding these activities affects self-esteem and leads to social isolation. Often, Orthodox individuals with agoraphobia also experience increased anxiety associated with certain aspects of synagogue attendance. Lengthy religious services may lead to anxiety because the person feels trapped. Men may be honored with requests to lead prayers or read from the Torah in front of the congregation. However, this honor can cause an increase in anxiety because the man is unable to leave the synagogue and he becomes the focus of the congregation's attention (Greenberg, Stravynski, & Bilu, 2004).

The observation of Sabbath rituals can also lead to increased anxiety. For instance, a 34-year-old Orthodox woman with OCD was unable to invite guests to her home for Sabbath meals, a culturally expected gesture, owing to OCD symptoms that included hoarding and eating rituals. Her dining room had become overrun with clutter, and hosting any guests grew very awkward. Furthermore, the client ate her meals in a ritualized fashion and was particular about which foods could come into contact with other foods. Her eating symptoms caused her and her family great embarrassment, and they avoided all offers to eat meals at others' homes. Treatment was not considered a success until she was both able to eat at a friend's home and then reciprocate the offer.

Advantages of CBT

There are many advantages of CBT for anxiety disorder with Orthodox Jews. CBT is generally shorter than insight-oriented therapy and focuses on reducing symptoms and promoting adaptive functioning, all necessary to fulfill family and community roles. By identifying goals and promoting coping skills, the therapist is able to establish a trusting relationship with the client. Clients often choose not to continue treatment, even when recommended by the therapist, after these goals are achieved (Paradis et al., 1996).

Exposure and response prevention have also been found effective for Orthodox Jews with OCD because it emphasizes the return to functioning without challenging religious beliefs directly (Greenberg, 1984). The therapist may need to include a rabbinical consultation if the client has scrupulosity, a form of OCD in which the rituals exceed the requirements of religious law and lead the client to neglect their religious or community obligations.

Limitations of CBT

There are some limitations specific to providing CBT to Orthodox Jewish clients. Group therapy, when incorporated into treatment, often needs to be single gender and focused on specific goals (Silverstein, 1995). Because of feelings of shame, it may be difficult to create an appropriate group, and most clients prefer individual treatment. As suggested previously, in vivo exercises need to be arranged outside of the client's neighborhood to minimize the possibility of gossip and to lessen the embarrassment of a chance encounter. In addition, it is important that the therapist not treat clients with exposure to situations proscribed by religious law. This may be an issue for clients with OCD. If unsure of the possible cultural and religious implications of an intervention, details of exposure exercises should be checked with the client's rabbi. Owing to confidentiality issues, Orthodox clients may feel isolated from others who have anxiety disorders, and it can be helpful to recommend readings from Orthodox Jewish clinicians as adjuncts to treatment (Twersky, 1993).

CONCLUSION

Orthodox Jews with anxiety and other psychological disorders are generally underserved by the mental health system (Trappler, Greenberg, & Friedman, 1995). Because of the stigma regarding mental illness, most avoid seeking treatment until the symptoms interfere significantly with functioning. Clients are also less open to considering psychotropic medications as an adjunct to therapy because of the fear of being seen as sick or mentally ill.

These concerns need to be addressed in treatment. In our clinical experience, CBT is quite successful when the Orthodox Jewish client's values and practices are understood, respected, and incorporated into the treatment.

REFERENCES

Cinnirella, M., & Loewenthal, K. M. (1999). Religious and ethnic group influences on beliefs about mental illness: A qualitative interview study. *British Journal of Medical Psychology, 72,* 505–524.

Gall, T. L. (Ed.). (1998). *Worldmark encyclopedia of culture and daily life: Vol. 3. Asia and Oceania.* Cleveland, OH: Eastword Publications Development.

Greenberg, D. (1984). Are religious compulsions religious or compulsive: A phenomenological study. *American Journal of Psychotherapy, 38,* 524–532.

Greenberg, D., & Shefler, G. (2002). Obsessive compulsive disorder in ultra-Orthodox Jewish patients: A comparison of religious and non-religious symptoms. *Psychology and Psychotherapy: Theory, Research and Practice, 75,* 123–130.

Greenberg, D., Stravynski, A., & Bilu, Y. (2004). Social phobia in ultra-Orthodox Jewish males: Culture-bound syndrome or virtue? *Mental Health, Religion and Culture, 7,* 289–305.

Greenberg, D., & Witztum, E. (2001). Treatment of strictly religious patients. In M. T. Pato & J. Zohar (Eds.), *Current treatments of obsessive–compulsive disorders* (2nd ed., pp. 173–191). Washington, DC: American Psychiatric Press.

Heilman, S. (2000). *The defenders of the faith: Inside ultra-Orthodox Jewry.* Berkeley: University of California Press.

Heilman, S. C., & Witztum, E. (1997). Value-sensitive therapy: Learning from ultra-Orthodox patients. *American Journal of Psychotherapy, 51,* 523–541.

Heilman, S. C., & Witztum, E. (2000). All in faith: Religion as the idiom and means of coping with distress. *Mental Health, Religion and Culture, 3,* 115–124.

Hirsch, S. R. (1967). *The Pentateuch.* New York: Judaica Press.

Loewenthal, K., Goldblatt, V., Gorton, T., Lubitsch, G., Bicknell, H., Fellowes, D., & Sowden, A. (1995). Gender and depression in Anglo-Jewry. *Psychological Medicine, 25,* 1051–1063.

Margolese, H. C. (1998). Engaging in psychotherapy with the Orthodox Jew: A critical review. *American Journal of Psychotherapy, 52,* 37–53.

Ostrov, S. (1978). Sex therapy with Orthodox Jewish couples. *Journal of Sex and Marital Therapy, 4,* 266–278.

Paradis, C. M., Friedman, S., Hatch, M. L., & Ackerman, R. (1996). Cognitive behavioral treatment of anxiety disorders in Orthodox Jews. *Cognitive and Behavioral Practice, 3,* 271–288.

Rosen, E. J., & Weltman, S. F. (1996). Jewish families: An overview. In M. McGoldrick & J. Giordano (Eds.), *Ethnicity and family therapy* (2nd ed., pp. 611–630). New York: Guilford Press.

Shafranske, E. P. (1996). *Religion and the clinical practice of psychology.* Washington, DC: American Psychological Association.

Silverstein, R. (1995). Bending the conventional rules when treating the ultra-Orthodox in the group setting. *International Journal of Group Psychotherapy, 45,* 237–249.

Trappler, B., Greenberg, S., & Friedman, S. (1995). Treatment of Hassidic Jewish patients in a general hospital medical-psychiatric unit. *Hospital and Community Psychiatry, 46,* 833–835.

Twersky, A. J. (1993). *I am I.* Brooklyn, NY: Shar Press/Mesorah.

Wikler, M. (1986). Pathways to treatment: How Orthodox Jews enter therapy. *Social Casework: The Journal of Contemporary Social Work, 67,* 113–118.

Witztum, E., & Buchbinder, J. T. (2001). Strategic culture sensitive therapy with religious Jews. *International Review of Psychiatry, 13,* 117–124.

Ukeles, J. B., & Miller, R. (2004, October). *The Jewish study of New York: 2002* (Final report, final text, exhibits, and an expanded research note on methodology). New York: Ukeles Associates for UJA Federation of New York.

II

COGNITIVE–BEHAVIORAL THERAPY WITH PEOPLE OF ADDITIONAL MINORITY CULTURES

8

COGNITIVE–BEHAVIORAL THERAPY WITH CULTURALLY DIVERSE OLDER ADULTS

ANGELA W. LAU AND LISA M. KINOSHITA

Currently, one in every eight Americans is 65 years or older, and it is predicted that by 2030 the proportion of older adults in the United States will grow to 20% of the general population (Administration on Aging, 2000; Siegel, 1999). By the year 2030, 25% of United States elders will be from ethnic minority cultures—a 328% increase in the older ethnic minority population (American Association of Retired Persons, 1997; Haley, Han, & Henderson, 1998). In part, this latter growth is because of post–World War II legislation that enabled ethnic minorities to immigrate to the United States in record numbers many years ago (e.g., the War Bride Act, GI Fiancées Act, Refugee Relief Act of 1953, and U.S. Refugee Act of 1980). Also adding to the increase has been the improved mortality of ethnic minorities living in the United States and an increase in the number of adult immigrants sponsoring aging parents to come to the United States and live with them.

Several empirical and case studies suggest that cognitive–behavioral therapy (CBT) is effective with older adults (Gatz et al., 1998; Knight & Satre, 1999). CBT modified to accommodate older adults has been effective for late-life depression (Gatz et al., 1998), generalized anxiety disorder (Durham, Chambers, MacDonald, Power, & Major, 2003), and insomnia

(Morin, Kowatch, Barry, & Walton, 1993). A cognitive–behavioral approach has been effective in reducing anxiety, anger, and depression in middle-aged and older adult caregivers of patients with dementia (Gallagher-Thompson et al., 2000). Researchers are beginning to demonstrate the utility of CBT with medically ill elders in primary care settings and skilled nursing facilities (Cook, 1998; Stanley et al., 2003). And cognitive and behavioral therapies also appear effective in treating cognitively impaired elders (Cohen-Mansfield, 2001; Teri, Logsdon, Uomoto, & McCurry, 1997).

However, despite the growth in cognitive–behavioral research with older adults, the majority of the work focuses on European American elders (Areán & Gallagher-Thompson, 1996). In a literature review, Arean and Gallagher-Thompson found that only 22% of controlled treatment outcome studies for older adults with mental disorders included ethnic minority participants. This lack of inclusion is due in part to the difficulties in recruiting and retaining older minority participants (Lau & Gallagher-Thompson, 2002). However, the results of the few studies that do include diverse elders are promising. Specifically, CBT has been found effective in the treatment of anxiety and depression in Japanese and Asian Indian elders (Gupta, 2000, 2003; Kinoshita & Gallagher-Thompson, 2004), in reducing depressive symptoms and somatic complaints in community-dwelling Chinese American elders (Dai et al., 1999), and in the treatment of depression in diverse ethnic minority elders (Arean & Miranda, 1996). Furthermore, the results of these studies emphasize the importance of understanding the interaction between age and culture within the clinical process, and the need to tailor assessment and therapy to incorporate clients' traditions, worldviews, cultural practices, and beliefs (Hays, 1995; Sue & Sue, 2003).

Before embarking on a discussion of culturally diverse groups, it is important to acknowledge the variability within these populations; there is great diversity within ethnic groups in terms of culture, language, immigration and acculturation histories, and life experiences based on particular cohorts. Thus, not all members of these groups will fit into the categories that will be mentioned throughout this chapter. The groupings are discussed as a model for the reader. CBT therapists are responsible for conceptualizing each of their culturally diverse clients' cases with the particular individual's life experiences and worldviews in mind. Although the focus of this chapter is on CBT with elders of ethnic minority cultures, the information presented is also relevant to elders of European American heritage, elders who identify with more than one (dominant or minority) culture, and ethnic minority elders who identify more with the dominant culture than with their ethnic minority origin.

TREATMENT ISSUES WITH ETHNIC MINORITY ELDERS

The issues mentioned in this section are generally more apparent among less acculturated elders of ethnic minority groups. First, members of ethnic minority cultures often hold explanatory models of illness that differ from the biomedical model of the dominant United States culture (Kleinman, 1980). These different explanatory models contribute to different concepts of what constitutes appropriate treatment and functional coping strategies. For example, many individuals of Chinese, Mexican, and Native American heritage believe that illnesses are the result of imbalances in one's life. Proper treatment involves restoring balance through diet, herbal remedies, religious practices, and environmental manipulation (Braun & Browne, 1998; Gallagher-Thompson, Talamantes, Ramirez, & Valverde, 1996; Harris, 1998). African American, Native American, and Latino/Hispanic elders are also more likely to believe spiritual or mystical forces are responsible for their maladies and therefore seek folk medicine or a spiritual practitioner rather than pharmaceutical relief or psychotherapy (Harris, 1998; Parks, 2003).

Some ethnic minority elders believe that psychological difficulties are the result of moral misconduct by an individual or by one's ancestors (Braun & Browne, 1998; Gallagher-Thompson et al., 1996). Such a belief decreases the likelihood that the individual will seek mental health services because admission of these problems would bring shame and stigma to the family (Gallagher-Thompson et al., 1996). For example, a Chinese family that believes Alzheimer's disease is punishment for an individual not complying with Confucian traditions and values may not seek help for the individual with dementia. Moreover, if the dementia is considered a justified punishment by spiritual forces (e.g., ancestors, gods, spirits), family members may choose to experience the difficulties as atonement rather than seek support services to improve the condition or circumstances.

Elders, especially ethnic minority elders, are also less likely to seek or accept help from "outsiders," especially mental health providers. In response to experiences of discrimination, abuse, and exploitation, minority communities have often developed their own institutions and support networks to meet the physical and emotional needs of their members. These supports can include religious communities and institutions, extended family including non-blood-related kin, and aid societies. Ethnic minority elders and their families also may strongly subscribe to cultural expectations regarding the responsibility and obligation of younger generations to care for their elders (Gallagher-Thompson et al., 2000).

When ethnic minority elders do finally reach out to mainstream systems of care, they are more likely to see a medical doctor than a mental health specialist (Black, 2000; Cooper-Patrick et al., 1999). Furthermore, older adults, including ethnic minority elders, are more likely to be brought in by a concerned family member or referral from a primary care physician rather than by self-referral (Baker, 1990, as cited in Baker & Takeshita, 2001; Hindrichsen & Dick-Siskin, 2000). Given the cautiousness with which many elders approach mental health services, therapists will need to take special care in the initial stages of therapy to develop rapport with and engage older clients.

Finally, regardless of culture, ethnic minority elders are often experiencing a decline in physical and cognitive functioning. Therapists must be sensitive to possible sensory losses (e.g., impaired hearing and vision), slower cognitive processes (e.g., slowed motor responding and the need for more time to recall information), and other physical changes (e.g., in sleep, appetite, and libido). Therapists should also be aware of life changes and stressors that are more common in later life, including loss (e.g., retirement, death of family members and friends), chronic and acute illness, disability caused by or exacerbated by chronic or acute medical conditions, and a shift in or renewal of interests and relationships (e.g., volunteerism, travel).

COMMON PRESENTING PROBLEMS

There are a number of mental health issues with which older clients commonly present, and being prepared for these and how different cultures understand these issues will aid therapists in treating these populations. These problems are shared by older adults of most cultural and ethnic groups: somatization, depression, dementia, grief, bereavement, intergenerational conflict, and caregiver stress. There are also a number of mental health conditions that may develop secondary to the physical illness or disability common among this population. We discuss all of these issues in this section.

Somatization

Somatization is negatively correlated with level of acculturation; that is, somatic complaints are more common among individuals who are less acculturated to the dominant European American culture in the United States (Gonzalez & Griffith, 1996; Lam, Pacala, & Smith, 1997). For example, more traditionally oriented elders of Asian and Latino heritage are more likely to express depression, anxiety, stress, and anger in more culturally accepted somatic forms such as headaches, backaches, fatigue, gastrointestinal problems, and insomnia (Gonzalez & Griffith, 1996; Lam et al., 1997; Sue & Sue, 2003). To ensure appropriate treatment and at the same time reassure elders that their somatic complaints are being taken seriously, it is essential that therapists thoroughly explore possible medical causes for somatic symptoms. At the same time, the better understanding the therapist has of his or her client's worldview and explanatory model of the illness, the more effective the therapist can be.

Depression

Studies have found that ethnic minority elders report higher rates of depression and depressive symptoms than do European American elders (see

Black, 2000), with a strong negative correlation between level of acculturation and depression (Lam et al., 1997; Zamanian et al., 1992). Ethnic minority elders may be more susceptible to depression because of life stressors that include racism, language barriers, limited education and finances, and, as a result of immigration, smaller support networks and intergenerational conflict within the family. Depression in older adults is also strongly associated with the loss in functional status resulting from physical illness or disability (Zeiss, Lewinsohn, Rohde, & Seeley, 1996). Therapists need to be aware that depression can cause mild to moderate cognitive impairments (e.g., difficulty with short-term memory, impaired ability to focus and sustain attention) that may be misdiagnosed as dementia. However, with successful treatment of the depression, these impairments can improve (Meyers, 1998).

Dementia

Dementia is the most common mental disorder in older adults, with prevalence rates increasing exponentially with each decade after age 65 (Evans et al., 1989). Ethnic minority families are less likely to seek help for an older family member with Alzheimer's disease or a related dementia (Gallagher-Thompson et al., 2000; McCormick et al., 1996). Reasons for this reticence include the belief that cognitive impairment is a part of the normal aging process, that there is no hope for the condition, and that seeking outside assistance would bring further shame and stigma to the family. However, individuals in the early stages of dementia are likely to experience depression and anxiety that can be treated. Early-stage dementia patients may also benefit from memory-enhancement strategies that capitalize on their existing strengths and compensate for cognitive weaknesses (Clare & Woods, 2004). Although some older adults will present with concerns about declining memory, it is more likely that family members will bring the elder's cognitive difficulties to the attention of a health care professional. As the disease progresses, families may seek and benefit from assistance in managing difficult behaviors exhibited by the older adult, such as agitation, aggression, paranoia, hallucinations, wandering, or other unsafe behaviors.

Caregiver Stress

Ethnic minority families are more likely to keep a disabled or ill elder in the community and provide care at home than to hire a paid caregiver or place the older adult in a skilled nursing facility or other external living arrangement (Lockery, 1991; McCormick et al., 1996). As a result, many caregivers are spouses or adult children who are also older adults. Caregivers often experience social isolation and frustration from their caregiving responsibilities and the cultural expectations placed on them as caregivers (e.g., to provide care without complaint or assistance). The stress and burden of caregiving can result in depression, anxiety, anger, increased somatic complaints, and the exacerbation of existing health problems (Ory, Yee, Tennstedt, & Schulz, 2000).

Grief and Bereavement

With advancing age, it is inevitable that older adults will experience losses caused by death. Losing a spouse, relatives, friends, and even adult children becomes more common. Also, it is not unusual for an older adult to begin to experience anticipatory grief for someone who is in the dying process or has been placed outside the home or, in the case of people with Alzheimer's disease, is functionally no longer the same person.

Intergenerational Conflict

Ethnic minority elders who are less acculturated and abide by traditional values and role expectations are more likely to experience conflict with younger generations who have become acculturated to Western values and worldviews. These older adults are likely to experience increased stress, anxiety, and depression because of the conflict. Unfortunately, the culture gap also may reduce the older adult's support system and ability to engage in formerly effective coping or problem-resolution strategies, particularly if the elder does not learn English while younger generations forget their native language or never learn it. The shame of a perceived loss in authority or culturally expected role may further prevent the ethnic minority elder from seeking support from others.

Mental Disorders Secondary to Physical Illness or Disability

Older adults are at greater risk for developing psychological difficulties secondary to physical illness or disability because they are more likely to experience medical problems. Over 75% of older adults have at least one chronic health problem, and 50% have multiple medical conditions (Fried & Wallace, 1992, as cited in Black, 2000). Adjustment disorder, major depression, and anxiety disorders are common reactions to losses associated with a change in functional status. Common medical conditions that result in changes in functional status include diabetes mellitus, hypertension, stroke, chronic obstructive pulmonary disorder, cardiovascular disease, insomnia, cancer, sexual dysfunction, and chronic pain (Sarkisian, Hays, Berry, & Mangione, 2001). These conditions are also associated with symptoms of depression and anxiety (Finch, Ramsay, & Katona, 1992; Zeiss et al., 1996).

Ethnic minority status is significantly related to poorer health outcomes as a result of a lack of preventative care and treatment, poorer quality of life (e.g., because of inadequate pain management), increased disability, and increased mortality (see Institute of Medicine, 2003). Of note is a pattern of discrimination in the physical and mental health treatment of minority clients that cannot be attributed to known factors other than race and ethnicity (e.g., access to health care; Institute of Medicine, 2003). It is clear that ethnic minority elders are at risk for mental disorders secondary to physical illness and disability.

Cohort-Specific Problems

Therapists will also want to be aware of mental health problems within specific cohorts of ethnic minority elders. For example, many immigrant populations, including refugees from Central America, Southeast Asia, and Africa, have experienced trauma associated with political oppression, civil unrest, and war. Consequently, these individuals are more susceptible to posttraumatic stress disorder (PTSD) and its sequelae. Older ethnic minority veterans are also more likely to experience PTSD than are European American veterans, possibly as a result of racial discrimination that placed them in greater danger with less support (Allen, 1986; Loo, 1994).

Culture-Bound Syndromes

Therapists need to be aware that certain symptom clusters are more common in particular cultures. These clusters are recognized in the most recent revision of the *Diagnostic and Statistical Manual of Mental Disorders* (4th ed., text rev.; *DSM–IV–TR*) as culture-bound syndromes but are not formal *DSM–IV–TR* diagnoses (American Psychiatric Association, 2000). However, these syndromes are widely accepted and formally recognized in many non-Western cultures. Less acculturated individuals are more likely to present with a culture-bound syndrome than are more acculturated older adults.

Advantages of CBT With Ethnic Minority Elders

CBT is structured, psychoeducational, oriented toward problem solving, and directive in its treatment approach, all of which are compatible with the style of relating of many ethnic minority groups (Hays, 1995; Lin, 2001). At the same time, CBT allows for creativity in adapting each treatment plan to individual needs and resources. CBT's focus on the present, specific behaviors, goal-setting, skill practice, and evaluation can decrease clients' anxiety regarding the ambiguity and vulnerability that often arise during therapy (Lin, 2001). And conceptualizing therapy as "going to class" can help to decrease the stigma associated with mental health care (Gallagher-Thompson et al., 1997; Lin, 2001).

CBT emphasizes listening to the client and understanding his or her worldview. It also encourages therapists to interface with the client's environment and support network to identify appropriate change mechanisms for a successful treatment plan. This approach lends itself well to elders who hold a collective worldview and whose thoughts, feelings, and behaviors are intertwined with those of other family and community members. Working with the client's support network has the added benefit of helping the therapist gain the trust of the elder and his or her family, which in turn facilitates learning and increases the likelihood that the new behavior will be maintained over time.

Limitations of CBT

Ethnic minority elders may lack the formal education necessary to be comfortable with the record keeping, homework assignments, and other school-related behaviors typical of a cognitive–behavioral treatment plan. Many immigrant elders from rural areas and developing countries will have limited literacy skills in English and their native language. Moreover, because of social and economic barriers related to segregation and racism, members of ethnic minority groups who grew up and were educated in the United States are also likely to have had less formal education than European Americans.

Another limitation of CBT is its assumption that the client holds an internal locus of control (i.e., sees himself or herself as an agent of change). An internal locus of control requires a sense of autonomy and independence in relation to the external world. In contrast, ethnic minority elders from cultures that value collectivism and interdependence often experience the world with an external locus of control, and thus may have difficulty accepting and engaging with cognitive–behavioral treatment.

The need to identify and address affect in CBT may also be difficult for older adults from cultures in which disclosure of one's emotions is considered a sign of weakness or shameful. Similar difficulties may arise when such elders are asked to isolate, identify, and admit to negative cognitions.

COGNITIVE–BEHAVIORAL THERAPY WITH ETHNIC MINORITY ELDERS

A number of interventions can enhance the assessment process when working with culturally diverse older adults. In this section, we review assessment methodologies, discuss ways to adapt CBT interventions for this population, and conclude with a case example that illustrates a culturally sensitive approach to CBT.

Initial Assessment

In the initial assessment, it is important to schedule extra time to develop rapport so that the elder is more likely to openly report information and engage with therapy. In addition, obtaining elders' personal histories takes longer because elders' histories *are* longer. Because elders may experience some embarrassment in revealing personal information to a stranger, the therapist may wish to emphasize the confidential nature of all therapy sessions. A therapist may establish trust and a personal relationship with the client through some ritual of reciprocity (e.g., an exchange of personal information or a "gift" in the form of helpful information). For example, with a Mexican American elder, sharing some personal information while engaging in small talk (*plática*) can help to establish trust (*confianza*) with the client. At the same time, clinical information can be gathered during this informal conversation.

A source of discomfort for some ethnic minority elders may be the identity of the therapist. Older clients in general may have less confidence in a therapist who is significantly younger than they are. Similarly, ethnic minority elders may have difficulty trusting therapists who are ethnically different from themselves. A therapist can work to overcome this distrust by learning as much as possible about the client's culture, working to understand the elder's explanatory model of his or her illness, and, as much as possible, incorporating this model into the therapist's explanation of the problem and the treatment plan. For example, interviewing techniques such as the LEARN model (**Listen** with sympathy and understanding to the patient's perception of the problem, **Explain** your preception of the problem, **Acknowledge** and discuss the differences and similarities, **Recommend** treatment, **Negotiate** agreement; Berlin & Fowkes, 1983, p. 934) and the work by Kleinman and colleagues have been used to elicit a person's explanatory model and to negotiate treatment compliance (Berlin & Fowkes, 1983; Carillo, Green, & Betancourt, 1999; Kleinman, Eisenberg, & Good, 1978).

Incorporating a client's cultural beliefs and vocabulary regarding feelings and emotions is crucial when working with clients who speak English as a second language. Given that individuals tend to be more comfortable expressing intense emotions in their primary language, it can be helpful to allow clients to express their feelings in their native language, although this places responsibility on the therapist for learning the meaning of the words. It may also be helpful to use analogies or stories from the client's culture, life history, or past experiences to help the elder understand the therapist's point and to engage and motivate the client in the therapy process. Therapists should keep in mind that ethnic minority elders may adopt a passive communication style when asked questions. As a result, therapists need to be careful to avoid pathologizing verbal and nonverbal responses that are acceptable within the client's context (e.g., lack of eye contact, difficulty verbalizing feelings, being overly agreeable with the therapist, denial of negative experiences).

Although confidentiality is important, in many ethnic groups the immediate and the extended family are an important aspect of the older client's worldview and value system. Therefore, with the client's consent, interviewing the client's family, friends, and other members of the support system can provide valuable information and help the therapist to better understand the client's values, beliefs, strengths, and community. Such information also helps in determining whether particular thoughts and behaviors are culturally congruent or not. In some cases, inclusion of a traditional healer or religious leader will enhance the elder's acceptance of therapeutic recommendations and commitment to therapy.

After rapport is established, it is important for the therapist to set a clear expectation of the client's role. In the first few sessions, the therapist should introduce the CBT model, educate the client about the importance of therapy compliance and homework, emphasize the client's active role in therapy, and explain effective agenda setting. Some clients may believe that the therapist will "fix them" like a physician. Therefore, it is helpful for the therapist to discuss his or her role in therapy as a guide and active collaborator who will coach the client throughout therapy.

Because older adults are more likely to fatigue, taking short breaks during formal cognitive assessments and extensive clinical interviews is important. This time can also be used to develop rapport with the older adult.

Standardized Assessments

The use of standardized tests with older adults requires caution for at least three reasons (Hays, 1996). First, older adults frequently experience standardized tests as intimidating, confusing, or simply irrelevant. Second, older people referred for mental health problems frequently have physical health problems that can interfere with the attention and concentration required for such tests. Finally, few standardized assessments include age-appropriate norms for older people, particularly elders of ethnic minority cultures. When a standardized assessment is necessary, written assessment tools in the client's native language can help to reduce the probability of the client misunderstanding questions in a second language.

Assessing Affect

Likert and Likert-type rating scales can be less biased in assessing mood states than formal assessment measures and can provide a less threatening medium for disclosure. For example, rating scales that use pictures to depict the anchor points have more face validity and may be perceived as a more innocuous request for information (e.g., using a continuum of happy to sad or angry faces). Another strategy for assessing affect involves asking the client to describe his or her feelings from the point of view of a third party (e.g., "If Mrs. X were [in a similar situation], how and what do you think she would feel, think, or act?"). This may allow the client to feel more distance and therefore increased comfort in talking about emotions.

Adapting Cognitive–Behavioral Interventions

A number of adaptations to CBT can be helpful when working with culturally diverse elders. Given the cognitive changes that arise as a result of the aging process, adapting CBT approaches to accommodate how older adults learn and recall information has been effective (Knight & Satre, 1999). To enhance the learning of specific skills, the therapist will want to keep sessions simple and structured, with regular review of important concepts. Recall of therapy concepts can be enhanced by the use of visual aids such as boards, charts, and handouts, with enlarged print when needed. Allowing the older adult to take notes or audiotape sessions can facilitate the maintenance of behavior change at home. For clients who have impaired vision or hearing, the therapist may use and recommend a magnifying glass with good lighting and a pocket-talker to enhance the therapist's voice for clearer understanding.

In general, older adult clients prefer sessions during the daytime rather than the evening when visual difficulties may make it hard to travel to and from the therapist's office. A number of older adults experience a change in their circadian rhythms that results in an advanced sleep phase pattern in which they are most alert and active in the morning (Ancoli-Israel et al., 2003). Reliance on family members or the use of public transportation means that therapists will need to be flexible regarding the scheduling of appointments. For some clients who are too physically weak or ill to travel, conducting therapy sessions in the client's home or nursing facility may be necessary.

When assigning homework, therapists need to consider what is normal within the client's cultural context and daily routine. Therapists should be careful to keep homework assignments as culturally compatible as possible, assigning tasks that fit easily into the client's existing activities. Tasks may be stigmatizing if too far outside the norms of the client's life, or if they require too much external assistance to complete. However, enlisting the assistance of the client's significant others can facilitate the completion of homework.

When addressing the affective or cognitive components of CBT, using analogies, a third-party example (see the *Assessing Affect* section in this chapter), or examples from folktales, historic lore, or cultural proverbs may help the client to feel more comfortable and increase the person's ability to understand the concepts. Therapists may need to be more directive in the beginning of therapy to point out and provide examples of the client's maladaptive thoughts and their consequences to model and guide the client in his or her ability to attend to metacognitions.

CASE EXAMPLE

The client, AC, was an 82-year-old Chinese American man referred to therapy by his primary care physician for increasing somatic complaints. Initially, AC reported having difficulty caring for his wife, who was in the moderate stage of Alzheimer's disease. When asked, AC denied feeling depressed but reported physical symptoms of upset stomach, low back pain, frequent headaches, insomnia, and heart palpitations. His medical history was significant for hypertension and Type II diabetes mellitus, both managed with medications. He had no prior history of mental illness or psychological treatment.

During the initial assessment, AC reported the following. He and his family had emigrated from mainland China to the United States 40 years ago, in search of better economic opportunities. In China, he had had 8 years of formal education and worked as a deliveryman for various businesses. After moving to the United States, he and his family settled in San Francisco's Chinatown. AC worked as a butcher a block away from his residence and rarely left the community, even after retiring. His primary language was Mandarin, and he spoke some limited English. He denied having a hearing impairment but frequently asked the therapist to repeat herself. He required glasses when reading.

With AC's consent, his daughter Mei was included in the intake process as a source of additional information. Mei worked full time and lived in a separate house with her two teenaged children. She helped to care for her mother to the extent that she could, and AC had become increasingly dependent on her for the management of their household. Contrary to AC's self-report, Mei described him as increasingly irritable, emotionally labile, and apathetic. She reported that he frequently exhibited depressed mood, hopelessness, and passive suicidal ideation. She said that he was becoming more isolated because of his caregiving responsibilities. On the basis of AC's self-reported symptoms, Mei's description, and the therapist's observations, the therapist diagnosed AC with major depressive disorder.

Initially, AC was uncomfortable with the idea of therapy because he did not perceive the therapist as having any credibility. Although the therapist was Chinese American, he believed that she could not be competent because she was a woman and much younger than he. After the first session, AC did not attend the next scheduled session. When the therapist called to reschedule his missed appointment, she carefully listened to his concerns regarding his wife, gave empathic responses, and provided information regarding how behavioral interventions could help him to better manage his wife. This informational exchange was meant to be a form of gift giving aimed at building rapport and trust with AC, and it worked. After the interaction, AC began attending therapy sessions regularly. Over time, he was able to learn more about the therapist as a person and to experience her knowledge and empathy regarding his immigration experiences. To reinforce his willingness to attend sessions, the therapist was careful to accommodate AC's scheduling needs, which involved relying on his daughter for transportation. This also allowed for the opportunity to occasionally include AC's daughter in the therapy sessions.

The therapist assessed AC's comfort and proficiency with the English language and found that although AC was not fluent in English, his comfort level and grasp of the language were sufficient to continue therapy together. To better understand her client's explanatory model of illness, she asked AC what he believed caused his somatic problems and what he believed would result in their resolution. AC stated he believed that his physical problems were caused by an imbalance of his *chi* (i.e., energy or life force). He explained that he was not eating right or exercising regularly as he did before caring for his wife. He did not see how he would benefit from mental health services, as he believed he could eliminate his symptoms if he made a concerted effort to eat a balanced diet and exercise daily. The therapist did not challenge his explanatory model of illness. She instead used his belief in the interaction of body and mind to describe his presenting problems, and she incorporated elements of his explanatory model (e.g., the importance of enhancing one's chi during times of stress) to describe the rationale for the treatment plan. Although the therapist's knowledge of the basic principles of Chinese medicine facilitated the therapeutic process, it was her solicitation of and listening to AC's explanatory model, and the incorporation of his beliefs, that resulted in AC's engagement in the therapy process.

The therapist spent four sessions educating AC about the CBT model, emphasizing the importance of homework assignments and agenda setting, and discussing therapy goals. She also explained her role as his therapist. She said that the sessions would be very structured, using an agenda. They decided collaboratively that his goals would be to reduce his physical distress and to improve his ability to cope with his caregiving responsibilities. They agreed that they would focus a portion of each session on caregiving concerns (i.e., questions about behavior management regarding his wife), and the rest of the session would be dedicated to attaining his goals of reducing the physical distress and improving his coping skills.

Initially, AC's mood was assessed weekly via his verbal self-report and completion of the Chinese version of the Geriatric Depression Scale (Stokes, Thompson, Murphy, & Gallagher-Thompson, 2001). However, his self-report and responses on the questionnaire were not congruent with his clinical presentation or with his daughter's report. Consequently, the therapist changed her approach to incorporate a Likert-type rating scale anchored by a happy face and a sad face. This method of assessment appeared to more closely reflect the therapist's observations and his daughter's reports and was incorporated into the weekly assessment of AC's stress and somatic symptoms.

Because of AC's apathy at the beginning of therapy, behavioral rather than cognitive interventions were the initial focus. The therapist asked AC to complete the Older Person's Pleasant Event Schedule (OP-PES; Gallagher & Thompson, 1981) at home. The OP-PES is a self-report measure that asks the client to rate the frequency and enjoyment of a number of activities that older people often find enjoyable (e.g., kissing, touching, showing affection, listening to birds sing). Although Mei helped translate unfamiliar words while he completed the scale, AC did not endorse many of the items because they were not culturally relevant to him. At the next session, the client and therapist collaboratively developed a list of pleasant events on the basis of his response to the OP-PES, and he was asked to complete at least three of the pleasant events on his list. The next week he reported that he did not do any of the activities. When the therapist explored his homework noncompliance, he reported that he did not like the activities listed. In the session, the therapist asked him to create a list of activities he enjoyed. This list included items such as doing tai chi and Chinese calligraphy, walking, reading the Chinese newspaper, and visiting Chinatown and his friends. After revising the list, his homework compliance was 100%. Within a month, his mood had improved as assessed by his daily mood ratings, his daughter's report, and the therapist's observations; he reported fewer somatic symptoms and reduced caregiver stress; and he showed an increased ability to manage his wife's problematic behaviors.

Once AC became more behaviorally engaged, the therapist began to introduce cognitive interventions into therapy. AC appeared to have several maladaptive thoughts that contributed to his depressed mood. One of these was the belief that his daughter's refusal to drop her employment and other responsibilities, to provide full-time care for her parents, was a reflection on his authority as head of the family. He believed that it was shameful that she was not more willing to fulfill her obligation to her parents according to Confucian laws. He expressed some catastrophic thoughts that Mei's behavior was evidence that he had lost his potency as a father and as a man, and that none of his children would care for him if or when he became ill or disabled. The therapist recognized that within AC's culture, such a situation *would* be seen as pitiful and shameful. A related belief held by AC was that men should not be engaged in "women's work"; his difficulty performing traditionally female responsibilities only added to his feelings of inadequacy.

The therapist helped AC complete thought logs that specified his beliefs, thoughts, and feelings regarding his daughter's behavior, the caregiving situation, and his role within the family. She explained how what people believe and think about something affects how they feel. She also pointed out how feelings can include emotions (e.g., his frustration with his daughter) and physical symptoms (e.g., the stomachache he experienced when frustrated). She then helped AC to look for and record evidence of the many ways in which his daughter did provide support.

In addition, with the therapist's help, AC was able to engage his other two children to assist in the caregiving responsibilities for their mother. To facilitate this, the therapist asked all three adult children to attend a family session in which the client's request for increased support was reinforced by the therapist. Finally, via several discussions of the cultural norms regarding traditional roles and responsibilities for men in AC's culture, the therapist helped AC to reframe the tasks he considered traditionally feminine as acceptable for a strong husband who wishes to provide for his wife.

At the end of his 20-week treatment, AC's depressive and somatic symptoms had decreased significantly, and he reported his caregiving role to be less stressful and burdensome. He described feeling more competent in his ability to care for his wife and to manage his household effectively. He was also receiving more help from his children.

CONCLUSION

The population of elders and particularly ethnic minority elders in the United States is growing rapidly. To provide effective care, therapists need to be culturally competent and knowledgeable regarding the diversity of older adults. This chapter offered suggestions for modifying cognitive–behavioral assessment and interventions with culturally diverse elders. Although it may take more time, effort, and patience, working with ethnic minority elders can be a rewarding experience for both the client and the therapist.

REFERENCES

Administration on Aging. (2000). *A profile of older Americans*. Washington, DC: Author.

Allen, I. M. (1986). Posttraumatic stress disorder among Black Vietnam veterans. *Hospital and Community Psychiatry, 37*, 55–61.

American Association of Retired Persons. (1997). *A profile of older Americans: 1997*. Washington, DC: U.S. Department of Health and Human Services.

American Psychiatric Association. (2000). *Diagnostic and statistical manual of mental disorders* (4th ed., text rev.). Washington, DC: Author.

Ancoli-Israel, S., Cole, R., Alessi, C., Chambers, M., Moorcroft, W., & Pollack, C. P. (2003). The role of actigraphy in the study of sleep and circadian rhythms. *Sleep, 26*, 342–392.

Areán, P., & Gallagher-Thompson, D. (1996). Issues and recommendations for the recruitment and retention of older ethnic minority adults into clinical research. *Journal of Consulting and Clinical Psychology, 64*, 875–880.

Areán, P., & Miranda, J. (1996). The treatment of depression in elderly primary care patients: A naturalistic study. *Journal of Clinical Geropsychology, 2*, 153–160.

Baker, F. M., & Takeshita, J. (2001). The ethnic minority elderly. In W. Tseng & J. Streltzer (Eds.), *Culture and psychotherapy: A guide to clinical practice* (pp. 209–222). Washington, DC: American Psychiatric Press.

Berlin, E. A., & Fowkes, W. C., Jr. (1983). A teaching framework for cross-cultural health care: Application in family practice. *Western Journal of Medicine, 139*, 934–938.

Black, S. A. (2000). The mental health of culturally diverse elderly: Research and clinical issues. In I. Cuellar & F. A. Paniagua (Eds.), *Handbook of multicultural mental health: Assessment and treatment of diverse populations* (pp. 325–339). San Diego, CA: Academic Press.

Braun, K. L., & Browne, C. V. (1998). Perceptions of dementia, caregiving, and help-seeking among Asian and Pacific Islander Americans. *Health and Social Work, 23*, 262–274.

Carillo, J. E., Green, A. R., & Betancourt, J. R. (1999). Cross-cultural primary care: A patient-based approach. *Annals of Internal Medicine, 130*, 829–834.

Clare, L., & Woods, R. T. (2004). Cognitive training and cognitive rehabilitation for people with early-stage Alzheimer's disease: A review. *Neuropsychological Rehabilitation, 14*, 385–401.

Cohen-Mansfield, J. (2001). Nonpharmacologic interventions for inappropriate behaviors in dementia: A review, summary, and critique. *American Journal of Geriatric Psychiatry, 9*, 316–381.

Cook, A. J. (1998). Cognitive–behavioral pain management for elderly nursing home residents. *Journals of Gerontology, Series B: Psychological Sciences and Social Sciences, 53B*, 51–59.

Cooper-Patrick, L., Gallo, J. J., Powe, N. R., Steinwachs, D. S., Eaton, W. W., & Ford, D. E. (1999). Mental health services utilization by African Americans and Whites: The Baltimore Epidemiologic Catchment Area follow-up. *Medical Care, 37*, 1034–1045.

Dai, Y., Zhang, S., Yamamoto, J., Ao, J., Belin, T. R., Cheung, F., et al. (1999). Cognitive behavioral therapy of minor depressive symptoms in elderly Chinese Americans: A pilot study. *Community Mental Health Journal, 36*, 537–542.

Durham, R. C., Chambers, J. A., MacDonald, R. R., Power, K. G., & Major, K. (2003). Does cognitive–behavioural therapy influence the long-term outcome of generalized anxiety disorder? An 8–14 year follow-up of two clinical trials. *Psychological Medicine, 33*, 499–509.

Evans, D. A., Funkenstein, H. H., Albert, M. S., Scherr, P. A., Cook, N. R., Chown, M. J., et al. (1989). Prevalence of Alzheimer's disease in a community population of older persons: Higher than previously reported. *Journal of the American Medical Association, 262*, 2552–2556.

Finch, E., Ramsay, R., & Katona, C. (1992). Depression and physical illness in the elderly. *Clinics in Geriatric Medicine, 8*, 275–287.

Gallagher, D., & Thompson, L. W. (1981). *Depression in the elderly: A behavioral treatment manual*. Los Angeles: University of Southern California Press.

Gallagher-Thompson, D., Areán, P., Coon, D., Menendez, A., Takagi, K., Haley, W. E., et al. (2000). Development and implementation strategies for culturally diverse caregiving populations. In R. Schulz (Ed.), *Handbook on dementia caregiving: Evidence-based interventions for family caregivers* (pp. 151–185). New York: Springer Publishing Company.

Gallagher-Thompson, D., Leary, M. C., Ossinalde, C., Romero, J. J., Wald, M. J., & Fernandez-Gamarra, E. (1997). Hispanic caregivers of older adults with dementia: Cultural issues in outreach and intervention. *Group, 21,* 211–232.

Gallagher-Thompson, D., Talamantes, M., Ramirez, R., & Valverde, I. (1996). Service delivery issues and recommendations for working with Mexican American family caregivers. In G. Yeo & D. Gallagher-Thompson (Eds.), *Ethnicity and the dementias* (pp. 137–152). Washington, DC: Taylor & Francis.

Gatz, M., Fiske, A., Fox, L. S., Kaskie, B., Kasl-Godly, J. E., McCallum, T. J., & Wetherell, J. L. (1998). Empirically validated psychological treatments for older adults. *Journal of Mental Health and Aging, 4,* 9–46.

Gonzalez, C., & Griffith, E. H. (1996). Culture and the diagnosis of somatoform and dissociative disorders. In J. E. Mezzich, A. Kleinman, H. Fabrega, & D. Parron (Eds.), *Culture and psychiatric diagnosis: A DSM–IV perspective* (pp. 137–150). Washington, DC: American Psychiatric Press.

Gupta, R. (2000). Treatment of depression in an elderly Asian Indian male: A cognitive behavioral approach. *Clinical Gerontologist, 22,* 87–90.

Gupta, R. (2003). Cognitive behavioral treatment on driving phobia for an Asian Indian male. *Clinical Gerontologist, 26,* 165–171.

Haley, W. E., Han, B., & Henderson, J. N. (1998). Aging and ethnicity: Issues for clinical practice. *Journal of Clinical Psychology in Medical Settings, 5,* 393–409.

Harris, H. L. (1998). Ethnic minority elders: Issues and interventions. *Educational Gerontology, 24,* 309–324.

Hays, P. A. (1995). Multicultural applications of cognitive behavior therapy. *Professional Psychology: Research and Practice, 26,* 309–315.

Hays, P. A. (1996). Culturally responsive assessment with diverse older clients. *Professional Psychology: Research and Practice, 27,* 188–193.

Hindrichsen, G. A., & Dick-Siskin, L. P. (2000). The treatment of late-life mental health problems. In S. K. Whitbourne (Ed.), *Psychopathology in later life* (pp. 323–353). New York: Wiley.

Institute of Medicine, Board of Health Sciences Policy, Committee on Understanding and Eliminating Racial and Ethnic Disparities in Health Care. (2003). In B. D. Smedley, A. Y. Stith, & A. R. Nelson (Eds.), *Unequal treatment: Confronting racial and ethnic disparities in health.* Washington, DC: National Academies Press. Retrieved November 17, 2003, from http://nap.edu/books/030908265X/html/

Kinoshita, L. M., & Gallagher-Thompson, D. (2004). Japanese American caregivers of individuals with dementia: An examination of Japanese cultural values and dementia caregiving. *Clinical Gerontologist, 27*(1/2), 87–102.

Kleinman, A. (1980). *Patient and healers in the context of culture: An exploration of the borderland between anthropology, medicine, and psychiatry.* Berkeley: University of California Press.

Kleinman, A., Eisenberg, L., & Good, B. (1978). Culture, illness, and care: Clinical lessons from anthropologic and cross-cultural research. *Annals of Internal Medicine, 88,* 251–258.

Knight, B. G., & Satre, D. D. (1999). Cognitive behavioral psychotherapy with older adults. *Clinical Psychology, 6,* 188–203.

Lam, R. E., Pacala, J. T., & Smith, S. L. (1997). Factors related to depressive symptoms in an elderly Chinese American sample. *Clinical Gerontologist, 17,* 57–70.

Lau, A. W., & Gallagher-Thompson, D. (2002). Ethnic minority older adults in clinical and research programs: Issues and recommendations. *The Behavior Therapist, 25*(1), 10–16.

Lin, Y. (2001). The application of cognitive–behavioral therapy to counseling Chinese. *American Journal of Psychotherapy, 55,* 46–58.

Lockery, S. A. (1991). Caregiving among racial and ethnic minority elders: Family and social supports. *Generations: Journal of the American Society on Aging, 15*(4), 58–62.

Loo, C. M. (1994). Race-related PTSD: The Asian American Vietnam veteran. *Journal of Traumatic Stress, 74,* 637–656.

McCormick, W. C., Uomoto, J., Young, H., Graves, A. B., Vitaliano, P., Mortimer, J. A., et al. (1996). Attitudes toward use of nursing homes and home care in older Japanese-Americans. *Journal of American Geriatrics Society, 44,* 769–777.

Meyers, B. S. (1998). Depression and dementia: Comorbidities, identification, and treatment. *Journal of Geriatric Psychiatry and Neurology, 11,* 201–205.

Morin, C. M., Kowatch, R. A., Barry, T., & Walton, E. (1993). Cognitive–behavior therapy for late-life insomnia. *Journal of Consulting and Clinical Psychology, 61,* 137–147.

Ory, M. G., Yee, J. L., Tennstedt, S. L., & Schulz, R. (2000). The extent and impact of dementia care: Unique challenges experienced by family caregivers. In R. Schulz (Ed.), *Handbook of dementia caregiving* (pp. 1–32). New York: Springer Publishing Company.

Parks, F. M. (2003). The role of African American folk beliefs in the modern therapeutic process. *Clinical Psychology: Science and Practice, 10,* 456–467.

Sarkisian, C. A., Hays, R. D., Berry, S. H., & Mangione, C. M. (2001). Expectations regarding aging among older adults and physicians who care for older adults. *Medical Care, 39,* 1025–1036.

Siegel, J. S. (1999). Demographic introduction to racial/Hispanic elderly populations. In T. P. Miles (Ed.), *Full-color aging: Facts, goals, and recommendations for America's diverse elders* (pp. 1–19). Washington, DC: Gerontological Society of America.

Stanley, M. A., Hopko, D. R., Diefenbach, G. J., Bourland, S. L., Rodriguez, H., & Wagener, P. (2003). Cognitive–behavior therapy for late-life generalized anxiety disorder in primary care: Preliminary findings. *American Journal of Geriatric Psychiatry, 11,* 92–96.

Stokes, S. C., Thompson, L. W., Murphy, S., & Gallagher-Thompson, D. (2001). Screening for depression in immigrant Chinese-American elders: Results of a pilot study. *Journal of Gerontological Social Work, 36,* 27–44.

Sue, D. W., & Sue, D. (2003). *Counseling the culturally diverse: Theory and practice* (4th ed.). New York: Wiley.

Teri, L., Logsdon, R. G., Uomoto, J., & McCurry, S. M. (1997). Behavioral treatment of depression in dementia patients: A controlled clinical trial. *Journal of Gerontology: Psychological Sciences, 52,* 159–166.

Zamanian, K., Thachrey, M., Starrett, R. A., Brown, L. G., Lassman, D. K., & Blanchard, A. (1992). Acculturation and depression in Mexican-American elderly. *Clinical Gerontologist, 11,* 109–121.

Zeiss, A. M., Lewinsohn, P. M., Rohde, P., & Seeley, J. R. (1996). Relationship of physical disease and functional impairment to depression in older people. *Psychology and Aging, 11,* 572–581.

9

COGNITIVE–BEHAVIORAL THERAPY AND PEOPLE WITH DISABILITIES

LINDA R. MONA, JENNIFER M. ROMESSER-SCEHNET, REBECCA P. CAMERON, AND VERONICA CARDENAS

The American Psychological Association (2002) has included cultural competence in working with people with disabilities as a standard in its "Ethical Principles of Psychologists and Code of Conduct." However, the field is still in its infancy in achieving such cultural competence, with few disabled people represented in the field of clinical psychology and little formal training available for conducting therapy with disabled people. The goal of this chapter is to move beyond the individually oriented deficit model in conceptualizing the difficulties experienced by clients with disabilities and discuss the utility of cognitive–behavioral therapy (CBT) with disabled people. To foster a broader conceptualization, we discuss the emerging recognition of disability as a cultural identity and contrast it with historical perspectives on disability, followed by research on psychological resources that aid people living with disability. Finally, examples of the use of behavioral and cognitive strategies to improve adjustment among persons with disabilities are described and illustrated. (Note that we have chosen to use the terms *disabled people, disability community,* and *people with disabilities* interchangeably. We believe that exclusively using person-first language—that is, *people with dis-*

abilities—ignores the recognition of disability as a cultural identity and the fact that many are proud to call themselves *disabled people*.)

Traditional models of disability have assumed that psychological difficulties experienced by people with disabilities originate within the affected individual and reflect the person's failure to adapt to the nondisabled world (Olkin, 1999, p. 25). Clinical interventions are often geared toward changing the individual to better approximate "normal" functioning. In contrast, more recent *interactionist* models conceptualize disability as a consequence of interactions between physical differences or impairments and multiple contexts (e.g., family, housing, transportation, and social situations; Olkin & Pledger, 2003). Such models offer a more comprehensive approach to working with clients, highlighting issues of person–environment fit and calling for the use of multiple intervention strategies.

There is an additional perspective emerging from sociopolitical frameworks and the field of disability studies that goes beyond the interactionist viewpoint to acknowledge that the experience of disabled people is that of belonging to a minority cultural group (Olkin & Pledger, 2003). This cultural perspective addresses issues of identity that arise from environmental and social deficits that limit full self-determination and participation by people with disabilities. It also recognizes the interplay between biological, social, and environmental factors in creating the disability experience.

Clinical psychology has yet to fully embrace the cultural perspective on disability, although change is occurring. The gradual incorporation of ethnicity as a core area of competence for psychologists suggests that awareness of disability perspectives may improve slowly over the next few decades. One challenge to comprehensive models of disability is that the term *disability* includes the shared cultural experiences of people with a range of differences, including physical, sensory, psychological, addictive, cognitive, developmental, and other chronic health conditions. However, much of the research relevant to clinical work with people with disabilities is undertaken with relatively homogeneous samples of people within specific categories of impairment or even within specific diagnostic groups (Andersson, 2000; Devins, Camerson, & Edworthy, 2000; Durand, Tanner, & Christopher, 2000; Fitzgerald, 2000; Jackson & Taylor, 2000; Kearney & McKnight, 2000; Tirch & Radnitz, 2000; Van Dorsten, 2000). In addition, studies of psychological functioning and psychotherapeutic intervention with disabled people have focused on individuals with acquired disabilities and have rarely addressed cultural variables that are unique to the disability experience (Craig, Hancock, Chang, & Dickson, 1998).

Although the issues we present are broadly applicable across diverse impairments, we have chosen to focus primarily on physical and sensory disabilities. We begin with a brief overview of the components of disability culture, followed by a discussion of the ways in which disability has been conceptualized within psychology and other disciplines, thus setting the stage for examining CBT applications within this diverse community.

DISABILITY CULTURE

Definitions of shared cultural experiences have typically been ascribed to people with similar ethnic backgrounds and familial lineage. In contrast, people with disabilities often grow up looking and feeling different from family members and having life experiences that vary significantly from those of their family of origin. Given this, what constitutes and lends support to the notion of disability culture? According to Gill (1995), there are eight core values that underlie political struggles, are reflected in art, are included within conversations, and become a part of the goals and the behaviors of people with disabilities. These eight core values shed light on the foundation of disability culture and are summarized as follows:

1. an acceptance of human variation (e.g., physical, functional, racial, intellectual, economic class);
2. a matter-of-fact orientation toward using assistance and an acceptance of human vulnerability and interdependence as part of life;
3. a tolerance for lack of resolution for dealing with the unpredictable and living with uncertainty or less-than-desired outcomes;
4. disability humor, including the ability to laugh at the oppressor as well as one's own experiences, with a keen sense of absurdity in even the most dire circumstances;
5. skills in managing multiple problems, systems, technology, and personal assistants;
6. a sophisticated future orientation involving the ability to construct complex plans taking into account multiple contingencies and realistically anticipated obstacles;
7. a carefully focused capacity for closure in interpersonal communication and the ability to read others' attitudes and conflicts to sort out, fill in the gaps, and grasp the latent meaning in contradictory social messages; and
8. a flexible, adaptive approach to tasks and a creativity stimulated by both limited resources and experience with nontraditional modes of operating. (Gill, 1995)

These values reflect the adaptive value of psychological flexibility among people with disabilities and also suggest the types of social constraints that may lead to mental health issues. Many of these values are consistent with those that guide the work of cognitive–behavioral therapists, particularly those values that counter rigid or perfectionistic standards for human functioning. Familiarity with these ideals of disability culture can facilitate the development of a more culturally responsive approach to CBT.

Disability culture is transmitted by means of shared life experiences among members of this group. For example, political issues affecting resources available to disabled people, the availability of accessible affordable housing, transportation, personal assistance services, and the availability and quality of structured living facilities all greatly affect the everyday life experiences of people with disabilities (Fine & Asch, 1988; Gill, 1995). Given the importance of belonging to a constituent community in developing a collective voice advocating for political change, Gill (1995) specifically described four purposes of disability culture that lend support to the development of this community. From a psychological perspective, these tenets function in the following fashion.

First, disability culture serves to fortify people with disabilities through the definition and expression of community self-worth, which leads to greater enrichment and resilience among disabled people, increasing endurance against oppression. Second, disability culture serves to unify disabled people through cultural activities that affirm shared values, a common heritage, and mutual support that is available in community with other disabled people. Third, disability culture serves to communicate the unique qualities of people with disabilities within and beyond the disability community through the development of art, language, symbols, and rituals. Finally, disability culture promotes "coming out" or "recruitment" by converting social marginalization into a celebration of distinctness. Although certain components of these functions are unique to the disability community, the themes are similar to other marginalized groups such as gay, lesbian, and bisexual people. Awareness of these avenues of cultural transmission for people with disabilities can help cognitive–behavioral therapists to more fully support identity development and political and community solidarity as adjuncts to or goals within traditional therapeutic approaches.

PARADIGMS OF DISABILITY

How one defines disability affects one's view of disability culture and people with disabilities. In this section we discuss the three most commonly used paradigms of disability: the moral, medical, and social models.

Moral Model

Several theoretical frameworks have shaped disability-related cultural discourse. The oldest of these paradigms is the moral model of disability. As presented by Olkin (1999, pp. 25–26), this view is based on the assertion that disability is a physical manifestation of sin or moral lapse. Under this model, disability may also be constructed as a test of faith or a divine opportunity for spiritual growth and increased enlightenment. The moral model was often used as justification for the social ostracism and isolation of disabled people, as their physical difficulties were perceived to be an outward reflection of their own moral character. Aspects of this model still resonate in the conceptualization of disability. For example, people with disabilities often feel pressured to overcompensate for their impairment because of a deeply ingrained cultural belief that they are inherently inferior to their nondisabled counterparts.

Medical Model

The medical model of disability was a direct consequence of an increased emphasis on rehabilitative medicine following the Civil War. As described by Longmore and Umansky (2001), the medical model is inextricably linked to modern social arrangements regarding disability. This approach places almost exclusive emphasis on the responsibility of the individual to overcome her or his disability. People with disabilities are culturally mandated by the mainstream to work as hard as possible to emulate the nondisabled norm.

The current emphasis on the medical aspects of disability has direct consequences on the allocation of social and economic resources. Specifically, generous financial resources are allocated to developing cures for medical conditions that factor into the experience of disability, but support for the kinds of resources that would be needed to create fully accessible communities is limited. The goal of eliminating disability is more culturally consistent with Western ideals than is the more immediate goal of embracing and supporting individuals presently living with disability.

Social Model

The social model of disability, currently identified with the field of disability studies, directly addresses the limitations of both the moral and medical models by framing disability as a social construction rather than an individual malady. The social model rejects the definition of disability as disorder and instead frames the experiences of disabled people as similar to those of other minority groups. This similarity includes a history of disempowerment in the form of restricted access to economic and cultural institutions and repeated experiences of stigma and discrimination. Discrimination experienced by disabled people has included restrictions on reproductive rights, inadequate health care and other socioeconomic resources, underrepresentation in political and economic spheres, and an increased incidence of hate crimes (Olkin, 1999, p. 42).

However, the social model is not limited to an awareness of disadvantage. This model also offers an affirming view of disability, with a focus on health, resilience, and an improved quality of life via enhanced social policies and civil rights protections (Olkin, 1999, p. 314). As with other minority-group studies, disability studies focus on the development of "a definition of self (i.e., Who are we?), preferred language (i.e., What do we call ourselves?), and the training and research agenda for the field" (Olkin & Pledger, 2003, p. 297).

PSYCHOSOCIAL VARIABLES RELEVANT TO SUBGROUPS OF DISABLED PEOPLE

Following the medical model of disability, most psychological studies of people with disabilities address adaptation to acquired disability in relation to groups defined by impairment or medical diagnosis. This approach has yielded useful data regarding adjustment to specific acquired impairments. However, the data are limited in their usefulness regarding the understanding of psychological issues and adjustment related to lifelong disability, the role of environmental factors in adjustment, and the nature of shared cultural experiences affecting the mental health status of disabled people.

Physical Disabilities

Numerous studies have examined the relationship between various psychological factors and adjustment in individuals with physical impairments. The majority of these studies have focused on factors that facilitate adjustment following spinal cord injury (SCI; Elliot, Godshall, & Herrick, 1991; Hancock, Craig, Dickson, Chang, & Martin, 1993; Rintala, Young, & Hart, 1992; Thompson, Coker, Krause, & Henry, 2003). Studies examining coping styles and adjustment in people with SCI have found that healthy coping strategies, including active coping, problem solving, and acceptance, were predictive of positive emotional adjustment (Elliot et al., 1991; Kennedy, Marsh, & Lowe, 2000; Moore, Bombardier, Brown, & Patterson, 1994). Coping can influence the degree to which an individual will experience subjective distress postinjury at both short-term (6 weeks) and long-term (4 years) follow-up (Kennedy et al., 2000).

Personality variables such as locus of control and self-esteem are also relevant to adjustment after injury (Hancock et al., 1993). Specifically, locus of control and self-efficacy can affect a person's perceived ability to meet the demands of his or her life situation, affecting the coping strategies the person chooses to implement (Hancock et al., 1993). For example, a disabled person who views her or his situation as challenging may use information seeking or positive reframing, whereas someone who views her or his situation as threatening may deny, withdraw, or disengage (Hancock et al., 1993). The personal resource of assertiveness and the interpersonal resource of social support may also be protective against depression within the SCI population (Elliot et al., 1991; Rintala et al., 1992).

Sensory Disabilities

Studies of individuals who have experienced total or partial loss of vision have demonstrated that the onset of visual impairment is often accompanied by some degree of emotional distress (Needham, 1988). In a study examining adults who lost their vision, over half of the participants experienced depression, anxiety, anger, somatic complaints, suicidal ideation, or insomnia in their first year of blindness (Fitzgerald, 1971). At a 4-year follow-up, approximately 40% to 50% of these individuals still had symptoms of anxiety and depression (Fitzgerald, Ebert, & Chambers, 1987). Psychological variables that have implications for intervention have been identified. Specifically, the use of denial as a coping strategy was found to be ineffective, resulting in barriers to rehabilitation and adjustment (Fitzgerald, 1970). A sense of high self-efficacy and an internal locus of control are factors that have been found to predict better adjustment in this group (Dodds, Flannigan, & Ng, 1993). These personality variables affect an individual's appraisal of his or her situation and perceived ability to meet demands, both of which affect adjustment and rehabilitation efforts (Dodds & Ferguson, 1994). For example, an individual with poor self-efficacy and an external locus of control may feel little control over her or his current or future situation and may attribute gains made in rehabilitation to the therapist or to luck rather than to her or his own efforts.

In addition to negative psychological sequelae, loss of vision can affect experiences relevant to one's quality of life, including compromised psychological security, physical integrity, monetary resources, and occupational opportunities. Visual impairment can also affect a person's self-worth, independence, and family role (Jackson & Taylor, 2000).

Adjustment to a hearing impairment is a similarly complex process. Although researchers have not identified psychological disturbances occurring directly as a result of hearing loss, adverse effects on social and interpersonal functioning have been identified (Andersson, 2000). Additionally, Andersson, Melin, Lindberg, and Scott (1995) found that health problems, hearing problems, and psychological problems are correlated, and the combination of these factors can hinder adjustment to hearing impairment.

Implications for Psychological Intervention

Collectively, these findings have implications for psychological treatment aimed at increasing the well-being of people with physical and sensory disabilities. Psychological interventions that focus on intrapersonal factors such as enhancing positive coping strategies and assertiveness, and on interpersonal factors such as increasing social support, may benefit disabled people who need strengthening in these areas. However, such approaches are incomplete if they focus solely on correcting apparent deficits among people with disabilities. A broader awareness of the social and environmental context of disablement is critical for culturally competent therapy. This includes a consideration of barriers that prevent optimal coping, reduce the likelihood of assertive behavior, and impede the development of social support networks among people with disabilities.

COGNITIVE–BEHAVIORAL MODEL OF PSYCHOTHERAPY

The cognitive–behavioral model focuses on the influence of cognitions and cognitive processes on an individual's emotions and behavior (A. T. Beck, 1976; J. S. Beck, 1995). Cognitions occur at a number of levels, as articulated by J. S. Beck (1995). Core beliefs are developed from early childhood experience. They operate at a fundamental level typically outside of awareness and give rise to intermediate beliefs in the form of rules, attitudes, and assumptions (J. S. Beck, 1995; Ellis & Grieger, 1986). Some of these beliefs and assumptions are rigid, dysfunctional, and maladaptive, whereas others are positive. Of primary interest to cognitive–behavioral therapists are the dysfunctional beliefs that contribute to the development of psychological disorders (J. S. Beck, 1995). These beliefs can skew information processing and lead to a negative triad of perceptions about oneself, the future, and the world (A. T. Beck, 1976).

For example, a client who accepts standards of beauty that are defined by the nondisabled world might believe that to be attractive she must look as nondisabled as possible. In this case, having a disability that interferes with adherence to beauty norms (e.g., using assistive equipment such as a wheelchair, cane, or crutches) may significantly affect the way that the client thinks about herself ("I am ugly"), the future ("I will be alone forever"), and the world ("Other people will reject me"). These thoughts will likely result in negative emotions such as sadness and anger and could lead to maladaptive behaviors such as social withdrawal or substance abuse (Galvin & Godfrey, 2001).

Physical barriers and the negative attitudes of others may interact with beliefs to increase the likelihood of developing cognitive distortions. For example, if this woman holds the culturally based belief that women should dress stylishly when leaving the house, she may feel the need to dress up and wear makeup to feel good about herself. However, in her attempt to do so, she may encounter physical barriers in transportation, retail stores, dressing rooms, display counters, and public restrooms. She may find herself being treated as if she is not worthy of respect by merchants, and she may be patronized regarding her efforts to dress well "despite everything." These kinds of experiences may feed into the types of distortions previously noted in which negative experiences and invalidating feedback come to be viewed as universally prevalent, permanent, and accurate assessments of one's self-worth.

Beliefs about illness and disability that vary greatly between cultures may conflict with current disability culture norms. For example, a dominant view within some ethnic groups may include the beliefs that people with disabilities should not marry, that disability status should be denied rather than acknowledged, that a cure should be hoped for as the ultimate goal, or that disability is a spiritual burden. This can lead to dilemmas in resolving multiple identities and reconciling competing belief systems for those individuals subscribing to both ethnic and disability culture norms. For example, a Chinese American adolescent living with rheumatoid arthritis may feel very connected to Chinese cultural values of family loyalty and support and receive all of her personal assistance with daily living activities from family members. However, she may also subscribe to disability culture norms in her desire to be on her own as an adult and may wish to experiment with assistance outside of the family to prepare for this transition. The individually tailored approach that characterizes CBT can be especially helpful in such instances.

Radnitz and Tirch (1997) integrated many of the important factors to be considered in working with disabled people in a model that focuses on the interactional relationship between preexisting factors (i.e., cognitive and attributional style), environmental elements (i.e., physical barriers, social barriers, and cultural milieu), and the psychological consequences of living with a disability (i.e., body image disturbance, lifestyle disruption, and feelings of loss). Although this model is derived primarily from clinical experience with the SCI population, it may be helpful with people with varying types of acquired conditions. It is important to note that this model is not meant to capture all aspects of the disability experience, but its interactional perspective provides a starting place for cognitive–behavioral conceptualizations of clients adjusting to disability. When treating people with disabilities, the role of the cognitive–behavioral therapist is to help clients face the psychological distress and sequelae that accompany the disability experience. Disability may not be central to the presenting problem for every disabled person who seeks therapy, but disability is part of the context in which the presenting problem occurs and in which treatment will take place (i.e., as gender, ethnicity, and social class would be for nondisabled clients).

Cognitive Distortions

Living with a disability affects the spectrum of interactions that a person has with her or his world (Tirch & Radnitz, 2000). What are of particular interest to a cognitive–behavioral therapist are the irrational cognitions and negative assumptions contributing to negative emotional states. As described in the model presented earlier, the stressors and limitations of living with a disability interact with preinjury factors (i.e., cognitive and attribution factors) and external factors (e.g., physical barriers, attitudes of others), increasing the likelihood of developing cognitive distortions. Although various authors have characterized cognitive distortions that are typical to people experiencing a range of psychological difficulties (e.g., A. T. Beck, Rush, Shaw, & Emery, 1979; J. S. Beck, 1995), there have also been relatively recent efforts to describe cognitive distortions that may be uniquely shaped by the experience of disability (Needham, 1988; Radnitz & Tirch, 1997; Tirch & Radnitz, 2000).

Radnitz and Tirch (1997) identified six categories of cognitive distortions relevant to people with disabilities. Rather than considering these to be universally present among all people with physical disabilities, these may be thought of as a starting point for assessment. If present, these types of distortions may significantly affect psychological well-being and social adjustment.

The first category concerns an overly negative view of the world and others (Tirch & Radnitz, 2000). People with disabilities may be at risk of believing that all people they encounter are insensitive, reducing the likelihood of positive social interactions. Although biases against people with disabilities are present in our culture, it is the pervasiveness of these beliefs that may be distorted.

The second cluster of distortions is based on the person's appraisal of her or his own self-worth (Tirch & Radnitz, 2000). This category involves feelings of inadequacy related to perceived lack of ability and reliance on others. An individual's premorbid beliefs about people with disabilities (and the meaning of accepting help) will likely influence the way that she or he feels about herself or himself (Van Dorsten, 2000).

The third type of cognitive distortion is the expectation and perception of rejection (Tirch & Radnitz, 2000). Again, predisability beliefs play a role and may combine with personal sense of self-worth (Tirch & Radnitz, 2000) to shape an individual's expectations about how others will perceive and treat him or her. People with disabilities may anticipate that others will reject them on the basis of their disability and consequently may perceive neutral interactions as negative and rejecting in nature. These expectations are likely to permeate initial interactions with the social environment, reducing the likelihood of disconfirming experiences (Van Dorsten, 2000).

The fourth type of cognitive distortion that may arise is that of hopelessness, the expectation of consistent failure (Tirch & Radnitz, 2000). Faced with considerable physical and social obstacles and the risk of frequent disappointment, a disabled person may give up hope of happiness or reasonable social, occupational, or personal achievement (Tirch & Radnitz, 2000). Such hopelessness can lead to depression, anxiety, and despair, which can in turn have a marked effect on rehabilitation efforts, adjustment, and overall well-being.

The fifth type of distortion concerns a sense of personal entitlement (Tirch & Radnitz, 2000). Some people with disabilities feel that they have received a raw deal in life and that others should therefore go out of their way for them. Such entitlement serves to emotionally distance them from the limitations of disability by externalizing their painful emotions (Tirch & Radnitz, 2000).

The sixth distortion centers on feelings of vulnerability, potentially arising from postdisability experiences that are experienced as dangerous or embarrassing (Tirch & Radnitz, 2000). The fact that people with disabilities are at increased risk for poverty and consequently may live in high-crime neighborhoods can also increase their potential for vulnerability and victimization (Tirch & Radnitz, 2000). Although there may be a reality basis for feelings of vulnerability, some individuals with disabilities may overestimate risks, leading to pervasive fearfulness.

Needham (1988) and colleagues identified several cognitive distortions and irrational beliefs that may be experienced by visually impaired individuals in particular. From material gathered in group and individual therapy sessions, Needham identified four general categories of irrational beliefs. The first type of distortion is based on the person's appraisal of her or his own self-worth and value, similar to the second category described earlier in this chapter by Tirch and Radnitz (2000). This category involves feeling that people with visual impairment are different from sighted people in their self-worth and value (e.g., that "losing one's sight means losing one's self"). The second type of distortion involves a feeling that people with visual impairment have a unique psychological constitution (e.g., that "only the blind can understand the blind"). The third type of distortion involves the idea that the visually impaired have a special relationship with other people and society in general (e.g., "blind people don't need to know how to cook or clean for themselves"); this is similar to Tirch and Radnitz's fifth category of entitlement. The fourth type of cognitive distortion identified by Needham involves the idea that there are magical circumstances about visual impairment (e.g., "with the right medicine, blindness can be cured").

The cognitive model proposes that an individual's emotions and behaviors are influenced by her or his perceptions of events (J. S. Beck, 1995). The situation itself does not directly determine how the individual feels; instead, her or his emotional reaction is a function of her or his perception of the situation (J. S. Beck, 1995). The cognitive distortions discussed earlier in this chapter are relevant to people with disabilities and can play a role in the development of distress and maladaptive coping in response to the demands of adapting to a disabling condition. Maladaptive coping behaviors may include avoidance, withdrawal, and substance abuse, which in turn may contribute to decreased motivation, excessive helplessness, or outward hostility. Any of these are counterproductive to the varied goals that people with disabilities may have, including rehabilitation, adaptation, and thriving. The goal of cognitive–behavioral therapists is to identify and target these cognitive distortions in treatment while balancing empathy and validation.

The Therapeutic Relationship

An important component of therapy with all clients is the therapeutic relationship. Genuineness, warmth, empathy, and positive regard can facilitate the application and success of CBT (A. T. Beck, 1976). Given the scarcity of therapists who are also disabled, empathic therapeutic relationships can also provide a client with positive experiences relating to a nondisabled person. This can be a direct source of evidence countering the perception that people without disabilities will be rejecting. When working with persons with disabilities, it is important that therapists spend time and energy on building the therapeutic relationship and openly talking about the cultural differences between themselves and the client.

Behavioral Techniques

Cognitively oriented therapists use a variety of behavioral techniques to assist clients in regaining a sense of control and effectiveness in daily activities. These include activity scheduling, engaging in activities that provide feelings of pleasure and mastery, graded task assignments, cognitive rehearsal, and problem solving. Behavioral strategies may also focus on enhancing interpersonal effectiveness (e.g., assertiveness training) or on improving physiological functioning (e.g., relaxation training; A. T. Beck, 1976; Young, Weinberger, & Beck, 2001).

When working with disabled people, it is important to be sensitive to clients' feelings about trying new activities. For example, an avid surfer and runner with a newly acquired physical disability would be likely to experience a profound sense of loss about the fact that she can no longer participate in these activities. It would be important that the therapist validate the client's emotional experience while still encouraging her to try new activities. The therapist should also recognize that she might not enjoy or master all activities that she tries. The client's trial-and-error process of identifying new pursuits or activities must be normalized to avoid supporting thoughts such as "I won't be good at anything anymore." A graded task approach in which simpler tasks are assigned and mastered prior to undertaking more complex ones, and cognitive rehearsal in which clients mentally rehearse the steps required to achieve specific goals, can be particularly useful for clients with disabilities. These approaches help clients to realistically pace themselves and to assist in the process of anticipating and addressing the physical, social, and cognitive roadblocks they may encounter.

For clients to benefit from therapy, cognitive–behavioral therapists encourage clients to practice the skills they are learning in therapy in their day-to-day surroundings (J. S. Beck, 1995). Practicing these skills first in the office can prepare clients for situations and individuals that may be rejecting and discriminatory. If negative situations do occur, therapy time can be used to process the experience to decrease the likelihood that it will be regarded as confirmatory evidence that "the world is an unsafe place" or "people are hostile."

Cognitive Techniques

The thought record is a central tool for restructuring negative and dysfunctional automatic thoughts, and eventually modifying intermediate and core beliefs (J. S. Beck, 1995). This multistep strategy helps clients to gain awareness of negative thoughts and their connection to negative mood states, then to develop proficiency in examining the validity of these negative thoughts and devising more adaptive responses (J. S. Beck, 1995; Greenberger & Padesky, 1995). Over time, clients learn to treat their thoughts as hypotheses rather than facts.

In considering the distortions that may occur at each level of cognitive functioning, it is important to recognize the objective aspects of situations that clients encounter. As Beck and colleagues have argued, the goal of CBT is to become more realistic, not simply more positive (A. T. Beck et al., 1979). Substituting realistic thinking for cognitive distortions allows for coping responses that are more likely to match the situation, yielding optimal outcomes. Thus, the client becomes more empowered and better able to appraise the accurate extent of stressors being experienced. People with disabilities have often experienced highly aversive interpersonal situations, such as prejudice, discrimination, hostility, and victimization, which tend to promote distorted or catastrophic thinking. If the therapist's interventions appear to minimize these experiences, the client may feel misunderstood and interpret the therapist's minimization as evidence that others cannot understand the phenomenology of disability.

Two central aspects of identity and belief have to do with self-acceptance and perceptions of family support. In his work with people who have experienced a limb amputation, Van Dorsten (2000) highlighted the need to reframe these cognitions and decatastrophize the impact of the disability (Van Dorsten, 2000). In addition, it may be beneficial to help clients recognize the personal factors that have not been changed by the disability, thus challenging the distortion that "nothing will ever be the same" (Van Dorsten, 2000). However, it is essential for the cognitive–behavioral therapist to take a cross-cultural perspective in evaluating such beliefs and attend to the environmental context that gives rise to such beliefs rather than place emphasis entirely on the client's cognitions as the root of distress.

An important final consideration is the need to adapt the mechanics of therapeutic interventions to the abilities of the client. For example, the thought record and other interventions are designed to be paper-and-pencil tasks, which may pose difficulties for clients with visual impairments or motor limitations. Therapists need to be prepared to offer alternative modalities, for example, via computer disk, large print, audiotape, or assistance from another person to complete the task.

The following examples present clinical data from two individuals with disabilities who received CBT. These examples were chosen to illustrate the multiple layers of identity that are frequently relevant to clients with disabilities. Rather than provide a detailed account of the course of therapy, our goal is to highlight the ways that disability influences the focus and process of therapy.

CASE EXAMPLE 1: FRANK

Frank, a 50-year-old divorced Latino male, was born in El Salvador and came to the United States at the age of 12. Frank was the youngest in a family of five children and the only son. Frank was diagnosed with cerebral palsy (CP) at birth. CP is a term that describes a group of impairments that affect movement control. In recent years, his condition had deteriorated to the extent that he had increased difficulty walking, and his speech had become increasingly slurred.

Frank sought therapy because he was feeling "sad and anxious" over the fact that he was unemployed. He explained that he had worked as an accountant for the past 25 years but quit his job because he had been promoted to a senior position that required him to speak in public and entertain out-of-town guests for the company. He was so self-conscious about his slurred speech and what he believed was an awkward appearance that he started to have panic attacks at work, with symptoms that included hyperventilation and rapid heartbeat. His coworkers noticed his symptoms but never discussed the situation with him. When Frank finally decided to quit, his coworkers did not seem upset, and therefore Frank concluded that they wanted him to leave.

During the first few sessions the therapist allowed Frank to tell her more about himself and his past. Frank shared that during his upbringing in El Salvador, his father was a successful businessman. However, because of political strife, Frank and his family were forced to flee their country and seek asylum in the United States. When asked how his family viewed his disability while growing up, Frank replied,

> It was rarely talked about. When I asked why I was different from the other children, I was told that when I was an infant, my mother had

accidentally dropped me on a concrete floor and this caused my cerebral palsy. My parents were constantly telling me that I should not think of myself as disabled and I should try to achieve things that nondisabled people strive for. It was not until I was an adult that I learned what really caused this condition.

Frank described how his family's *"creencias Latinas"* (Latin beliefs) dictated certain expectations regarding his role within the family given that he was the youngest child and the only son. Frank stated,

My family was proud to be in the United States where there was more opportunity. They made it very clear to me when we arrived that I would be the one who everyone would work very hard for to send to college. I really had no say in the matter and just did everything I could to get myself through school. During college, I had difficulty keeping up with the pace of work and I knew it had to do with my disability. When I would explain to my parents why it was taking me longer to finish, they would say, "Don't worry about it, just finish." It took me 10 years to complete what other students were doing in 4.

At age 40, Frank fell in love with a woman who had recently immigrated to the United States from Peru, marrying her 6 months after they met. Frank believes that the main reason she married him was because she wanted to be legalized in this country. Frank explained that during the first 2 months of their marriage, his wife avoided his sexual advances. During this time, Frank became very self-conscious about his body, thinking that perhaps his wife was "repulsed when she looked at it." However, after several discussions, his wife admitted that she feared "becoming pregnant and giving birth to a child with his *enfermedad* (disease)." Frank understood her concerns and set up a medical appointment in which he had a physician explain to her the cause of CP and the fact that there was a low probability of their children inheriting this condition. After this occurred, Frank and his wife began to engage in sexual activity; however, Frank continued to believe that there were parts of him that his wife was not attracted to. For example, Frank stated,

I never felt that I could please her as a woman because I could not move my body during sex the same way that other men do. Most of the time, I would run out of breath and needed her to help me out in order to give her pleasure. It is very hard to be part of a culture that sometimes expects men to be very strong and dominating in the bedroom. I never felt like I could live up to that *macho* image we Latin men are given.

Despite these concerns, Frank and his wife were able to conceive and give birth to three daughters.

Frank remained married for 8 years, after which his wife filed for divorce. Frank explained that the divorce was "very nasty" as his wife attempted to get full custody of their children, claiming that he was unfit to be a parent. Frank shared,

> I will never forget the day I asked my lawyer on what grounds she was accusing me of being a bad parent and he told me that it was because of my cerebral palsy. Up until this point in my life, I had never thought about my condition being a serious issue in my life. I fought this custody battle with everything I had and fortunately the court granted me partial custody. But after this episode, I was changed. I began to have a hard time concentrating at work and started feeling like everyone was noticing things about my disability. It was then that I began to question what other ways my condition was affecting me.

Frank's primary focus in psychotherapy was to reduce anxiety to facilitate a return to the workforce. It was determined that CBT would be an effective approach for Frank as it would allow him to explore his thoughts and feelings related to his anxiety at work and also about his disability.

Frank had gone through much of his life without a significant level of anxiety or depression. The accumulation of negative life events including the onset of his divorce, the custody battle, and the loss of his job appeared to have triggered some of his negative core beliefs. Until this time, his compensatory strategies (i.e., working very hard and not identifying himself as a disabled person) had helped to keep his negative core beliefs at bay. Core beliefs included "Being disabled means that I am not good enough" and "My disability makes me unattractive." Intermediate beliefs (which mediate between core beliefs and automatic thoughts) included "I must work very hard to show people that I am good enough" and "If I identify myself as a disabled man, I will be rejected."

Core cultural beliefs also were identified during therapy, such as "Being the only male in my family, I should be able to prosper and make my family feel proud of me" and "As a Latino male, I should be the one who has the most physical strength in the marriage to please my wife and make her feel safe." These beliefs are not inherently negative, particularly within the cultural context that gives rise to them; however, they became a source of vulnerability for Frank given his CP, his unemployment, and the breakup of his marriage. In Frank's case, when these beliefs were applied inflexibly, they led to shame and dysphoria. The goal in therapy was to expand these beliefs rather than to attempt to change Frank's identification with his Latin culture. For example, a more helpful version of these beliefs for Frank was, "I can make my family proud by having integrity and being a good father, not just by achieving financial success" and "As a male, I can respect and care for a woman in a way that makes her feel safe and protected." Thus, Frank's traditional views of his roles as son, husband, and father were made more flexible and concordant with his strengths as a disabled person.

Frank had initial concerns about completing thought records because his motor impairment meant that writing was extremely difficult. The therapist suggested completing thought records in session with the therapist writing, which proved to be a successful strategy. A typical thought record dealt with Frank's anxiety facing a professional situation that involved mingling with a large group of people. Frank experienced a particularly distressing automatic thought, "These people are uncomfortable because I am not able to reach out and shake their hand the way normal people do," along with emotions of nervousness, embarrassment, and shame. Frank weighed evidence supporting the thought ("I can tell that people's expressions and body gestures change when I come into the room or approach them" and "They seem to avoid making eye contact and they become stiffer when I get close to them"). He considered evidence contradicting the thought ("There are some people who will sometimes smile and come over to speak to me," "No one has actually ever said that I make them uncomfortable and walked away," and "Not everyone expects a handshake"). Ultimately, his conclusions were more balanced: "There are some people who may be uncomfortable being around me but they will still make an effort to acknowledge my existence and speak to me," "There are quite a few people who do seem to enjoy greeting me and asking me what I think about something," and "These people always smile at me and are not staring at my body."

By the time the therapy ended, Frank had a better understanding of what his disability meant to himself and others. After decades of experiencing his disability as a potential source of shame and inadequacy, something to be minimized as much as possible, he began to experience it both as a more central part of his identity and, at the same time, as a less dire and threatening reality. This gentler and more matter-of-fact approach suggested that he was beginning to adopt a belief system more characteristic of disability culture values. In fact, Frank had been somewhat avoidant of befriending other people with disabilities because of his belief in the importance of presenting himself as a nondisabled person. Over the course of therapy, he found himself reaching out to a neighbor about 15 years older than himself. This man, also Salvadoran American, had lost his eyesight secondary to diabetes but was happily married and integrated into the Latin community. Although Frank and this neighbor did not speak directly about their experiences with disability, Frank found himself viewing this man as an older male role model.

Frank came to understand that his assumption that others would dislike him because of his disability also meant that he did not experience himself as likable. By examining the global nature of his assumption, he was able to see his situation with greater nuance. He recognized that many but not all people would respond negatively to him because of his difference, and that although socially painful encounters were inevitable, he did not have to base his self-image on the insensitive behavior and comments of others. His self-esteem improved as he was able to devote more of his mental attention to the people in his life whose feelings toward him reflected a more complete picture of his personality and character. The completion of the thought records allowed Frank to realize that many people genuinely liked him, including family members, neighbors, and former coworkers. This support served as a buffer against some of the thoughtless remarks he received from others.

Frank also benefited from completing several home practice assignments that helped him to generate evidence challenging his beliefs. The homework assignments involved engaging in social activities to test whether people were really rejecting him. For example, he attended a parent–teacher conference at his daughters' school. He was very nervous about this event, but he forced himself to go and then felt proud about it afterward. Despite his divorce and the difficult custody battle, Frank's relationship with his children continued to provide him with a sense of himself as a family man, which was particularly important to him given his Latino upbringing that emphasized family roles. As he became less anxious and more self-confident, he began to realize that his experiences of social rejection and self-doubt made him particularly empathic to his daughters' trials and tribulations, and he relished their willingness to talk with him about their fears, anxieties, and triumphs.

Another homework assignment involved going to several job interviews for positions in which he had little interest. This activity gave him the opportunity to notice how new people really did react to him. After several interviews he started to feel more relaxed. He began to attend less to his own perceived inadequacies and more to whether the potential employers seemed aware of legal requirements regarding workplace accommodations for people with disabilities. Over time, Frank stopped waiting for the therapist to give him homework assignments and started taking risks on his own, signaling his readiness to terminate therapy.

CASE EXAMPLE 2: LISA

Lisa was a 55-year-old European American woman and a single parent of a 30-year-old son with Down's syndrome. Lisa grew up in a family with strong conservative Christian values. Both her parents were active participants in the church and expected Lisa and her older brother to follow the faith. At age 25, Lisa gave birth to her son without the help of a partner. Her family and friends expressed disappointment and warned her that it would be very difficult to raise a disabled child as a single parent. Lisa was hurt by their lack of encouragement and thought, "I will show everyone that it is possible to care for my son with or without family assistance." For the next 30 years, Lisa devoted herself to working full time in retail jobs to provide for her son. She took pride in the fact that she was "always able to hold a job and simultaneously raise a child with a disability."

At the age of 54, Lisa had a stroke and began using a wheelchair. Her realization that she could no longer walk contributed to feelings of depression, and she decided to quit her job. She began to tell herself, "I am no longer the woman I used to be. I am of no use to anyone." In describing the feelings that led her to seek therapy, Lisa also reported experiencing guilt because she could no longer physically provide care for her son and was forced to make arrangements for him in a special assisted living facility. Thoughts that accompanied this decision included self-condemnation, such as "I am a horrible mother because I cannot take care of my son anymore."

Lisa's depression and anger began to take a toll on her friendships and eventually led her to seek therapy. She indicated that she was feeling "impatient and temperamental" with people around her. Her irritability led her to yell at people when they made mistakes or failed to show up on time. Lisa said that she recently spent a lot of time crying while viewing photographs of her life before the stroke. She reported a loss of interest in pleasurable activities and fears that she would be "unhappy and alone" for the remainder of her life. During the first session, she also briefly mentioned that although she found herself "a little attracted to women" most of her life, these feelings had become stronger, and she was feeling confused and ashamed because of her traditional religious beliefs. At the time that she entered therapy, Lisa was living in an apartment that was minimally wheelchair accessible, and she had volunteer personal assistance services to help her with activities of daily living (e.g., shopping, cooking, bathing).

Lisa had several core beliefs that contributed to her depression and anxiety, including "I am only worthwhile if I am self-sufficient," "I am a failure if I am not able to care for my son perfectly," and "Having a disability means others will not love me or find me attractive." Her intermediate beliefs included: "If I do not care for my son, my family will be right about me," "I will never be the woman that I used to be," and "Being attracted to women is wrong."

Throughout Lisa's life, these intermediate and core beliefs about being a failure, a disappointment, and not good enough motivated her to work hard and to be an involved mother. Additionally, her success in maintaining an excellent work history, providing for her son's financial needs, and physically and emotionally caring for her son full time enabled her to feel good about herself despite holding some negative core beliefs. Her stroke and subsequent concerns about disappointing her son and family, distress about being unemployed, uncertainty about the future, difficulty coping with architectural barriers at her apartment, and confusion about being attracted to women undermined her ability to function in the way that she had previously and led to emotional distress.

The beginning of therapy focused on building rapport, discussing cultural differences related to her Christian upbringing that might affect therapy, and introducing the CBT model. Homework consisted of activity logging to better understand how Lisa was currently spending her time. Lisa's completed activity log suggested that she spent much of her time at home alone, which contrasted greatly with a typical day before her stroke. As she explained, "Six months ago, my schedule was packed with work activities, appointments for my son, lunch dates with my girlfriends, and house chores. Now I cannot do any of that."

The therapist spent time exploring and validating Lisa's feelings about her inability to do some of the things that she previously enjoyed doing (e.g., jogging, physically caring for her son in her own home). The therapist recognized the importance of not only challenging the automatic thought but also identifying the grain of truth in the thought and addressing the subsequent reality-based feelings of loss. Together, Lisa and her therapist examined her negative automatic thought, "I cannot do the things that I used to enjoy doing." An automatic thought record was introduced, and evidence for and against the accuracy of this thought was examined. With help from her therapist, Lisa was able to challenge this thought and create the more balanced statement, "I can still do many of the things that I like to do while using a wheelchair." Over time, the therapist assisted Lisa to challenge and restructure her beliefs about being a bad mother because of her disability and a failure as a person because of her attraction to women.

Behavioral strategies were also implemented, beginning with activity scheduling. Lisa was asked to schedule two pleasurable activities into her day and rated the amount of mastery and pleasure that she anticipated she would feel prior to engaging in the activity. She was then asked to rerate her pleasure and mastery while doing the activity. As predicted, Lisa's anticipatory ratings for going out to lunch with her friends were significantly lower (pleasure = 3, mastery = 4) than her feelings while at lunch (pleasure = 8, mastery = 7).

Lisa was encouraged to schedule not only pleasant events but also tasks that would allow her to feel accomplished and worthy. For example, Lisa took the initiative to make arrangements to receive public transportation to visit her son every other day. Being able to see her son and provide even a small amount of care for him had a dramatic effect on Lisa's mood. Lisa reported that now that she was spending less time alone and getting more things done, her feelings of sadness and frustration lessened. These behavioral strategies were continued until Lisa was regularly engaging in pleasurable activities and her mood had improved.

Lisa was also taught problem-solving strategies aimed at facilitating adjustment to her disability. Assertiveness training was provided to help Lisa express herself in a more effective manner. Specifically, Lisa was asked to focus on the difficulties she was having in communicating with the people around her. When asked what interactions were particularly troubling, Lisa said, "I am mostly bothered when someone treats me like I'm some sort of alien." She provided an example of a waiter treating her differently by avoiding eye contact and using a different tone of voice than he used with her companion. She reported feeling very upset and complaining to the manager, whose response was invalidating and rejecting. She said she then yelled at the manager and left the restaurant feeling misunderstood, discriminated against, and ostracized.

The therapist validated Lisa's anger and provided the opportunity for Lisa to discuss her experience of discrimination and resulting feelings. Lisa described a sense of helpless anger mixed with self-denigration. The therapist asked Lisa to consider whether she could have expressed her anger differently and discussed with her the difference between passive, assertive, and aggressive communication. Lisa agreed that being assertive rather than aggressive could have improved the communication. Lisa was willing to role-play and practice her new assertive style of communication with the therapist over several sessions. With practice, Lisa learned to express her thoughts and feelings without losing control of her temper.

Becoming more assertive did not always yield satisfactory outcomes in situations Lisa encountered, but overall it did work well. For example, when she finally moved to an apartment that was supposed to be wheelchair accessible, she found that the bathroom door was installed so that it opened into the bathroom, making it impossible for her to shut the door while inside. The apartment manager initially responded with indifference to the fact that she would be unable to have privacy, but Lisa was able to persist until he realized how unacceptable the situation was and arranged for the door to be installed appropriately. Throughout this experience, despite feeling intensely upset at times, Lisa was able to retain a sense of humor about the absurdity of the situation and the manager's oppressive response. She eventually concluded that she had had a deep positive influence on the manager by shaking up his assumptions and helping him to experience an empathic response.

This successful experience led Lisa to modify her beliefs to include the thought, "I can advocate for meaningful change." She eventually became a local community advocate for accessibility, frequently writing to city officials about the need for accessible housing, curb cuts, and increased funding for the public transportation she had found to be so helpful. Lisa used her own cultural experiences of living with disability and her knowledge of being a mother of a disabled child to promote awareness and change for others living with disability.

As Lisa progressed in developing a positive identity as a disabled person, the therapist periodically asked about her feelings of attraction to women, so as to normalize same-gender desires and relationships. When Lisa expressed that she was unsure of her readiness to explore this topic, the therapist directed Lisa to general readings and resources on same-gender attraction and relationships, including information on gay, lesbian, and bisexual persons with disabilities.

CONCLUSION

The multicultural life experiences of people with disabilities were presented in this chapter for the purposes of describing the use of CBT with this diverse population. We aimed to highlight the complexity of disability by paying close attention to the social context of the disability and the ways in which thoughts, feelings, and behaviors can be addressed in therapy. Although negative beliefs may be rooted in real-life oppressive and discriminatory situations, the chapter emphasized the importance of challenging the interpretations of these negative experiences so that more adaptive functioning can be facilitated. The richness of disability culture with its shared history of language, meanings, art, and symbols was also discussed as a foundation for understanding disability cultural ideals. It is our hope that the information presented in this chapter is a step toward the creation of a larger body of clinical work more critically exploring the conceptualization, approach, and treatment of people with disabilities from a cultural lens.

REFERENCES

American Psychological Association. (2002). Ethical principles of psychologists and code of conduct. *American Psychologist, 57,* 1060–1073.

Andersson, G. (2000). Hearing impairment. In C. L. Radnitz (Ed.), *Cognitive behavioral therapy for persons with disabilities* (pp. 183–204). Northvale, NJ: Jason Aronson.

Andersson, G., Melin, L., Lindberg, P., & Scott, B. (1995). Dispositional optimism, dysphoria, health, and coping with hearing impairment in elderly adults. *Audiology, 34,* 76–84.

Beck, A. T. (1976). *Cognitive therapy and the emotional disorders.* New York: International University Press.

Beck, A. T., Rush, A. J., Shaw, B. F., & Emery, G. (1979). *Cognitive therapy of depression.* New York: Guilford Press.

Beck, J. S. (1995). *Cognitive therapy: Basics and beyond.* New York: Guilford Press.

Craig, A. R., Hancock, K., Chang, E., & Dickson, H. (1998). Immunizing against depression and anxiety after spinal cord injury. *Archives of Physical Medicine and Rehabilitation, 79,* 375–377.

Devins, G. M., Camerson, J. I., & Edworthy, S. M. (2000). Chronic disabling disease. In C. L. Radnitz (Ed.), *Cognitive behavioral therapy for persons with disabilities* (pp. 105–140). Northvale, NJ: Jason Aronson.

Dodds, A., & Ferguson, E. (1994). The concept of adjustment: A structural model. *Journal of Visual Impairment and Blindness, 88,* 487–498.

Dodds, A. G., Flannigan, H., & Ng, L. (1993). The Nottingham Adjustment Scale: A validation study. *International Journal of Rehabilitation Research, 16,* 177–184.

Durand, V. M., Tanner, C., & Christopher, E. (2000). Autism. In C. L. Radnitz (Ed.), *Cognitive behavioral therapy for persons with disabilities* (pp. 207–226). Northvale, NJ: Jason Aronson.

Elliot, T. R., Godshall, F. J., & Herrick, S. M. (1991). Problem solving appraisal and psychological adjustment following spinal cord injury. *Cognitive Therapy and Research, 15,* 387–398.

Ellis, A., & Grieger, R. (1986). *Handbook of rational–emotive therapy* (Vol. 2). New York: Springer Publishing Company.

Fine, M., & Asch, A. (1988). *Women with disabilities: Essays in psychology, culture, and politics.* Philadelphia: Temple University Press.

Fitzgerald, R. G. (1970). Reactions to blindness: An exploratory study of adults with recent loss of sight. *Archives of General Psychiatry, 22,* 370–379.

Fitzgerald, R. G. (1971). Visual phenomenology in recently blind adults. *American Journal of Psychiatry, 127,* 1533–1539.

Fitzgerald, T. E. (2000). Pain related occupational musculoskeletal disability. In C. L. Radnitz (Ed.), *Cognitive behavioral therapy for persons with disabilities* (pp. 77–104). Northvale, NJ: Jason Aronson.

Fitzgerald, R. G., Ebert, J. N., & Chambers, M. (1987). Reactions to blindness: A four year follow-up study. *Perceptual and Motor Skills, 64,* 363–378.

Galvin, L. R., & Godfrey, H. P. D. (2001). The impact of coping on emotional adjustment to spinal cord injury (SCI): Review of the literature and application of a stress appraisal and coping formulation. *Spinal Cord, 39,* 615–627.

Gill, C. J. (Fall, 1995). A psychological view of disability culture. *Disability Studies Quarterly.* Retrieved February 24, 2004, from http://www.independentliving.org/docs3/gill1995.html

Greenberger, D., & Padesky, C. A. (1995). *Mind over mood: Change how you feel by changing the way you think.* New York: Guilford Press.

Hancock, K. M., Craig, A. R., Dickson, H. G., Chang, E., & Martin, J. (1993). Anxiety and depression over the first year of spinal cord injury: A longitudinal study. *Paraplegia, 31,* 349–357.

Jackson, W. T., & Taylor, R. E. (2000). Visual impairment. In C. L. Radnitz (Ed.), *Cognitive behavioral therapy for persons with disabilities* (pp. 183–204). Northvale, NJ: Jason Aronson.

Kearney, C. A., & McKnight, T. J. (2000). Mental retardation. In C. L. Radnitz (Ed.), *Cognitive behavioral therapy for persons with disabilities* (pp. 227–244). Northvale, NJ: Jason Aronson.

Kennedy, P., Marsh, N., & Lowe, R. (2000). A longitudinal analysis of psychological impact and coping strategies following spinal cord injury. *British Journal of Health Psychology, 5,* 157–172.

Longmore, P. K., & Umansky, L. (Eds.). (2001). *The new disability history.* New York: New York University Press.

Moore, A. D., Bombardier, C. H., Brown, P. B., & Patterson, D. R. (1994). Coping and emotional attributions following spinal cord injury. *International Journal of Rehabilitation Research, 17,* 39–48.

Needham, W. E. (1988). Cognitive distortions in acquired visual loss. *Journal of Vision Rehabilitation, 2,* 45–54.

Olkin, R. (1999). *What psychotherapists should know about disability.* New York: Guilford Press.

Olkin, R., & Pledger, C. (2003). Can disability studies and psychology join hands? *American Psychologist, 58,* 296–304.

Radnitz, C. L., & Tirch, D. D. (1997). Physical disability. In R. L. Leahy (Ed.), *Practicing cognitive therapy: A guide to interventions* (pp. 373–389). Northvale, NJ: Jason Aronson.

Rintala, D. H., Young, M. E., & Hart, K. A. (1992). Social support and the well-being of persons living with spinal cord injury in the community. *Rehabilitation Psychology, 37,* 155–163.

Thompson, N. J., Coker, J., Krause, J. S., & Henry, E. (2003). Purpose of life as a mediator of adjustment after spinal cord injury. *Rehabilitation Psychology, 48,* 100–108.

Tirch, D. D., & Radnitz, C. L. (2000). Spinal cord injury. In C. L. Radnitz (Ed.), *Cognitive behavioral therapy for persons with disabilities* (pp. 183–204). Northvale, NJ: Jason Aronson.

Van Dorsten, B. (2000). Amputation. In C. L. Radnitz (Ed.), *Cognitive behavioral therapy for persons with disabilities* (pp. 59–76). Northvale, NJ: Jason Aronson.

Young, J. E., Weinberger, A., & Beck, A. T. (2001). Cognitive therapy for depression. In D. H. Barlow (Ed.), *Clinical handbook of psychological disorders: A step by step treatment manual* (3rd ed., pp. 264–308). New York: Guilford Press.

10

AFFIRMATIVE COGNITIVE–BEHAVIORAL THERAPY WITH LESBIAN, GAY, AND BISEXUAL PEOPLE

KIMBERLY F. BALSAM, CHRISTOPHER R. MARTELL,
AND STEVEN A. SAFREN

Cognitive–behavioral therapy (CBT) is highly effective for a wide range of problems; however, few studies address its use with lesbian, gay, or bisexual clients. Furthermore, although many cognitive–behavioral techniques are similar for heterosexual and nonheterosexual clients, cultural sensitivity and knowledge will enhance the use of CBT techniques and, if neglected, can hinder treatment. This chapter addresses the use of a culturally sensitive, affirmative CBT in treating lesbian, gay, and bisexual clients.

TERMINOLOGY

Because nonheterosexual people are a stigmatized group, an awareness of terms can help to promote an affirmative environment for therapeutic

---

For a more comprehensive treatment of affirmative cognitive–behavioral therapy with lesbian, gay, and bisexual clients see Martell, Safren, and Prince (2004).

work. *Sexual orientation* is an umbrella term that describes the gender or genders of a person's emotional and sexual attractions. *Sexual identity* is a more specific term that refers to a person's self-identification, usually including recognition of one's sexual orientation and sexual behaviors and the meanings one places on them. The acronym *LGB* is often used to refer to lesbian, gay, and bisexual individuals and communities and is used throughout the remainder of this chapter.

It is important to keep in mind that these terms do not universally apply to people of all cultural backgrounds. For example, among Native Americans who may have sexual or affectional attractions to people of the same gender, the term *two-spirit* is often used in place of LGB. This term makes reference to the historical acceptance of sexual and gender diversity and the traditional social role for these individuals in some Native communities (Jacobs, Thomas, & Lang, 1997; Tafoya & Wirth, 1996). Although a vibrant African American gay and lesbian community is emerging (Icard, 1996), there are many African American men who live apparently heterosexual lives while having sex with other men "on the down low" (King, 2004). Women may maintain sexual or affectional attractions to other women but not define themselves as lesbian. Greene (1994) suggested that many African American women cite their African American identity as primary over identification with a lesbian community. In some Latino cultures, a man may have sex with men but not consider himself to be homosexual if he is the active rather than the passive partner sexually (Zamora-Hernández & Patterson, 1996).

Other terms used to refer to LGB people include *sexual minority, homosexual,* and *queer. Sexual minority* refers to individuals who are marginalized on the basis of their sexual identity or sexual behavior and is often used as an umbrella term to refer to LGB people in general. The term *homosexual* was historically used by the mental health community to describe and diagnose anyone with a same-sex orientation as pathological; for this reason American Psychological Association (2001) guidelines now recommend avoiding its use. The term *queer,* once used pejoratively, has been reclaimed by some LGB individuals and youth communities as an affirmative self-identification inclusive of lesbian, gay, bisexual, and transgender identities. As with the term homosexual, queer may carry a negative connotation for some people in the LGB community, and therapists are advised to be cautious regarding its use.

Separate but related to sexual identity is an individual's sexual behavior. A person may engage in same-sex sexual behavior without self-identifying as lesbian, gay, or bisexual. Conversely, a person might identify as LGB without having any previous same-sex sexual experience. As with sexual behavior, sexual attraction may or may not be congruent with sexual identity. Indeed, in a population-based sample of urban women, Meyer, Rossano, Ellis, and Bradford (2002) found that only 33% of women with any same-sex orientation reported all of the following three components of sexual orientation: same-sex identity, same-sex behavior, and same-sex attractions.

Sexual orientation also differs from gender identity. *Gender identity* is defined as the internal identification with maleness and femaleness and the presentation of such feelings (and their subsequent roles) to the external world (Gainor, 2000). Although *transgender* individuals (who identify with a gender different from their biological sex) and *intersex* individuals (whose biological sex is ambiguous) are currently considered sexual minorities, a discussion of the unique issues facing these individuals is beyond the scope of this chapter. The reader is referred to Elkins and King (1998) for more information about the unique issues facing these individuals.

Although LGB people are diverse in terms of social demographics and life experiences, there are some commonalities that stem from growing up and living in a society that assumes heterosexuality as the norm. The term *heterosexism* refers to an ideological system that denies, denigrates, and stigmatizes any nonheterosexual form of behavior, identity, relationship, or community (Herek, 1990). A similar but related term is *homophobia*, used to refer to irrational fear, hatred, and intolerance of homosexuality (Weinberg, 1972). This term indicates a negative conditioned emotional response to homosexuality (Spencer & Hemmer, 1993), and some behaviorists have suggested that it is not truly a phobic response and thus should not be used (Rowan, 1994). Rowan also noted that the term suggests that those individuals who disapprove of homosexuality for religious reasons have a pathological diagnosis.

Whether or not fear and hatred of LGB people is a diagnosable condition, and regardless of terminology, discrimination against LGB people has negative effects on the LGB individual. For many LGB people, oppression on the basis of their sexual orientation intersects with other oppressions such as racism, classism, and sexism. Bisexual people are also subject to *biphobia*, defined by Ochs (1996, p. 217) as the "discrimination, hostility, and invalidation" experienced by bisexuals in both the lesbian/gay and heterosexual communities.

DEVELOPMENTAL ISSUES AND CHALLENGES

Unlike people of ethnic and cultural minorities whose families typically share their minority status, LGB individuals often grow up in a household that lacks LGB role models and in which gender norms for behavior are enforced. For young girls and boys who have interests in cross-gender behavior or who become aware of same-sex attractions, a great deal of confusion can result. From a cognitive–behavioral perspective, children and adolescents who display such behaviors typically experience punishments from their environment in the form of rejection, criticism, and even verbal and physical abuse (D'Augelli, 1998). Conversely, children are rewarded through praise and social support for conforming to norms for heterosexual behavior. Negative societal messages about nonheterosexual orientations affect the way LGB individuals think and feel about themselves. This is referred to as *internalized homophobia* or *internalized homonegativity* and has been linked empirically to psychological distress (Szymanski, Chung, & Balsam, 2001).

Another distinguishing feature of this group is that unlike many other minorities, LGB people have the option of concealing or disclosing their stigmatized status. The process of becoming aware of one's sexual orientation and disclosing this to others is referred to as *coming out.* It is important to understand that coming out is a continuous process over the life span, as LGB individuals negotiate their identities and decisions about disclosure on a day-to-day basis. Furthermore, this process varies across cultures (Smith, 1997). Preliminary research suggests that greater *outness* (self-disclosure to others) is associated with lower psychological distress (Morris, Waldo, & Rothblum, 2001).

The impact of heterosexist oppression on an individual is a function of a range of individual differences, including race, ethnicity, gender, socioeconomic status, and degree of outness. For example, an African American gay man may experience competing loyalties to the LGB community and the African American community, perhaps receiving messages that "Black men aren't gay" from his family and friends. A lesbian woman working in a traditionally male-dominated field may feel physically threatened by her coworkers and may fear reprisal if she comes out at work. A bisexual woman who is visible and politically active in the LGB community may be distressed by homophobic comments from her neighbors and periodic hate mail that she receives, whereas her more closeted bisexual friend who is married to a man may be distressed at her relative "invisibility" and by the assumption of heterosexuality that her marital status confers.

LGB INDIVIDUALS IN THERAPY

LGB adults are more likely to attend psychotherapy and take psychiatric medications than their heterosexual counterparts (Balsam, Beauchaine, Mickey, & Rothblum, 2005; Cochran, Sullivan, & Mays, 2003). This finding may be due to a number of factors, including cultural acceptance within LGB communities of therapy and the self-exploration and personal growth associated with the sexual identity formation process (Bradford, Ryan, & Rothblum, 1994). Regardless of the reason, CBT practitioners are likely to encounter LGB clients in the course of their practice, whether or not they advertise in the LGB community. As with any client population, LGB clients may present with a wide range of concerns that may or may not be directly related to their sexual orientation. Recent population-based studies of LGB adults have found slightly elevated rates of depressive and anxiety disorders, suicide attempts, and substance use disorders in comparison with heterosexual populations (see Cochran, 2001, for a review). LGB clients may also present for help with stressors related to their sexual orientation, including discrimination, rejection by family members and friends, conflict between sexual orientation and religious beliefs, and internalized homophobia. Such concerns were found in a mental health chart review of gay men seeking mental health services in an urban LGBT health center (Berg, Mimiaga, & Safren, in press).

The impact of sexual orientation-based oppression on the individual LGB person has been referred to as *minority stress* and linked to mental health problems (Meyer, 2003). Additionally, recent research has demonstrated that LGB people experience relatively high rates of interpersonal trauma over the life span, including bias-related victimization (Herek, Gillis, Cogan, & Glunt, 1997), childhood abuse (Corliss, Cochran, & Mays, 2002; Tomeo, Templer, Anderson, & Kotler, 2002), and sexual assault in adulthood (Hughes, Johnson, & Wilsnack, 2001; Tjaden, Thoeness, & Allison, 1999). These experiences are associated with a number of different psychological disorders and symptoms and may prompt contact with a mental health professional.

STRENGTHS AND LIMITATIONS OF CBT WITH LGB INDIVIDUALS

There are a number of advantages to using CBT with LGB clients. First, the history and development of cognitive and behavioral approaches to therapy are grounded in empirical findings, with strong support for treatment of many of the disorders (e.g., depression and anxiety) prevalent in LGB populations. Second, unlike therapeutic approaches that locate the source of psychopathology within the individual's psyche, contemporary CBT pays close attention to the environmental and social context of clients' lives. Third, CBT allows therapists to take a collaborative, problem-solving approach to therapy, helping clients to develop and test hypotheses about problems and try out new behaviors in everyday life. Living in a society that assumes heterosexuality, LGB clients frequently do not fit the dominant culture's expectations and may particularly benefit from an approach that allows them to voice their unique perspectives. Fourth, the skills-training focus of some CBT approaches can give clients concrete tools to cope with stressors related to minority status. Fifth, CBT does not conceptualize behavior as good or bad but rather as functional or not functional. This nonjudgmental approach is especially appropriate with clients who experience judgment from their social environment. Sixth, cognitive–behavioral techniques are useful in countering the assumption that internalized homophobic beliefs represent "the truth" and in reconceptualizing these beliefs as thoughts that can be changed.

Although the benefits of using CBT with LGB clients are numerous, a few limitations require mention. First of all, behavior therapy techniques were historically used to assist some LGB clients to change their sexual orientation (Adams, Tollison, & Carson, 1981). Behavioral case studies suggest that people may change their sexual behavior as a result of aversive conditioning, but there is no evidence that treatment has any impact on sexual orientation (Haldeman, 1994). Behavior therapy may propose to create an aversion to sexual arousal to individuals of the same sex or to achieve positive erotic conditioning to members of the opposite sex (Wolpe, 1990), but it is doubtful that these conditioned responses constitute more than a change in arousal patterns or sexual behavior, neither of which constitutes sexual orientation per se. Furthermore, these types of treatments often result in serious psychological consequences for those who attempt them (Shidlo & Schroeder, 2002). They also promote a heterosexist agenda that assumes different sexual orientations should be treated (Davison, 1976). Some LGB clients, particularly those who came out in the pre-Stonewall[1] era, may consequently approach behavior therapy with skepticism and mistrust. The American Psychiatric Association (2000), the National Association of Social Workers (1996), and the American Psychological Association (2000) directly oppose or strongly recommend against the use of therapies that attempt to change sexual orientation. A professional fact sheet for working with LGBT (i.e., LGB and transgender) individuals provides information about the potential for harm with these approaches (Association of Behavior and Cognitive Therapy, in press).

Numerous studies have been conducted on CBT for specific disorders, but these studies have not assessed for sexual orientation and have not included specific approaches for addressing developmental concerns of LGB clients. Combining an understanding of CBT and the LGB literature has allowed several writers to offer empirically grounded suggestions for working with this population (Martell, Safren, & Prince, 2004; Padesky, 1989; Purcell, Campos, & Perilla, 1996), but more research is needed in this area. In addition, few behaviorally oriented graduate programs offer training in LGB issues (Anhalt, Morris, Scotti, & Cohen, 2003). Conversely, graduate programs that emphasize diversity and provide training in LGB issues typically do not provide adequate training in CBT. Thus, trained CBT clinicians who can approach LGB people in a culturally sensitive manner may be difficult to find.

---

[1]The Stonewall riots refer to an altercation that occurred on June 27, 1969, in Greenwich Village, New York, between patrons of the Stonewall Inn (a gay bar) and police. Prior to this event, police raids on gay and lesbian bars and establishments were common in the United States. The Stonewall riots marked a turning point in the modern gay rights movement because it was the first time that a significant number of gay men resisted arrest and fought back during a police raid.

ADAPTING COGNITIVE–BEHAVIORAL THERAPY

Assessment and case conceptualization play an important role in cognitive–behavioral treatment. As with any cognitive–behavioral approach, therapists working with LGB clients are advised to develop a problem list; gain an understanding of the environmental, historical, behavioral, cognitive, and physiological variables that may be affecting the client's problems; and work collaboratively with the client to develop a treatment plan that addresses the problems and fits with the client's goals. In addition, therapists working with LGB clients must consider the role of sexual orientation in the client's presenting problem and treatment.

For some clients, sexual orientation may play a prominent role in the presenting problem and may be a central focus of treatment (Martell et al., 2004; Padesky, 1989; Purcell et al., 1996). For example, a 35-year-old heterosexually married woman may present for treatment to understand her emerging same-sex attractions, address anxiety related to internalized homophobic beliefs, and explore her options regarding relationships and identity. On the other end of the spectrum, sexual orientation may have very little to do with the presenting problem. For example, a 45-year-old gay man who has been out for 25 years may present with a panic disorder that has nothing to do with his sexual orientation. In such cases, it is possible for the therapist to overemphasize sexual orientation, which can also be considered a form of bias (Garnets, Hancock, Cochran, Goodchilds, & Peplau, 1991). For many LGB clients, sexual orientation has some significance to the presenting problem but does not play a central role. For example, a 25-year-old lesbian diagnosed with a generalized anxiety disorder reports that she worries about her health, world events, and her performance at work and that some of her worries focus on being rejected by others because of her sexual orientation.

Key to LGB affirmative therapy is the assessment of the role of sexual orientation in the presenting problem. The assessment should include questions about identity, behavior, and attractions, as well as the client's thoughts and feelings about any discrepancies between these dimensions of sexual orientation. Regarding historical factors, the therapist might inquire about the client's sexual identity development process, asking when and how the client became aware of his or her sexual orientation, how and when they disclosed to others, and what were the key events or turning points in this process. In assessing the role of the current environment, the therapist would need to determine the extent to which the client is out and feels accepted in various settings and by important people in his or her life. The therapist will also want to know the degree to which these environmental factors, along with the client's own beliefs about being LGB, might be causing distress. This may include questions regarding possible discrimination, harassment, or victimization and the extent to which the client attributes these experiences to their sexual orientation.

Some common outcome measures used in CBT are useful with all clients regardless of gender or sexual orientation, such as the first and second editions of the Beck Depression Inventory (Beck, Steer, & Brown, 1996; Beck, Ward, Mendelson, Mock, & Erbaugh, 1961), the Beck Anxiety Inventory (Beck, Epstein, Brown, & Steer, 1988), the Addiction Severity Index (McLellan et al., 1992), and the Quality of Life Inventory (Frisch, 1994). These instruments are more appropriate because they do not ask questions specific to sexual orientation, and they are gender neutral.

Anxiety inventories that ask questions about social anxiety using phrases such as "discomfort with members of the opposite sex" make an implicit assumption that people who have anxiety about dating will be anxious interacting in mixed company. It is better to ask if there is discomfort "around a person to whom I was physically or emotionally attracted." Likewise, couple inventories frequently use forms for "husband" and "wife" that are inappropriate for same-sex couples. "Partner A" and "Partner B" differentiate the two people in the couple without promulgating the idea that couples are always of mixed genders (e.g., see the Frequency and Acceptability of Partner Behavior scale by Christensen & Jacobson, 1997, and the Dyadic Adjustment Scale by Spanier, 1976).

In conducting CBT with LGB clients, it is recommended that therapists take a culturally sensitive approach similar to those recommended for ethnically diverse clients (Purcell et al., 1996). Toward this end, therapists need to be informed about their clients' cultural norms. For example, among men in same-sex relationships, consensual nonmonogamy is not uncommon and should not be assumed to be problematic for the client (Solomon, Rothblum, & Balsam, 2005). Another area in which cultural norms may play a role is in the client's definition of family. Because LGB clients may have experienced rejection by or hostility from their families or cultural communities, friendship circles may be their family of choice (Bepko & Johnson, 2000; Weinstock, 2000).

Another key element in culturally sensitive treatment with LGB clients involves attention to the social context of homophobia and heterosexism and, when appropriate, helping clients to identify sources of oppression in their environment. It is imperative that therapists listen carefully to clients and not jump too quickly to recommendations that could lead to harmful consequences, for example, encouraging a client to come out without a full understanding of the client's context. However, it is helpful to examine areas in which a client may be engaging in avoidant behavior related to sexual orientation. For example, a woman who works in a large office may avoid casual conversations with coworkers out of fear that they will ask questions about her relationship status. In such cases, clinicians may conduct a functional analysis of avoidant behaviors and help the client to develop alternative behavioral responses. Cognitive restructuring, a key intervention in CBT, can also be used to counter negative beliefs about self or the LGB community that may be based on stereotypes or internalized homonegativity.

Another area of clinical focus with LGB clients is social support, including the client's connection with a community. Social support has been linked cross-culturally to positive mental health among LGB adults and youths (Kaminski, 2000; Vincke & vanHeeringin, 2002; Zea, Reisen, & Poppen, 1999). For some LGB people, fear of living more openly as LGB may be linked to a fear of losing supportive relationships. Additionally, some relationships may be supportive in some domains yet unsupportive of the client's sexual orientation. To assist clients in finding LGB-affirmative social supports, clinicians need to be knowledgeable about local LGB community resources.

CASE EXAMPLE 1: ROBIN

Robin was a 26-year-old European American lesbian of Scandinavian and German descent who lived alone in an apartment near the university campus in a northwestern city. At the time she presented for treatment, she was in graduate school studying for her PhD in history. She had been active in the LGBT rights movement for several years, volunteering for a national organization and publishing a local newsletter. Robin had been dating Jenna, a woman she met at school, for about 5 months. Her parents and younger brother all lived in the Midwest, in the town where she was born.

Robin presented for therapy after finding the therapist's phone number in an LGBT business directory. Her initial complaints were of "sleep problems and stress." On assessment, she revealed that her sleep problems were largely due to nightmares and feelings of agitation at the slightest sound in her apartment. She reported that she was having difficulty concentrating on her schoolwork and had been spending less time socializing with Jenna and other friends. She had become increasingly irritable and reported tearfully that lately she was "snapping" at her girlfriend for no reason. Robin also reported experiencing symptoms consistent with a panic attack on at least two recent occasions.

Suspecting a diagnosis of PTSD, the therapist inquired about a history of trauma. With some hesitation, Robin acknowledged that a male friend had sexually assaulted her at the age of 19 in her dorm room at college. This incident occurred after the two had been drinking together at a party on campus. According to Robin, at the time she was beginning to recognize her attractions to women and to develop feelings for an openly lesbian young woman in one of her classes. Although she enjoyed the company of this man, she turned down his sexual advances after he walked her home from the party. After attempting to verbally coerce her and calling her a "dyke," he used physical force to rape her. Although she experienced a great deal of psychological distress in the following months, Robin never told anyone about the incident.

After the incident, staying at that school was difficult. She transferred to another college the following year. The development of her sexual orientation became more and more salient to her, and she slowly chose to come out to her parents, her siblings, and her friends. She tried, with difficulty, to bury the sexual assault into the past. In the ensuing years, she had intermittent nightmares but generally managed to push away thoughts and feelings about the rape during the day. She generally tried to avoid reading about or watching any accounts of rape on television because this would make the nightmares increase. She also rarely drank alcohol and avoided parties and other large gatherings where people were drinking. Periodically, she experienced homophobic street harassment, which triggered memories of the rapists' slurs.

According to Robin, 3 months prior to treatment, she walked into one of her classes and was shocked to discover that the professor bore a striking resemblance to the man who had raped her. Her symptoms immediately increased, and she began to have intrusive thoughts about the rape, particularly when she was sitting quietly trying to study. She stated that she was beginning to feel pretty hopeless about her situation and referred to herself as "weak" for letting this incident bother her so much. Robin stated that she blamed herself for the assault because she should have known not to drink with this man and should have been able to fight him off. She stated that she never wanted to tell anyone about her history for fear that they would also see her as weak and that they would attribute her lesbian identity to the experience. Although Jenna suspected that something was wrong and had encouraged her to seek therapy, Robin feared that if she knew about the rape, Jenna would not respect her.

The therapist diagnosed Robin as having posttraumatic stress disorder (PTSD) secondary to the traumatic experience of rape. A diagnosis of PTSD is based on a person's reaction to a traumatic event in which the individual "experienced, witnessed, or was confronted with an event or events that involved actual or threatened death or serious injury, or a threat to the physical integrity of self or others" and the person experienced "intense fear, helplessness, or horror" (American Psychiatric Association, 1994, p. 209). These experiences are not uncommon in the general population; epidemiologic studies indicate that approximately 69% of the population will experience at least one such event in their lifetime (Norris, 1992). Compared with heterosexuals, LGB persons are at elevated risk for interpersonal trauma experiences such as rape, childhood abuse, and physical assault over the life span (Balsam, Rothblum, & Beauchaine, 2005; Corliss et al., 2002; Tjaden et al., 1999). Thus, therapists working with LGB clients are likely to see clients for whom a traumatic event or events play a prominent role in their presenting concerns. For some clients, this may manifest clinically as PTSD. Kessler,

Sonnega, Bromet, Hughes, and Nelson (1995) found that 20.4% of women and 8.2% of men who experience a traumatic event will go on to develop PTSD.

LGB clients who present for therapy with trauma-related problems may also experience additional symptoms related to thoughts and feelings about their sexual orientation. For example, assaults that are perceived to be bias-related produce more stress than do other types of assaults (Herek, Gillis, & Cogan, 1999). LGB individuals must also contend with pervasive cultural myths regarding the "cause" of minority sexual orientations (Balsam, 2003). For example, in one study, nearly half of LGB survivors of childhood sexual abuse reported that at one time they had questioned whether the abuse "made them" LGB (Balsam, 2002). Furthermore, PTSD and other trauma-related symptoms may be exacerbated by additional experiences of trauma. Daily experiences of discrimination and stigmatization among LGB people have been theorized to constitute a form of trauma (Neisen, 1993). Although social support is an important factor in reducing symptoms after trauma, some LGB people who are not out or who are isolated from their families or cultural communities may lack this support.

After learning Robin's history, the therapist asked her to complete the PTSD Symptom Scale—Self-Report (Foa, Riggs, Dancu, & Rothbaum, 1993) and then followed up with a clinical interview to arrive at the diagnosis of PTSD. The therapist looked for symptoms of depression, other anxiety disorders, and substance abuse and assessed changes in Robin's life following the event, including her beliefs about the rape and its role in her life. As the therapist presented her clinical summary, Robin expressed some relief at finally understanding the source of her distress. The therapist provided Robin with some handouts describing common reactions to rape; this gave Robin the feeling that she was not alone with her reactions and some hope that she could reduce her symptoms through treatment.

The therapist's approach to treatment with Robin was based on Foa and Rothbaum's (1998) *prolonged exposure therapy*. This treatment has demonstrated empirical support with survivors of rape (Foa, Rothbaum, Riggs, & Murdock, 1991) as well as other traumatic events. Prolonged exposure therapy targets avoidance of trauma-related environmental cues and memories of the trauma using exposure-based techniques. The rationale for the treatment is that PTSD symptoms are reduced as the client habituates to the traumatic memories. Like many other clients, Robin was initially skeptical about this approach and reluctant to engage in treatment that would require her to relive the rape event. The therapist discussed Robin's reluctance and provided her with information about the rationale and efficacy of exposure-based treatment.

Prolonged exposure therapy includes both imaginal and in vivo exposure. During imaginal exposure, Robin relived the rape during therapy sessions by describing aloud the details of the event in the present tense to the therapist. The therapist tape-recorded the description, and Robin was instructed to listen to these tapes daily at home between sessions. The following is an excerpt from Robin's first in-session imaginal exposure exercise:

Robin: Now we're in my dorm room . . . I turn on the light and thank Joe for walking me home. . . . He doesn't leave . . . now he's coming toward me and he smells like beer (pause) . . . He said that he knew I wanted to have sex with him . . . (pause)

Therapist: He's *saying* that he *knows* I want to have sex with him . . .

Robin: Right, present tense, okay, I . . . I tell him that I just want to be his friend . . . I don't know what to think . . . he's standing so close to me . . . he's rubbing my back . . . (starts to wring her hands)

Therapist: You're doing just fine, Robin. Stay with this image.

Robin: I tell him to stop. . . . He's squeezing my arm. . . . Now he's starting to . . . he's calling me names, he's saying "you f***ing dyke" . . . (breathing rapidly)

Therapist: Okay, what is your anxiety level now on the 0 to 100 scale?

Robin: It's . . . I think it's 90.

Therapist: Good, now keep going.

Robin: I don't know what to do . . . he's trying to kiss me . . . he's pushing me onto the bed . . . I don't want to do this, I just want him to leave me alone . . . (long pause)

Therapist: Stay with your feelings

Robin: I don't feel anything . . . I just want him to leave . . . (long pause)

Therapist: I know this is difficult. Keep going . . .

During this initial imaginal exposure exercise, the therapist's focus was on gently prompting Robin to stay in the present tense and keep the narrative going. During later sessions, the therapist used more prompts to help Robin activate feelings of distress and confront the aspects of the event that were most fear-producing for her. After several weeks of imaginal exposure exercises in session and at home, Robin's distress decreased, and she reported fewer intrusive thoughts and nightmares about the rape.

For in vivo exposure, Robin developed a hierarchy of feared and avoided situations and gave each situation a Subjective Units of Distress (SUDS) rating. Robin's hierarchy included talking to friends about the first college she attended (with a SUDS rating of 50), going to class with the professor who resembled the perpetrator (60), reading a newspaper article about a rape (70), talking to her girlfriend about the rape event (80), attending a social event where people are drinking alcohol (90), and going back to the campus where the rape occurred (90). The therapist and Robin worked together to plan exposures to these stimuli between sessions.

Robin's clinical presentation included feelings of guilt and shame accompanied by distorted cognitions such as "It was my fault that I was raped" and "A strong woman wouldn't feel scared." Foa and Rothbaum (1998) suggested adding a cognitive restructuring component to prolonged exposure treatment for clients with PTSD who have this clinical presentation. Robin's therapy included standard elements of cognitive restructuring, including identifying and challenging distorted beliefs about the rape, herself, and her relationships with others. The therapist addressed Robin's belief that others might attribute her sexual orientation to the rape via cognitive restructuring techniques and by asking Robin to read written accounts of other lesbian and bisexual women's experiences of sexual assault. Robin was eventually able to talk with Jenna about the experience. The support and empathy she received from Jenna on disclosure was useful in challenging the belief that she was somehow at fault or that the rape showed that she was "weak."

The therapist also worked with Robin to develop a proactive coping response to situations in which she experienced homophobic harassment or slurs. Using the guided self-dialogue technique (Foa & Rothbaum, 1998), Robin learned to talk herself through potentially stressful situations, use coping self-statements (e.g. "I can handle this"), and provide herself with reinforcement for successfully managing stressful situations.

By the end of treatment, Robin reported a dramatic reduction in PTSD symptoms and no longer met criteria for the disorder. She no longer avoided class and was better able to concentrate on her studies. Discussing the rape with Jenna increased her feelings of intimacy, and the two planned to move in together the following summer. Although she was still somewhat guarded about discussing the event, Robin also made a phone call to a long-time friend and disclosed the rape to her and reported relief at doing so. She also felt empowered by her ability to reconcile her traumatic history with her self-image as a strong woman and LGBT activist. At the time of her final session, she was investigating an opportunity to write for a national newsletter on violence against LGBT people.

CASE EXAMPLE 2: ED

Ed was a 39-year-old African American man who, at the time of his initial session, had been working in an administrative position at a legal office for over a year. Ed reported that he had previously been unemployed for significant periods of time. He grew up in Virginia with his mother, grandmother, and aunt and described his upbringing as religious and strict. His family still lived in Virginia. He was currently living in a large northeastern city.

On the telephone prior to the first session, Ed described his presenting problem as depression with some anxiety. Ed stated that his depression was affecting his ability to get to work on time and to complete projects he was assigned. He reported that he eventually wanted to return to college but that he felt too depressed to take any steps toward this goal. As a result of his depression, he also reported that he had been less involved with his 13-year-old son than he would like.

When Ed arrived for the first session, the therapist explained the process of the evaluation for CBT, which included a diagnostic interview followed by feedback, and then a discussion of what CBT might entail. The therapist used questions from the Structured Clinical Interview for DSM–IV (First, Spitzer, Gibbon, & Williams, 1995) as well as the Anxiety Disorders Interview Schedule (Brown, DiNardo, & Barlow, 1994). Ed met criteria for a major depressive disorder, recurrent, of moderate severity, and for a mild panic disorder (controlled with medications). While assessing Ed's depressive symptoms including his libido, a discussion about dating situations and romantic relationships emerged. Ed stated that he did not date often. He added that he avoided situations in which he would meet potential dates because he believed that many (White) men were either not interested in Black men or were interested only in sex.

Because this was a general outpatient clinic and Ed had not previously mentioned sexual orientation as an issue, it had not occurred to the therapist that Ed might be gay. As a result, up until this point the therapist had conducted an assessment typical of many cognitive and behavioral intake assessments. However, after Ed made this comment, the therapist was able to go back and obtain additional information. This example illustrates why assessing sexual orientation should be a part of most general intake interviews.

The therapist subsequently learned from Ed that he had struggled with his sexuality throughout his life. Owing to pressure from his family and community, he had dated women until he was in his late 20s. He was sexual with several different women, and one of them became pregnant with his son. During the time he dated women socially and sexually, Ed was also sexual with men. These relationships were kept secret, as both he and his partners were not out. During this time, Ed struggled with alcohol abuse, which cost him several jobs.

A complete cognitive–behavioral case formulation revealed that Ed's depression was exacerbated by social isolation, his desire for a meaningful relationship with another man, and negative core beliefs he had about himself related to his sexual orientation. Although he had previously struggled with both alcohol and finances, Ed had been alcohol-free for several years and had an income on which he could live. Ed still struggled to reconcile his religious beliefs and the messages he grew up with in a devout family with his current sexual identity and behaviors.

As his panic disorder was under control with medication, and the alcohol problem was stable, cognitive–behavioral treatment focused on the depression. One of the early interventions involved mood and activity monitoring. Investigation revealed that his mood was much better during the day when he was at work, where he would socialize with his coworkers. However, his mood dropped when he was at home without plans and was the worst over the weekend. During the weekend, there was a small elevation when he went to the gym one afternoon, but his mood was the worst on Saturday night when he was home alone watching television. This led to a discussion about the need to find enjoyable nonwork-related activities. Ed's main exposure to other gay men had been in bars and clubs, where he found it difficult to meet men who were not only interested in sex. He had felt on more than one occasion that White gay men had the tendency to view Black gay men as sexual objects and that he did not have much in common with openly gay Black men as they had a tendency to be college-educated, younger, and wealthy.

Over the course of several sessions Ed agreed with some reluctance to consider alternative ways of meeting other gay men. Ed and the therapist came up with several suggestions, including a hiking club, a gay running club, and volunteering. Ed rejected the idea of a hiking club because he said he hated the outdoors, he thought the running club would be too difficult to start off with, but he thought he could probably volunteer at a local AIDS community center. Ed had heard about volunteering there but had some ambivalence. The following discussion emerged as part of a cognitive restructuring intervention.

Therapist: Let's try to figure out exactly what it is that is making you reluctant to try this out. Let me ask you to, for a minute, pretend that you have called and made an appointment with the volunteer coordinator.

Ed: Okay.

Therapist: You have an appointment to go next week and learn about the kinds of things they offer. Picture yourself going in to the appointment. What is going through your head?

Ed: Oh my God, I can't believe I am doing this.

Therapist: Okay, why, in your head, are you thinking that you can't believe you are doing this?

Ed: This guy is not going to like me.

Therapist: Okay, what else?

Ed: If this guy is gay, he is going to wonder why the f*** I am there, since I am so different from other gay men.

Therapist: What else is going through your head?

Ed: Well, the other thing is that if he does like me, it will only be because he is interested in me sexually. And, if I am too friendly, he is going to think that I am interested in him sexually, or that I'm just there to meet men.

Therapist: And why, in your head, would that be bad?

Ed: Because it is lame.

Therapist: Why is it lame?

Ed: Because only someone totally f***** up would need to resort to going to a place like that to meet friends.

One of the first steps in cognitive restructuring procedures is to list the thoughts that make one feel depressed or anxious. This was covered earlier in this chapter. Additional steps include identifying distortions or errors in one's thinking and learning to use objective evidence to dispute the thoughts and come up with a rational response. Ed was able to recognize that he was using "all-or-nothing thinking" and "mind reading" in making assumptions that volunteer coordinators would either dislike him or only accept him because they were sexually attracted to him (although he was not completely convinced that he was incorrect about this view). He also made some gains with respect to his mood, structuring his weekend and after-work activities (although not always social activities). Over time, he was able to use conversations like the one earlier in this chapter to test out his negative predictions about social situations. In turn, this led to decreased avoidance of social situations and increased satisfaction with these interactions.

Throughout the course of treatment, Ed gradually built on his early success with activity planning. He eventually began volunteering at a local organization for HIV, where he was well liked among the staff, and his negative predictions did not come true. This allowed him to become more open to other cognitive restructuring exercises aimed at increasing his social activities including slowly meeting friends and maintaining friendships and dating relationships. It was important to Ed that he was able to make friends both within the LGB community and maintain and build on relationships with other individuals, such as his coworkers, who were heterosexual. By becoming more integrated into the LGB community and feeling better about being gay, he also felt he could be more honest about who he was to his heterosexual friends, and therefore, these relationships could grow.

CONCLUSION

LGB individuals face a variety of stressors related to their sexual orientation. When presenting for mental health treatment, many LGB individuals may also have difficulties similar to individuals who are not LGB, including anxiety, depression, relationship problems, and coping with stress. Although cognitive–behavioral techniques can be applied to this population, an adequate knowledge base about LGB issues is important to assist in formulating a functional analysis and case conceptualization. Sometimes stress related to one's sexual orientation is the primary cause for the need for treatment, at other times it is a peripheral cause, and at yet other times it has nothing to do with the presenting problem. We included two case examples to illustrate some of the presenting concerns of LGB clients and some of the ways in which CBT approaches might be implemented in a culturally sensitive manner. It is important to note that much of the literature on CBT interventions does not report on sexual orientation, and it appears that it is not routinely assessed in these studies. Hence, the therapeutic techniques described in this chapter are based on the general CBT literature, case studies, and our clinical experience. It will be important for future research to investigate further the presenting concerns of LGB clients and to develop and test approaches to address these concerns.

REFERENCES

Adams, H. E., Tollison, C. D., & Carson, T. P. (1981). Behavior therapy with sexual deviations. In S. M. Turner, K. S. Calhoun, & H. E. Adams (Eds.), *Handbook of clinical behavior therapy* (pp. 318–346). New York: Wiley.

American Psychiatric Association. (1994). *Diagnostic and statistical manual of mental disorders* (4th ed.). Washington, DC: Author.

American Psychiatric Association. (2000). *American Psychiatric Association Commission on Psychotherapy by Psychiatrists position statement on therapies focused on attempts to change sexual orientation (reparative or conversion therapies)*. Washington, DC: Author.

American Psychological Association. (2000). *Guidelines for psychotherapy with lesbian, gay and bisexual clients*. Washington, DC: Author.

American Psychological Association. (2001). *Publication manual of the American Psychological Association* (5th ed.). Washington, DC: Author.

Anhalt, K., Morris, T. L., Scotti, J. R., & Cohen, S. H. (2003). Student perspectives on training in gay, lesbian, and bisexual issues: A survey of behavioral clinical psychology programs. *Cognitive and Behavioral Practice, 10,* 255–263.

Association of Behavior and Cognitive Therapy, LGBT Special Interest Group. (in press). *Fact sheet for working with LGBT clients*. New York: Author.

Balsam, K. F. (2002). *Traumatic victimization: A comparison of lesbian, gay, and bisexual adults and their heterosexual siblings*. Unpublished doctoral dissertation, University of Vermont.

Balsam, K. F. (2003). Traumatic victimization in the lives of lesbian and bisexual women: A contextual approach. *Journal of Lesbian Studies, 7*(1), 1–14.

Balsam, K. F., Beauchaine, T. D., Mickey, R., & Rothblum, E. D. (2005). Mental health of lesbian, gay, bisexual, and heterosexual siblings: Effects of gender, sexual orientation, and family. *Journal of Abnormal Psychology, 114,* 471–476.

Balsam, K. F., Rothblum, E. D., & Beauchaine, T. (2005). Victimization over the life span: A comparison of lesbian, gay, bisexual, and heterosexual siblings. *Journal of Consulting and Clinical Psychology, 73*, 477–487.

Beck, A. T., Epstein, N., Brown, G., & Steer, R. A. (1988). An inventory for measuring clinical anxiety: Psychometric properties. *Journal of Consulting and Clinical Psychology, 49*, 448–454.

Beck, A. T., Steer, R. A., & Brown, G. K. (1996). *Manual for the BDI–II.* San Antonio, TX: Psychological Corporation.

Beck, A. T., Ward, C. H., Mendelson, M., Mock, J., & Erbaugh, J. (1961). An inventory for measuring depression. *Archives of General Psychiatry, 4*, 561–571.

Bepko, C., & Johnson, T. (2000). Gay and lesbian couples in therapy: Perspectives for the contemporary family therapist. *Journal of Marital and Family Therapy, 26*, 409–419.

Berg, M., Mimiaga, M., & Safren, S. A. (in press). Mental health concerns of HIV-negative gay and bisexual men seeking services. *Journal of Homosexuality.*

Bradford, J., Ryan, C., & Rothblum, E. D. (1994). National lesbian health care survey: Implications for mental health care. *Journal of Consulting and Clinical Psychology, 62*, 228–242.

Brown, T. A., DiNardo, P. A., & Barlow, D. H. (1994). *Anxiety Disorders Interview Schedule for DSM–IV: Adult version.* Albany, NY: Graywinds.

Christensen, A., & Jacobson, N. S. (1997). *Frequency and acceptability of partner behavior.* Unpublished questionnaire. (Available from Andrew Christensen, University of California, Department of Psychology, Los Angeles, CA 90095)

Cochran, S. D. (2001). Emerging issues in research on lesbians' and gay men's mental health: Does sexual orientation really matter? *American Psychologist, 56*, 931–947.

Cochran, S. D., Sullivan, J. G., & Mays, V. M. (2003). Prevalence of mental disorders, psychological distress, and mental services use among lesbian, gay, and bisexual adults in the United States. *Journal of Consulting and Clinical Psychology, 71*, 53–61.

Corliss, H. L., Cochran, S. D., & Mays, V. M. (2002). Reports of parental maltreatment during childhood in a United States population-based survey of homosexual, bisexual, and heterosexual adults. *Child Abuse and Neglect, 26*, 1165–1178.

D'Augelli, A. R. (1998). Developmental implications of victimization of lesbian, gay, and bisexual youths. In G. M. Herek (Ed.), *Stigma and sexual orientation: Understanding prejudice against lesbians, gay men, and bisexuals* (pp. 187–210). Thousand Oaks, CA: Sage.

Davison, G. C. (1976). Homosexuality: The ethical challenge. *Journal of Consulting and Clinical Psychology, 44*, 157–162.

Elkins, R., & King, D. (1998). Blending genders: Contributions to the emerging field of transgender studies. In D. Denny (Ed.), *Current concepts in transgender identity* (pp. 97–115). New York: Garland.

First, M., Spitzer, R. L., Gibbon, M., & Williams, J. (1995). *Structured Clinical Interview for DSM–IV Axis I disorders: Patient edition*. New York: New York State Psychiatric Institute, Biometrics Research Department.

Foa, E. B., Riggs, D. S., Dancu, C. V., & Rothbaum, B. O. (1993). Reliability and validity of a brief instrument for assessing post-traumatic stress disorder. *Journal of Traumatic Stress, 6*, 459–473.

Foa, E. B., & Rothbaum, B. O. (1998). *Treating the trauma of rape: Cognitive–behavioral therapy for PTSD*. New York: Guilford Press.

Foa, E. B., Rothbaum, B. O., Riggs, D. S., & Murdock, T. B. (1991). Treatment of posttraumatic stress disorder in rape victims: A comparison between cognitive–behavioral procedures and counseling. *Journal of Consulting and Clinical Psychology, 59*, 715–723.

Frisch, M. B. (1994). *The Quality of Life Inventory: Manual and treatment guide*. Minneapolis, MN: National Computer Systems.

Gainor, K. A. (2000). Including transgender issues in lesbian, gay, and bisexual psychology: Implications for clinical practice and training. In B. Greene & G. L. Croom (Eds.), *Education, research, and practice in lesbian, gay, bisexual, and transgendered psychology* (pp. 131–160). Thousand Oaks, CA: Sage.

Garnets, L., Hancock, K. A., Cochran, S. D., Goodchilds, J., & Peplau, L. A. (1991). Issues in psychotherapy with lesbians and gay men: A survey of psychologists. *American Psychologist, 46*, 964–972.

Greene, B. (1994). Lesbian women of color: Triple jeopardy. In L. Comas-Díaz & B. Greene (Eds.), *Women of color: Integrating ethnic and gender identities in psychotherapy* (pp. 389–427). New York: Guilford Press.

Haldeman, D. C. (1994). The practice and ethics of sexual orientation conversion therapy. *Journal of Consulting and Clinical Psychology, 62*, 221–227.

Herek, G. M. (1990). The context of anti-gay violence: Notes on cultural and psychological heterosexism. *Journal of Interpersonal Violence, 5*, 316–333.

Herek, G. M., Gillis, J. R., & Cogan, J. C. (1999). Psychological sequelae of hate-crime victimization among lesbian, gay, and bisexual adults. *Journal of Consulting and Clinical Psychology, 67*, 945–951.

Herek, G. M., Gillis, J. R., Cogan, J. C., & Glunt, E. K. (1997). Hate crime victimization among lesbian, gay, and bisexual adults. *Journal of Interpersonal Violence, 12*, 195–215.

Hughes, T. L., Johnson, T., & Wilsnack, S. C. (2001). Sexual assault and alcohol abuse: A comparison of lesbians and heterosexual women. *Journal of Substance Abuse, 13*, 515–532.

Icard, L. D. (1996). Assessing the psychosocial well-being of African American gays: A multidimensional perspective. In J. F. Longres (Ed.), *Men of color: A context for service to homosexually active men* (pp. 25–49). New York: Harrington Park Press.

Jacobs, S., Thomas, W., & Lang, S. (1997). *Two-spirit people: Native American gender identity, sexuality, and spirituality*. Urbana, IL: University of Chicago Press.

Kaminski, E. (2000). Lesbian health: Social context, sexual identity, and well-being. *Journal of Lesbian Studies, 4*, 87–101.

Kessler, R. C., Sonnega, A., Bromet, E., Hughes, M., & Nelson, C. B. (1995). Post-traumatic stress disorder in the National Comorbidity Survey. *Archives of General Psychiatry, 52*, 1048–1060.

King, J. L. (2004). *On the down low: A journey into the lives of "straight" Black men who sleep with men.* New York: Broadway Books.

Martell, C. R., Safren, S. A., & Prince, S. E. (2004). *Cognitive–behavioral therapies with lesbian, gay and bisexual clients.* New York: Guilford Press.

McLellan, A. T., Kushner, H., Metzger, D., Peters, R., Smith, I., Grissom, G., et al. (1992). The fifth edition of the Addiction Severity Index. *Journal of Substance Abuse Treatment, 9*, 199–213.

Meyer, I. H. (2003). Prejudice, social stress, and mental health in lesbian, gay, and bisexual populations: Conceptual issues and research evidence. *Psychological Bulletin, 12*, 674–697.

Meyer, I. H., Rossano, L., Ellis, J. M., & Bradford, J. (2002). A brief telephone interview to identify lesbian and bisexual women in random digit dialing sampling. *Journal of Sex Research, 39*, 139–144.

Morris, J. F., Waldo, C. R., & Rothblum, E. D. (2001). A model of predictors and outcomes of outness among lesbian and bisexual women. *American Journal of Orthopsychiatry, 71*, 61–71.

National Association of Social Workers. (1996). *Code of ethics of the National Association of Social Workers.* Retrieved October 2, 2000, from http://www.naswdc.org/pubs/code/default.asp

Neisen, J. H. (1993). Healing from cultural victimization: Recovery from shame due to heterosexism. *Journal of Gay and Lesbian Psychotherapy, 2*, 49–63.

Norris, F. (1992). Epidemiology of trauma: Frequency and impact of different potentially traumatic events on different demographic groups. *Journal of Consulting and Clinical Psychology, 60*, 409–418.

Ochs, R. (1996). Biphobia: It goes more than two ways. In B. A. Firestein (Ed.), *Bisexuality: The psychology and politics of an invisible minority* (pp. 217–239). Thousand Oaks, CA: Sage.

Padesky, C. A. (1989). Attaining and maintaining a positive lesbian self-identity: A cognitive therapy approach. *Women & Therapy, 8*(1–2), 145–156.

Purcell, D. W., Campos, P. E., & Perilla, J. L. (1996). Therapy with lesbians and gay men: A cognitive behavioral perspective. *Cognitive and Behavioral Practice, 3*, 391–415.

Rowan, A. (1994). Homophobia: A new diagnosis for *DSM–V? The Behavior Therapist, 17*, 183–184.

Shidlo, A., & Schroeder, M. (2002). Changing sexual orientation: A consumer's report. *Professional Psychology: Research and Practice, 33*, 249–259.

Smith, A. (1997). Cultural diversity and the coming out process: Implications for clinical practice. In B. Greene (Ed.), *Ethnic and cultural diversity among lesbians and gay men* (pp. 279–300). Thousand Oaks, CA: Sage.

Solomon, S. E., Rothblum, E. D., & Balsam, K. F. (2005). Money, housework, sex, and conflict: Same-sex couples in civil unions, those not in civil unions, and heterosexual married siblings. *Sex Roles, 52,* 561–575.

Spanier, G. B. (1976). Measuring dyadic adjustment. *Journal of Marriage and the Family, 38,* 15–28.

Spencer, S. B., & Hemmer, R. C. (1993). Therapeutic bias with gay and lesbian clients: A functional analysis. *The Behavior Therapist, 16,* 93–97.

Szymanski, D. M., Chung, Y. B., & Balsam, K. F. (2001). Psychosocial correlates of internalized homophobia in lesbians. *Measurement and Evaluation in Counseling and Development, 34,* 27–38.

Tafoya, T., & Wirth, D. A. (1996). Native American two-spirit men. In J. F. Longres (Ed.), *Men of color: A context for service to homosexually active men* (pp. 51–67). New York: Harrington Park Press.

Tjaden, P., Thoeness, N., & Allison, C. J. (1999). Comparing violence over the life span in samples of same-sex and opposite-sex cohabitants. *Violence and Victims, 14,* 413–425.

Tomeo, M. E., Templer, D. I., Anderson, S., & Kotler, D. (2002). Comparative data of childhood and adolescent molestation in heterosexual and homosexual persons. *Archives of Sexual Behavior, 30,* 535–541.

Vincke, J., & vanHeeringin, K. (2002). Confidant support and the mental wellbeing of lesbian and gay young adults: A longitudinal analysis. *Journal of Community and Applied Social Psychology, 12,* 181–193.

Weinberg, G. (1972). *Society and the healthy homosexual.* New York: St. Martin's Press.

Weinstock, J. S. (2000). Lesbian friendships at midlife: Patterns and possibilities for the 21st century. *Journal of Gay and Lesbian Social Services: Issues in Practice, Policy and Research, 11,* 1–32.

Wolpe, J. (1990). *The practice of behavior therapy* (4th ed.). New York: Pergamon.

Zamora-Hernández, C. E., & Patterson, D. G. (1996). Homosexually active Latino men: Issues for social work practice. In J. F. Longres (Ed.), *Men of color: A context for service to homosexually active men* (pp. 69–91). New York: Harrington Park Press.

Zea, M. C., Reisen, C. A., & Poppen, P. S. (1999). Psychological well-being among Latino lesbians and gay men. *Cultural Diversity and Ethnic Minority Psychology, 5,* 371–379.

III

ASSESSMENT AND SUPERVISION ISSUES

11

CULTURAL CONSIDERATIONS IN COGNITIVE–BEHAVIORAL ASSESSMENT

SUMIE OKAZAKI AND JUNKO TANAKA-MATSUMI

A large body of research points toward the utility of evidence-based psychological assessment and interventions for ethnic minority populations (Miranda et al., 2005). However, cultural influences in the assessment of psychopathology still present a challenge for cognitive–behavioral therapists given the legitimate critique that cognitive–behavioral assessment measures (as well as treatments) have not been adequately validated in minority cultures (Bernal & Scharron-del-Rio, 2001; Hall, 2001; Haynes & O'Brien, 1990; Iwamasa, 1997; Wood, Garb, Lilienfeld, & Nezworski, 2002). Of course, cognitive–behavioral assessment is not alone in this regard; most measures of personality and psychopathology are limited in their cross-cultural validity. Moreover, the clinical self-report assessment instruments that have the best cross-cultural validation are the Minnesota Multiphasic Personality Inventory (MMPI) and the MMPI–2 (Wood et al., 2002), which are not as widely used in cognitive–behavioral therapy (CBT).

Recognizing these limitations, this chapter provides an overview of major issues that may be helpful in conducting cognitive–behavioral assessments with culturally diverse clients. We include both self-report and behavioral measures, as CBT involves the evaluation of clients' cognitions in various forms and behavioral performance. First, information is provided regarding cross-cultural differences in self-reported affect, behavior, and well-being—research that has important implications for cognitive–behavioral assessments that rely heavily on self-report data. Second, the use of cognitive–behavioral instruments for assessing specific disorders, cognitive styles, and behavior with ethnic minority clients is discussed with special attention to one of the most commonly used self-report measures, the Beck Depression Inventory (BDI) and the BDI–II. Finally, several clinical approaches to culturally responsive cognitive–behavioral assessment are described, including functional analysis, the Culturally Informed Functional Assessment (CIFA) interview, the ADDRESSING framework, the Multicultural Assessment Procedure (MAP), the Explanatory Model Interview Catalogue (EMIC), and a bicultural evaluation procedure used in New Zealand. A case example is used to illustrate functional analysis and the CIFA interview.

CROSS-CULTURAL FINDINGS REGARDING SELF-REPORT DATA

Multiple studies have documented the tendency of people from East Asian cultures to not endorse high levels of positive affect and, in contrast, the tendency of people from Latin American cultures to report high levels of positive affect (Diener, Oishi, & Lucas, 2003). Perceived norms within cultures have also been found to affect self-reports differentially across cultures, with East Asians reporting levels of subjective well-being consistent with their beliefs about the normative desirability of positive and negative emotions (Diener, Suh, Smith, & Shao, 1995). An examination of possible reasons for the lower subjective well-being reported by Japanese, South Korean, and Chinese people (compared with Americans) led researchers to conclude that these cross-national differences were not due to differences in income, extreme response set, humility, or social desirability (Diener et al., 1995).

In a study of cross-national differences in self-reported emotions, people from nations described as more individualistic (Australia, Austria, Denmark, Finland, Germany, Hungary, Italy, the Netherlands, Norway, Puerto Rico, South Africa, Spain, and the United States) were compared with those of more collectivistic nations (Bahrain, China, Colombia, Ghana, Indonesia, South Korea, Nepal, Nigeria, Pakistan, Peru, Singapore, Thailand, and Zimbabwe; Suh, Diener, Oishi, & Triandis, 1998). Results showed that the individuals from individualistic nations relied primarily on their own subjective emotional experiences to make global judgments about their life satisfaction, whereas individuals from the collectivistic countries used cultural norms about the desirability of life satisfaction as a basis for such judgments, in addition to their own emotions.

Similar differences have been found in retrospective reports of well-being and behavior. In a series of studies with Japanese, European American, and Asian American students, Oishi (2002) found that although there were no cultural differences in momentary or day-to-day reports of well-being, European Americans reported a higher level of life satisfaction than Asian Americans in retrospective and global judgments of well-being. East–West cultural differences have also been noted in the nature of representations of the self in long-term memory (Cohen & Gunz, 2002; Wagar & Cohen, 2003). For example, Asian Canadians were slower than European Canadians to recognize personal traits encoded in relation to self than collective traits (e.g., social roles) encoded in relation to self (Wagar & Cohen, 2003). Asian Canadians were also more likely than European Canadians to have third-person memories of personal events (i.e., imagining the scene from an observer perspective rather than an actor's perspective; Cohen & Gunz, 2002). Finally, cross-cultural differences have been found in the extent to which one's *situation* influences reported levels of affective experiences and in the importance placed on an individual's self-view being consistent across situations (Oishi, Diener, Scollon, & Biswas-Diener, 2004; Suh, 2002).

Taken together, these studies show cultural variations in multiple areas of self-report: (a) normative levels of self-reported happiness and distress, (b) the importance of perceived norms regarding happiness and distress, (c) retrospective judgments of one's past affective states, and (d) the desirability of consistency between one's emotions and identity across situations. These findings clearly demonstrate the need for caution when using self-report scores in assessment.

ACCULTURATION AND COGNITIVE–BEHAVIORAL ASSESSMENT

Acculturation is a critical construct in understanding the psychological functioning of immigrants and ethnic minorities. There is a volume of research on theories and measurement of acculturation as well as research examining the relationship between acculturation (and related constructs such as assimilation and enculturation) and various assessment measures (see, e.g., Chun, Balls Organista, & Marín, 2002; Dana, 2000). Acculturation scales are typically designed to assess the person's language(s), social support network, and participation in certain ethnic and cultural activities. Cognitive–behavioral therapists use these available measures of acculturation to assess the possible relationship between cultural adjustment difficulties and presenting problems. Recent theories have pointed to the complexities and inconsistencies in the pattern of relationships between acculturation and various measures of adaptive behavior (Rudmin, 2003). A review of this literature is beyond the scope of this chapter; however, it is important for clinicians to note that clients' acculturation status can shape not only their behavior, affect, and cognitions but also their responses to various assessment tools.

THE UTILITY OF ASSESSMENT INSTRUMENTS
WITH DIVERSE CLIENTS

Within the vast literature documenting the effectiveness of CBT, an enormous number of instruments have been developed for assessing symptoms associated with specific disorders (Anthony & Barlow, 2002), including some that have been used successfully in primary care settings in the United States and other countries (e.g., the Patient Health Questionnaire; Spitzer, Kroenke, & Williams, 1999). A number of diagnostic instruments have been developed specifically for international use (e.g., the Composite International Diagnostic Interview; World Health Organization, 1991) and used successfully with ethnic minority populations in the United States (e.g., Jackson et al., 2004). A review of these instruments is not feasible in this chapter owing to space limitations. However, we provide information regarding the self-report measure of depressive symptoms most widely used in conjunction with the cognitive–behavioral treatment of depression (the BDI and BDI–II; Beck, Ward, Mendelson, Mock, & Erbaugh, 1961) and information on several instruments for assessing cognitive styles and behavior. Whenever possible, we discuss the applicability and usefulness of these instruments with regard to the three largest U.S. ethnic minority groups for which there are data: African Americans, Latinos, and Asian Americans.

The BDI and BDI–II

African Americans

Although no comprehensive validation studies have been published regarding the BDI or the BDI–II with African Americans, several studies have found adequate reliability with African Americans (e.g., Carr, Gilroy, & Sherman, 1986; Molock, Kimbrough, Blanton Lacy, McClure, & Williams, 1994). However, there are mixed findings regarding the comparability of mean scores on the BDI between African Americans and European Americans. Whereas some studies have found comparable mean BDI scores (e.g., Lester & DeSimone, 1995; Trent, Rushlau, Munley, Bloem, & Driesenga, 2000), others have reported higher scores among African Americans (e.g., Cavanaugh, 1983).

In an item analysis to examine for possible test bias in the BDI, Ayalon and Young (2003) compared depressive symptoms reported on the BDI between 278 African American outpatients seeking psychotherapy and a matched sample of 278 European American outpatients. Of the 21 items, 10 were reported differently. At equal levels of depression, African Americans reported more insomnia, loss of libido, appetite loss, and feelings of being punished and less pessimism, self-blame, suicidal ideation, and dissatisfaction than did European Americans. On 6 items (primarily cognitive symptoms), ethnic differences in symptom severity were not related to depression severity, suggesting test bias on these items.

Latino Populations

There have been several approaches to establishing equivalence, validity, and utility of the BDI with Spanish-speaking populations. Many of the studies used their own translations of the BDI into Spanish, making direct comparisons across studies difficult.

One attempt to establish item-level equivalence between English and Spanish translations found bias in four items of the BDI (Azocar, Areán, Miranda, & Muñoz, 2001). The Spanish-speaking group (a heterogeneous sample of immigrants and U.S.-born Latinos) was more likely to endorse the items of feeling like they are being punished, feeling like crying, and believing they "look ugly" and less likely to endorse not being able to work than was the English-speaking group.

In another study, the BDI was revised and modified to be more consistent with the *Diagnostic and Statistical Manual of Mental Disorders* (4th ed., *DSM–IV*; American Psychiatric Association, 1994) diagnostic criteria for major depressive disorder in Puerto Rican populations (Bonilla, Bernal, Santos, & Santos, 2004). The revised measure (BDI-S) was translated into Spanish and administered, along with a number of other measures, to 351 university students from the University of Puerto Rico. The authors reported adequate internal consistency and correlations with other depression scales and concluded that the BDI-S provides a reliable and valid measure of depressive symptoms, with psychometric properties comparable with the English version of the BDI.

Beck, Steer, and Brown (1996) published a Spanish-translated version of the BDI–II, which is commercially available from the same test publisher that publishes the English BDI–II. In a study of 122 primarily Mexican American medical patients receiving hemodialysis, the Spanish BDI–II was found to have adequate internal consistency (Penley, Wiebe, & Nwosu, 2003). Acculturation to the U.S. culture was negatively associated with Spanish BDI–II total scores, but this effect was no longer significant when socioeconomic status was partialed out. Examination of response patterns on the English and the Spanish versions of the BDI–II completed by 23 bilingual patients found the total scores from both versions to be highly correlated, with mean scores not significantly different from one another.

Asian Americans

The BDI has been translated into a number of Asian languages, primarily for use in East Asia (e.g., China, Korea, and Japan).[1] Here again, researchers have often translated the scales themselves for their local population, making comparisons difficult. The absence of official translations has limited the use of the BDI in clinical practice with Asian language speakers.

In a series of studies with college students, Okazaki (2002) found that Asian Americans tended to report higher levels of depression than European Americans on self-report inventories such as the BDI–II. In addition, perceived cultural norms about depression were related to depressive symptom reports among Asian Americans but not among European Americans (Okazaki & Kallivayalil, 2002).

The Chinese translation of the BDI (CBDI; Zheng, Wei, Goa, Zhang, & Wong, 1988) used with 503 immigrant Chinese American patients was found to be an effective screening tool for depression (Yeung, Howarth, et al., 2002). In a related study with the same group of patients, the CBDI was compared with the Chinese Depression Inventory (CDI; Zheng & Lin, 1991) toward the goal of constructing a more culturally valid instrument (Yeung, Neault, et al., 2002). Yeung, Neault, et al. concluded that the CBDI and the CDI, when administered by raters, were comparable in their abilities to screen for clinically diagnosable depression in recently immigrated Chinese people in the United States. It seems important to note that the researchers found that their initial approach of leaving patients in the clinic's waiting area with the depression questionnaire elicited little willingness among less acculturated patients to complete the questionnaire. The more personal approach of research assistants sitting with the patient, introducing the study, and then verbally administering the questionnaire resulted in a higher participation rate.

Finally, in response to critiques that existing depression scales such as the BDI are Western in origin and thus may not fully capture distress in non-Western populations, several culture-specific measures of depression have been developed: the Vietnamese Depression Scale (Kinzie et al., 1982), the Kim Depression Scale for Korean Americans (Kim, 2002), and the Hmong Adaptation of the Beck Depression Inventory for use with Hmong Lao refugees in the United States (Mouanoutoua, Brown, Cappelletty, & Levine, 1991). Regarding the last scale, to make the scale more easily understood by the Hmong (many of whom could not read), response options had to be changed from severity to frequency of the occurrence of symptoms. Although the psychometric properties for these three scales appear promising, it is dif-

---

[1]See Leong, Okazaki, and Tak (2003) for a review of anxiety and depression measures and their use with overseas East Asian populations. Also see a Web site titled "Psychosocial Measures for Asian American Populations: Tools for Direct Practice and Research" (http://www.columbia.edu/cu/ssw/projects/pmap/), which collects and organizes information on the use of self-report measures with Asian American populations.

ficult to know to what extent these measures have been disseminated or have gained usage in practice.

Standardized Assessment of Cognitive Styles

Although there is a large empirical literature on dysfunctional cognitions (e.g., automatic beliefs, cognitive schemas) and their relationship to psychological symptoms among European Americans, little research has been conducted with ethnic minorities. One study notable for its culturally based examination of these constructs examined whether self-attention, as assessed by a modified version of the Introspectiveness Scale (Hansell & Mechanic, 1985), mediates the influence of acculturation on depressive symptoms in first-generation Chinese American and Japanese American immigrants (Chen, Guarnaccia, & Chung, 2003). Results indicated that the more acculturated participants were more likely to report more affective and fewer somatic symptoms of depression, and that the changes in symptom expression that accompanied acculturation were mediated by changes in the attention given to affective versus somatic aspects of the self.

Two additional studies addressed the utility of cognitive–behavioral assessment tools with African Americans. In the first study (Schoeder, 2002), 258 African American students were administered the BDI, the Dysfunctional Attitudes Scale (DAS; Oliver & Baumgart, 1985), and the Automatic Thoughts Questionnaire (ATQ; Hollon & Kendall, 1980) to examine Beck's cognitive theory of depression (i.e., that depressive thoughts lead to depressed mood). Schoeder found that the ATQ but not the DAS mediated the relationship between negative life events and depressive symptoms in this sample. In the second study, 213 African American female caregivers completed the Depressive Cognition Scale (Zauszniewski, 1995), which was found to have adequate internal consistency and construct validity for detecting depression in these African American women (Zauszniewski, Fulton Picot, Debanne, Roberts, & Wykle, 2002).

Behavioral Assessment

Behavioral assessment refers to strategies that range from individualized tests of specific behaviors (e.g., an impromptu public speech to assess social phobia) to formal rating systems such as the Social Performance Rating Scale used to rate videotaped performances of socially anxious patients in public-speaking tasks (Fydrich, Chambless, Perry, Buergener, & Beazley, 1998; Harb, Eng, Zaider, & Heimberg, 2003). Here again, very little research has been conducted on the reliability, validity, and utility of behavioral assessment measures with diverse populations (Tanaka-Matsumi, 2004). One aspect of behavioral assessment that has received some attention is how the clinically relevant behavior of ethnic minorities may be perceived by others.

For example, Gonzalez, Cauce, and Mason (1996) examined the behavioral ratings by African American and non-African American coders on measures of maternal support, maternal restrictive control, and parent–adolescent conflict with 57 African American mothers and their adolescent daughters. The study found African American coders' ratings to be more consistent with the perceptions of the African American mothers and adolescents themselves than were the ratings made by non-African American coders. Okazaki, Liu, Longworth, and Minn (2002) examined the behavioral ratings of White American and Asian American college students engaged in a social performance task. Although there were no ethnic differences in the microlevel behavior rated by trained coders (e.g., frequency of eye contact, length of uncomfortable silence), Asian Americans were rated by the coders to be more anxious than White Americans.

MODELS FOR CULTURALLY RESPONSIVE COGNITIVE–BEHAVIORAL ASSESSMENT

In a recent conversation with one of the authors about cultural competence issues, a Latina student related an anecdote in which she had encountered a clinician who, in an initial phone conversation with the student, identified herself as also a Latina and remarked to the student, "Oh, as a Latina, you must be dealing with *marianismo*." The student, taken aback by such a facile (and in this case, inaccurate) application of a cultural and religious stereotype, thought, "What do YOU know about my family? What do YOU know about me?" It is clear that, in this situation, the clinician had mismanaged the communication surrounding possible roles that culture, race, and ethnicity may play in the student's life. However, we could just as easily imagine another Latina who would feel a sense of rapport with a clinician who communicates a similar sentiment. How does one conduct a cognitive–behavioral assessment that walks this fine line?

Culturally responsive cognitive–behavioral therapists have addressed the question of cultural differences and value implications in behavior therapy, noting two major tasks (Evans, 1997; Forehand & Wierson, 1993; Kanfer & Scheft, 1988). First, the therapist needs to evaluate the client's presenting problems using functional analysis, and, second, the therapist must assess the larger context of the client's social network with attention to cultural influences. These influences are conceptualized as criteria for cultural accommodation to psychotherapy and include (a) cultural definitions of the problem behavior, (b) knowledge of accepted norms of role behavior, (c) cultural acceptability of behavior change techniques, and (d) culturally approved behavior change agents (Tanaka-Matsumi, Higginbotham, & Chang, 2002). The following section describes how these cultural criteria are considered as part of a functional analysis.

Functional Analysis

The goal of functional analysis is the "identification of important, controllable, causal functional relationships applicable to a specified set of target behaviors for an individual client" (Haynes & O'Brien, 1990, p. 654). In other words, the therapist collaboratively works with the client and significant others to identify factors that may cause, contribute to, or exacerbate a particular problem behavior. This information is then used to develop a treatment plan aimed at extinguishing (i.e., eliminating) the problem behavior and strengthening positive behaviors and coping skills. The inclusion of data from multiple sources (i.e., people) and situations (cultural contexts and mediating factors) makes functional analysis highly useful in cross-cultural settings. Consider the following example.

The parents of a 7-year-old Japanese boy, who moved with his family to the United States because of his father's business assignment, described in Japanese to the bilingual cognitive–behavioral therapist the following concern: "His classroom teacher calls frequently to tell us that our son Kenta is acting out in school and they cannot control him. Kenta comes home and tells us nothing about school. We never heard of such a complaint about our son in Japan." The therapist collected additional information from Kenta's parents concerning his "acting out," and then she interviewed the child. Once this information was gathered, the therapist obtained the parents' consent to contact the child's school. The purpose of calling Kenta's school was to assess the specific behaviors labeled as "acting out" and the situations in which Kenta exhibited these behaviors. The therapist sought information concerning (a) specific descriptions of the acting-out behaviors, (b) their antecedent events and situations, and (c) the consequences of the acting-out behaviors in the classroom.

The therapist identified that the acting out involved talking loudly in Japanese when the teacher asked for class participation and standing on the chair when the teacher continued to repeat the instruction in English. The consequent events included other students clapping their hands when Kenta stood up on the chair and the teacher reprimanding the class in English for the disruption of her class. At other times, it was reported that Kenta put his head down on his desk with his fingers covering his ears. Subsequently, behavioral observation was conducted by the therapist at the school. The therapist looked for the relationships between antecedent events, the target behavior, and the consequent events within Kenta's new school environment and his new cultural context.

On the basis of her observations of Kenta's classroom behavior, the therapist explained to Kenta's teacher the likelihood that his acting-out behavior was being maintained by his inability to follow the teacher's English directions and the attention directed to his acting-out behavior by his peers in class. The therapist designed a program focusing on the teacher's contingent positive attention for Kenta's good behaviors. The teacher also created chances for Kenta to display his talents without having to use difficult English in the classroom (e.g., drawing, playing the recorder). Children were told not to clap when Kenta stood on his chair. Instead, they were to help Kenta whenever he had difficulty because of the language barrier. His parents were informed of Kenta's daily activities and his progress in school. Gradually, Kenta's behavior improved in class and he made friends with his American peers.

The Culturally Informed Functional Assessment Interview

Although 90% of behavior therapists report using interviews as part of their assessments (Spiegler & Guevremont, 1998), only a few interview guidelines have been developed that specify the *content* of behavioral interviews. Not surprisingly, even less attention has been given to cross-cultural content in behavioral interviews.

The Culturally Informed Functional Assessment (CIFA) interview (Tanaka-Matsumi, Seiden, & Lam, 1996) was designed to facilitate the integration of cultural observations into cognitive–behavioral assessment and treatment planning (Tanaka-Matsumi et al., 2002). Specifically, it aims to increase the cultural relevance of a case formulation by generating detailed, culturally relevant information regarding observable events that are potentially connected to the client's presenting problem. The CIFA involves eight successive stages:

1. assessment of the client's cultural identity and level of acculturation;
2. assessment of the client's presenting problems;
3. elicitation of the client's conceptualization of the problems and possible solutions;
4. functional analysis of the antecedent–target–consequence sequence;
5. negotiation of similarities and differences between the functional analysis and the client's causal explanation of the problems;
6. development of a treatment plan that is acceptable to all parties involved, including culturally different individuals and reference groups;
7. data gathering that facilitates ongoing assessment of the client's progress; and
8. discussion of treatment duration, course, and expected outcome.

At each stage, the therapist compares and contrasts the perspectives of the client, the family, cultural reference groups, and the therapist's own emerging case formulation (Tanaka-Matsumi et al., 2002). Returning to the case of Kenta, the bilingual therapist recognized that Kenta was relatively unacculturated to the dominant U.S. culture and acknowledged the role of his limited English in the situation. She considered the differing perspectives of Kenta's cultural reference groups (i.e., his Japanese parents and the European American teacher and school system). She made an assessment of his presenting problem (the acting-out behavior) that included the parents' and the teacher's conceptualizations of the problem. She conducted a functional analysis of the relationship between his problem behaviors (e.g., talking loudly in Japanese when the teacher was talking, standing on his chair) and the antecedents (not understanding the teacher's directions in English), situation (the new cultural context of the American classroom), and reinforcement of the problem behaviors (other children clapping their hands, the teacher's attention albeit negative). The therapist developed a treatment plan that built on Kenta's strengths and abilities (drawing, playing the recorder) and was acceptable to the parents, the teacher, and Kenta. Finally, she collected data that allowed her to assess Kenta's responsiveness to the interventions.

Using guidelines adapted from the CIFA, Seiden (1999) evaluated the reliability of cross-cultural behavioral case formulations of four Chinese clients who met criteria for the Chinese syndrome of *neurasthenia* (a condition characterized by mental and physical fatigue and accompanied by a range of other neuropsychological and mood symptoms as well as nonspecific physical symptoms) and had multiple somatic problems. Each client was interviewed by a Chinese behavioral therapist in Chinese. In a typical interview, one of the men described his immigration to the United States, his changed social status from a surgeon to a restaurant kitchen worker, excessive working hours, renewed family problems, and a series of somatic complaints including back and leg pains. As the interview proceeded, in response to the Chinese interviewer's probes, the client described his sense of personal loss, loneliness, and dejected mood and his inability to cope with many overwhelming situations in the United States. This case illustrates how the systematic attention given to cultural influences in the CIFA interview can facilitate the interview process, helping the interviewer to build rapport and thus increase the likelihood of obtaining more accurate information.

In the same study, 18 Chinese American and 31 European American behaviorally oriented clinicians individually watched an English-subtitled videotape of a functional assessment interview such as the one with the Chinese client previously discussed (Seiden, 1999). Each clinician was asked to identify the problems, their antecedents and consequences, and recommended treatments. A majority consensus was found between and within clinician cultures on specific cross-culturally validated categories for antecedents and consequences of target *problems* (e.g., headaches and fatigue). However, the content of agreed-on *intervention* targets and *treatments* varied between patients. These results suggest that the CIFA interview guidelines are useful in gathering a rich amount of data that must then be used to develop individually oriented treatment plans and interventions.

In another example, Tanaka-Matsumi et al. (1996) presented the stepwise assessment of a cross-cultural marital case in which the Spanish wife complained of her own depression and her Japanese husband's inability to communicate with her at home. In a typical interaction, the wife would become increasingly upset at her husband for not talking with her, until she would decide to leave home for a few hours. When she returned, her worried husband would apologize, which temporarily improved her depression and the marital dissatisfaction. By using the CIFA guidelines, the therapist called attention to the cultural differences in each individual's expectations regarding communication and hypothesized a functional relationship between the antecedent (the husband's lack of communication with his wife), the presenting problem (the marital distress and the wife's depression), and the consequence (the husband's apology and attention).

In summary, the greater the therapist's knowledge of the client's cultural definitions of problem behavior and cultural norms regarding behavior, change strategies, and the change agents (i.e., the criteria for cultural accommodation to psychotherapy), the more accurate and useful an assessment will be. Although functional analysis and assessment are highly amenable to such cross-cultural uses, they have not routinely taken cultural influences into account. The CIFA interview provides a systematic approach to integrating these influences into cognitive–behavioral assessment.

The *DSM–IV–TR* Outline for Cultural Formulation

Today, a majority of cognitive–behavioral therapists use the *DSM–IV Text Revision* (*DSM–IV–TR*; American Psychiatric Association, 2000) for the purposes of assessment, diagnosis, and professional communication. In fact, most of the empirically supported treatment guidelines are organized according to specific, behaviorally based *DSM* categories (Nelson-Gray & Paulson, 2004). The *DSM–IV* was the first edition to include a systematic approach to the assessment of psychopathology in minority cultures in the form of the Outline for Cultural Formulation and Glossary of Culture-Bound Syndromes (American Psychiatric Association, 1994). The outline specifies five areas for gathering information: (a) the client's cultural background; (b) cultural explanations of the client's illness (e.g., cultural idioms of distress); (c) cultural factors related to the psychosocial environment and levels of the client's functioning; (d) cultural elements of the relationship between the client and the clinician; and (e) the overall cultural assessment necessary for diagnosis and care. The glossary consists of a list of 25 culture-bound syndromes commonly reported in particular cultures.

Although these sections represent an attempt to address cultural issues in the assessment and diagnostic process, they suffer from several problems.

One, the cultural outline is placed in the appendix, where it is generally not used. Two, by placing the culture-bound syndromes in a separate section rather than integrating them into the body of the DSM, their inclusion seems to suggest that cultural influences are only relevant to people of ethnic minority cultures. Three, as the DSM–IV–TR itself notes, many of the culture-bound syndromes would fit under more recognized disorders (e.g., *ataque de nervios* under general anxiety disorder, *taijin kyfusho* under social phobia, and *shenjing shuairuo* under mood or anxiety disorder; Hays, 2001). If these syndromes had been more integrated into the multiaxial system, they might have gained greater recognition (not to mention reimbursement by insurance companies). At present, the use of the cultural outline and culture-bound syndromes for clinical purposes is rare (Hays, 2001).

The Multicultural Assessment Procedure

Ridley, Li, and Hill (1998) noted that there is a large body of literature that has raised consciousness within the helping professions concerning the importance of cultural sensitivity in clinical assessment. However, Ridley et al. argued that many of these suggestions have failed to adequately guide the average clinician in conducting culturally sensitive assessments for three reasons. One, the multicultural assessment field lacks a coherent conceptual framework. Two, the majority of the existing recommendations identify what needs to happen but fail to direct clinicians on how to accomplish the goals. Three, many of the recommendations do not have a solid scientific basis.

To address these shortcomings, Ridley et al. (1998) developed a set of clearly defined and conceptually coherent guidelines for conducting culturally sensitive assessments called the Multicultural Assessment Procedure (MAP). The MAP consists of four progressive phases: (a) identifying cultural data, (b) interpreting cultural data, (c) incorporating cultural data, and (d) arriving at a sound assessment decision. Within each of the first three phases, Ridley et al. provided step-by-step microprocess recommendations, many of which have been described elsewhere in the multicultural literature. Although it is not described as cognitive–behavioral, the MAP is a data-driven, hypothesis-testing approach that could easily be adapted to cognitive–behavioral assessment with people of diverse cultures.

The ADDRESSING Framework

The ADDRESSING framework was developed as a means of helping therapists to systematically consider multidimensional cultural influences on the therapist, on the client, and on the therapeutic process (Hays, 2001). This approach places a great deal of responsibility on therapists to increase their cross-cultural competence. The ADDRESSING acronym summarizes the multiple dimensions of culture that have been neglected in psychological research and practice, and that therapists are advised to be *addressing* in their work: Age and generational influences (including cohort and role influences), Developmental and acquired Disabilities, Religion and spirituality, Ethnicity, Socioeconomic status, Sexual orientation, Indigenous heritage, National origin, and Gender. Specific guidelines are given for establishing rapport, conducting assessments, using standardized tests and the *DSM–IV* in diagnosis, and developing and choosing interventions with people of diverse cultural identities.

In one example, Hays (2001) described the assessment of a 70-year-old second-generation Korean American man who was brought by his adult daughter to see a 37-year-old Latina clinician (pp. 120–123). The client gave little eye contact and denied or minimized the problems reported by his daughter. Sensing that her next assessment method of a brief mental status exam would increase the mounting tension and further alienate him, the therapist chose instead to take a break and meet separately with the client, engaging him in conversation about his family's medical and social history through the collaborative generation of a family genogram. Throughout this process, rather than asking the client directly about symptoms and problems, the therapist used the ADDRESSING framework to formulate hypotheses about the behaviors she observed in the client. For example, she asked herself, "Does he know information that most Korean American men his age would know, and do I know enough about his particular cohort to assess this?" "Might there be cultural explanations for behaviors or beliefs that appear to me to be unusual or abnormal, that is, explanations related to his age or generation, possible disability, religion, or spiritual orientation, or any of the other ADDRESSING influences?" (p. 122).

As the therapist observed his behaviors and responses during construction of the genogram, she recognized that she had made an incorrect assumption that his general demeanor might be a sign of dementia. By the end of the assessment, she concluded that his limited eye contact was a function of his cultural identity as an older Korean American man in relation to her identity as a younger woman, combined with some embarrassment regarding his daughter's complaints. She also realized that his minimization of problems was more likely related to cultural beliefs, including the view of emotional restraint as a sign of maturity, and Buddhist beliefs about the inevitability of pain and suffering. Through this less direct approach of behavioral observation, she was able to obtain most of the information she needed to complete the assessment.

The Explanatory Model Interview Catalogue

Knowledge of indigenous views and explanatory models of illness is fundamental to understanding the cultural context of presenting problems. The Explanatory Model Interview Catalogue (EMIC) consists of a semistructured interview for gathering data regarding patterns of distress and perceived causes, help-seeking behavior and treatment, general illness beliefs, and specific queries concerning the problem (Weiss et al., 1992). The culturally relevant, descriptive information gathered by the EMIC can be useful in cognitive–behavioral assessment as it provides therapists with information regarding the client's local language and cultural idioms of distress. For example, Yeung, Chang, Gresham, Nierenberg, and Fava (2004) used the EMIC to learn more about the illness beliefs of Chinese American primary care patients diagnosed with depression. The researchers found that although the majority of the patients endorsed depressed mood on the BDI, most did not consider depressed mood to be a symptom to report to their physicians, and many were unfamiliar with depression as a treatable psychiatric disorder. It is clear that this sort of information would be important for the therapist who is attempting to understand a patient's behavior and develop an appropriate treatment plan.

Bicultural Evaluation

In their work with bicultural Maori people of New Zealand, Evans and Paewai (1999) proposed a cognitive–behavioral model for case conceptualization that aims to build rapport, ensure cultural fairness, and use multiple sources of data. Their approach makes use of a 15-point checklist of quality indicators for a culturally sensitive approach to functional analysis. These criteria include assessment of the client's cultural identity, idioms of distress, and motivation for change; assessment of culturally relevant social support including conflicting demands within the social environment; and automatic thoughts and triggers in relation to their cultural contexts. In addition, information regarding the client's cultural and ancestral heritage is included in the treatment description, and attention is given to culturally desirable alternative behaviors as replacements for maladaptive behaviors. This approach could be helpful in functional analyses with people of diverse, bicultural, and multicultural identities.

CONCLUSION

Cognitive–behavioral assessment with diverse populations is still a new area of investigation and innovation, with much to be learned regarding the cross-cultural applicability of instruments and procedures. In the next decade, we will probably see an increase in indigenous cognitive–behavioral measures and procedures that are developed from the ground up and thus incorporate the norms of specific ethnic cultures. Miranda et al. (2005) have suggested that cultural adaptation studies hold promise for increasing the application of evidence-based CBT among ethnic minority clients. In this chapter, we have pointed to some of the critical issues that must be considered in the use and development of such measures. In the tradition of the scientist-practitioner model that is at the heart of CBT, we encourage cognitive–behavioral therapists to be both scientifically minded and aware of the larger social consequences and implications of their attempts to conduct culturally responsive assessments (Messick, 1995; Sue, 1998).

REFERENCES

American Psychiatric Association. (1994). *Diagnostic and statistical manual of mental disorders* (4th ed.). Washington, DC: Author.

American Psychiatric Association. (2000). *Diagnostic and statistical manual of mental disorders* (4th ed., text rev.). Washington, DC: Author.

Anthony, M. M., & Barlow, D. H. (Eds.). (2002). *Handbook of assessment and treatment planning for psychological disorders*. New York: Guilford Press.

Ayalon, L., & Young, M. A. (2003). A comparison of depressive symptoms in African Americans and Caucasian Americans. *Journal of Cross-Cultural Psychology, 34*, 111–124.

Azocar, F., Areán, P., Miranda, J., & Muñoz, R. F. (2001). Differential item functioning in a Spanish translation of the Beck Depression Inventory. *Journal of Clinical Psychology, 57*, 355–365.

Beck, A. T., Steer, R. A., & Brown, G. K. (1996). *Manual for the Beck Depression Inventory—II*. San Antonio, TX: Psychological Corporation.

Beck, A. T., Ward, C. H., Mendelson, M., Mock, J., & Erbaugh, J. (1961). An inventory for measuring depression. *Archives of General Psychiatry, 4*, 561–571.

Bernal, G., & Scharron-del-Rio, M. R. (2001). Are empirically supported treatments valid for ethnic minorities? Toward an alternative approach for treatment research. *Cultural Diversity and Ethnic Minority Psychology, 7*, 328–342.

Bonilla, J., Bernal, G., Santos, A., & Santos, D. (2004). A revised Spanish version of the Beck Depression Inventory: Psychometric properties with a Puerto Rican sample of college students. *Journal of Clinical Psychology, 60*, 119–130.

Carr, J. G., Gilroy, F. D., & Sherman, M. F. (1986). Silencing the self and depression among women: The moderating role of race. *Psychology of Women Quarterly, 20*, 375–392.

Cavanaugh, S. V. (1983). The prevalence of emotional and cognitive dysfunction in a general medical population: Using the MMSE, GHQ, and BDI. *General Hospital Psychiatry, 5*, 15–24.

Chen, H., Guarnaccia, P. J., & Chung, H. (2003). Self-attention as a mediator of cultural influences on depression. *International Journal of Social Psychiatry, 49*, 192–203.

Chun, K. M., Balls Organista, P., & Marín, G. (Eds.). (2002). *Acculturation: Advances in theory, measurement, and applied research*. Washington, DC: American Psychological Association.

Cohen, D., & Gunz, A. (2002). As seen by the other. . . : Perspectives on the self in the memories and emotional perceptions of Easterners and Westerners. *Psychological Science, 13,* 55–59.

Dana, R. H. (Ed.). (2000). *Handbook of cross-cultural and multicultural personality assessment.* Mahwah, NJ: Erlbaum.

Diener, E., Oishi, S., & Lucas, R. E. (2003). Personality, culture, and subjective well-being: Emotional and cognitive evaluations of life. *Annual Review of Psychology, 54,* 403–425.

Diener, E., Suh, E. M., Smith, H., & Shao, L. (1995). National differences in reported subjective well-being: Why do they occur? *Social Indicators Research, 34,* 7–32.

Evans, I. M. (1997). The effect of values on scientific and clinical judgment in behavior therapy. *Behavior Therapy, 28,* 483–493.

Evans, I. M., & Paewai, K. (1999). Functional analysis in a bicultural context. *Behaviour Change, 16,* 20–36.

Forehand, R., & Wierson, M. (1993). The role of developmental factors in planning behavioral interventions for children: Disruptive behavior as an example. *Behavior Therapy, 24,* 117–141.

Fydrich, T., Chambless, D. L., Perry, K. J., Buergener, F., & Beazley, M. B. (1998). Behavioral assessment of social performance: A rating system for social phobia. *Behaviour Research and Therapy, 36,* 995–1010.

Gonzalez, N. A., Cauce, A. M., & Mason, C. A. (1996). Interobserver agreement in the assessment of parental behavior and parent–adolescent conflict: African American mothers, daughters, and independent observers. *Child Development, 67,* 1483–1498.

Hall, G. C. N. (2001). Psychotherapy research with ethnic minorities: Empirical, ethical, and conceptual issues. *Journal of Consulting and Clinical Psychology, 69,* 502–510.

Hansell, S., & Mechanic, D. (1985). Self-awareness and adolescent symptom reporting. *Journal of Human Stress, 11,* 165–176.

Harb, G. C., Eng, W., Zaider, T., & Heimberg, R. G. (2003). Behavioral assessment of public-speaking anxiety using a modified version of the Social Performance Rating Scale. *Behaviour Research and Therapy, 41,* 1373–1380.

Haynes, S. H., & O'Brien, W. H. (1990). Functional analysis in behavior therapy. *Clinical Psychology Review, 10,* 649–668.

Hays, P. (2001). *Addressing cultural complexities in practice: A framework for clinicians and counselors.* Washington, DC: American Psychological Association.

Hollon, S. D., & Kendall, P. C. (1980). Cognitive self statements in depression: Development of an automatic thoughts questionnaire. *Cognitive Therapy and Research, 4,* 383–395.

Iwamasa, G. Y. (1997). Behavior therapy and culturally diverse society: Forging an alliance. *Behavior Therapy, 28,* 347–358.

Jackson, J. S., Torres, M., Caldwell, C. H., Neighbors, H. W., Nesse, R. M., Taylor, R. J., et al. (2004). The National Survey of American Life: A study of racial, ethnic and cultural influences on mental disorders and mental health. *International Journal of Methods in Psychiatric Research, 13*, 196–207.

Kanfer, F. H., & Scheft, B. K. (1988). *Guiding the process of therapeutic change.* Champaign, IL: Research Press.

Kim, M. T. (2002). Measuring depression in Korean Americans: Development of the Kim Depression Scale for Korean Americans. *Journal of Transcultural Nursing, 13*, 109–117.

Kinzie, J. D., Manson, S. M., Vinh, D. H., Nguyen, T. T., Anh, B., & Pho, T. N. (1982). Development and validation of a Vietnamese-language depression rating scale. *American Journal of Psychiatry, 139*, 1276–1281.

Leong, F. T. L., Okazaki, S., & Tak, J. (2003). Assessment of depression and anxiety in Asia. *Psychological Assessment, 15*, 290–305.

Lester, D., & DeSimone, A. (1995). Depression and suicidal ideation in African American and Caucasian American students. *Psychological Reports, 77*, 18.

Messick, S. (1995). Validity of psychological assessment: Validation of inferences from persons' responses and performances as scientific inquiry into score meaning. *American Psychologist, 50*, 741–749.

Miranda, J., Bernal, G., Lau, A., Kohn, L., Hwang, W., & LaFromboise, T. (2005). State of the science on psychosocial interventions for ethnic minorities. *Annual Review of Clinical Psychology, 1*, 113–142.

Molock, S. D., Kimbrough, R., Blanton Lacy, M., McClure, K. P., & Williams, S. (1994). Suicidal behavior among African American college students: A preliminary study. *Journal of Black Psychology, 20*, 234–251.

Mouanoutoua, V. L., Brown, L. G., Cappelletty, G. G., & Levine, R. V. (1991). A Hmong adaptation of the Beck Depression Inventory. *Journal of Personality Assessment, 57*, 309–322.

Nelson-Gray, R. O., & Paulson, J. F. (2004). Behavioral assessment and the DSM system. In S. N. Haynes & E. M. Heiby (Eds.), *Comprehensive handbook of psychological assessment: Vol. 3. Behavioral assessment* (pp. 470–488). New York: Wiley.

Oishi, S. (2002). The experiencing and remembering of well-being: A cross-cultural analysis. *Personality and Social Psychology Bulletin, 28*, 1398–1406.

Oishi, S., Diener, E., Scollon, C. N., & Biswas-Diener, R. (2004). Cross-situational consistency of affective experiences across cultures. *Journal of Personality and Social Psychology, 86*, 460–472.

Okazaki, S. (2002). Self–other agreement on affective distress scales in Asian Americans and White Americans. *Journal of Counseling Psychology, 49*, 428–437.

Okazaki, S., & Kallivayalil, D. (2002). Cultural norms and subjective disability as predictors of symptom reports among Asian Americans and White Americans. *Journal of Cross-Cultural Psychology, 33*, 482–491.

Okazaki, S., Liu, J. F., Longworth, S. L., & Minn, J. Y. (2002). Asian American–White American differences in expressions of social anxiety: A replication and extension. *Cultural Diversity and Ethnic Minority Psychology, 8*, 234–247.

Oliver, J. M., & Baumgart, E. P. (1985). The Dysfunctional Attitude Scale: Psychometric properties and relation to depression in an unselected adult population. *Cognitive Therapy & Research, 9*, 161–167.

Penley, J. A., Wiebe, J. S., & Nwosu, A. (2003). Psychometric properties of the Spanish Beck Depression Inventory—II in a medical sample. *Psychological Assessment, 15*, 569–577.

Ridley, C. R., Li, L. C., & Hill, C. L. (1998). Multicultural assessment: Reexamination, reconceptualization, and practical application. *Counseling Psychologist, 26*, 827–910.

Rudmin, F. W. (2003). Critical history of the acculturation psychology of assimilation, separation, integration, and marginalization. *Review of General Psychology, 7*, 3–37.

Schoeder, R. M. (2002). The cognitive roles of dysfunctional attitudes and automatic thoughts in depression: A study of African American college students. *IFE Psychologia: An International Journal, 10*, 60–71.

Seiden, D. Y. (1999). *Cross-cultural behavioral case formulation with Chinese neurasthenic patients.* Unpublished doctoral dissertation, Hofstra University, Hempstead, NY.

Spiegler, M. D., & Guevremont, D. C. (1998). *Contemporary behavior therapy* (3rd ed.). Pacific Grove, CA: Brooks/Cole.

Spitzer, R. L., Kroenke, K., & Williams, J. B. W. (1999). Validation and utility of a self-report version of PRIME-MD: The PHQ Primary Care Study. *Journal of the American Medical Association, 282*, 1737–1744.

Sue, S. (1998). In search of cultural competence in psychotherapy and counseling. *American Psychologist, 53*, 440–448.

Suh, E. M. (2002). Culture, identity consistency, and subjective well-being. *Journal of Personality and Social Psychology, 83*, 1378–1391.

Suh, E., Diener, E., Oishi, S., & Triandis, H. C. (1998). The shifting basis of life satisfaction judgments across cultures: Emotions versus norms. *Journal of Personality and Social Psychology, 74*, 482–493.

Tanaka-Matsumi, J. (2004). Behavioral assessment and individual differences. In M. Hersen, S. Haynes, & E. M. Heiby (Eds.), *The comprehensive handbook of assessment: Vol. 3. Behavioral assessment* (pp. 359–393). New York: Wiley.

Tanaka-Matsumi, J., Higginbotham, H. N., & Chang, R. (2002). Cognitive–behavioral approaches to counseling across cultures: A functional analytic approach for clinical applications. In P. B. Pedersen, W. J. Lonner, J. G. Draguns, & J. E. Trimble (Eds.), *Counseling across cultures* (5th ed., pp. 337–354). Thousand Oaks, CA: Sage.

Tanaka-Matsumi, J., Seiden, D., & Lam, K. (1996). The Culturally Informed Functional Assessment (CIFA) interview: A strategy for cross-cultural behavioral practice. *Cognitive and Behavioral Practice, 3*, 215–233.

Trent, C. R., Rushlau, M. G., Munley, P. H., Bloem, W., & Driesenga, S. (2000). An ethnocultural study of posttraumatic stress disorder in African American and White American Vietnam war veterans. *Psychological Reports, 87*, 585–592.

Wagar, B. M., & Cohen, D. (2003). Culture, memory, and the self: An analysis of the personal and collective self in long-term memory. *Journal of Experimental Social Psychology, 39,* 468–475.

Weiss, M. G., Doongaji, D. R., Siddhartha, S., Wypij, D., Pathare, S., Bhatawdekar, M., et al. (1992). The Explanatory Model Interview Catalogue (EMIC) contribution to cross-cultural research methods from a study of leprosy and mental health. *British Journal of Psychiatry, 160,* 819–830.

Wood, J. M., Garb, H. N., Lilienfeld, S. O., & Nezworski, M. T. (2002). Clinical assessment. *Annual Review of Psychology, 53,* 519–543.

World Health Organization. (1991). *Composite international diagnostic interview.* Geneva, Switzerland: Author.

Yeung, A. S., Chang, D. F., Gresham, R. L., Jr., Nierenberg, A. A., & Fava, M. (2004). Illness beliefs of depressed Chinese American patients in primary care. *Journal of Nervous and Mental Disease, 192,* 324–327.

Yeung, A., Howarth, S., Chan, R., Sonawalla, S., Nierenberg, A. A., & Fava, M. (2002). Use of the Chinese version of the Beck Depression Inventory for screening depression in primary care. *Journal of Nervous and Mental Disease, 190,* 94–99.

Yeung, A., Neault, N., Sonawalla, S., Howarth, S., Fava, M., & Nierenberg, A. A. (2002). Screening for major depression in Asian-Americans: A comparison of the Beck and the Chinese Depression Inventory. *Acta Psychiatrica Scandinavica, 105,* 252–257.

Zauszniewski, J. A. (1995). Development and testing of a measure of depressive cognitions in older adults. *Journal of Nursing Measurement, 3,* 31–41.

Zauszniewski, J. A., Fulton Picot, S. J., Debanne, S. M., Roberts, B. L., & Wykle, M. L. (2002). Psychometric characteristics of the Depressive Cognition Scale in African American women. *Journal of Nursing Measurement, 10,* 83–95.

Zheng, Y., & Lin, K.-M. (1991). Comparison of the Chinese Depression Inventory and the Chinese version of the Beck Depression Inventory. *Acta Psychiatrica Scandinavica, 84,* 531–536.

Zheng, Y., Wei, L., Goa, L., Zhang, G., & Wong, C. (1988). Applicability of the Chinese Beck Depression Inventory. *Comprehensive Psychiatry, 29,* 484–489.

12

MULTICULTURAL COGNITIVE– BEHAVIORAL THERAPY SUPERVISION

GAYLE Y. IWAMASA, SHILPA M. PAI, AND KRISTEN H. SOROCCO

Cognitive–behavioral therapy (CBT) has become one of the most influential forms of psychotherapy in many countries, and within the United States, it is now mandated for the training of psychiatry residents. At the same time, little empirical data exist that demonstrate the appropriateness, efficacy, or effectiveness of CBT with cultural minorities. Yutrzenka and colleagues have called for the need to emphasize ethnic and cultural diversity in the training of mental health professionals if the field is to keep up with the changing demographics (Yutrzenka, 1995; Yutrzenka, Todd-Bazemore, & Caraway, 1999). Psychology as a profession has recognized the importance of these issues, as demonstrated by the *Guidelines on Multicultural Education* adopted by the American Psychological Association in 2002. Although the need for more culturally competent services is clear, few resources exist for ameliorating the dearth of culturally competent service providers.

Although many books and manuals have been published on CBT, few include information on the supervision of students in training (e.g., Beck's, 1995, widely used book *Cognitive Therapy: Basics and Beyond*). Books on supervision do a better job of including cognitive–behavioral approaches. For example, Watkins's (1997) *Handbook of Psychotherapy Supervision* contains chapters on supervision in behavioral, cognitive, and rational emotive behavior therapy (Fruzzetti, Waltz, & Linehan, 1997; Liese & Beck, 1997; Woods & Ellis, 1997, respectively). This same volume also contains one chapter separately devoted to cultural competence in supervision (López, 1997).

The multicultural therapy literature has paid greater attention to supervision (i.e., than has the CBT literature) but primarily from a contextual rather than a theoretical perspective. At present, there are no books on multicultural issues in CBT supervision. Practitioners trained within specific models of therapy generally learn about multicultural applications as the "special case," whereas those who attend training programs that emphasize diversity rarely receive training in specific therapies such as CBT.

In summary, the CBT *research* includes little information regarding supervision and even less on cultural diversity; the *multicultural literature* addresses supervision but neglects theoretical approaches such as CBT; and the *supervision literature* includes cognitive–behavioral approaches but neglects cultural influences. The segregation of these three domains means that there is currently no cognitive–behavioral approach to supervision that integrates cultural considerations. Toward the goal of developing such an integration, this chapter provides information regarding each area beginning with an overview of the supervision research in CBT, followed by information from the multicultural therapy field on culturally competent supervision, and finally, several suggestions regarding the integration of these areas.

COGNITIVE–BEHAVIORAL SUPERVISION

In one exploratory content analysis of cognitive–behavioral supervision (Milne, Pilkington, Gracie, & James, 2003), 14 themes were extracted:

1. agenda setting for the supervision experience;
2. instructions regarding behavioral interventions such as role-plays;
3. the reevaluation of thoughts and the search for evidence by supervisees;
4. collaboration;
5. the development of conceptualization skills;
6. the provision of feedback to the supervisee;
7. the gathering of information about the client;
8. goal-setting and clarification of learning objectives;
9. provision of information intended to educate the supervisee;
10. modeling;
11. reflecting (thoughtfulness);
12. socialization to the CBT model;
13. summarization and clarification; and
14. supporting/understanding the supervisee.

These themes are exemplified in the following summary of supervision within specific CBT approaches.

Liese and Beck (1997) suggested that ongoing supervision is essential to ensure that therapists do not "drift" from the treatment standards of cognitive therapy (CT). (CT is a specific type of CBT—see Beck, 1995.) Supervision should be structured, focused, and educational in nature, and responsibility for the content and structure of supervision is shared by the supervisor and supervisee. Supervision is typically weekly and 60 minutes per session, with at least one client discussed in depth and issues generalized to other clients with whom the supervisee is working. The recommended structure of the supervision session mirrors that of a CT session: check-in, agenda-setting, bridging from previous supervision, case management of previously discussed cases, homework review, prioritization and discussion of agenda, assignment of new homework, summary of the session by the supervisor, and feedback from the supervisee.

CT supervisors often require that supervisees tape-record sessions that are reviewed by supervisors prior to the supervision session. Supervisors also use standardized measures such as the Cognitive Therapy Adherence and Competence Scale (Liese, Barber, & Beck, 1995) to evaluate supervisees. This scale assesses supervisees' abilities in four areas: structuring the therapy, developing a collaborative relationship with the client, developing and applying a cognitive case conceptualization, and implementing cognitive and behavioral techniques.

Liese and Beck (1997) also addressed interpersonal influences in supervision, including the supervisee's personal concerns, the supervisor's personality style, and the interaction between supervisee and supervisor. They identify possible supervisee problems, such as an inability to focus and passive, avoidant, defensive, or aggressive behaviors. They acknowledge supervisors' limitations and summarize three problematic approaches: (a) the "Mister Rogers Supervisor" who is good natured but fails to provide substantive feedback or education to the supervisee; (b) the "Attila the Supervisor" who is rigid and believes in "my way or the highway"; and (c) the "How do you feel? Supervisor" who overly emphasizes the supervisee's personal feelings about the client. When difficulties occur in supervision, it is the supervisor's responsibility to carefully conceptualize and problem solve so that changes can be made to improve the student's supervision experience.

Woods and Ellis (1997) emphasized the educational process of rational emotive behavior therapy (REBT) supervision and stressed that supervision should begin by teaching the REBT model. Supervisors provide trainees with the literature on REBT, followed by close supervision of the model being implemented in therapy. REBT supervision focuses on general goals and skills of therapy, such as the development of the therapist–client relationship, empathy, knowledge, and patience. REBT supervisees are asked to "set aside" previously learned techniques from other treatment modalities, such as strict behavioral or nondirective approaches. Supervisors focus on developing specific REBT skills that teach clients (a) to understand cause-and-effect relationships; (b) that emotions and behaviors are the result of cognitions such as ideas and beliefs (the ABCs of REBT); (c) to become aware of and acknowledge the specific causes of one's distress; (d) that thoughts can be questioned and challenged; and finally, (e) that irrational thoughts can be reduced and replaced with rational thoughts. It is the supervisor's responsibility to ensure that the client is able to identify the ABCs and progress in their therapy with clients.

According to the REBT philosophy, the supervisee's own irrational thoughts (e.g., self-deprecation, evaluation, and performance anxiety) can impede his or her training. Thus, these difficulties should be dealt with by the supervisor, emphasizing the implementation of REBT principles by the supervisee in his or her own personal life. Evaluation should also occur in an accepting and tolerant atmosphere. Supervisors are encouraged to apply REBT principles to themselves to maintain professionalism with the supervisee.

Fruzzetti et al. (1997) summarized supervision issues related to dialectical behavior therapy (DBT; Linehan, 1993) for the treatment of clients who have a history of suicidal thoughts or behavior and a diagnosis of borderline personality disorder. This therapy is hierarchical and occurs in three stages. Stage 1 focuses on addressing and decreasing maladaptive client behaviors while increasing client skills. After these goals are met, Stage 2 focuses on reducing stress, both past and current. Stage 3 focuses on increasing client self-respect and improvement regarding life goals.

According to Fruzzetti et al. (1997), DBT is unique in that supervision is provided in a team format that conceptualizes the supervision as a form of treatment for the therapist. Supervision roughly parallels DBT, with attention to the therapeutic aspects of interactions among the therapist, members of the supervision team, and clients. The major components of supervision are therapist skill acquisition and application, with specific supervision and consultation targets. Therapists acquire skills through coursework and experiential learning (i.e., clinical practica). Skills are applied through the DBT supervision–consultation team, with all members agreeing to (a) use a dialectical approach (i.e., there is no absolute truth), with an emphasis on validation, synthesis, and effective action; (b) consult with the client on effective behaviors; (c) not expect consistency in the therapy process; (d) view the client's behavior contextually and with empathy; (e) accept that all therapists are fallible; and (f) observe one's own personal and professional limits in the conduct of DBT.

The structure of DBT's supervision–consultation team is that it meets weekly for 1 to 2 hours, with a minimum of two members. An agenda is set at the beginning of the meeting, with a focus on following the stages of treatment, positive reinforcement, development and maintenance of DBT skills such as communication strategies, case management strategies, dialectics, and use of the DBT Expert Rating Scale.

CULTURALLY COMPETENT SUPERVISION

D'Andrea and Daniels (1997) described multicultural supervision as involving a supervisory relationship in which the supervisor, supervisee, and client, or both, are of different cultural, ethnic, or racial backgrounds. They contended that multicultural supervision is consistent with traditional models of supervision but with greater emphasis on the role of the supervisor's, supervisee's, and client's identity development in the therapy and supervision process.

In contrast, López (1997) emphasized the development of cultural competence, which he defined as the "therapist's ability to treat people of diverse cultural backgrounds in ways that respect, value, and integrate their sociocultural context" (p. 570). López discussed the problems associated with over- and underpathologizing clients on the basis of culture. A clinician's cultural competence lies in the ability to move between his or her own cultural lens and that of the client, and to use this information to understand the client in context (which López called process orientation). The therapist and client are able to maintain their own culture-specific frameworks, and both are respected and valued.

López (1997) also incorporated Kleinman's (1988) ethnographic emphasis on the therapist's ability to take the client's perspective in understanding the psychological meanings of the client's experience. López applied this notion to four areas of clinical practice: engagement, assessment, theory, and method. In the *engagement* phase, the culturally competent therapist seeks to understand the client's perspective on the problem and what the client hopes to gain from therapy. It is the therapist's responsibility to validate the client's definition of the problem and develop a plan to address the problem in therapy. In the *assessment* phase, López indicated that although formal assessment procedures can be used, culturally competent assessment and interpretation must incorporate two sets of cultural norms: those of the client's culture and those of mainstream culture. The *theory* phase incorporates the client's explanatory model of his or her own psychological functioning into an understanding of how therapy can assist with behavior change. Finally, the *method* phase involves the therapist's ability to develop and adapt interventions that are consistent with the client's cultural belief system. Of importance here is the therapist's ability to communicate verbally and nonverbally in a manner that is respectful to clients' cultural values and practices. This phase requires openness to considering the possibility that one's methods may be inconsistent with the client's cultural context. López concluded by indicating that it is the supervisor's responsibility to model appropriate professional behavior by being knowledgeable about and inquiring about the role of culture with the supervisee's clients.

> Suzanne, a 34-year-old European American woman from an upper-middle-class background was a staff psychologist at a small private university counseling center. She was excited about serving as supervisor for students in the master's program in psychology. In a supervision session with Diane, a third-generation Mexican American, Suzanne asked Diane to explain her treatment plan regarding Marco, an 18-year-old Puerto Rican man who was experiencing anxiety regarding his desire to tell his family that he was gay. Diane indicated that she was not familiar with sexual orientation issues among Latino men and asked Suzanne for some references. Suzanne was surprised, became defensive, and responded that, as a Latina, Diane should be the one to know about such issues, not Suzanne.

Ancis and Ladany (2001) suggested that multicultural competence in supervision is an ethical issue supported by a variety of professional ethics codes in the fields of psychology and counseling. According to these authors, the following domains constitute multicultural supervision competencies:

1. supervisor-focused personal development (e.g., "Supervisors actively explore and challenge their attitudes and biases toward diverse supervisees," p. 81);
2. supervisee-focused personal development (e.g., "Supervisors help supervisees understand the impact of social structures on supervisee and client behavior, including how class, gender, and racial privilege may have benefited the counselor," p. 81);
3. conceptualization (e.g., "Supervisors facilitate supervisees' understanding of culture-specific norms, as well as heterogeneity within groups," p. 82);
4. skills/interventions (e.g., "Supervisors encourage an appreciation of multiple sources of support, including indigenous helping networks," p. 82);
5. process (e.g., "Supervisors model respect for diversity and equality with supervisees and clients," p. 83); and
6. outcome/evaluation (e.g., "Supervisors recognize their responsibility for ensuring that their supervisees provide multiculturally competent counseling," p. 83).

Ancis and Ladany (2001) presented their *heuristic model of nonoppressive interpersonal development*, which they stated is not intended to replace traditional models of supervision but rather to provide guidance regarding the incorporation of issues related to client demographics. They suggested that with any given demographic variable, individuals may belong to a socially oppressed group (SOG), a socially privileged group (SPG), or in the case of people with multicultural identities, both groups (e.g., a European American woman). Their model suggests that individuals progress through means of interpersonal functioning (MIF) that include identity-based behaviors and thoughts and feelings about the self. People can be more advanced in MIF with regard to one aspect of identity (e.g., race) than another (e.g., gender). For example, an African American man may be more aware of the effects of racism on African Americans and less aware of the impact of sexism on African American women.

A supervisor's development of cultural competence in supervision is thought to occur in four stages: adaptation, incongruence, exploration, and integration. In the *adaptation* phase, both SOG and SPG supervisors actively deny and dismiss culturally related concerns regarding themselves, the supervisee, and the supervisee's clients. Anxiety occurs when diversity issues are raised by the supervisee or client, but the supervisor is unwilling to admit the discomfort. As a result, blaming the client and discounting the role of cultural context are likely to occur.

In the *incongruence* stage, SOG and SPG supervisors and trainees experience dissonance between their previously held views and new information or experiences. Denial of oppression is replaced by minimization and rationalization. Supervisors in this stage are also unlikely to discuss diversity concerns in supervision or, at most, address them only minimally. Supervisees in this stage are likely to be aware of cultural issues but unlikely to bring them up, especially if they perceive the supervisor to be disinterested.

The third stage involves active *exploration* of one's own SOG or SPG status. Both SOG and SPG supervisors are more likely to address diversity issues in supervision and attempt to actively facilitate supervisees' multicultural awareness. They may initiate self-exploration of cultural influences for the trainee and be open to exploration of diverse conceptualizations and interpretations based on cultural differences. A risk is that cultural influences may be overemphasized, and the supervisor may have difficulty providing support for the supervisee as the supervisor continues his or her own personal exploration. Supervisees at this phase are interested in exploring multicultural issues but may also overemphasize culture at the expense of other influences.

In the final stage of *integration*, SOG and SPG supervisors possess multicultural integrity, awareness, and proficiency in interacting with and understanding a variety of SOG groups. They recognize oppression when it occurs and can accurately empathize with feelings of oppression. They may advocate against oppression and willingly use their privilege to promote equality. They are adept at facilitating multicultural development in their supervisees and may reach out to other SOGs for mentoring. Trainees in this stage are able to conceptualize their clients in a complex fashion that integrates the client's multiple identities. They are able to challenge their own biases, explore how such biases affect their work with clients, and differentiate between their own personal issues and client-based concerns.

Grace, a 37-year-old third-generation Japanese American faculty member, supervised practicum students in a traditional scientist-practitioner PhD program that emphasized CBT. Amanda, a third-generation Swedish American student in her third year of practicum, summarized an intake session with Bin, a 25-year-old chemistry student from China. Bin was experiencing anxiety and some depression related to how his lab partners were treating him. The students were asked by their graduate advisor to complete several experiments by a certain date. The group met several times but were unable to successfully complete the experiments. Subsequently, Bin stayed up late several nights and was able to complete the experiments on his own. Although he informed the graduate advisor that the work was a result of the team's efforts, the other graduate students, all European American, were upset with Bin and accused him of trying to make himself look better than them. In group supervision, Grace asked Amanda to consider whether cultural factors might have influenced the situation, including Bin's behaviors, the other students' behaviors, and Bin's premature discontinuation of therapy. With the group's help, Amanda was able to recognize how the cultural perspective of Bin (which emphasized collectivism and self-sacrifice) contrasted with the cultural perspective of his lab partners (who valued individualism and competition), and how everyone's lack of understanding regarding these differences contributed to the conflict. Amanda also realized that her own European American perspective contributed to her unintentional reinforcement of the dominant cultural values. In this case, the supervisor was operating from the integrated stage of MIF, and was thus able to facilitate Amanda's multicultural awareness in the context of a supportive group supervision session.

SUPERVISOR RESPONSIBILITIES

We believe that it is the supervisor's responsibility to address and invite discussion of diversity issues in supervision, much as it is the supervisor's responsibility to train the student in the CBT model. Discussions concerning multiculturalism are necessary at the beginning of supervision to avoid assumptions and misconceptions that may undermine the supervision process (Hird, Cavalieri, Dulko, Felice, & Ho, 2001). These early conversations help to establish rapport between the supervisor and supervisee, emphasize the significance of culture in supervision and therapy, and create a mutual language concerning cultural issues (McRoy, Freeman, Logan, & Blackmon, 1986).

The failure to incorporate multicultural topics can contribute to a supervisee's frustration and, ultimately, resistance in supervision. Although either member of the supervisory dyad may introduce multicultural concerns, the power differential warrants initiation by the supervisor (Hird et al., 2001). Moreover, research indicates that supervisees may withhold potentially critical cultural information from their supervisors (Ladany, Hill, Corbett, & Nutt, 1996). The supervisor's deliberate attention to culture helps to create a climate of safety and comfort within the supervisory relationship.

The lack of attention to diversity in supervision may result from the lack of multicultural training among supervisors (Ancis & Ladany, 2001). However, by being willing to reveal this as an area of weakness and discuss the steps one is taking to address it, the supervisor can further facilitate an accepting learning environment. Supervisors who examine their own knowledge, assumptions, attitudes, perceptions, and feelings are more able to assist the supervisee as he or she engages in a similar process (Garrett, 2001).

> David, a 42-year-old European American clinical psychologist, was supervising Kelly, a 22-year-old male practicum student. Kelly's new client was an 18-year-old single Laotian mother who was pregnant with her second child. David was fairly certain that Kelly, who was raised in an upper-middle-class suburb of Chicago, had little exposure to Laotian culture or single parenting. David also had little experience in these areas. Thus, he contacted several individuals, including a Chinese American classmate from graduate school, and conducted a PsycINFO search on Laotians and single parenting, to be prepared for his supervision session with Kelly.

Faubert and Locke (2003) proposed a model of reciprocal supervision in which supervisees succeed in an environment of open communication, support, and challenge. They described a structured environment in which the supervisor provides supervisees with a list of counselor and client behaviors from which they select skills for further work. The supervisor may also select skills that he or she believes the supervisee needs to improve or learn. Skills are developed through the use of videotapes and practice. The supervisor facilitates cultural learning by modeling culturally competent skills, attitudes, and behaviors. At times, self-disclosure and a willingness to share power are necessary. The supervisor may also need to normalize common reactions such as guilt, anger, and insecurity. Supervisors must be able to honestly evaluate their own abilities and cultural competence and be committed to ongoing personal and professional growth.

In the past 2 decades, researchers have developed several measures to assess supervisees' cultural competence. These include the Multicultural Awareness–Knowledge–Skills Survey (D'Andrea, Daniels, & Heck, 1991), the Multicultural Counseling Inventory (Sodowsky, Taffe, Gutkin, & Wise, 1994), the Multicultural Counseling Awareness Scale (Ponterotto, Rieger, Barrett, & Sparks, 1994), and the Cross-Cultural Counseling Inventory (LaFromboise, Coleman, & Hernandez, 1991). Although each scale requires further research regarding its validity and reliability, it may provide supervisors with a general baseline assessment of various skills and assist in tracking the supervisee's progress in developing multicultural awareness, knowledge, and skills.

INTEGRATION OF MULTICULTURAL INFLUENCES
IN CBT SUPERVISION

Obviously, the main goal for a supervisor integrating diversity issues into CBT supervision is the development of culturally competent therapists. The question is, how do CBT supervisors achieve this goal? As mentioned previously, the supervisor must start with himself or herself. However, given that cultural competency is an ongoing process, we believe that a supervisor does not have to be "the expert" in multicultural therapy as long as he or she is willing to model the steps toward increasing one's level of multicultural competence. Included in this work is an understanding of the role of one's culture and its effects on communication, as cultural differences in communication may lead to misunderstandings with the supervisee (Adler, Rosenfeld, & Towne, 1989).

Sources of information that CBT supervisors may find useful include guidelines and standards for multicultural training (e.g., American Psychological Association, 2002). For example, within the multicultural counseling field, Lee (1997) suggested that professionals need to accomplish four steps to begin the process of becoming multiculturally competent: (a) become aware of one's own cultural background, (b) be aware of and understand cultural biases that may interfere with helping effectiveness, (c) learn about the history and culture of diverse groups, and (d) develop new skills. To accomplish these four steps, Lee suggested that future training in multiculturalism needs to focus on three areas. The first is skill development, including the integration of awareness and knowledge into therapeutic skills. Second, supervisors should incorporate experiential teaching, including in vivo cultural experiences. Third, supervisors need to move beyond a monolithic conceptualization of identity and recognize within-group differences. These three areas are strengthened when cultural diversity is incorporated throughout the training curriculum, not solely in supervision.

In addition, CBT supervisors can draw from multicultural models of treatment, many of which incorporate elements of CBT. For example, González (1997) suggested use of a postmodern model of supervision in which the supervisor functions as a partial learner. Constantine (1997) advocated a supervision framework in which specific questions regarding the cultural identities of the supervisor and supervisee are used as a foundation for supervision. Fong and Lease (1997) provided suggestions specific to European American supervisors working with culturally different supervisees.

Garrett (2001) proposed a supervision paradigm called VISION that emphasizes the following:

> V: how the supervisee and supervisor examine their values and beliefs
> I: how they interpret experiences
> S: how they structure preferences (i.e., the supervisor structures the goals of supervision)

I: how they interact (verbal and nonverbal communication)

O: how they operationalize strategies (selecting and collaboratively working toward supervision goals)

N: how they discuss perceived needs (mental, physical, emotional, and environmental)

These are but a few of the existing models that suggest the need for a supervision format that is designed to increase knowledge, offer open discussion of beliefs, and assist in the development of culturally appropriate case conceptualizations. Ideally, supervisors and supervisees will have had the opportunity to attend a general course on cultural diversity and psychology early in their training to enable them to start with basic knowledge. However, whether or not this is possible, increasing knowledge and discussing belief systems can be obtained through a combination of personal experiences and group and individual supervision. Group supervision can emphasize readings and student presentations on diversity, foster discussions on culturally appropriate research, and create an environment in which it feels safe to openly discuss one's personal beliefs. A supervision format that incorporates group supervision (1–2 hours per week) and individual supervision (1 hour per week) is recommended.

> Steve, a 42-year-old European American supervisor, realized that he did not have much experience supervising cases in which clients presented with issues related to sexual orientation and ethnic identity development. Anticipating that his supervisees would have increasingly culturally diverse clients, he decided to focus his group supervision on these topics. He structured group supervision so that the first hour would consist of student presentations on a specific topic followed by group discussion with questions and answers. At the first group supervision of the year, he presented the following topics for students to select from: the coming-out process, single parenting, ethnic identity, racial identity, biracial individuals, and disability issues. His students were excited, as this was the first time a practicum supervisor had acknowledged that these issues were potentially important in the therapy process.

The topics to be covered in both group and individual supervision depend on the cultural competence of the CBT supervisor as well as the supervisee. Regardless of the level of cultural competence, an important CBT point is the idea that culture serves as a filter through which individuals identify their thoughts, feelings, and behaviors. During the beginning stages with a new supervisee, a supervisor should consider an assessment of cultural competence either formally through standardized assessment measures or informally through individual supervision. This topic may be continued in group supervision with a discussion of how one's level of cultural competence can negatively or positively affect rapport with a client from a different cultural background.

TABLE 12.1
Sample Topics for Beginning and Later Stages of Cultural Competence

Beginning stages	Later stages
Supervisee self-assessment of own values, beliefs, practices	Discussion of articles on culturally appropriate research and treatment
Definitions of multicultural competence	Case presentation (by supervisee using different case conceptualizations and treatment approaches related to cultural influences)
Identification of stereotypes across cultural groups, level of personal contact and experience	
Impact of level of multicultural competence on therapeutic rapport	Other roles therapists can take to better serve culturally diverse populations
Traditional components of therapy	Impact of sociocultural context on culturally diverse populations (e.g., attempts to ban gay marriage, affirmative action, etc.)
Potential barriers to treatment	
Verbal and nonverbal communication styles of different cultures	

Table 12.1 provides a listing of potential topics for discussion during the beginning and later stages of multicultural competence. Such topics can be covered in both group and individual supervision, depending on the supervisor's assessment of group and individual needs. For example, in the beginning stages of multicultural competence, supervisees are encouraged to consider barriers to the treatment of culturally diverse populations. To begin this discussion, the supervisor may discuss the fact that traditional therapies have been developed from a Eurocentric point of view, and many components do not lend themselves well to cultural minority populations (Sue & Sue, 2002). As a group, the components of traditional therapies could be identified (e.g., openness to emotions, emphasis on long-range goals, distinction between physical and mental well-being, therapy setting occurring away from the client's environment). Follow-up discussions might compare and contrast how people of different cultures might react to these components. In later stages of multicultural competence, supervisees could present a current case from another cultural perspective.

CONCLUSION

The CBT supervision literature lacks coverage of multicultural competence, whereas the multicultural therapy supervision literature has an atheoretical basis. This chapter summarized both CBT and multicultural approaches to supervision. To provide culturally competent CBT supervision, supervisors must first be willing and able to examine their own values, beliefs, attitudes, and worldview. This foundation of self-awareness and the ongoing assessment it involves will increase the supervisor's comfort in raising and addressing cultural questions with supervisees. Given the lack of integration between the CBT and multicultural therapy supervision information, culturally competent CBT supervision is an excellent focus for further research.

REFERENCES

Adler, R. B., Rosenfeld, L. B., & Towne, N. (1989). *Interplay: The process of interpersonal communication* (4th ed.). New York: Holt, Rinehart & Winston.

American Psychological Association. (2002). *Guidelines on multicultural education, training, research, practice, and organizational change for psychologists.* Washington, DC: Author.

Ancis, J. R., & Ladany, N. (2001). A multicultural framework for counselor supervision. In L. J. Bradley & N. Ladany (Eds.), *Counselor supervision: Principles, process and practice* (3rd ed., pp. 63–90). Philadelphia: Brunner-Routledge.

Beck, J. S. (1995). *Cognitive therapy: Basics and beyond.* New York: Guilford Press.

Constantine, M. G. (1997). Facilitating multicultural competency in counseling supervision: Operationalizing a practical framework. In D. B. Pope-Davis & H. L. K. Coleman (Eds.), *Multicultural counseling competencies: Assessment, education and training, and supervision* (pp. 310–324). Thousand Oaks, CA: Sage.

D'Andrea, M., & Daniels, J. (1997). Multicultural counseling supervision: Central issues, theoretical considerations and practical strengths. In D. B. Pope-Davis & H. L. K. Coleman (Eds.), *Multicultural counseling competencies: Assessment, education and training, and supervision* (pp. 290–309). Thousand Oaks, CA: Sage.

D'Andrea, M., Daniels, J., & Heck, R. (1991). Evaluating the impact of multicultural counseling training. *Journal of Counseling & Development, 70,* 143–150.

Faubert, M., & Locke, D. C. (2003). Cultural considerations in counselor training and supervision. In G. Roysircar (Ed.), *Multicultural competencies: A guidebook of practices* (pp. 51–63). Alexandria, VA: Association for Multicultural Counseling and Development.

Fong, M. L., & Lease, S. H. (1997). Cross-cultural supervision: Issues for the White supervisor. In D. B. Pope-Davis & H. L. K. Coleman (Eds.), *Multicultural counseling competencies: Assessment, education and training, and supervision* (pp. 387–405). Thousand Oaks, CA: Sage.

Fruzzetti, A. E., Waltz, J. A., & Linehan, M. M. (1997). Supervision in dialectical behavior therapy. In C. E. Watkins (Ed.), *Handbook of psychotherapy supervision* (pp. 84–100). New York: Wiley.

Garrett, M. T. (2001). Multicultural SuperVISION: A paradigm of cultural responsiveness for supervisors. *Journal of Multicultural Counseling and Development, 29,* 147–159.

González, R. C. (1997). Postmodern supervision: A multicultural perspective. In D. B. Pope-Davis & H. L. K. Coleman (Eds.), *Multicultural counseling competencies: Assessment, education and training, and supervision* (pp. 350–386). Thousand Oaks, CA: Sage.

Hird, J. S., Cavalieri, C. E., Dulko, J. P., Felice, A. A., & Ho, T. A. (2001). Visions and realities: Supervisee perspectives of multicultural supervision. *Journal of Multicultural Counseling and Development, 29,* 114–130.

Kleinman, A. (1988). *Rethinking psychiatry: From cultural category to personal experience.* New York: Free Press.

Ladany, N., Hill, C. E., Corbett, M. M., & Nutt, E. A. (1996). Nature, extent, and importance of what psychotherapy trainees do not disclose to their supervisors. *Journal of Counseling Psychology, 43,* 10–24.

LaFromboise, T. D., Coleman, H. L., & Hernandez, A. (1991). Development and factor structure of the Cross-Cultural Counseling Inventory—Revised. *Professional Psychology: Research and Practice, 22,* 380–388.

Lee, C. C. (1997). New approaches to diversity: Implications for professional counseling training and research. In C. C. Lee (Ed.), *Multicultural issues in counseling: New approaches to diversity* (2nd ed., pp. 353–360). Alexandria, VA: American Counseling Association.

Liese, B. S., Barber, J., & Beck, A. T. (1995). *The Cognitive Therapy Adherence and Competence Scale.* Unpublished instrument, University of Kansas Medical Center, Kansas City.

Liese, B. S., & Beck, J. S. (1997). Cognitive therapy supervision. In C. E. Watkins (Ed.), *Handbook of psychotherapy supervision* (pp. 114–133). New York: Wiley.

Linehan, M. M. (1993). *Cognitive–behavioral treatment of borderline personality disorder.* New York: Guilford Press.

López, S. R. (1997). Cultural competence in psychotherapy: A guide for clinicians and their supervisors. In C. E. Watkins (Ed.), *Handbook of psychotherapy supervision* (pp. 570–588). New York: Wiley.

McRoy, R. G., Freeman, E. M., Logan, S. L., & Blackmon, B. (1986). Cross-cultural field supervision: Implications for social work education. *Journal of Social Work Education, 22,* 50–56.

Milne, D. L., Pilkington, J., Gracie, J., & James, I. (2003). Transferring skills from supervision to therapy: A qualitative and quantitative analysis. *Behavioral and Cognitive Psychotherapy, 31,* 193–202.

Ponterotto, J. G., Rieger, B. P., Barrett, A., & Sparks, R. (1994). Assessing multicultural counseling competence: A review of instrumentation. *Journal of Counseling & Development, 72,* 316–322.

Sodowsky, G. R., Taffe, R. C., Gutkin, T. B., & Wise, S. L. (1994). Development of the Multicultural Counseling Inventory: A self-report measure of multicultural competencies. *Journal of Counseling Psychology, 41,* 137–148.

Sue, D. W., & Sue, D. (2002). *Counseling the culturally different: Theory and practice* (4th ed). New York: Wiley.

Watkins, C. E. (1997). *Handbook of psychotherapy supervision.* New York: Wiley.

Woods, P. J., & Ellis, A. (1997). Supervision in rational emotive behavior therapy. In C. E. Watkins (Ed.), *Handbook of psychotherapy supervision* (pp. 101–113). New York: Wiley.

Yutrzenka, B. A. (1995). Making a case for training in ethnic and cultural diversity in increasing treatment efficacy. *Journal of Consulting and Clinical Psychology*, *63*, 197–206.

Yutrzenka, B. A., Todd-Bazemore, E., & Caraway, S. J. (1999). Four winds: The evolution of culturally inclusive clinical psychology training for Native Americans. *International Review of Psychiatry*, *11*, 129–135.

AUTHOR INDEX

Numbers in italics refer to listings in the references.

Felice, A. A., 274, *280*
Fellowes, D., *174*
Ferguson, E., 205, *220*
Fernandez-Gamarra, E., *195*
Fhagen-Smith, P. E., 102, *115*
Fienup-Riordan, A., 48, 49, 50, 51, 53, 56, 69
Finch, E., 184, *194*
Fine, M., 202, *221*
Fink, C. M., 107, *112*
First, M., 236, *241*
Fischer, A. R., 100, *112*
Fiske, A., *195*
Fitzgerald, R. G., 205, *221*
Fitzgerald, T. E., 200, *221*
Flannigan, H., 205, *220*
Fleming, C. M., 27, 28, 32, *42, 43, 44*
Foa, E. B., 133, *137*, 233, 235, *241*
Fong, M. L., 276, *279*
Fong, R., 5, *15*
Ford, D. E., *194*
Forehand, R., 254, *263*
Forman, B. D., 123, *139*
Fossett, M. A., 106, *114*
Fowkes, W. C., Jr., 187, *194*
Fox, L. S., *195*
Franklin, A. J., 98, 109, *112*
Freeman, A., 5, *14*
Freeman, E. M., 274, *280*
French, C., 32, *41*
Frewat-Nikowitz, S., 141, *158*
Friedman, A., 146, *158*
Friedman, E. K., 100, *112*
Friedman, S., 163, 173, *174, 175*
Frisch, M. B., *241*
Fruzzetti, A. E., 268, 270, *279*
Fudge, R. C., 103, 104, 105, 106, 107, 110, 111, *113*
Fuentes, R. M., 78, *96*
Fuertes, J. N., 5, *18*, 58, *70*
Fujino, D. C., 77, *96*
Fukuyama, M. A., 6, 13, *15, 16*
Fulton Picot, S. J., 253, *266*
Funkenstein, H. H., *194*
Fydrich, T., 253, *263*

Gainor, K. A., 225, *241*
Gall, T. L., *174*
Gallagher, D., 191, *194*
Gallagher-Thompson, D., 180, 181, 183, 185, 191, *193, 194, 195, 196*
Gallo, J. J., *194*

Galvin, L. R., 206, *221*
Gamba, R., 123, *139*
Garb, H. N., 247, *266*
Garcia, J. G., 74, *95*
Gardner, K. A., *112*
Garnets, L., 229, *241*
Garrett, M. T., 27, *42*, 275, 276, *279*
Gatz, M., 179, *195*
Gawboy, C., 25, *44*
Gay, J., 56, *69*
Geist-Martin, P., 122, *137*
Gerjevic, S., 60, *69*
Gerton, J., 10, *16*
Gibbon, M., 236, *241*
Gill, C. J., 201, 202, *221*
Gillis, J. R., 227, 233, *241*
Gilroy, F. D., 250, *262*
Gim, R. H., 128, *137*
Giordano, J., 5, *17*, 101, *114*
Glunt, E. K., 227, *241*
Goa, L., 252, *266*
Godfrey, H. P. D., 206, *221*
Godshall, F. J., 204, *221*
Goh, M., 122, *137*
Goldblatt, V., *174*
Goldfried, M. R., 103, *114*
Gone, J., 29, *42*
Gonzalez, C., 182, *195*
González, G., 78, *96*
Gonzalez, J., 25, *42*
Gonzalez, N. A., 254, *263*
Gonzalez, R. C., 276, *279*
Good, B. J., 76, *95*, 187, *196*
Goodchilds, J., 229, *241*
Goodstein, R., 102, *113*
Gopaul-McNicol, S. A., 6, *16*
Gordon, L. C., *115*
Gorman, J. M., 77, *95*
Gorsuch, R. L., 35, *44*
Gorton, T., *174*
Gracie, J., 268, *280*
Graves, A. B., *196*
Green, A. R., 187, *194*
Greenberg, D., 169, 172, 173, *174*, 211
Greenberg, R. L., 4, *14*
Greenberg, S., 173, *175*
Greenberger, D., 5, 7, 8, *17, 221*
Greene, B., 5, *15*, 224, *241*
Gresham, R. L., Jr., 261, *266*
Grieger, R., 206, *221*
Griffith, E. H., 182, *195*
Grissom, G., *242*

Joiner, T. E., Jr., 102, *113*
Jones, A. C., 110, *113*
Jones, R. T., 98, *113*
Jumper-Thurman, P., 27, *44*

Kallivayalil, D., 252, *264*
Kaminski, E., 231, *242*
Kanfer, F. H., 254, *264*
Kanfer, G., 38, *43*
Kantrowitz, R. E., 7, *16*
Kaskie, B., *195*
Kasl-Godly, J. E., *195*
Kataoka, S. H., 78, *95*
Katona, C., 184, *194*
Kawagley, O. A., 48, 49, 56, 59, *70*
Kazarian, S., 120, *138*
Kearney, C. A., 200, *221*
Kelly, S., 98, 99, 106, 109, 110, *113*
Kendall, P. C., 253, *263*
Kennedy, P., 204, *221*
Kessler, R. C., 74, *95*, 232, *242*
Khadivi, A., 141, *158*
Kiecolt, K. J., 106, *114*
Kim, A. U., *111*
Kim, B. S. K., 123, *139*
Kim, M. T., 252, *264*
Kim, S. C., 4, 10, *16*
Kim, S. J., 128, *137*
Kim, U., 125, *139*
Kimbrough, R., 250, *264*
King, D., 225, *240*
King, J. L., 224, *242*
Kinoshita, L. M., 180, *195*
Kintner, E. K., 98, *113*
Kinzie, J. D., 252, *263*
Kiselica, M. S., 128, *139*
Kleinman, A., 76, *95*, 181, 187, *195*, *196*,
    271, *280*
Klonoff, E. A., 98, 102, *114*
Knight, B. G., 179, 189, *196*
Koch, W. J., 133, *139*
Kohn, L. P., *95*, 106, *114*, *264*
Kotler, D., 227, *243*
Kowatch, R. A., 180, *196*
Kozak, M. J., 133, *137*
Krause, J. S., 204, *222*
Krauss, M. E., 53, *70*
Krieger, N., 98, *114*
Kroenke, K., 250, *265*
Kurasaki, K., 75, *95*
Kurtines, W. M., 78, *96*, *194*
Kurtz, D. A., 100, *114*

Kushner, H., *242*
Kwate, N. O., 98, *114*

Ladany, N., 272, 275, 279, *280*
LaDuke, W., 26, *43*
LaFromboise, T., 10, *16*, 27, 28, *43*, *95*, *264*,
    275, *280*
Lam, K., 256, *265*
Lam, R. E., 182, 183, *196*
Lamchichi, A., 142, *159*
Landrine, H., 98, 102, *114*
Landrum-Brown, J., *111*
Lang, S., 224, *241*
Langdon, S. J., 48, 51, 53, 54, 56, *70*
Lassman, D. K., *197*
Laszloffy, T. A., 99, 107, *114*
Lau, A. W., *95*, 180, *196*, *264*
Leaf, P. J., 74, *95*
Leary, M. C., *195*
Lease, S. H., 276, *279*
Leavitt, D., 106, *114*
Ledley, D. R., 5, *16*
Lee, C. C., 5, *16*, 276, *280*
Lee, E., 6, *16*, 118, 119, 121, *139*
Leong, F. T. L., 252n, *264*
Lester, D., 250, *264*
Levant, R., 6, *17*
Levine, R. V., 252, *264*
Levy, D., 125, *139*
Lewinsohn, P. M., 183, *197*
Lewis, E. L., 100, *112*
Li, L. C., 259, *265*
Liao, M., *121*
Liese, B. S., 4, *15*, 268, 269, *280*
Lilienfeld, S. O., 247, *266*
Lin, K.-H., *115*
Lin, K.-M., 252, *266*
Lin, Y., 185, *196*
Lindberg, P., 205, *220*
Linehan, M. M., 5, *17*, 268, 270, *279*, *280*
Liu, J. F., 254, *264*
Locke, D. C., 275, *279*
Lockery, S. A., 183, *196*
Loewenthal, K. M., 167, *174*
Logan, S. L., 274, *280*
Logsdon, R. G., 180, *197*
Longmore, P. K., 203, *221*
Longworth, S. L., 254, *264*
Lonner, W. J., 5, *17*
Loo, C. M., 185, *196*
López, S. R., 268, 271, *280*
Lowe, R., 204, *221*

Steinwachs, D. S., *194*
Stephenson, E., 101, *115*
Stevenson, H. C., 57, *70*
Stewart, C., 35, *43*
Stickle, T. R., 105, *111*
Stokes, S. C., 191, *196*
Stravynski, A., 172, *174*
Sue, D. W., 5, 6, *18*, 29, *44*, 124, *139*, 180,
    182, *197*, 278, *280*
Sue, S., 6, *18*, 77, 96, 104, 108, *115*, 127,
    139, 262, *265*
Suh, E. M., 248, 249, *263*, *265*
Suinn, R. M., 5, *18*
Suleiman, M. W., 143, 144, *159*
Sullivan, J. G., 226, *240*
Sutton-Tyrrell, K., 98, *115*
Swan Reimer, C., 6, *18*, 48, 60, *70*
Swenson, L. P., 98, *112*
Swift Hawk, P., 36, *43*
Swinomish Tribal Community, 6, 10, *18*, 30,
    31, *44*, 59, *71*
Szymanski, D. M., 128, *137*, 226, *243*

Taffe, R. C., 275, *280*
Tafoya, T., 29, *44*, 224, *243*
Tak, J., 252n, *264*
Takagi, K., *194*
Takeshita, J., 181, *193*
Takeuchi, D. T., 74, 77, 95, *96*
Talamantes, M., 181, *195*
Talleyrand, R., 123, *138*
Tanaka-Matsumi, J., 253, 254, 256, 257, 258,
    265
Tanner, C., 200, *221*
Taylor, R. E., 200, 205, *221*
Taylor, R. J., 100, *115*, *263*
Taylor, S., 133, *139*
Templer, D. I., 227, *243*
Tennstedt, S. L., 184, *196*
Teri, L., 180, *197*
Tevendale, H. D., 98, *112*
Thachrey, M., *197*
Therrien, M., 74, *96*
Thoeness, N., 227, *243*
Thomas, L., *70*
Thomas, W., 224, *241*
Thompson, L. W., 191, *194*, *196*
Thompson, N. J., 204, *222*
Thorn, B. E., 4, *18*
Thurman, P., 24, 29, *44*
Tien, L., 120, *139*
Tirch, D. D., 200, 207, 208, 209, *222*

Tjaden, P., 227, 232, *243*
Todd-Bazemore, E., 267, *281*
Tollison, C. D., 228, *239*
Tomeo, M. E., 227, *243*
Toporek, R. L., 5, *18*, 58, *70*
Torres, M., *263*
Tower, E., 49, *71*
Towne, N., 276, *279*
Tran, M., 135, *138*
Trappler, B., 173, *175*
Trent, C. R., 250, *265*
Triandis, H. C., 30, *44*, 248, *265*
Trimble, J. E., 5, *17*, 24, 25, 27, 29, 32, *41*,
    43, *44*
Troxel, W. M., 98, *115*
Tseng, W. S., 120, *140*
Tu, W., *95*
Turner, M. A., 97, *115*
Turner, S. M., 30, *43*, 55, *70*, 107, *112*
Turtle-Song, I., 30, *41*
Twersky, A. J., 173, *175*

Uba, L., 6, *18*, 118, 119, 120, 123, 124, *140*
Ukeles, J. B., ix, xi, *175*
Ullman, J. B., 98, *114*
Um, K., *138*
Umansky, L., 203, *221*
United States Census Bureau, xi, 5, *18*, 24,
    45, 54, *71*, 74, 117, *140*
United States Department of Health and
    Human Services, 5, *18*, 28, *45*, 69,
    98, *115*
United States Department of the Interior, 24,
    45
Uomoto, J., 180, 196, *197*

Valdes Dwyer, E., 77, *96*
Valdimarsdottir, H. B., 98, *114*
Valverde, I., 181, *195*
Vandiver, B. J., 102, 108, *115*
Van Dorsten, B., 200, 208, 211, *222*
Van Sickle, T., 141, *158*
Venables, R. W., 25, 27, *45*
Vincke, J., 231, *243*
Vinh, D. H., *264*
Vitaliano, P., *196*
Vrasidas, C., 25, *45*

Wagar, B. M., 249, *266*
Wagener, P., *196*
Wald, M. J., *195*
Waldo, C. R., 226, *242*

SUBJECT INDEX

Asian Indians, 180
Assertiveness training, 32, 82, 89–92, 218–219
Assessment, 9–12, 32–33, 35–36, 56–63, 191, 229–230, 247–262
Assessment instruments, 250–254
Assessment models, 254–261
Assimilation, 10
    American Indians, 26–27
    Arab Americans, 147
Authority figure, therapist as, 76, 148–149
Automatic Thoughts Questionnaire (ATQ), 253
Ayalon, L., 250–251

Balance, as cultural value, 120, 125, 181, 191
Balfour Declaration (1917), 143
Balls Organista, P., 75
Beauty norms, 206
Beck, A. T., 211, 251
Beck, J. S., 206–212, 269
Beck Anxiety Inventory, 230
Beck Depression Inventory (BDI and BDI-II), 35, 230, 248, 250–253
Bedouins, 147
Behavioral assessment, 253–254
Behavioral contract, 89, 92
Behavioral interventions, 154–155, 210–211
Beidel, D. C., 107
Bereavement, 184
Bernal, G., 78–79
Bicultural competence model, 10–11
Biculturalism, 28, 32–33, 35, 54–55, 57, 148.
        See also Multicultural competence
Biopsychosocial model of health, 125
Biphobia, 225
Bisexuals. See LGB people
Boarding school system, 26–27, 50
Boyd-Franklin, N., 109
Bradford, D. T., 122
Bradford, J., 224
Bromet, E., 233
Brown, G. K., 251
Buddhism, 260
Burns, D. D., 85

Cambodians, 133–136. See also Asian Americans
Caregiver stress, 183–184, 189–193
Casas, J. M., 5
Case consultation, 106
Case histories, x, 3–4, 12

African Americans, 103–105, 107–109
Alaska Natives, 60–61, 63–68
American Indians, 34–40
Arab Americans, 151–156
Asian Americans, 133–136
    culturally competent supervision, 272, 274–275, 277
    culturally responsive assessment, 255–257
    disabled people, 212–219
    ethnic minority elders, 189–193
    Latinos, 82–94
    LGB people, 231–238
Cauce, A. M., 254
Cerebral palsy (CP), 212–216
Chang, D. F., 261
Change, individual vs. social, 79–80
Child rearing, 146. See also Family; Family roles
Chin, J. L., 122
Chinese Americans, 118, 121, 180–181, 189–193, 257, 261. See also Asian Americans
Chinese Depression Inventory (CDI), 252
Christensen, A., 108–109
Christianity, 49–50, 100, 142, 144
Chumrah, 169–170
Churches, African American, 100
Clarification of problem, 60–62
Clergy, African American, 110
Cognitive–behavioral therapy (CBT)
    adapting, x, 80–82, 106–108, 188–189, 229–231
    advantages, 58–63, 76–82, 102–104, 127, 151, 173, 185–186, 227–228
    disadvantages, x, 58–63, 127, 151, 173, 186, 227–228
Cognitive–behavioral therapy (CBT), characteristics of, 62–63
    collaborative nature, 103
    culturally responsive approach, 8–9
    educational approach, 76, 151, 185–186
    emphasis on contextual factors, 127
    emphasis on empowerment, 103
    emphasis on rationality, 59, 105, 151
    emphasis on understanding client's worldview, 185–186
    empirical grounding, 227
    Eurocentrism, 104–105, 151
    focus on content, 227
    focus on here-and-now, 151
    individualistic focus, 105, 127

neglect of culture, 4–5
neutrality, 104
nonjudgmental approach, 227
problem-solving approach, 127, 151, 227
reliance on written assignments, 127
skills-training focus, 227
universal applicability, 104
verbal emphasis, 59
Cognitive–behavioral therapy (CBT) with
    diverse populations, ix–x, 6–13. See
    also Case histories
    African Americans, 102–111
    Alaska Natives, 56–63
    American Indians, 29–33
    Arab people, 148–151
    Asian Americans, 126–133
    disabled people, 206–212
    Latinos, 76–82
    LGB people, 226–231
    older adults, 179–193
    Orthodox Jews, 167–173
Cognitive challenging, 131–132
Cognitive distortions, of disabled people,
    207–210
Cognitive impairment, 183
Cognitive problems, 11–12
Cognitive restructuring, 8, 38, 59, 63, 66–
    68, 82, 85–89, 151, 153, 155–156,
    230–231, 235, 238
Cognitive skills, learning, 131
Cognitive styles, 124–125, 253
Cognitive techniques, for disabled people,
    211–212
Cognitive therapy (CT), 269
Cognitive Therapy Adherence and Compe-
    tence Scale, 269
Cohort-specific problems, of older adults, 185
Coining, practice of, 134
Coleman, H. L. K., 10
Collectivism, 30, 37, 81–82, 121–124, 145,
    186, 248
"Colorblind" approach, 104
Comas-Díaz, L., 5, 78, 82, 90
Coming out, 226, 232
Communication issues, 39, 59–60, 84, 86,
    122, 187. See also Language issues
Community, African American, 105–106
Community, LGB, 231
Complexity of problems, 12–13, 64, 76–77,
    93, 130–131, 220
Composite International Diagnostic Inter-
    view, 250

Conceptualization of problem, 9–12, 122,
    229
Confidentiality, 122, 168, 170–171, 173, 187
Conflicting messages, cultural, 155–156
Consolacion, T., 127
Constantine, M. G., 276
Contraception, 166–167, 171
Coping strategies, of disabled people, 204–
    205
Core beliefs, identifying, 88–89
Core values, of disability culture, 201–202
Counseling, use of term, 62
"Counting coup," 36
Couple therapy, 103, 109
Courtship, 166, 170–171
Creation stories
    Alaska Natives, 48–49
    American Indians, 24–25
Credibility, client perception of, 108
Critical thinking, 149
Cross, T. L., 61
Cross-cultural competence, 32–33, 77–78, 271.
    See also Multicultural competence
Cross-Cultural Counseling Inventory, 275
Cross-cultural equivalence, of psychological
    disorders, 28
Cuban Americans, 74–75. See also Latinos
Cultural beliefs, 144–146, 213–214
Cultural diversity, defining, x–xi
Cultural identification, of American Indians,
    27–28, 32–33
Cultural identity, of Alaska Natives, 51–55
Cultural influences, 254
Cultural information, 3–4, 55–58, 61, 67,
    129. See also Multicultural compe-
    tence
Culturally Informed Functional Assessment
    (CIFA) interview, 248, 256–258
Cultural norms, as basis for self-reporting, 248
Cultural responsiveness, in CBT assessment,
    247–262
Cultural values, Latino, 80–82
Culture, use of term, 73
Culture-bound syndromes, 126, 185, 258–
    259
"Culture brokering," 93
Culture gap, 184
Cupping, practice of, 125

D'Andrea, M., 271
Daniels, J., 271
Dating, 166, 170–171, 235–238

Deficit model of disability, 199–200
Dementia, 180, 183
Denial, as coping strategy, 205
Depression, 82–94, 151–156, 216–219, 227, 235–238, 250–253
  assessment issues, 250–253
  late-life, 179, 182–184, 189–193
Depressive Cognition Scale, 253
Developmental disabilities, 57
Developmental issues, for LGB people, 225–226
Dialectical behavior therapy (DBT), 270–271
Dillard, Denise, 60
Disability. *See also* Disabled people
  as cultural identity, 199
  cultural perspective on, 200–202
  paradigms of, 202–204
  as part of treatment context, 207
  physical, 204–205
  sensory, 205
Disability, use of term, 200
Disability community, use of term, 199–200
Disability culture, 201–202, 215, 220
Disability Studies, 203–204
Disabled people, 199–220
Disabled people, use of term, 199–200
Disclosure. *See* Coming out; Confidentiality; Shame; Trust
Discrimination, 185. *See also* Anti-Arab sentiment; Anti-Semitism; Hate crimes
  experienced by disabled people, 203
  against LGB people, 225, 233
Disease, 49
Disharmony, American Indian concept of, 30–31
Divorce, 145, 166, 171, 213–214
Down syndrome, 216–219
Dowry, 145
Draguns, J. G., 5
Droby, R. M., 48
Dropout, 107
Drug abuse, 34, 56
DSM–IV, 9, 251
DSM–IV–TR, 76, 126, 185
  Outline for Cultural Formulation, 258–259
Duncan, J. W., 78, 82, 90
Dwairy, M. A., 150
Dyadic Adjustment Scale, 230
Dysfunctional Attitudes Scale (DAS), 253
Dysfunctional beliefs, of disability, 206–207

East Asians, 248. *See also* Asian Americans
Ecological niche, 73
Education, 26–27, 50, 106, 144, 164
Elders, of ethnic minorities, 59–60, 88, 110, 122, 165–166, 179–193. *See also* Older adults; Respect, as cultural value
Elkins, R., 225
Ellis, A., 86, 269
Ellis, J. M., 224
Emigration, Arab, 147. *See also* Immigrants
Empathy, 85
Ending therapy sessions, 132–133
Environmental conditions, 9–10
Environmental interventions, 154–155
Environmental problems, 9–11
Epidemics, 49
Erickson, C. D., 146, 149
Eskimo, use of term, 51
Essence reflection, 129
Ethical issues, 272–274
Ethnic identity
  Alaska Natives, 57
  Arab peoples, 146–148
  Asian Americans, 123
Ethnicity, relevance of, 3–4
Eurocentrism, 5, 41, 104–105, 180, 253, 278
Evans, I. M., 261
Explanatory Model Interview Catalogue (EMIC), 248, 260–261
Explanatory models of illness, 181, 191
Exposure, 173
Extended family, 83, 99–100, 124, 145–146

Facial expressions, 60
Falicov, C. J., 73
Familismo (familism), 81–82, 88
Family, 90–92, 108–111, 144–145, 151–156, 192, 212–216, 230. *See also* Older adults
Family dynamics, assessing, 90–92
Family-focused interventions, 90–92
Family roles, 120–121, 145–146, 164–167
Family size, 166–167, 171
Family structure, 120–122
Family therapy, 150
Family types, 121
Fatigue, among older adults, 188
Faubert, M., 275
Fava, M., 261
Fear network theory, 133

Fetal alcohol syndrome (FAS), 57
Fienup-Riordan, A., 50
Fink, C. M., 107
Fleming, C. M., 28
Foa, E. B., 233, 235
Follow-up phone calls, 132–133
Fong, M. L., 276
Fong, R., 5
Franklin, A. J., 109
Frequency and Acceptability of Partner Behavior scale, 230
Friendship circles, as family, 230
Fruzzetti, A. E., 270
Fudge, R. C., 104, 111
Fuentes, R. M., 78
Fujino, D. C., 77
Functional analysis, 254–256
Fusion model, 10

Gallagher-Thompson, D., 180
Garrett, M. T., 27–28, 276–277
Gays. See LGB people
Geist-Martin, P., 122
Gender, 58
Gender identity, use of term, 225
Gender-neutrality, 230
Gender-related conflict, 150
Gender roles, 122–123, 164–165, 192
Gender stereotypes, 101, 111
Generational influences, 57
Geriatric Depression Scale, 191
Gerton, J., 10
Gift-giving practices, 40, 89, 150, 187, 190
Gill, C. J., 201–202
Giordano, J., 5
Giving, client's perception of, 108
Goals, therapeutic, 129–130
Goh, M., 122
Gone, J., 29
Gonzalez, G., 78
Gonzalez, N. A., 254
Gonzalez, R. C., 276
Gossip, avoidance of, 166
Greene, B., 5, 224
Gresham, R. L., Jr., 261
Grief, 184
Grooper, J., 66
Group supervision, 277
Group therapy, 173
Guided self-dialogue technique, 235
Guilt, 235
Gulf War, 143

Hakim-Larson, J., 150
Handshake styles, 59
Hardy, K. V., 99
Harmony, American Indian concept of, 30–31
Hate crimes against Muslims, 143
Hays, P. A., 5, 260
Healers, traditional, 36–37, 188
Healing, traditional, 38–39, 125–126
Health beliefs, Asian American, 125–126
Hearing impairment, 205
Heilman, S., 164
Helms, J. E., 123, 128
Helpfulness, concept of, 67–68
Heterosexism, 225, 228, 230–231
Heuristic model of nonoppressive interpersonal development, 272–274
Hill, C. L., 259
Hmong Adaptation of Beck Depression Inventory, 252
Holidays, Orthodox Jewish, 169, 172
Hollywood, and image of American Indians, 36
Home care, for elders, 183–184
Homework, 38–39, 189, 192, 216–218, 234
Homophobia, 225–226, 230–231
Homosexual, use of term, 224
Homosexuality. See Same-gender attraction
Hootch v. Alaska State Operated School System (Molly Hootch decree), 50
Hopelessness, feelings of, 208–209
Howard, K. I., 76
Howard-Hamilton, M. F., 5
Hu, L., 77
Hughes, M., 233

Identity. See Ethnic identity; Racial identity
Illness, explanatory models of, 181, 191
Imaginal practice, 233–234
Immigrants, 179
    Arab, 144
    Asian American, 118–119
    Black, 101
    Jewish, 162–163
    Latino, 213
    Palestinian, 151–152
Immigrants, use of term, 119
Imprisonment, 34–35
Indigenous heritage, 57–58
Individual supervision, 277
Initial assessment, 186–188
Initial therapy sessions, 129–130

Matsumoto, D., 30
McClanahan, A. J., 57
McGoldrick, M., 5
McMullin, R., 37
Means of interpersonal functioning (MIF), 273
Mechanics, of therapeutic intervention, 212, 215
Medical model of disability, 203
Melin, L., 205
Men
    African American, 106
    Latino, 88
Mental health issues
    African Americans, 98–99
    American Indians, 28–29
    Arab Americans, 149–150
    Asian Americans, 121–122
    Latinos, 75
Mental illness
    secondary to physical illness or disability, 184–185
    stigmatized, 149, 168, 170–171, 181
Mexican Americans, 74–75, 82–94, 181. See also Latinos
Meyer, I. H., 224
Middle therapy sessions, 130–132
Migration, rural-urban, 97
Military combat experience, 34, 39–40, 185
"Mind reading," 238
Minn, J. Y., 254
Minnesota Multiphasic Personality Inventory (MMPI and MMPI-2), 247
Minority stress, 227
Mio, J. S., 5
Miranda, J., 77–78, 94, 261
Missionaries, Christian, 49–50, 54
Modesty, as cultural value, 167–168
Mohammed, Prophet, 142
Mohammedan, use of term, 142
Mohatt, G., 27
Mood and activity monitoring, 237
Moral model of disability, 202–203
Multicultural Assessment Procedure (MAP), 248, 259
Multicultural Awareness–Knowledge–Skills Survey, 275
Multicultural competence, 33, 36, 39–40, 55, 57, 106–108, 127–128, 148–149, 187, 190, 254–261, 271–278
Multicultural Counseling Awareness Scale, 275

Multicultural Counseling Inventory, 275
Multicultural model, 10
Multicultural therapy (MCT), 5–7, 268
Multiple identities, 101–102, 207, 212
Multiplex model of panic generation, 133–134
Muñoz, A., 122
Muñoz, R. F., 73–74, 78, 106
Muslim, use of term, 142
Muslims, 141, 143, 151–156. See also Arab peoples

Nassar-McMillan, S. C., 150
National Association of Social Workers, 228
National origin, 58
Native Americans. See Alaska Natives; American Indians
Neault, N., 252
Needham, W. E., 209
Negative attitudes of others, disabled people and, 206–207
Nelson, C. B., 233
Nervios (nerves), 76
Neurasthenia, 257
Nidah, 165
Nierenberg, A. A., 261
Nolen-Hoeksema, S., 85
Nomadic cultures, 147
Nonverbal symbols, 84, 86
Northern Plains Bicultural Inventory (NPBI), 32–33

Obsessive–compulsive disorder (OCD), 169–172
Ochs, R., 225
Oden, T., 106
Oil revenues
    Alaskan, 50–51
    Arab, 147
Oishi, S., 249
Okazaki, S., 252, 254
Old age, and decline in function, 182
Older adults, 179–193
Older Person's Pleasant Event Schedule, 191–192
Olkin, R., 203
Oppression, experience of
    African Americans, 97, 99
    American Indians, 31–32
    LGB people, 225–226, 230–231
Organista, K. C., 73–75, 78, 80
Orientation, pretherapy, 81

Response prevention, 173
Ridley, C. R., 259
Risk vs. protective factors, 83
Rivers, R. Y., 5
Robinson, A., 106
Robinson, T. L., 5
Role-playing, 38–39, 89, 93
Role preparation, 76
Rossano, L., 224
Rossello, J., 78–79
Rothbaum, B. O., 233, 235
Rowan, A., 225

Sabbath, Orthodox Jewish, 172
Same-gender attraction, 216–219, 231–232,
    235–238. *See also* LGB people
    negative attitudes toward, 225–226
    terminology issues, 223–225
Scheduling issues, 189–190
Schema, 8
Schoeder, R. M., 253
Scott, B., 205
Scrupulosity, 169–170
Security object, 172
Seiden, D. Y., 257
Self-acceptance, 211
Self-care, 62–63, 156
Self-efficacy, 204–205
Self-esteem, 204, 215–216
Self-exploration, therapist and, 106
Self-identification, as Alaska Native, 54–55,
    57–58
Self-monitoring, 40, 86
Self-report data, cross-cultural findings for,
    248–249
Self-worth, 208–209
Separation, between sexes, 165
Separation, from mainstream American so-
    ciety, 163–164
Sexual assault, 231–235
Sexual behavior, attempts to change, 228
Sexual identity, and sexual behavior, 223–
    225
Sexual identity, use of term, 224
Sexual minority, use of term, 224
Sexual orientation, 57, 228–230, 236, 239
Sexual orientation, use of term, 224
Shame, 168, 181, 184, 186, 192, 213–215,
    235
Shanda, 168
Shared beliefs, among Orthodox Jews, 163–
    164

Silence, role of, 60
Simek-Morgan, L., 5
simpatía (smooth communication), 82, 89
Skilled nursing facilities, 180
Slavery, 97
Sliverman, W. K., 78
Smith, T., 5
Snowden, L., 80
Social behaviors, Asian American, 126
Social class, in Arab culture, 147
Social dominance and cognition, American
    Indians and, 31–32
Social model of disability, 203–204
Social Performance Rating Scale, 253
Socially oppressed group (SOG), 272–274
Socially privileged group (SPG), 272–274
Socioeconomic status
    African Americans, 100–101
    Alaska Natives, 57
    Latinos, 74
Somatization, 182
Sonnega, A., 233
Spinal cord injury (SCI), 204–205
Spirituality
    African American, 100, 110
    Alaska Native, 59
    American Indian, 30
    Asian American, 120
Standardized tests, and older adults, 188
State–Trait Anxiety Inventory (STAI), 35
Steer, R. A., 251
Stonewall riots, 228n
Strengths, client, 61, 83, 99–100, 109, 151–
    152
Stroke, 216–219
Structured Clinical Interview for *DSM–IV*,
    236
Subjective emotional experiences, as basis for
    self-reporting, 248
Subjective Units of Distress (SUDS), 234–235
Subsistence, 49
Substance abuse, 64, 227. *See also* Alcohol
    abuse; Drug abuse
Sue, D. W., 6
Sue, S., 77, 104, 108, 127
Suicide attempts, 227
Supervision, 106, 267–279
    cognitive–behavioral, 268–271
    culturally competent, 271–274
    and evaluation, 269–270
    integration of diversity issues, 276–278
    interpersonal influences in, 269

"Wind overload," 134
Witchcraft, American Indians and, 31
Wohl, J., 5
Women
    African American, 106
    Arab, 145–146, 151–156
    Asian American, 122–123
    Orthodox Jewish, 165
Woods, P. J., 269
Worldview
    African American, 99
    Alaska Native, 49
    American Indian, 30

negative, 208
World War II, 53, 143–144

X, Malcolm, 111

"Yes, but" technique, 82, 87
Yeung, A. S., 252, 261
Yin and yang, concepts of, 120, 124–125
Young, M. A., 250–251
Yutrzenka, B. A., 267
Yuuyaraq (subsistence), 49

Zane, N. W. S., 77, 108

ABOUT THE EDITORS

Pamela A. Hays, PhD, completed a doctorate in clinical psychology from the University of Hawaii; a year of study at the University of North Wales, United Kingdom; a certificate in French from La Sorbonne, Paris, France; and a postdoctoral fellowship in geropsychology from the University of Rochester School of Medicine, Rochester, New York. Her research has included work with Arab women in North Africa and Southeast Asian refugees in the United States, and she is the author of *Addressing Cultural Complexities in Practice* (American Psychological Association, 2001). She currently works at Central Peninsula Counseling Services in Kenai, Alaska, and serves as adjunct faculty for the University of Alaska in Anchorage and Antioch University in Seattle, Washington.

Gayle Y. Iwamasa, PhD, is associate professor in the Department of Psychology at DePaul University in Chicago, Illinois. She has published numerous articles and chapters on multicultural mental health across the life span and is coeditor with Jeffery Mio of *Culturally Diverse Mental Health* (2003). She has served as president of the Asian American Psychological Association, program chair for the American Psychological Association's Society for the Psychological Study of Ethnic Minority Issues, and coordinator of the Membership Committee and the Academic and Professional Issues Committee of the Association for Behavioral and Cognitive Therapies.